The Intellectual Powers

The Intellectual Powers:
a Study of Human Nature

P. M. S. Hacker

Fellow of St John's College · Oxford

WILEY Blackwell

This edition first published 2013
© 2013 John Wiley & Sons, Ltd.

Blackwell Publishing was acquired by John Wiley & Sons in February 2007. Blackwell's publishing program has been merged with Wiley's global Scientific, Technical, and Medical business to form Wiley-Blackwell.

Registered Office
John Wiley & Sons Ltd, The Atrium, Southern Gate, Chichester, West Sussex, PO19 8SQ, UK

Editorial Offices
350 Main Street, Malden, MA 02148-5020, USA
9600 Garsington Road, Oxford, OX4 2DQ, UK
The Atrium, Southern Gate, Chichester, West Sussex, PO19 8SQ, UK

For details of our global editorial offices, for customer services, and for information about how to apply for permission to reuse the copyright material in this book please see our website at www.wiley.com/wiley-blackwell.

The right of P. M. S. Hacker to be identified as the author of this work has been asserted in accordance with the UK Copyright, Designs and Patents Act 1988.

Library of Congress Cataloging-in-Publication Data
Hacker, P. M. S. (Peter Michael Stephan)
   The intellectual powers : a study of human nature / P. M. S. Hacker.
       pages cm
   Includes index.
   ISBN 978-1-4443-3247-6 (cloth) – ISBN 978-1-118-65121-6 (pbk.)
1. Philosophical anthropology. 2. Philosophy of mind. 3. Thought and thinking. I. Title.
   BD450.H23555 2013
   128'.3–dc23
                                          2013016694

A catalogue record for this book is available from the British Library.

Cover design by Design Deluxe.

Set in 10.5/12.5 Sabon by Toppan Best-set Premedia Limited
Printed in Malaysia by Ho Printing (M) Sdn Bhd

1   2013

For

Herman Philipse

Contents

Preface

In 2007 I published a volume entitled *Human Nature: the Categorial Framework*. It belonged to the genre the Germans call 'philosophische Anthropologie' – a broader domain than philosophy of mind. In it, I investigated the nature of substance, causation, power and agency, as well as teleological and rational forms of explanation of behaviour. The book concluded with an examination of the nature of the mind and the body, and an elucidation of the concept of a person. This set the stage for further investigations. I announced in the Preface my intention of continuing the study with a book entitled *Human Nature: the Cognitive and Cogitative Powers*. This is that book, although the title has changed due to the exigencies of computer cataloguing. *The Intellectual Powers: a Study of Human Nature* pays homage to, and deliberately echoes the title of, Thomas Reid's great work. My aim was to map the landscape of cognitive and cogitative concepts, and thereby to illuminate the nature of our cognitive and cogitative powers. I hope that others will find my maps helpful in finding their way around this unruly and intellectually perilous terrain. I have tried to plot not only the safe routes, but also the many inviting pathways that lead to quicksands, chasms and seas of nonsense. Including sensation and perception among the intellectual powers is perhaps eccentric, and would be disapproved by Aristotelians and scholastics. Nevertheless, human sensibility is not only a primary source of knowledge – it is also concept-saturated and thought-ridden. These features of our sensible powers are the warrant for including two chapters on these themes.

This book presupposes the conclusions of the previous investigation, but has been designed to be read independently of it. Consequently, there is occasional overlap between the two books. Sometimes

I recapitulate conclusions previously reached. Sometimes I pick up threads left dangling there, and weave them into the larger tapestry. *Human Nature: the Categorial Framework* investigated the most general categories in terms of which we think about ourselves. The present book examines our sensory and perceptual powers, our ability to attain and retain knowledge, our doxastic propensities, the relations of knowledge and belief, our cogitative powers and the gift of imagination with which we are endowed. I hope to complete these studies with a third volume entitled *The Moral Powers: a Study of Human Nature*. Collectively they will constitute a comprehensive essay in philosophical anthropology.

As in *Human Nature: the Categorial Framework*, each chapter is accompanied by tree diagrams, tables and lists. These are often no more than illustrations to the text, sometimes oversimplifying for the sake of surveyability. As I noted in the Preface to that book, they are meant to illuminate the argument as a picture illustrates a story, not to be a substitute for it. I have also introduced marginalia (as in *Philosophical Foundations of Neuroscience*) to facilitate surveyability, to make it easier to follow the argument, and to assist in locating topics.

Writing this volume took longer and was more laborious than I had anticipated. I am grateful to the friends and colleagues who encouraged me in my endeavours, gave me invaluable advice, and saved me from so many errors. Erich Ammereller, George Barton, Jonathan Beale, Terence Cave, Gerhard Ernst, Eugen Fischer, Anthony Kenny, Rick Peels, Dennis Patterson, Dan Robinson and David Wiggins all read and commented upon one or more (and sometimes many more) chapters. I owe a special debt to Hanoch Ben-Yami, Hans Oberdiek and Herman Philipse, who read the whole draft and gave me detailed comments, powerful criticisms and illuminating suggestions. I am grateful to my college, St John's, for the support and assistance it has given me.

P. M. S. Hacker
St John's College, Oxford
September 2012

For any man with half an eye
What stands before him may espy;
But optics sharp it needs I ween,
To see what is not to be seen.

John Trumball

Introduction:
The Project

We are substances – animate spatio-temporal continuants, consisting of matter, with active and passive causal powers. We are sentient, self-moving agents, with the ability to act or refrain from acting at will. Being language-using creatures with rational capacities, we adopt and pursue goals for reasons. We have projects and interests, we make choices and decisions, act voluntarily and intentionally, and are responsible for what we do. So we are persons. Our deeds are explained teleologically by reference to our goals and purposes, and by the reasons and motives for which we act. We have a mind and a body. The body we *have* consists of the somatic features of the body (the animate material substance) that we *are*. The mind we have is not a substance (a *res cogitans*) or a part of a substance (the brain). To have a mind is to have and exercise an array of first- and second-order intellectual and volitional abilities. The conceptual network that underlies these categorial observations was described in detail in *Human Nature: the Categorial Framework* (2007).

That book provided, as it were, the *mis-en-scène* for the play that will begin to unfold here. But the lighting still had to be put in place. This is the role of the three chapters of the Prolegomena: 'Consciousness', 'Intentionality' and 'Mastery of a Language'. Both consciousness and intentionality have been invoked to explain what it is to have a mind, and to characterize the mental. Both concepts are sources of ramifying confusions. Eradicating these confusions is

The Intellectual Powers: A Study of Human Nature, First Edition. P. M. S. Hacker.
© 2013 John Wiley & Sons, Ltd. Published 2013 by John Wiley & Sons, Ltd.

necessary before investigating the nature of our cognitive and cogitative powers. What *is* distinctive of humanity, what above all distinguishes us from other animals, is that we are language-using creatures.
Hence, the nature of language and of linguistic abilities need to be
clarified before moving on to the main themes of the investigation.

The subject of consciousness was introduced into philosophy by
Descartes, who held (against the Aristotelians) that consciousness is
the mark of the mind. Consciousness assumed even greater importance in the writings of Locke, who held it to be the glue binding our
past to our present experience, which makes each of us a person. It
was assigned supreme importance by Kant, who held it to be the
source of the transcendental unity of experience. Over the last decades,
consciousness has been variously presented – as the last remaining
obstacle to a satisfactory 'scientific conception of the world', as a
mystery that is beyond the powers of the human mind to resolve, and
as the feature (the 'what-it's-likeness of experience') that distinguishes
us from automata. I shall show that the early modern discussion of
the subject from Descartes to Kant was enmired in confusion. There
is no mystery about consciousness, and current debates on the subject
are no more than the excited buzzing of flies in a fly-bottle. In place
of these misconceptions, I shall advance a comprehensive *connective
analysis* of this *multi-focal concept*. Connective analysis (see Appendix) consists in describing the manifold logical connections between
a given expression (and its cognates) and other expressions with
which it is associated, or with which it is likely to be confounded. A
focal concept (exemplified by Aristotle's analysis of health) is one
with a focal point (e.g. the health of a being) around which are clus-
tered a variety of logically related extensions of the concept (e.g.
healthy exercise, healthy food, healthy environment). A multi-focal
concept is a concept with multiple centres of variation. A centre of
variation need not have a focal point. It is more commonly a focus
of points.

Brentano revived the medieval concept of intentionality and argued
that intentionality is the mark of the mental. This too is mistaken.
What is true is that the intentionality of *some* mental or psychological
concepts that characterize our nature is a source of widespread misunderstanding. Intentionality and *intentional in-existence* require elucidation, and intentional phenomena and their grammar need to be
characterized. This I shall try to do. What it is that we believe when
we believe falsely is a persistent source of confusion. Do we believe
facts, states of affairs, propositions or sentences? How are our beliefs

related to what makes them true? And how are they related to what makes them false? How do we know what we believe? The problems of intentionality ramify. How can we believe what is not the case? For if it is not the case, there is nothing to believe. This tangle of problems will be unravelled.

The final chapter of the Prolegomena brings us to the source of all that is distinctive about us and that differentiates us from the rest of the animal kingdom. We are *unique* in nature in being language-using creatures. In *Human Nature: the Categorial Framework* I argued that it is because we have a developed language that we are capable of self-consciousness, that we can reason – and think, feel and act for reasons, that we can apprehend truths of mathematics and logic, that we know good and evil and can have a moral conscience, that we have autobiographies and a socio-historical sense of identity. Our nature is the product of our animality *qua hominidae*, of our mastery of a developed language that endows us with rational powers, and of our histories *qua* social and cultural beings. Much confusion surrounds the ideas of language and linguistic skills, of speaking and understanding language and of meaning something by words and utterances. The debates on these matters over the last century are polarized between two conceptions of language: (i) as a meaning calculus (e.g. Frege, Russell in *Principia*, Wittgenstein in the *Tractatus*, Carnap, Davidson, Dummett), and (ii) conceptions of language as a form of human behaviour (Wittgenstein in the *Investigations*, Austin, Grice, Strawson). The former conception gives primacy to assertion, truth, truth-conditions of sentences, and to understanding conceived as a computational process or its resultant state. The latter conception gives primacy to the use of words in the stream of life, to the practice of communication conceived intentionally and contextually, and to understanding conceived as akin to an ability rather than to a process or state. We shall investigate the questions that lead to these different conceptions.

With the discussion of these three great themes, the lighting for the stage is prepared, and the play can begin. At stage centre stand *knowledge* and *belief*. Neither is a mental state. They are not brain states either. Nor are they attitudes towards propositions. Knowing-how and knowing-that are two different forms knowledge may take. The former is not in general reducible to the latter. Practical knowledge is an essential and irreducible element of our agential nature. Both forms of knowledge have a kinship with ability – hence with potentiality rather than actuality. Knowing things to be so is distinct from knowing things to be true. In so far as knowledge can be said to aim at anything, it aims at reality – at how things are, and only secondarily at what is true. Received analyses of knowledge in terms of truth, belief and justification (or certainty, or a right to be sure) are defective. What is needed is not such a *definitional analysis* of knowledge, but a *connective analysis* that displays the place of knowledge in the network of epistemic concepts. An examination of the needs met and purposes satisfied by the uses of 'know' and 'believe' reinforces the connective analysis. Not only is belief not a mental state, it is not a feeling or a disposition either. Once the doxastic map is drawn, the complex relationship between knowledge and belief falls into place. Although belief is the default position when knowledge fails, knowledge – the possession of information – is not a species or form of belief at all. Since believing is neither an act nor an activity, the question of voluntariness of belief must be addressed and the fact that we are responsible for our beliefs explained. Finally, the epistemology of belief and the nature of self-deception demand clarification.

Without sensibility, there would be no knowledge. With us, but not with other animals, sensation and perception are concept-laden. Concepts (unlike ideas) are creatures of the intellect (or, on Kant's account, of the understanding), and our perceptual experience is unavoidably run through with concepts and judgement. We see the world around us in terms of the concepts we employ in describing it. Both sensation and perception are primary sources of knowledge. Their logical geography needs to be mapped, their relations clarified, their voluntariness investigated and their cognitive potentialities described. The causal theory of perception has long seemed irresistible, or, if resistible, then only at the price of idealism. The familiar flaws of the classical representational causal theory and of its current neuroscientific variants are sketched. The modern Grice/Strawson analytic form of the causal theory is examined and shown to be untenable. That concepts of perception are not causal concepts, and that perceiving something is not an experience caused by what one sensibly seems to perceive, do not imply that scientific investigations into the causal processes that endow us with our perceptual powers and that occur when we perceive things are faulty. The analytic causal theory of perception is a mistaken account of *concepts* of perception; the neuroscientific theory of perception is an empirical theory of the neural processes involved in perceiving. The latter does not imply the former. However, it is important to avoid the common neuroscientific mistake of reverting to the seventeenth-century representational causal theory of perception, and the equally common neuroscientific incoherence of ascribing perception to the brain. It is the living being as a whole that perceives. It is likewise important to deconstruct the idea of the necessity of a general sense (*sensus communis*) and its modern neuroscientific equivalent, the binding problem.

Memory is knowledge retained. In the absence of the power to retain knowledge, the horizon of possibilities for thought, affection and action would be very near – as it is with non-language-using animals. Without personal memory, human beings would not enjoy the moral status of persons, and would not be responsible for their deeds. Without the ability to recollect our past, we would lack any sense of our own identity over time. We would have no autobiography. Without personal memory, our social bonds, our loves and friendships, would be reduced to the inchoate forms of affection exhibited by other bonding animals. Without memory of the traditions and subjective history of our social group, we should have no sense of social identity.

The final part of the book deals with our cogitative powers. A connective analysis of thinking clarifies this multi-focal concept. We are naturally inclined to conceive of thinking as an activity of the mind – but that conception obliterates important distinctions. We are equally inclined to suppose that we think *in* some medium or other – in images, concepts or words. Representations do indeed require a medium. But thoughts are not representations – they are all message and no medium. A cousin of the misconceived idea that we must think *in* something is the doctrine that there must be a language of thought. That idea, which goes back at least as far as Ockham, was resurrected from its mouldy grave by Chomsky and Fodor. It needs, and will be given, decent burial. The question of whether non-human animals can think has much preoccupied scientists and philosophers in recent years. We shall give this due scrutiny. Finally, the connection between our cogitative powers and the idea of an 'inner life' must be explored. For human beings, unlike all other animals, have an inner life of thought and reflection, of daydreaming and recollecting, of hoping and fearing, and of deciding, forming intentions and planning.

Imagination too is a cogitative power. Philosophical reflection on the imagination is marred by the assimilation of our ability to think of novel possibilities to our ability to conjure up mental images. The latter is logically inessential to the creative imagination, but is a rich source of confusion. The relationship between images (drawings, paintings, photographs) and mental images must be clarified; otherwise, we shall wrongly suppose that mental images are a species of image. We must note the intelligibility of imagining something rotating and the unintelligibility of rotating something in the imagination; otherwise, we may be gulled into supposing (as psychologists and cognitive scientists do) that there is such a thing as rotating mental images in mental space. We must investigate the relationship between perceiving and imagining, lest we assign to the imagination impossible and unnecessary synthesizing tasks, as Hume and Kant did. Mental images are not faint perceptions. They may or may not be vivid, but they are not distinguishable from perceptions by their relative vivacity. Rather, the vivacity of mental images and the vivacity of perceptions are categorially different. Finally, the relationship between the imaginable, the conceivable and the possible require investigation.

It has in recent years become fashionable to conceive of ourselves as the helpless products of our genes; free will and responsibility are commonly thought an illusion, to be displaced by genetic and neural determinism; and the theory of evolution is invoked to explain morality and altruism in terms of natural selection. Our affinity with other *hominidae* has become a subject of extensive research, often aimed at cutting us down to size. The prowess of the great apes is exaggerated, often in order to narrow the perceived gap between animals and us. This development in the *Zeitgeist* is sadly understandable, but unwarranted. We are, of course, animals – but the only rational ones. We are, to be sure, *hominidae* – but the only language-using ones. No other creature has eaten of the fruit of the Tree of Knowledge of Good and Evil. We are animals, but the only animals who can aspire to live under the rule of law, and who can achieve happiness (as opposed to mere contentment). It is well that we should bear in mind our rational nature and what is distinctive about us – what makes us 'darkly wise and rudely great', 'a pendulum betwixt smile and tear', 'the glory and the shame of the universe'. Accordingly, I have paid considerable attention throughout this book to comparisons between man and beast, to the applicability and reasons for the applicability of many cognitive and cogitative concepts to human beings, and to their inapplicability to all other animals that are neither blessed with, nor cursed by possession of, the powers of reason, thought and understanding.

Such is the project of the current book. Its completion prepares the way for a further study – of the affective life of man, of the place of value in human life and of the moral powers with which we are endowed and the exercise of which gives meaning to our lives.

The methodology of these essays on human nature was explained and defended in *Human Nature: the Categorial Framework*, chapter 1. Further detailed explanation of the methods here used and a general defence of the venerable Way of Words is to be found in the Appendix. Those who have qualms about the Way of Words, those who cannot see that scrutiny of linguistic usage can clarify concepts and those who cannot grasp how conceptual clarification could shed light upon the nature of things are advised to read the Appendix before proceeding further. Others are invited to eat the pudding before investigating the cooking.

Prolegomena

1

Consciousness as the Mark of the Mental

1. Consciousness as a mark of modernity

The ancients did not characterize the mind in terms of consciousness
Although the ancients raised questions about our own knowledge of our perceptions and thought, and introduced the idea of an inner sense, they had no word for consciousness and they did not characterize the mind as the domain of consciousness. Aristotelians conceived of the mind as the array of powers that distinguish humanity from the rest of animate nature. The powers of self-movement, of perception and sensation and of appetite are shared with other animals. What is distinctive of humanity, and what characterizes the mind, are the powers of the intellect – of reason and of the rational will. Knowledge of these powers is not obtained by 'consciousness' or 'introspection', but by observing their exercise in our engagement with the world around us. The medievals followed suit. They too lacked a term for consciousness, but they likewise indulged in reflection upon 'inner senses', arguably – in the wake of Avicenna's distinguishing five such senses – to excess.

Descartes's introduction of the term and redefinition of the mind
Descartes's innovations with regard to the uses in philosophy of the Latin 'conscientia' (which had not hitherto signified consciousness at all), as well as the French 'la conscience', were of

The Intellectual Powers: A Study of Human Nature, First Edition. P. M. S. Hacker.
© 2013 John Wiley & Sons, Ltd. Published 2013 by John Wiley & Sons, Ltd.

capital importance.[1] For it was he who introduced the novel use of the term into the philosophical vocabulary. He invoked it in order to account for the indubitable and infallible knowledge which he held we have of our Thoughts (*cogitationes*) or Operations of the Mind. His reflections reshaped our conception of the mind and redrew the boundaries of the mental. Thenceforth consciousness, as opposed to intellect and sensitivity to reasons in thought, affection, intention and action, was treated as *the mark of the mental* and *the characteristic of the mind*.

The expressions 'conscius' and the French 'conscient', and the attendant conception of consciousness, caught on among his correspondents and successors (Gassendi, Arnauld, La Forge, Malebranche). So too 'consciousness' and 'conscious' caught on among English philosophers, churchmen and scientists (Stanley, Tillotson, Cumberland, Cudworth and Boyle). But it is to Locke that we must turn to find the most influential, fully fledged, *philosophical* conception of consciousness that, with some variations, was to dominate reflection on the nature of the human mind thenceforth. This conception was to come to its baroque culmination in the writings of Kant. In the Lockean tradition, consciousness is an *inner sense*. Unlike outer sense, it is indubitable and infallible. It is limited in its objects to the operations of the mind. The objects of consciousness are private to each subject of experience and thought. What one is thus conscious of in inner sense constitutes the subjective foundation of empirical knowledge. Because consciousness is thus confined to one's own mental operations, it was conceived to be equivalent to self-consciousness – understood as knowledge of how things are 'subjectively' ('privately', *in foro interno*) with one's self.

Development of the ordinary use The ordinary use of the English noun 'consciousness' and its cognates originates in the early seventeenth century, a mere three or four decades prior to the Cartesian introduction of a novel sense of 'conscius' and 'conscient' into philosophy in the 1640s. So it evolved side by side with the philosophical use – but, on the whole, in fortunate independence of it. For the ordinary use developed, over the next three centuries, into a valuable if specialized instrument in our toolkit of cognitive concepts. By contrast, as we shall see, philosophical usage sank deeper and deeper into quagmires of confusion and incoherence from which it has not recovered to this day.

[1] French to this day has only 'la conscience' to do the work of the distinct English nouns 'consciousness' and 'conscience'.

Multiple centres of variation   The ordinary use of 'conscious' evolved a number of related *centres of variation*: being conscious as opposed to unconscious; being perceptually conscious *of* something, or of some aspect of something, in one's environment; being conscious of one's feelings and inclinations; being conscious *that* as well as being conscious *of*; *conscious*, as opposed to *unconscious* mental attributes (such as belief or desire); *consciously doing* something *qua* agent, as well as *being conscious of doing* something *qua* spectator; and being *self-conscious*. These are not related as species to a genus. Nor are they different *senses* of 'consciousness', if that suggests that they are mere homonyms. Nor is consciousness an Aristotelian 'focal concept' (like *healthy*). Rather, there are multiple centres of variation, with various forms of connection between them (see fig. 1.1).

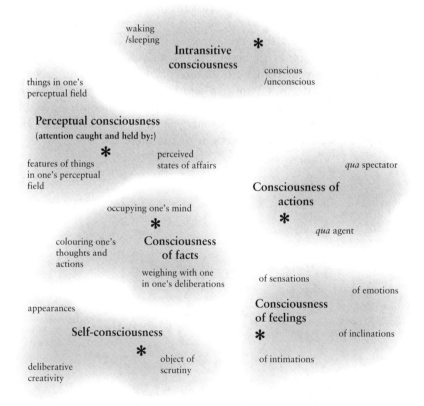

Figure 1.1 *Centres of variation in the normal use of 'consciousness'*

The most important of these centres of variation are far removed from the early modern philosophical idea of an inner sense that discerns 'operations of the mind'. They are equally far removed from the contemporary philosophical conception of *conscious experience* as possessing a unique qualitative character, of there being 'something that it is like' to enjoy such experience. Being perceptually conscious of something is actually a form of *cognitive receptivity* (see fig. 1.2). It is not to achieve knowledge, but to receive it (and hence is a cousin of *noticing*). The concept of *being conscious of* something belongs to the same family of concepts as *being aware of*, *noticing* and *realizing*, and is bound up with *taking cognizance* of something known. To become, and then to be, conscious of something or conscious that something is so, is either to *receive* knowledge as a result of one's attention *being caught and held by something*, or it is for knowledge already possessed to *weigh with one*, or *on one*, in one's deliberations, or for it to *colour one's thought and manner of acting*. It is not to *attain* knowledge by one's endeavours (as are discovering, discerning or detecting), but to be *given* it; or it is for knowledge *already possessed* to colour one's thoughts, enter into one's deliberations and modulate one's manner of acting. *Self-consciousness*, as ordinarily used, is far removed from both *apperception* and *consciousness of one's self*. 'Consciousness' and its cognates, far from signifying the general form, or ubiquitous accompaniment, of the mental, are highly specialized instruments of our language the focus of which is but rarely, and selectively, the operations of the mind.

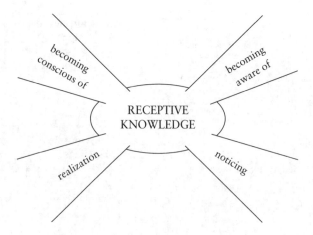

Figure 1.2   *Forms of cognitive receptivity*

Purpose of this chapter   The purpose of this chapter is to clarify the ordinary concept of consciousness, and to show that consciousness is not the mark of the mind. Further, I shall show that both the early modern philosophical account of consciousness as an inner sense whereby we know what passes in our minds,[2] and the contemporary conception of consciousness conceived as a property of experience, namely that there is something which it is like for the subject to have it, are equally incoherent. These *philosophical* conceptions of consciousness, far from identifying the defining mark of the mental, are themselves a mark of deep and ramifying conceptual confusions.

2. The genealogy of the concept of consciousness

History of the concept: Greek   The ancients had no word that can be translated as 'consciousness'. The closest the Greeks came to our abstract noun 'consciousness' is *suneidesis*. The corresponding verb derives from conjoining *oida* (I know) with *sun* or *xun* (with) to yield *sunoida*: 'I know together with', 'I share the knowledge that' or, if the prefix *sun* functions merely as an intensifier, 'I know well', or 'I am well aware'.[3] Of course, this does not mean that they did not struggle with the same philosophical phantasms as the early moderns did and as we do. Whether that implies that they had our *philosophical* concept of consciousness, despite lacking a word for it,

---

[2] Leibniz modified the Lockean conception of consciousness. He invented the French term 'apperception' as a substitute for Piere Coste's 's'apercevoir de' as a translation of Locke's 'perceiving one's perceptions'. Where Locke had argued that one cannot perceive without perceiving that one perceived, Leibniz held that there are innumerable *petites apperceptions* of which we are not conscious. Kant in turn modified Leibniz's conception of consciousness (apperception). He distinguished empirical from transcendental apperception, and held the Lockean/Leibnizean account of consciousness to be confined to empirical apperception. He agreed with Leibniz as against Locke that we can have unconscious representations, but insisted against Leibniz that it must be *possible* for us to be conscious of them. As he put it, the 'I think' need not accompany all my representations, but it must be capable of so doing. Nevertheless, it is arguable that Kant remained a prisoner of the incoherences of the philosophical notion of consciousness that originates with Descartes (see P. M. S. Hacker, 'Kant's Transcendental Deduction: a Wittgensteinian Critique', repr. in P. M. S. Hacker, *Wittgenstein: Comparisons and Context* (Clarendon Press, Oxford, 2013)).

[3] See C. S. Lewis, 'Conscience and Conscious', in his *Studies in Words* (Cambridge University Press, Cambridge, 1960), pp. 181–213.

depends upon whether, after careful analysis, it can be shown that we do have a coherent philosophical *concept* – or whether it will become clear that we are merely floundering about in incoherent conceptual confusion.

History of the concept: Latin   The Greek pattern is also exhibited by Latin, where the combination of *scio* (I know) and *cum* (with) yielded the verb *conscio*, the noun *conscientia*, and the adjective *conscius*. These too could be used in the sense of *shared knowledge*, or of *being privy* to information about something or someone (including oneself), as well as in the thin sense of *knowing well* or *awareness*. The idea of shared knowledge, or knowledge to which one is privy, drifted into the different idea of unshared knowledge to which one is privy – a drift from being a joint witness to being a single 'internal' witness, in particular, a witness against oneself inasmuch as one possesses knowledge of a guilty secret about oneself. Here is the origin of our idea of a *guilty conscience*. And it is from the idea of an internal witness that the idea of *conscience* as an internal law-giver was later to evolve. Note, however, that neither *suneidesis* nor *conscientia* was employed to signify the manner in which one is (according to the Cartesian and early modern conception) held to know of whatever is 'passing in one's mind' or to know (according to the contemporary conception) what it is like to have a given experience. Nor was what one was *sunoida* or *conscius* of restricted to operations or states of one's mind.

History of the concept: English   The emergence of the English expressions 'consciousness', 'being conscious of' and 'self-conscious' is surprisingly late.[4] 'Conscious' and its cognates occur nowhere in the writings of Shakespeare. Their earliest occurrences,

---

[4] The French *la conscience* (in the sense of 'consciousness') evolved from the second sense of *conscientia*, namely *knowing well* or *awareness*. Leibniz, writing about Locke in French in his *Nouveaux Essaies*, coined the term 'consciosité' (to avoid the ambiguity of la conscience), but it did not catch on. The German *Bewusstsein* is of even later coinage, and first appears in the early eighteenth century as 'bewust seyn' in the writings of Christian Wolff, as a rendering of the Cartesian use of 'la conscience' (and so quite distinct from 'Gewissen', i.e. conscience). 'Bewust' was derived from 'bewissen', an Early High German compound of 'wissen'. It is curious that Notker Teutonicus, in the eleventh century, used the Old High German 'wizzantheit' (derived from 'wizzan' – to know, to be aware of) as a translation of the epistemic sense of the Latin 'conscientia' (i.e. knowing well or being aware of) and used 'giwizzani' to signify conscience. But while *giwizzani* survived as *Gewissen*, *wizzantheit* was lost by the fourteenth century. (I am indebted to Joachim Adler for this philological history.)

according to the *Oxford English Dictionary*, are at the beginning of the seventeenth century, when 'to be conscious', like *conscius*, signified *being privy* to something or to some secret. It could be applied poetically to inanimate things or abstractions as sharing knowledge of, or being witness to, human actions – as in 'the conscious time' (Jonson, 1601), 'the conscious groves, the scenes of his past triumphs and his loves' (Denham, 1643), and 'under conscious Night, Secret they finish'd' (Milton, 1667). 'Being conscious', ascribed to a person, was used in the classical sense to signify sharing a secret, being privy to something with another person, as in Hobbes (*Leviathan*, 1651): 'Where two, or more men, know of one and the same fact, they are said to be Conscious of it one to another', or in South's discussion of friendship (*Sermons*, 1664): 'Nothing is to be concealed from the other self. To be a friend and to be conscious are terms equivalent.'

Sharing a secret, however, easily mutated into no more than *being privy to* or *witness to* something. This usage is evident already in the 1610s. The objects of *being conscious to oneself* could be facts about other people or states of affairs, or they could be facts about oneself, for example, one's weakness (1620). One was said to be *conscious to* the patience and wisdom of another (1649), or *conscious to* a murder (1658). Gradually the suffix 'to oneself' was dropped, and *consciousness to something* was transformed into *consciousness of something*. Already in the 1630s we find Massinger writing 'I am conscious of an offence', and in the 1660s Milton was writing of 'consciousness of highest worth'.

Ordinary use evolved independently of philosophical use In blissful independence of philosophical entanglements from the 1650s onwards, the common notion of consciousness continued to evolve in the public domain. The classical sense of being privy to a secret, of being 'in the know', continued into the early nineteenth century. Hence we find Jane Austen writing of Mrs Morland's 'conscious daughter', that is, the daughter who shared secret knowledge with another (*Northanger Abbey*, ch. 30), and of someone who 'looked conscious', that is, someone who, being privy to certain information, looked as if he was 'in the know' (ch. 18). But by the twentieth century this use had lapsed.

Outside philosophy, one use of 'to be conscious of' evolved in the late seventeenth and early eighteenth centuries into a first cousin of 'to be aware of'. So, unlike the simultaneously evolving philosophical conception of consciousness, that of which one might be said to be conscious was not confined to one's states of mind or mental operations. One could be said to be conscious of the rain clouds on the horizon, of the lateness of the hour, of the merits of a case, of the importance of the issue under consideration. Indeed, one could be said to be conscious of the mental state of another person, as when one is conscious of the irritability of another, or of their rising anger. Even where the object of consciousness was restricted to oneself, what one could be said to be conscious of did not have to be one's mental operations or mental states. It might well be past or present facts about oneself of which one felt ashamed or guilty, hence that one *kept privy to oneself*, or of which one felt proud and hence was 'conscious of one's worth'. But even when the objects of consciousness were one's own current mental operations, the range of mental operations of which one could be said to be conscious was, on the whole, limited to things that one could be said to *feel* – as when one is conscious of butterflies in one's stomach, of one's rising anxiety or of the increasing severity of one's pain. No one (other than philosophers) would have spoken of being conscious of thinking whatever one is thinking, or of *perceiving* (= *being conscious of*) one's perceiving (as opposed to sometimes becoming and being conscious of *what* one perceives), or of being conscious of intending to do whatever one intends to do.

The old link with being privy to something, and the phrases 'conscious to oneself' and 'conscious to something', slowly faded away. Since one could be said to *be* conscious of something, one could also be said to *become* conscious of something. This had important logico-grammatical ramifications with respect to the possible objects of consciousness (by contrast with the possible objects of *noticing*, *realizing* and *being aware of*). These will be examined later.

According to the *Oxford English Dictionary*, it was not until the middle of the nineteenth century that the term 'consciousness' came to be used to signify wakefulness, as when one speaks of *regaining consciousness* or *losing consciousness* (rather than of *regaining (or losing) one's senses*). Similarly, the common conceptions (as opposed to the philosophical notion) of being *self-conscious*, that is, being overly concerned with one's appearance and dress, or being aware that the eyes of others are upon one, and being affected thereby, seem likewise to be a nineteenth-century addition. Categories of dispositional consciousness, such as class-consciousness (1903), dress-consciousness (1918), money-consciousness (1933), are twentieth-century innovations.

Deviation of ordinary from philosophical use

The most striking feature of the genealogy of *con-sciousness* is the extent to which philosophical use deviated from common usage from its inception. This barely noticed fact should make us examine both with care. The autonomy of the philosophical use bodes ill. For it is not impossible that the philosophical use belongs to the same category of conceptual disasters as seventeenth-century *ideas* and twentieth-century *sense-data*. In 1707 Clarke wrote: 'Consciousness, *in the most strict and exact Sense of the Word*, signifies . . . the Reflex Act by which I know that I think and that my Thoughts and Actions are my own and not Another's' (emphasis added). In 1785 Reid felt confident in writing: 'Consciousness is a word used by Philosophers, to signify that immediate knowledge we have of our present thoughts and purposes, and, in general, of all the present operations of our minds.'[5] What philosophers held to be a special philosophical sense of the word may be no more than a special philosophical muddle.

3. The analytic of consciousness

Intransitive consciousness

We must distinguish first between *intransitive* and *tran-sitive* consciousness.[6] Being intransitively conscious is contrasted with various forms of being unconscious, for example, being comatose or anaesthetized. Consciousness is something one may lose (on fainting, when having a high fever, or being knocked out) and regain (on recovering consciousness). Being awake differs from being conscious in so far as it is contrasted with being asleep rather than with being unconscious. 'Is A unconscious?' and 'Has A recovered consciousness?' belong typically in the hospital, whereas 'Is A asleep?' and 'Has A woken up?' are more appropriate at home. Responsiveness during sleep is far greater than respon-siveness during periods of unconsciousness. There are, of course, borderline cases intermediate between intransitive consciousness and

[5] Thomas Reid, *Essays on the Intellectual Powers of Man* [1785] (Edinburgh University Press, Edinburgh, 2002), p. 24.

[6] The grammatical nomenclature is Norman Malcolm's, in his 'Consciousness and Causality', in D. M. Armstrong and N. Malcolm, *Consciousness and Causality* (Blackwell, Oxford, 1984), p. 3.

unconsciousness for which there is appropriate non-technical terminology (e.g. semi-conscious, barely conscious, groggy, dazed, sleep-walking) as well as technical nomenclature (e.g. hypnotic trance, fugue, epileptic automatism).

Unconsciousness is a state, consciousness a condition

Unconsciousness is a state of a creature, though not a mental one. Consciousness is a condition for being in any occurrent mental state. A conscious state (or state of consciousness) is not a state that is conscious, any more than a happy outcome is an outcome that is happy (as opposed to an outcome that makes someone happy) or a passionate belief is a belief that is passionate (as opposed to someone's believing passionately). Nor is it necessarily a mental state *of which one is conscious* – a state of intense concentration is a state of consciousness, but not one *of* which one is conscious (although one may later realize how intensely one had been concentrating, since one did not notice the clock striking twelve). Rather, it is a mental state one is in *while one is conscious* (e.g. concentrating on one's work, feeling excited or elated) as opposed to a dispositional mental state (e.g. being in a depression, being cheerful, or being anxious about something, for many weeks).

Criteria for intransitive consciousness

The criteria for another person's *regaining consciousness* and then *being conscious* are behavioural – namely appropriate forms of responsiveness to perceptual stimuli. We can normally see *that* a person is conscious (someone can pretend to be unconscious, but not to be conscious). However, there are and could be no criteria for saying 'I am conscious' or even 'I have regained consciousness'. That one is conscious is not evident to one by 'introspection'. Nor is it information one might acquire by having 'access' to one's consciousness (a misuse of the term 'access'). I may become and then be conscious of your regaining consciousness, but I cannot become and then be conscious of my regaining consciousness. There is no such thing as *being conscious of one's consciousness*. This is a form of words without sense. My own intransitive consciousness is not an object of possible experience for me, but a precondition for my having any experiences at all.

Transitive consciousness: dispositional and occurrent

Transitive consciousness is consciousness *of something*. It may be dispositional or occurrent. A person can be said to be class-conscious, that is, conscious of his own and others' social class (or money-conscious, or safety-conscious), if he is disposed to pay attention to the social class of others and frequently adverts to it and to his own (like Jane Austen's Sir Walter Elliot). Someone can be said to be conscious of their ignorance (like Harriet Smith) or superiority (like Mr Darcy) if they are prone to be preoccupied with their ignorance or superiority, if they tend to dwell on it and manifest this in what they do and say.

Occurrent transitive consciousness Occurrent transitive consciousness is not a disposition. It has different modes (see fig. 1.4 on p. 27):

(i)   *having one's attention caught and held* by something;
(ii) *giving one's attention* to one's own deliberate action;
(iii) *something's weighing with one* in one's current deliberation;
(iv) *something's occupying one's mind and knowingly colouring* one's thoughts, feelings and manner of behaving.

It is *these* aspects of transitive consciousness that are our concern. Let us first identify the categorial post at which this concept is stationed.[7]

Becoming and being conscious of something are not acts or activities To become and then to be conscious of something is not to perform *an act* of any kind. There is no such thing as an act of consciousness or an act of becoming conscious of something. So to become conscious of something is not to *pay* attention to it or to *give* one's attention to it. For one cannot voluntarily, deliberately or on purpose become conscious of something – whereas one can voluntarily, deliberately or on purpose pay attention to something. Hence, one cannot decide, or refuse, to be or become conscious of something, and one cannot have a reason for becoming or being conscious of something – whereas one can decide to give one's attention to something and one may have reasons for doing so. That is why, contrary to received philosophical misconceptions, *thinking about* one's Mental Operations or Thoughts is not to be conscious (or not conscious) of them, since one can voluntarily, intentionally and deliberately think about one's state of mind, and one can be asked or ordered to think about and reflect on one's mental operations. To become conscious of something is an occurrence at a given time, but it is not something one *does* – it is something that *happens* to one.

---

[7] The following analysis is indebted to, and is an elaboration of, A. R. White's *Attention* (Blackwell, Oxford, 1964), ch. 4.

Neither to become nor to be conscious of something is *an activity*. One cannot be engaged in becoming conscious of something, and one cannot be interrupted in the middle of, and later resume, being conscious of it. One cannot hurry up in being conscious of something and there are no means and methods of becoming conscious of anything.

Being conscious of something is not a mental state   To be conscious of something is not to be in *a mental state*, although what one is conscious of may, sometimes, be a mental state, as when one is conscious of one's anxiety. The reason for this is perhaps the conceptual link between being conscious of something and knowing something. For to know something to be so is not to be in a mental state of any kind, but *to be able to do various things* in the light of *what* one knows, that is, of information one possesses (see chapter 4). To be in receipt of knowledge, or for knowledge already possessed to weigh with one or affect one, is not in itself to be in any particular mental state.

Locus of the concept of consciousness in our conceptual scheme   This gives us a distinct idea of consciousness. But it does not yet give us a clear one. For that we must locate the idea in the web of our conceptual scheme, and examine its reticulations. The concept of transitive consciousness lies at the confluence of the concepts of *knowledge, receptivity, realization, awareness, attention caught and held, taking cognizance of* and *being affected by* knowledge already possessed.

Verbs of cognitive receptivity   As remarked, 'to be conscious of' belongs to the same family of cognitive verbs as 'notice', 'be aware of', 'realize', which are verbs of *cognitive receptivity*. These stand in contrast to the family of verbs of *cognitive achievement*, such as 'discover', 'discern', 'detect', which may signify the successful upshot of an intentional activity, often (but not always) an actual quest for knowledge. One may try to discover, detect and discern, and if one does so successfully, one has achieved knowledge. By contrast, verbs of cognitive receptivity, in particular in their application to modes of perception, signify not forms of *achieving* knowledge, but the manner in which knowledge is *given* one – by something's striking one, dawning on one, or catching and holding one's attention. So one can neither try to become conscious of something, nor endeavour to realize or to notice (as opposed to taking note of) something. For these verbs of cognitive receptivity do not signify acts that might be done voluntarily, intentionally or on purpose, since they do not signify acts at all (see fig. 1.3).

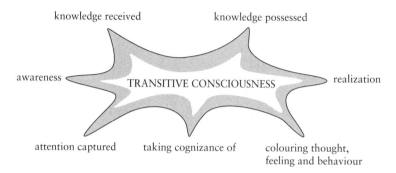

Figure 1.3   *The locus of the concept of transitive consciousness in the web of cognitive concepts*

Each of these verbs has a special role, even though they may sometimes overlap. For example, whatever one is conscious of, one is also aware of, but there is much one is perfectly aware of (since, say, one has been reliably informed) that one is not conscious of (since it is not 'before one's mind', and does not occupy one). Roughly speaking, to notice something is to be struck by it, to be aware of something is for it to sink in, to realize something is for it to dawn on one, and to be conscious of something is for it to be before one's mind. Each of these metaphorical characterizations needs to be (and can be) unpacked.

One may notice or realize something, but one may *become* aware or conscious of something. 'To be conscious of' is a result verb, not a success verb. It may signify the cognitive result of *becoming* perceptually conscious of something, or, in cases of non-perceptual consciousness of facts, the result of something of which one is already aware *coming before one's mind*.

The idea of *becoming* conscious of something has immediate logical consequences marking *perceptual consciousness* off from noticing and realizing something. For one may notice something instantaneous (a flash or a bang), but what one is perceptually conscious of must be something that lasts some time. Otherwise one could not *be* perceptually conscious of it. Moreover, it must pre-exist one's *being* conscious of it, otherwise one could not have *become* conscious of it.

The representational form of transitive consciousness

Realizing is exclusively of facts, since it is the upshot of putting two and two together. Consciousness is also *of things* (as well as of features, events and states of affairs). We may apprehend and become, and then be, conscious of Jack standing in the corner, of the ticking of the clock, of the smell of cooking, of the heat and humidity. Immediate apprehension is the normal *representational form* (even when it is not the matter) of transitive consciousness.[8] That is, we have a marked preference for 'consciousness of', as opposed to 'consciousness that'. This is no coincidence. We speak of being conscious of our ignorance, our weariness or our irritability; we may be conscious of the grief of others, of their vulnerability or of their peril; and we are conscious of impending danger, of the honour being done to us, of the importance of the situation. All these phrases can be transformed into *consciousness that* phrases: to be conscious of one's ignorance is to be conscious (of the fact) that one is ignorant, to be conscious of the grief of another is to be conscious (of the fact) that they are grieving, and to be conscious of the impending danger is to be conscious (of the fact) that danger is impending. Why then the preference for the abstract objectual form, rather than for the factual or propositional form? Precisely because the objectual abstraction emphasizes the affinity of *consciousness of* with immediate apprehension. For what one is *conscious of* is necessarily something 'present to the mind', something that holds one's attention, something that currently weighs with one in one's deliberation, or something that colours one's thoughts, feelings and behaviour. You may have to remind me of what I am already aware of, but you cannot remind me of what I am conscious of. Although consciousness is primarily of what is present, one can be conscious of things past too, as when one is conscious of yesterday's victory or of the good luck one had, if these past facts are now 'present to one's mind' and are affecting one's thoughts, behaviour and manner of behaving. Moreover, one may be conscious of one's own enduring characteristics – as when one is conscious of one's strength or weakness, of one's knowledge or ignorance. In such cases, one *feels* strong or weak, knowledgeable or ignorant, and one's feeling is right. One typically

---

[8] In the sense in which one may say that the representational form of knowledge is *possession*, that is, we *represent* knowledge as something we have, own, possess, can give away – this is the *picture* we use.

feels so when one is exhibiting or is about to exhibit the trait in question and realizes one is, or realizes one should refrain from, so doing.

Consciousness is polymorphous

Consciousness is polymorphous (like *obeying, working, practising*).[9] What it is to become conscious of something depends upon what it is that one has become conscious of – a sight, sound or smell, danger, weariness or a feeling of irritation. Being conscious of something may take the various forms of perceiving something – if what one perceives catches and holds one's attention; or it may take the form of dwelling on what one is conscious of – if one is occupied with it and it colours one's thoughts and behaviour. With some exceptions, contrary to the philosophical tradition, what one is conscious of may occur or obtain without one's being conscious of it, that is, without its catching and holding one's attention, and without one's dwelling on it. Of course, perceptual verbs are not polymorphous, and consciousness is not *a form of perception*. Consciousness can be of objects of sensible perception, but it is not an *outer sense*. And it is not an *inner sense* either. This will be made clear below.

Transitive consciousness is generally a form of knowledge of its object

Consciousness of something is generally *a form of knowledge of what one is conscious of*. It may be knowledge of the presence of someone or something, as when one is conscious of Jack standing in the corner, or of the rain clouds on the horizon. Or it may be knowledge that something is so, as when one is conscious of the boredom of one's audience, that is, conscious that they are bored, or conscious of the honour being done to one, that is, conscious that one is being honoured. Because it is a form of knowledge, what one is conscious of is so – that is, like 'to know', 'to be conscious of' is *factive*. One cannot be conscious of what is not the case. So consciousness, unlike belief, expectation, hope and fear, is *not intentional*, and its objects do not enjoy intentional *in-existence*.[10] However, ironically, it is precisely when the object of consciousness *is* a 'mental operation' – in particular

[9] The terminology is Ryle's: see 'Thinking and Language', repr. in his *Collected Papers* (Hutchinson, London, 1971).

[10] That is, one may believe that things are so, even though they are not – so this use of 'believe' is intentional. But one cannot be conscious that things are so if they are not – so 'to be conscious that' is not intentional and its objects do not enjoy 'intentional in-existence'. See chapter 2.

something one feels – that, contrary to the whole philosophical tradition, consciousness, though factive, *is not a form of knowledge at all*,
any more than forgetting one's troubles is a form of mnemonic deficiency. This singularity will be clarified below.

Differences between Although consciousness, unlike mere attention,
knowing and being is *generally* a form of knowledge, it is a very
conscious of something specific one. Whereas one can know something
well, thoroughly, intimately or in detail, one cannot be conscious of
something well, thoroughly, intimately or in detail. And while one
can be acutely, agreeably or uncomfortably conscious of certain
things, one cannot acutely, agreeably or uncomfortably know things.
The reason for this is because one form knowledge may take is skill
or competence – as when one knows Latin *well*. Another form of
knowledge is expertise – as when one has a *thorough and detailed*
knowledge of Tudor England. A further form knowledge possessed
may take is acquaintance – as when one knows Jack or Jill *intimately*.
But to be conscious of something is neither to possess a skill, nor to
be an expert in a given domain of knowledge, nor yet to be acquainted
with something or someone. One cannot be trained to become conscious of things – only trained in greater *receptivity*. There is no such
thing as being *skilful* at being conscious of things – only being more
sensitive. One can be good at learning, discovering, detecting or
finding out that things are thus-and-so, but one cannot be good at
becoming or being conscious of things. One can be conscious of
someone without being acquainted with him, and acquainted with
someone without being conscious of him. One can find out that one
knows something (e.g. the dates of the monarchs of England), but
one cannot find out that one is conscious of something, because one
cannot *find out* that one's attention is caught by something (as
opposed to finding out what has caught one's attention). One may
ask 'How do you know?' but not 'How are you conscious of . . . ?'
Rather one asks 'What made you conscious of . . . ?' For there are
sources of knowledge (e.g. perception, reason, testimony), but no
sources of what one is conscious of.

Objects of transitive Transitive consciousness may take many different
consciousness kinds of objects (see fig. 1.4). What one is conscious of may be:

(i)   What one sees, hears, smells, tastes or feels – both objectually
      and factually (i.e. both objects (properties and relations of
      objects) perceived, and things being perceived to be so (as well

as events being perceived to occur and processes being perceived to go on)). This I have called 'perceptual consciousness'.

(ii) Facts that one has *previously learnt* and that are currently occupying one's mind, weighing with one in one's deliberations, or colouring one's thoughts, behaviour or manner of behaving.
(iii) What one is doing.
(iv) What one is feeling, that is, a subset of traditional Mental Operations, which may be sensations, inclinations, felt dispositions to behave and, in certain circumstances, intimations (as when one feels it would be wrong to . . .).

Doubtless this crude classification can be refined. But for present purposes these distinctions suffice. Investigating them will bear fruit.

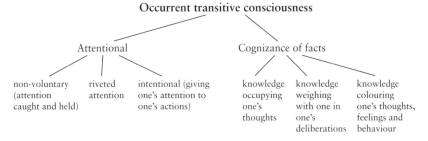

Figure 1.4 *Modes of occurrent transitive consciousness*

Perceptual consciousness: attention caught and held

The most prominent form of 'consciousness of something' in natural language is perceptual consciousness. To become and then be conscious of something in one's field of perception is *to have one's attention caught and held* by something one perceives. Just as one may perceive something or perceive that something is so, so too one may be conscious of someone or something (e.g. of Jack) or conscious that something is so (e.g. that Jack is standing in the corner). That of which one is conscious is what caught one's attention (a creature, a material thing, a sound or smell, an event or process). Its features are typically what hold one's attention (that it is located there, its movement or manner of movement, its striking appearance and so forth).

The incompatibility of intentional attention and perceptual consciousness

The nexus with attention determines the contours of the concept of perceptual consciousness. One cannot be conscious of many things at the same time, because one cannot attend to many things at the same time.[11] One cannot remain conscious of something that no longer holds one's attention (although one may be perfectly aware that things are as one was conscious of them as being). One cannot become and be conscious of something if one is *intentionally attending* to it, any more than one can involuntarily lie, discover something one already knows or detect something one has already found out. Of course, the fact that one cannot be said to become and be conscious of what one is *intentionally* attending to (since it has not caught and held one's attention) does not imply that one is *not* conscious of it, any more than the fact that one cannot be said to recognize one's wife every time one looks at her in the course of a conversation over the breakfast table means that one fails to recognize her. It means that the question of whether one is or is not conscious of what one is intentionally attending to anyway cannot arise.

Perceptual consciousness and peripheral attention

This is obvious once one realizes that perceptual consciousness is commonly a matter of *peripheral attention*. I cannot be said to be either conscious or not conscious of what you are saying if I am listening attentively to you, but I may become conscious of a buzzing noise in the background. (But not all perceptual consciousness is of what one peripherally perceives. For one may become and remain conscious of a hitherto unnoticed *feature* of something one is intentionally attending to.)

Perceptual consciousness and cognitive receptivity

Perceptual consciousness is not merely a matter of attention being caught and held. It is also a matter of *reception of knowledge*. Merely to have one's attention caught by something does not suffice for being conscious of that thing. For one must also *realize* what it is that has caught one's attention. One may perceive something and have one's attention caught by what one perceives, *without* being conscious of it – as when one perceives a shadow in the bushes and takes it to be a cat. Here one is neither conscious of a cat nor conscious of a shadow.

Of course, one may perceive something without its catching and holding one's attention at all – and in such cases one cannot be said to be conscious of what one perceives, although one may or may not have noticed it.

---

[11] But one can be aware of many things at the same time, since awareness of facts is not a form of attention, but of being well informed and adverting from time to time to what one knows.

To be perceptually conscious of something is not to be conscious *of perceiving it*, that is, it is not what Locke called 'perceiving one's perceptions', nor is it what Leibniz and later Kant called 'apperception'. It is, rather, to have one's attention caught and held by *what* one perceives. Hence one cannot remain *perceptually* conscious of what one no longer perceives, just as one cannot remain conscious of something that no longer holds one's attention. But in both cases, one may remain aware of what one was previously conscious. One can become and then be conscious of the boredom of one's audience, of the friendliness of the company and of the spectators' eyes upon one. These are cases of becoming conscious (*because* one comes to perceive) *that* something is so.

Self-consciousness:
1st sense
Self-consciousness, in *one* of the senses of the English phrase, is a form of thought or awareness. It is a matter of thinking (rightly or wrongly) that others are looking at one or of being aware that they are, of this causing one to feel embarrassed and affecting the naturalness of one's behaviour and manner. People who are self-conscious before a camera freeze, and cannot assume their normal expression. People who are self-conscious in company exaggerate their behaviour, their laughter is shrill or forced, or their shyness gets the better of them and so forth. In another sense of the phrase, to be self-conscious about one's appearance is to be *excessively concerned* with how one will look to others, especially with regard to dress.

Consciousness
that is knowledge
possessed
The cognitive receptivity of perceptual consciousness includes consciousness of perceived fact. As remarked, not all consciousness of fact involves *perceiving* things to be thus-and-so. Nor, indeed, is it always a case of cognitive *receptivity*. For it can equally well be a matter of knowledge *already possessed* coming to mind, occupying one and affecting one's thoughts, deliberations and feelings, as well as one's behaviour and manner of behaving. If one visits a recently widowed friend, well aware that her husband died and that she is grieving, one's consciousness of her grief and of her recent loss does not consist in one's attention being caught and held by something one perceives. Rather, it consists of knowledge one already possesses (things of which one is already well aware) *being before one's mind, colouring* one's thoughts and feelings, and *affecting one's manner of behaving*. That of which one is acutely conscious *in one's deliberations* is something that *weighs* with one and is a factor one may *take*

into account in one's decision. As noted, it is the immediacy of the influence of antecedently acquired knowledge that inclines us here towards the nominalized form 'I was conscious of her grief', rather than the more laboured 'I was conscious of the fact that she was grieving', or 'I was conscious of the honour being done to me' rather than 'I was conscious of the fact that I was being honoured'. Note that consciousness of facts incorporates realization or recollection of facts and reflection on things being as one realizes or remembers them to be. It includes a further form of self-consciousness, namely one's consciousness of one's own character traits, virtues and vices, folly or erudition, precisely to the extent that these tend to come to mind and one is prone to reflect on them.

Consciousness of one's action, qua spectator and qua agent

One may be conscious of what one is doing – and this in two ways: *qua* spectator and *qua* agent. *Qua* spectator what one becomes and then is conscious of is typically not something one is *intentionally* doing. When one realizes with dismay that one is repeating last week's lecture, or boring one's audience, or telling a joke one has already told before, one may become embarrassingly conscious of the fact. One's attention is drawn to what one is unintentionally doing, or to an unintended consequence or side effect of what one is doing. The affinities of this form of consciousness with perceptual consciousness are patent.

One may also be conscious of what one is doing *qua* agent. One may consciously do something, for example, crack a carefully rehearsed joke at one's lecture. Here the agent knows what he is doing, and is attending to the doing of it. The agent is acting in execution of his intention, and is occupied and absorbed in carrying out his intention – as is made vivid by the common conjunction 'consciously and deliberately'. Agential consciousness is therefore altogether different from perceptual consciousness. It is not a matter of having one's attention caught and held by something – indeed, it is *deliberately giving* one's attention to something. It is an off-shoot of the web of concepts of consciousness, called into being *in contrast* to spectatorial consciousness of one's action, which *is* a matter of one's attention being caught by a feature of whatever one is doing.

Self-consciousness: 2nd sense

A further strand is interwoven into the concept of agential consciousness, a strand that connects it with yet another aspect of the ordinary notion of self-consciousness. For we say of a painter or writer that they are highly self-conscious – that they deliberate at length over their work (like Leonardo), reflect deeply upon what they are doing (like Flaubert), that what they do is not spontaneous (as Picasso often was) and intuitive (like Jackson Pollock), but carefully thought through. This notion of a self-conscious writer or artist is evidently a dispositional cousin of the concept of agential consciousness of action.

Consciousness of operations of the mind The final class of objects of transitive consciousness consists of 'mental operations'. It was this that obsessed post-Cartesian philosophers to the exclusion of all else. La Forge (1666) already declared that 'conscience, ou connaissance intèrieure que chacun de nous ressent immédiatement par soi-même quand il s'aperçoit de ce qu'il fait ou de ce que se passe en lui'.[12] Malebranche (1674) identified *conscience* with 'internal sentiment'. Indeed, as we saw above, Samuel Clarke (1707) and Thomas Reid (1785) declared that *strictly speaking* consciousness is *only* of the operations of the mind. Consciousness thus conceived was 'apperception'. We shall examine this tangle of confusions below.

Its restriction to feelings In the natural use of 'conscious of', the operations of the mind of which one can intelligibly be said to be conscious are primarily feelings, in the broad sense of the term which incorporates sensations, moods, attitudes, emotions, motives and intimations. No one other than a philosopher would ever speak of being conscious of seeing, hearing, tasting or smelling something, as opposed to being conscious of what one saw, heard, tasted or smelled. No one outside philosophy would speak of being conscious of thinking, believing, knowing or remembering anything – *being able to say* that one is thinking or what one thinks is not a matter of being conscious of anything. If one were to say 'I think that such-and-such', and were asked whether one was conscious of thinking this – one would be bewildered. One might say 'yes', but only because if one said 'no', it might seem that one was claiming that one thought such-and-such, but was *not* conscious of so doing, that is, was ignorant of so doing – and *that* one would not want to say. To be sure, what one would probably say is, 'What do you mean?'

[12] Louis de La Forge, *Traité de l'esprit de l'homme* (1666), repr. in *Œuvres philosophiques*, ed. Pierre Clair (Paris, 1974), p. 112.

By contrast, one may well say that one is conscious or aware of the increasing pain in one's tooth, of the tickling sensation between one's shoulder blades, of the itch in one's neck. Sensations are not objects, let alone objects we perceive. But they do *catch and hold our attention.* One may be conscious or aware of one's posture and of the disposition or movements of one's limbs. And so too, one may be conscious of one's overall bodily condition, of one's feeling of exhaustion or of well-being – if one's exhaustion or sense of well-being impress themselves upon one. We may also become conscious or aware of our affections. For we may become conscious of our increasing irritation as the speaker drones on, of our feeling of jealousy as our spouse flirts with another and of our excitement as the race we are watching reaches its climax. We can, but need not, be conscious of our moods and their changes – as when we become conscious of the deepening of our depression, or of feeling exceptionally cheerful or unusually irritable. Affective consciousness usually takes the form of realization, rather than captured attention. For it often dawns on us that we are feeling jealous or irritable, and we may then dwell on it. Consciousness of the attitudes we feel, of our likes and dislikes, our approvals and disapprovals, are likewise typically the upshot of realization, the object of which then occupies us. We can become conscious of the misgivings we feel, of our feeling that it is time to go, or of our inclination to take another drink – if these cross our mind and we dwell on them prior to resolving what to do. It is interesting that 'to be aware of' sits more comfortably here than 'to be conscious of' (see fig. 1.5 for an overview of occurrent transitive consciousness).

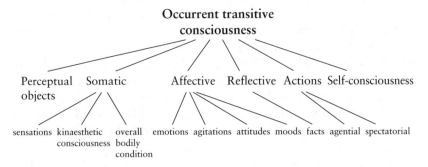

Figure 1.5   *Objects of occurrent transitive consciousness*

This aspect of the concept of transitive consciousness is a potent source of conceptual entanglement – for it is here above all that we confuse the ability *to say* how things are with us with the ability *to see*, by consciousness, apperception, introspection, or inner sense. This confusion lay at the heart of the novel early modern philosophical conception of consciousness.

4. The early modern philosophical conception of consciousness

Aristotle's questions on apperception and the general sense   As noted, the ancients lacked any term for 'conscious' and its cognates, and they did not conceive of consciousness as the mark of having a mind. Nevertheless, it would be mistaken to suppose that none of the confusions that give rise to *our* concern with consciousness were familiar to them. Aristotle raised the question of how one perceives (or apprehends) that one sees, hears or tastes (*De Anima*, 425^{b}12–25). Is it by the use of the same sense-faculty as that with which one respectively sees, hears or tastes, or is it by some other sense-faculty? He queried how we distinguish white from sweet if each is perceived by the use of a different sense organ ('On Sleep', 455^{a}15–22). And he asked how we perceive a single thing as being *both* white *and* sweet, given that each quality is perceived by the use of a different sense organ (*De Anima*, 426^{b}8–21). How, he wondered, is the separate information all brought together to form a unified perception of a white and sweet object? His answer to this latter question was that it is by means of the *koinê aisthêsis* (later called the 'sensus communis'), or the primary power of sense (*to prôton aesthêtikon*), the organ of which is the common or general sensorium (which Aristotle thought to be the heart and was later held to be the brain). However, these puzzling questions themselves are faulty.

The confusions underlying the questions   Not surprisingly, physiological questions were here conflated with conceptual ones. How neural impulses from the separate sense organs are processed by the brain to enable us to perceive as we do involves an array of legitimate empirical questions on which neuroscientists are still working. The question of how we perceive (or apprehend) that we see, hear, smell, etc. presupposes that we do *perceive* that we see, hear, smell, etc. whenever we do, or that our ability to *say* that we see or hear this or that rests on *apprehension* or *knowledge* that we are seeing or hearing. That is far from obvious. How we discriminate white from sweet, how we take different special sensibles to belong to one and the same object, and how we know that we are seeing or hearing, are conceptual questions of even more dubious legitimacy. Very briefly: what one cannot sensibly confuse or conflate, one cannot be said sensibly to distinguish either. Hence the question of what sense faculty is involved in distinguishing white from sweet makes no sense. The question of how, when we take and eat a lump of white sugar, we apprehend the same thing as being white, sweet, granular and cuboid presupposes the intelligibility, in these same circumstances, of sensing them as not being qualities of the same object, but as being qualities of different objects. But these presuppositions are unintelligible. We shall revert to this below.

The legacy: the general sense and the binding problem   Aristotle had opened a Pandora's box, releasing conceptual puzzles that were to occupy his successors among the Stoics, Epicureans and later the neo-Platonists for the next few centuries. Plotinus wrote of an 'inner perceptual ability' by means of which we know of our appetites (Plotinus 4.8.8.10–12). Augustine (*Confessions* vii, §17; *On Freedom of the Will* 2.2.8) held that we perceive our perception by means of an inner sense (*sensus interior*). It is the general sense (*sensus communis*), in animals and man alike, that synthesizes the information from the five external senses to form a unified perception and that enables us to perceive that we perceive. These questions were inherited from the medievals by the moderns. Descartes accepted the legitimacy of the question of how the 'information' from the different senses is synthesized to form a unified apprehension of a multiply qualified object. Indeed, he accepted a form of the Aristotelian solution that postulated a *sensus communis* to fulfil the synthesizing role. Kant endeavoured to answer the question in his account of transcendental psychology. He tried to explain the mechanisms by reference to a threefold synthesis: of apprehension, of reproduction in the imagination, and of recognition under a concept in apperception. It is this that yields self-conscious experience of unified phenomenal objects in a spatio-temporal framework. The same conceptually suspect puzzle has now transmuted into a neuroscientific question known as the 'binding problem' – namely: how does the brain bring all the 'information' from the separate senses together to form a 'single unified picture'? But this too is incoherent.[13]

Origins of the early modern philosophical conception of consciousness in Descartes

The early modern *philosophical* notion of consciousness was introduced by Descartes.[14] The term does not appear in his work prior to the *Meditations* (1641), and even there it occurs just once.[15] In the Third Meditation, it occurs not in relation to knowledge of one's 'thoughts' or 'operations of the mind', but in relation to lack of awareness of power to perpetuate one's own existence.[16] It was only under pressure from objectors to this single remark that Descartes was forced, in his 'Replies to Objections', to elaborate his ideas on knowing one's own 'thoughts'. He used the terms *conscientia*, *conscius*, and *conscio* to signify a form of knowledge, namely the alleged direct knowledge we have of what is passing in our minds. What we are conscious of, according to Descartes, are *Thoughts*, a term which he stretched to include thinking (as ordinarily understood), sensing or perceiving (shorn of factive force), understanding, wanting and imagining.

---

[13] See e.g. Francis Crick: 'we can see how the visual parts of the brain take the picture (the visual field) apart, but we do not yet know how the brain puts it all together to provide our highly organized view of the world – that is, what we see. It seems as if the brain needs to impose some global unity on certain activities in its different parts so that the attributes of a single object – its shape, colour, movement, location, and so on – are in some way brought together without at the same time confusing them with the attributes of other objects in the visual field' (*The Astonishing Hypothesis* (Touchstone, London, 1995), p. 22). But, of course, the brain doesn't take what we see apart, and what we see is no picture (unless we are looking at one). The brain *makes it possible* for us to use our eyes in order to see. To do that it does not, and could not, take a picture apart and put it together again. For detailed discussion, see M. R. Bennett and P. M. S. Hacker, *Philosophical Foundations of Neuroscience* (Blackwell, Oxford, 2003), pp. 137–43.

[14] The term was already used by Bacon, initially in the form 'conscient' (1612), and then in the form 'conscious' (1625) to signify being privy to knowledge about one's faults. But the concept had no role in his philosophy.

[15] I am indebted to Hanoch Ben-Yami's scholarship for this surprising information about Descartes.

[16] René Descartes, Fourth Meditation, in *The Philosophical Writings of Descartes*, trans. S. Cottingham, R. Stoothoff and D. Murdoch (Cambridge University Press, Cambridge, 1985), vol. II, p. 34 (subsequent references 'CSM'); *Œuvres de Descartes*, ed. C. Adam and P. Tannery, rev. edn (Vrin, Paris, 1964–70), vol. VII, p. 49 (subsequent references 'AT').

Because he held thinking to be the sole essential attribute of immaterial substances, he claimed that we are thinking all the time, waking or sleeping. He held that consciousness of operations of the mind is indubitable and infallible, and argued that the mind is, as it were, transparent. For, he wrote (CSM II, 150; AT VII, 214), it is *self-evident* that one cannot have a thought and *not* be conscious of it. Thinking is *self-presenting* – although the thoughts we have in sleep are immediately forgotten.

Descartes's epistemic conception of consciousness

Descartes's position was equivocal and indecisive. He equivocated between taking consciousness of a thought to be reflective thought about a thought ('Conversation with Burman', CSM III, 335), and elsewhere holding it to be identical with thinking ('Replies to Bourdin', CSM II, 382).[17] A corollary of this was that he equivocated between taking thoughts to be the objects of consciousness, that is, that *of which* one is conscious (so consciousness is an accompaniment of thought), and taking thoughts to be species (or forms) of consciousness in the sense in which seeing, hearing, smelling are species (or forms) of perceiving ('Replies to Hobbes', CSM II, 124; AT VII, 176: all acts of thought 'fall under the common concept' of consciousness). Above all, he had no explanation of the possibility of this extraordinary cognitive power, which, unlike *all* our other cognitive powers, is allegedly *necessarily exercised upon its objects*,[18] and both *infallible* and *indubitable*. Within the confines of one's mind, this cognitive power is, as it were, godlike – omniscient. How can this be? As Thomas Reid later remarked, if one were to ask Descartes how he knew that his consciousness cannot deceive him, he could answer only that 'the constitution of our nature forces this belief upon us irresistibly'.[19]

---

[17] The difficulty was inherited by his successors. Arnauld, sensitive to the issue, distinguishes *reflexion virtuelle* from *reflexion actuelle*. The former, he averred, 'accompanies all our perceptions', but in addition 'there is also something explicit, which occurs when *we examine* our perceptions by means of another perception' (*On True and False Ideas* [1683] (Manchester University Press, Manchester, 1990), p. 71). The latter, he said, is not consciousness, but voluntary reflection.

[18] It may seem that if acts of thought are species of consciousness, then it is obvious that if one thinks one must be conscious that one thinks, just as if one sees, one necessarily perceives. But that is a mistaken analogy. If one sees a tree, then what one perceives is not *one's seeing it*, but *the tree*. However, Descartes requires that the object of consciousness be the act of thinking, not merely *what* one is thinking.

[19] Reid, *Essays on the Intellectual Powers of Man*, Essay VI, ch. 7.

Locke's psychological Locke, writing almost half a century later, charac-
conception of terized consciousness not epistemically, in terms
consciousness as of indubitability and incorrigibility, but psycho-
inner perception logically, comparing consciousness to an 'internal
sense'[20] whereby we perceive that we perceive (a move already made
by others, such as Arnauld, La Forge and Cudworth). 'Consciousness', he explained, 'is the perception of what passes in a Man's own
Mind'.[21] We attain knowledge of what passes in our minds by the
exercise of an inner sense. We cannot perceive without perceiving that
we perceive.[22] He did not use the term 'introspection' to name this
alleged faculty of inner sense, but that should not be surprising, as
the term was barely yet in currency.

Locke's introduction Like Descartes, Locke held that one 'cannot think
of self-consciousness at any time, waking or sleeping without being
sensible of it'. 'To suppose the Soul to think, and
the Man not to perceive it is . . . to make two Persons in one
Man . . . For 'tis altogether as intelligible to say, that a body is
extended without parts, as that any thing *thinks without being conscious of it*, or perceiving that it does so.'[23] Unlike Descartes, he did
not suppose that we must be thinking for the whole of our existence.
And unlike Descartes, he did not limit the objects of consciousness
to the present or to the operations of the mind. He held us to be
conscious of our past mental operations and of our present as well
as our past actions whenever we remember our doing and thinking
whatever we did and thought. Consciousness is the glue that binds
together the fleeting perceptions of the mind into *one persisting self-
consciousness*, and is a necessary condition for responsibility for our
actions. It is noteworthy that consciousness has by now been indi-
vidualized. One can now speak of *a* consciousness, of the same and
of different consciousnesses, and of the numerical identity of a single
consciousness over time. Consciousness, thus reified, *has become the
mind*! According to Locke, consciousness is constitutive of the dia-
chronic identity of a person. In a striking passage in which he repudi-
ates the need for the same person to be the same substance, Locke
invokes the novel expression self-consciousness:

[20] Locke, *An Essay concerning Human Understanding*, 4th edn [1700], II. i. 4.

[21] Ibid., II. i. 19.

[22] Ibid., II. xxvi. 9.

[23] Ibid., II. i. 10; II. i. 19).

> Had I the same consciousness, that I saw the Ark and *Noah's* Flood,
> as that I saw an overflowing of the *Thames* last Winter, or as that I
> write now, I could no more doubt that I, that write this now, that saw
> the *Thames* overflow'd last Winter, and that view'd the Flood at the
> general Deluge, was the same *self*, than that I that write this am the
> same *my self* now whilst I write . . . I being as much concern'd, and
> as justly accountable for any Action was done a thousand Years since,
> appropriated to me now by this self-consciousness, as I am for what I
> did the last moment.[24]

Self-consciousness and consciousness are assimilated. Consciousness
evidently encompasses all 'operations of the mind'. But because Locke
conceived of personal identity as a forensic concept, and because he
linked personal identity with consciousness, he included among its
objects one's consciousness of one's own actions while performing
them ('consciousness . . . that I write now').

Descartes held that thinking (in his broad sense of the term) is the
defining essence of mental substances (minds), so he argued that one
must think (engage in mental operations) all the time, otherwise
one would cease to exist. Locke disagreed, denying that substances
are defined by a single essential property. But he agreed that one could
not think without perceiving that one thinks. Leibniz in turn disagreed with Locke, holding that there are multitudinous *petites perceptions* which we do not perceive, of which we are not conscious. But
he agreed with Locke (against Arnauld) in holding consciousness to
be a form of reflection (for which Reid was later to criticize him).

A Galtonian picture of the early modern philosophical conception

It was from these foundations that the eighteenth-
century debate developed. One may summarize,
in a *Galtonian picture*, the conception of consciousness that Kant, to his misfortune, inherited,
via Wolff, from the Cartesian and empiricist
tradition.[25]

---

[24] Ibid., II. xxvii. 16. The term 'self-consciousness' was initially a philosopher's
term of art. Locke was not the first to use the expression to mean the capacity for
reflexive knowledge of one's mental operations. Cudworth, in his *Treatise on Freewill*
(1688) wrote: 'We are certain by inward sense that we can reflect upon ourselves and
consider ourselves, which is a reduplication of life in a higher degree; for all cogitative
beings as such are self-conscious'. It is interesting that Pierre Coste translated 'self-
consciousness' by *conscience* and added the English term – which is indicative of the
novelty of the usage.

[25] For detailed investigation of Kant's conception of consciousness and self-
consciousness, see Hacker, 'Kant's Transcendental Deduction'.

(i)   Consciousness is the general form of Operations of the Mind, that is, one cannot 'think' without being conscious of one's 'thinking'.

(ii)   Consciousness is an *inner sense* – by the use of which we know how things are subjectively with us.

(iii)   The deliverances of consciousness are indubitable – one cannot doubt whatever one is conscious of.

(iv)   The deliverances of consciousness are infallible – one cannot make a mistake about what one is conscious of.

(v)   One can think things to be thus-and-so, and one is then unavoidably conscious of so thinking. But one cannot in turn think that one is conscious of thinking. It may sensibly seem to one that things are thus-and-so, but it cannot sensible seem to one that it sensibly seems to one that things are thus-and-so.

(vi)   Objects of consciousness are operations of the mind.

(vii)   Objects of consciousness are confined to the present.

(viii) The objects of consciousness are privately 'owned' (no one else can have my experiences – experiences are logically private, inalienable, property).

(ix)   The objects of consciousness are epistemically private – only I *really* know (because I have privileged access to) the operations of my mind.

(x)   One's consciousness of what passes in one's mind requires possession of ideas or concepts of mental operations. These ideas or concepts have no logical relationship to behaviour, since they are applied in inner sense without reference to one's behaviour. To possess them requires no more than consciousness of the ideas (Descartes[a]), or a private ostensive definition (Locke[b]).

(xi)   Consciousness of the operations of the mind is *self-consciousness* – consciousness of how things are with one's self *in foro interno*.

List 1.1   *A Galtonian representation of the early modern philosophical conception of consciousness*

So the mind is, as it were, *transparent*, and what is in the mind is, so to speak, *self-presenting*. So *mind is better known than matter*. Consequently, *the private is better known than the public*. Points (viii) to (x) commit the early moderns and their followers to the intelligibility of a logically private language. This fatal flaw will not be discussed here. Disagreements, which continued well into the nineteenth century, turned largely on the questions of (a) whether there are unconscious operations of the mind; (b) whether inner sense is contemporaneous with, or subsequent to, its objects (Comte, Spencer, Mill); and (c) whether consciousness is or is not infallible. In the post-Kantian and German idealist debate, attention was focused on the nature of transcendental self-consciousness and its ramifications. This will not be discussed here.

5. The dialectic of consciousness I

3 presuppositions of the early modern philosophical conception

Such was the conception of consciousness and self-consciousness that plagued philosophy in the Cartesian/Lockean tradition. The whole structure turns on three simple and correct thoughts.

First, the sincere first-person use of *many* psychological attributes is indubitable. If one feels a pain, one cannot doubt that one is in pain. If one thinks that it is time to go, one cannot doubt that one does. If one is afraid of tomorrow's examination, one cannot doubt

---

Notes a and b to List 1.1

[a] Descartes: 'Thus it would be pointless trying to define, for someone totally blind, what it is to be white: in order to know what that is, all that is needed is to have one's eyes open and to see white. In the same way, in order to know what doubt and thought are, all one need do is to doubt or to think. That tells us all it is possible to know about them, and explains more about them than even the most precise definitions' (*The Search after Truth* (CSM II, 417f.; AT X, 524).

[b] Locke: 'Such precise, naked appearances in the mind, without considering how, whence or with what others they came to be there, the understanding lays up (with names commonly annexed to them) as standards to rank real existences into sorts, as they agree with these patterns, and to denominate then accordingly' (*Essay*, II. ix. 9).

that one is. It makes no sense to say 'I doubt whether I am in pain', or 'I doubt whether I think that . . .'.

Secondly, in *many* cases, one cannot be mistaken. So, for example, one cannot be *mistaken* that one is in pain, any more than one can mistake a pain for a tickle; nor can one be mistaken that one thinks that 2 + 2 = 4, any more than one can misidentify one's thought that 2 + 2 = 4 as the thought that 2 + 2 = 22.

Thirdly, in those cases which Descartes held to be suitable as the premise of a *cogito* proof of his existence, that is, all the cases that seem to involve certainty and infallibility, *truthfulness guarantees truth*.

The logic of illusion   It is all too easy to follow the Cartesian tradition in supposing that if one cannot doubt things to be so with oneself and cannot be mistaken, then one must know with complete certainty that they are so. But this seemingly innocuous move is precisely where one goes wrong. For we mistake the impossibility of doubt for the presence of certainty, and the impossibility of mistake for the presence of infallible knowledge. To clarify this we must penetrate *the logic of conceptual illusion* – the dialectic of consciousness.

The logical exclusion of doubt excludes empirical certainty too   Doubt needs reasons. The possibility of doubting an empirical truth such as 'Jack is in pain' or 'Jill thinks that it is time to go' may be excluded by realization of the eliminability of all genuine alternatives in the circumstances. Here possible doubt is excluded by the available evidence. Here, it is quite certain (and one is quite certain) that things are as one takes them to be. But doubt may also be excluded by purely *logical* or *conceptual* considerations: by the fact that it *makes no sense* to doubt the kind of thing in question, or that it *makes no sense* to doubt in such circumstances. Here doubt is not excluded *de facto*, but *de jure*. For no sense has been given to the words 'I doubt' as a prefix to the empirical proposition in question, or in the circumstances in question. To give a few familiar examples: it makes no sense to doubt whether one exists (if someone said 'I am not sure I exist' or 'I doubt whether I exist' we should ask him what on earth he meant). Similarly, it makes no sense, in normal circumstances, as one walks through a wood of great oak trees, to doubt whether *this* is a tree or *this* is a tree, etc. If someone, as he touched each great tree, said 'I doubt whether this is a tree', we would think him deranged – or a philosopher. When doubt is excluded *de facto*, then it makes sense to speak of certainty, for certainty can be *established* by excluding alternative possibilities. But when it is *logically impossible* to doubt an empirical proposition – when it makes *no sense* to doubt, then it makes no sense to speak of certainty either. The satisfaction of the conditions of subjective certainty does indeed exclude all doubt, but if all doubt is *logically* excluded, there is nothing for subjective certainty to exclude. There is no room for certainty – the logical space, so to speak, has vanished. Similar considerations apply to the exclusion of mistake with regard to an empirical proposition. The logical impossibility of a mistake does not imply infallible knowledge, but the exclusion of knowledge *together with error*. This is precisely how things are with regard to first-person uses of the subset of psychological verbs that satisfy Descartes's demands on *cogitationes*. It is precisely because it *makes no sense* for someone to be in pain and doubt whether he is, or to mistake his thinking that it is time to go for his thinking that Paris is the capital of France, that it makes no sense to say that he is certain, or knows infallibly and incorrigibly, how things are with him in such respects.

That truthfulness guarantees truth does not imply knowledge   It is perfectly correct that with regard to avowals of pain, confessions of one's thoughts, assertions of how things sensibly appear to one to be ('It visually seems to me . . .'), truthfulness in general guarantees truth. In such cases, the speaker's word goes (although not always indefeasibly). It is all too easy to try explain this by reference to the idea that the speaker *knows* how things are with him because he has 'privileged access' to his mind by introspection, and that is why truthfulness guarantees truth. That is mistaken. The speaker's word goes, not because he is a *witness* to his own consciousness, but because he is an articulate *agent*. I shall elaborate.

Where knowledge is logically excluded, so is ignorance   Why do we cleave so adamantly to the idea that we *know* with certainty that things are so with us? Because it is altogether natural to feel that if it is not the case that we know, then we must be *ignorant* of what we are being said not to know. And for sure, when one is in severe pain, one *is not ignorant* that one is in pain. But it does not follow that one knows (with certainty) that one is. It follows that one neither knows *nor is ignorant*. It is not that we *don't* know that things are thus-and-so with us – it is that there is no such thing as *not knowing* in these cases. But by the same token, *there is no such thing as knowing either*. The truth of the matter is that being mature language users, we can – in all the cases relevant to the early modern debate on consciousness – *say* how things are with us. Our saying so is constitutive (not inductive) evidence *for others*, for things being so with us. And our sincere word therefore has a privileged status *for others* (it is *logically* good evidence for them). Such constitutive evidence is defeasible, but if not defeated, *it stands firm*. But this does not show that we *know* that things are as we say they are – for there is *no work* for the verb 'know' to do. It shows only that ignorance, *together with knowledge*, are here logically excluded.

The illusions of inner sense, apperception and introspection — Of course, if we assume, with the early modern tradition, that we know with certainty how things are ('subjectively') with us, then it is all too natural to ask *how* we know. Then we are strongly tempted to suppose that we do so by the exercise of a cognitive faculty. Moreover, since we can *say* how things are thus with us without any evidence, it is almost irresistible to suppose that this cognitive faculty is a form of perception – since to learn how things are by directly perceiving how they are involves no evidence either. So too it seems that we know how things are with us 'inwardly' by means of an *inner sense*, which we then dub 'apperception' or 'introspection'. As William James put it so wrongly in 1890, introspection 'means, of course, the looking into one's own mind and reporting there what we discover'.[26] It is by the use of this inner sense, it seems, that we perceive, apperceive, introspect or become conscious, of how things are with us. This inner sense is just like an outer sense, only

(i)   without a sense organ;
(ii)   its successful exercise is independent of observation conditions (there is here no 'more light, please', no looking more closely or using a telescope);
(iii)   it never fails us, but always yields knowledge;
∴ (iv) we know the mind better than the material world (cp. Descartes, Brentano, Husserl).

But there is no such thing as a cognitive faculty that is miraculously immune to error, and no such thing as a faculty of perception that enables us to perceive without any organ of perception and the

[26] W. James, *The Principles of Psychology* (Holt, New York, 1890), vol. 1, p. 185.

successful exercise of which is independent of circumstances of observation. 'To perceive', as well as 'to see', 'to hear', etc. have a legitimate use as success verbs – but there is no such thing as succeeding if there is no logical possibility of failing. (As noted, 'to be conscious of', although factive, is *not* a success verb – one cannot try to become or succeed in being conscious of something.)

There is indeed such a thing as introspection – but, *pace* James, it is not a form of perception and involves no 'looking into' one's mind. It is a form of self-reflection, at which some people, like Proust, are better than others. It involves reflecting on one's actions and character traits, on one's springs of action, likes and dislikes. It is a route to self-knowledge, but also a high road to self-deception. It is not exercised when one says that one has a headache or that one is thinking of going to London tomorrow. That a child has learnt to say 'Mummy, my head aches' does not show that he is becoming introspective. Nor does it show an advance in self-knowledge.

Of the importance of not confusing the ability to say with the ability to see

What is true is that if we are asked whether we are in pain, whether we want this or that, whether we think things to be so, or are thinking of something or other, we *can say so*. It is characteristic of Locke and his successors down to James, Brentano and Husserl, to confuse the ability to *say* how things are with one with the ability to *see* (by introspection) how things are with one. To be sure, when a human being, who has mastered the use of language, has a pain, he can normally say so. If asked whether he is in pain, he can reply. It is tempting to think that he can say that he has a pain in his foot, because he feels, that is, perceives, the pain. But to feel pain is not a form of perception. To feel a pain in one's foot, for one's foot to hurt, just *is* to *have a pain* – not to have a pain and in addition to perceive it. Truthfully to say 'My foot hurts' is no more an expression of something one has *perceived*, *learnt* or *come to know* than is a groan of pain. Of course, one is not *ignorant* of one's foot's hurting either. *Can* one intelligibly *say* 'I know I have a pain'? In appropriate circumstances, of course. But all it means is that I really do have a pain, that it is true that I have a pain. It does not mean that I have evidence for it, nor does it mean that I perceive it directly.

Saying what one thinks

A language-user can say what he is thinking. If asked 'A penny for your thoughts?' he can reply. So how does he know *that* he is thinking? Is it not by introspection? — No. Let us first ask how he knows *what* he thinks. Well, he may have weighed the evidence, and decided that the weight of evidence is in favour of things being thus-and-so; so he says that things are so – that is what he has concluded is the case. If he takes it to be a matter of opinion, or if he takes the evidence not to be decisive, he will affix an 'I think' to the sentence to indicate just that. So he says that he *thinks* things to be thus-and-so. 'I think' functions *here* as a qualifier which does not signify a mental operation currently taking place, but indicates (for others) the epistemic weight of the proposition to which it is affixed.[27]

Knowing and not knowing what one thinks or wants   Yes, but surely he *knows that he thinks what he thinks*! After all, do we not sometimes say 'I don't know what I think'? And if 'I don't know what I think' makes sense, then surely its negation 'I know what I think' makes sense too! — It is true that we sometimes say 'I don't know *what* I think'. But not to know what one thinks is not to think something and not to know what it is. If I don't know what I think about something or other, what I do is *not* 'peer into my mind' to find out. Rather, what I do is examine the evidence pertinent to the matter at hand, and make up my mind on the balance of evidence. 'I don't know what I think' is an expression of inability to judge ('I can't make up my mind', we say) – not of an introspective deficiency. It is a confession of not knowing *what to think*, which can be remedied only by looking again at the evidence.

All right; but still, we often proclaim that we don't know what we want. Here surely what we don't know is an operation of the mind! Don't we then quickly introspect and then say 'Now I know what I want'? — No. On the contrary: 'I don't know what I want' signifies *inability to decide* between desiderata. And finding out what one wants is not a matter of 'introspectively running over one's various desires', but rather of reflecting on the desirability characteristics of the available alternatives and choosing the most preferable. 'Now I know what I want!' amounts to the same as 'Now I have decided'.[28]

---

[27] Of course, there are other uses of this verb (see chapter 10).

[28] One might, provocatively, say that these uses of 'I know' are non-epistemic, in the sense in which 'While you were with me, I forgot all my troubles' is not an epistemic use of 'forget' – it does not signify a failure of memory and does not serve as a confession of epistemic fault. So too, 'I know I am in pain' or 'I know I intend to go' do not signify the upshot of a successful exercise of a cognitive faculty, and do not serve to make a cognitive claim. They serve merely to emphasize that I am indeed in pain, or to concede that I do indeed intend to go. 'You're in pain!' – 'Yes, I know' is a joke.

So, to return to the questionable questions of the ancients: When we see something or see something to be so, *how do we know that we do*? Do we perceive our seeing by sight? Or do we perceive our seeing by a general sense (a *sensus communis*)? — Neither. There is no such thing as confusing seeing with hearing or tasting. If someone were to say 'I think there is a sound coming from the bush, but I am not sure whether I see it or taste it', we would not know what he meant. We exercise our senses and use our sense-organs in making judgements about things in our vicinity. According to the sense-qualities we apprehend, and to the sense-organs we employ, we can affix an 'I see // I can see . . .', 'I hear // I can hear . . .', 'I smell // I can smell . . .' to the expression of one's perceptual judgement. These prefixes indicate the sense-faculty and sense-organ by the use of which one takes oneself to have acquired information. There is no such thing as *mistaking* sight for smell, or hearing for tasting. And if there is no room for *error*, and if there are no evidential grounds for saying 'I see a so-and-so' or 'I heard a sound from over there', then the question 'How do you know that you see (rather than hear or taste) something or other?' is, in the case of proper sensibles, to be rejected, and in the case of common sensibles to be answered by citing the sense-organ and sense-faculty used. But even in the latter case (say, of feeling the shape of something with one's fingers), one does not *perceive* that one perceives. Rather, one perceives with one's fingers, one's sense of touch, and *can say so*. Nor is one conscious *that one perceives*, although one may be *conscious of what one perceives* – if it catches and holds one's attention. One can *say* what one perceives – but to be able to say *what one perceives* is not to *perceive that one perceives*.

To be able to say that one perceives is not to perceive that one perceives

It is not that the 'I think' *must* accompany all my representations, as Descartes and Locke supposed. Nor is it even that it must be *possible* for the 'I think' to accompany all my representations, as Kant suggested. Rather, it must be possible for the 'I say' to accompany all my representations. Or, more perspicuously, it must be possible for me to say how things are with me. Therefore, I can also reflect on things being so with me – which is something non-language-using animals cannot do. But to reflect on things being thus-and-so with me is not the same as being conscious of things being thus-and-so, any more than reflecting on Julius Caesar's assassination is to be conscious of it. To reflect on things being thus-and-so

It must be possible for the 'I can say' to accompany all my representations

with me is a mental act, which I may be asked or ordered to perform, and may perform voluntarily, intentionally and deliberately. But I cannot intelligibly be asked or ordered to be conscious of things being thus-and-so with me, and to be conscious of things being thus-and-so is not an act, *a fortiori* not a voluntary or intentional one.

The illusion of consciousness as an inner sense

In brief, consciousness conceived as an inner sense is a fiction. Roughly speaking, anything that Descartes might, *with good reason*, wish to cite as an indubitably and infallibly known *act of thought* (*cogitatio*), everything 'inner' *for which truthfulness guarantees truth*, is something of which one *cannot* oneself be either ignorant or doubtful. By the very token of the *cannot*, one cannot know or be certain about it either. Consciousness, conceived as an inner sense with operations of the mind as its objects, is not the mark of a mind, but of thoroughgoing confusion.

Animal consciousness contrasted with human consciousness and self-consciousness

Given this confusion, the idea that consciousness is *the* mark of the mind collapses. So it should. After all, consciousness, properly understood, is characteristic of other animals than humans. All developed animals are sentient – they have the powers of sensation and perception, and are susceptible to pleasure and pain. They typically have a diurnal cycle of sleeping and waking, hence enjoy intransitive consciousness. They can have their attention caught and held by objects in their perceptual field, and so enjoy perceptual consciousness. But, of course, they are not language-users. Nor is there an 'I can say' that can accompany all their representations. They do not have an 'inner life' of reflection, recollection and articulate feeling. They are conscious, but not, in *this* sense, self-conscious beings. But it is precisely such features that characterize having a mind. Furthermore, many further attributes distinctive of creatures that *do* have a mind cannot be subsumed under the rubric of Cartesian thoughts (definitive of *Cartesian* consciousness) since these attributes are neither indubitable nor transparent. We have wide-ranging cognitive powers, but sometimes think we know something and are mistaken. We have beliefs, but sometimes deceive ourselves about what we really believe. We have mnemonic powers, but sometimes think wrongly that we remember something. Our powers of understanding are great, but we often mistakenly think we understand something. It is evident that only conscious creatures (properly so called) can be said to have a mind, but consciousness is not sufficient for having a mind.

6. The contemporary philosophical conception of consciousness

The decline and revival of interest in consciousness in the modern era

The Cartesian/empiricist conception of consciousness dominated philosophical thought concerning the mind well into the twentieth century. But among analytic philosophers of the Vienna Circle in the interwar years, and among Oxford philosophers of the postwar years, interest in consciousness waned. This was due partly to the rise of behaviourism, partly to a shift of interest away from philosophy of mind and towards philosophy of logic and language in the 1920s and 1930s, and partly to the powerful criticisms of the foundations of both Cartesianism and classical empiricism launched by Wittgenstein and Ryle in mid-century. Interest was reawakened by the emergence, first, of central state materialism in the writings of Smart, Place and Armstrong,[29] which identified types of mental states with types of brain states, and then by its successor, namely functionalism.

Functionalism, advanced in the USA, eschewed the identification of types of mental states with types of brain states. Philosophical functionalists hoped to explain the nature of any mental state solely by reference to its function in correlating causal inputs, behavioural outputs and its causal relations to other mental states (just as a Turing machine-table simultaneously defines the roles of all the machine states in causal terms without circularity). To be sure, any such individual mental state of a being is held to be contingently *token-*identical with whatever cortical or electro-mechanical vehicle realizes it. Functionalism seemed to offer the benefits of behaviourism (the correlation of stimuli (inputs) with behaviour (outputs)), and of materialism (the token-identity thesis), without denying the existence of internal mental states. But it construed internal mental states solely in *functional terms*. A mental state was to be defined in terms of the inputs and outputs it coordinates and its causal interaction with other internal states. This, as critics pointed out, conspicuously omitted

[29] U. T. Place, 'Is Consciousness a Brain Process?', *British Journal of Psychology*, 47 (1956), and J. J. C. Smart, 'Sensations and Brain Processes', *Philosophical Review*, 48 (1959); see also H. Feigl, 'The "Mental" and the "Physical" ', *Minnesota Studies in the Philosophy of Science*, vol. II (University of Minnesota Press, Minneapolis, 1958); D. M. Armstrong, *A Materialist Theory of Mind* (Routledge & Kegan Paul, London, 1968).

mention of the felt character of the experiences that sentient creatures enjoy – experiences of pain or pleasure, hunger, thirst, seeing and hearing, longing, expecting, being sad or joyful. Against the functionalist background, it *seemed* that it was perfectly intelligible to suppose that there might be creatures ('zombies'), just like us in all behavioural respects, subject to the same 'inputs' and yielding the same 'outputs', and having the same causal connections between internal, non-conscious 'machine-states' – but *without enjoying any experiences whatsoever*. It was in reaction to this illusion that the new wave of interest in consciousness emerged in the 1970s with a seminal paper by Thomas Nagel.[30] To save us from the fear that all others might be 'zombies', to save our humanity from reductive physicalism and soulless functionalism, consciousness was appealed to as the defining feature of the mind and the characteristic mark of the mental. For, it was now argued, what was irremediably missing from functionalism was *conscious experience* (see fig. 1.6).

Figure 1.6 *Zombies and us. It is striking how readily the metaphor of 'light inside our heads' comes to be used here. But, if there is any light, it is certainly not inside our heads*

An experience, it was averred, is conscious if there is something which it is like for the subject of the experience to have it. For is there not something it is like to be in pain, to feel joy, to see and hear? And a subject of experience is conscious if there is something that it is like for it to be that subject. For while there is nothing it is like for a brick to be a brick, or for an ink-jet printer to be an ink-jet printer, there is surely something it is like for a cat to be a cat, for a bat to be a bat, for us to be human and indeed for me to be me. *That* is the essence of consciousness and of conscious experience. What began as a ripple in the USA in the 1970s had acquired tsunami proportions by the 2010s, when 'consciousness studies' were all the rage and 'the what-it's-likeness of experience' the slogan.

[30] T. Nagel, 'What is It Like to be a Bat?', *Philosophical Review*, 83 (1974).

The contemporary philosophical conception of consciousness is no less incoherent than the early modern conception. If our humanity needs saving in the face of modernity, it is from far more serious things than functionalism – which is no more than a house of cards that will collapse under the weight of conceptual criticism.

3 pivotal theses of current philosophical misconceptions   Three salient theses determine the concept of consciousness advanced by contemporary philosophers and cognitive scientists:

1. *An experience is a conscious experience if and only if there is something it is like for the subject of the experience to have that very experience.*

What it is like for an organism to have a given experience is denominated 'the subjective character (or quality) of experience'. Knowing what it is like is dubbed 'phenomenal consciousness'.

2. *A creature is conscious or has conscious experience if and only if there is something it is like for the creature to be the creature it is.*

So, we all know that there is something which it is like for us to be human beings – although it is very difficult to say what it is like. On the other hand, no one (other than a bat) can even imagine what it is like to be a bat.

3. *The subjective character of the mental can be apprehended only from the point of view of the subject.*

Some clarification and elaboration is needed.

(a) Just as Descartes (and his successors) misguidedly extended the notion of Thought to include *perceiving* and *wanting something* (etc.) so the new conception of Conscious Experience is misguidedly extended to include *thinking, knowing, believing* and *understanding* (which are no more 'experiences' than perceiving and wanting are species or forms of thought).

(b) Each conscious experience is argued to have its own qualitative character – its distinctive *phenomenal feel*.[31] The individual feel of an

---

[31] The notion of 'raw feels', subservient to a very similar muddled thought, was introduced much earlier by the behaviourist psychologist E. C. Tolman in his *Purposive Behaviour in Animals and Men* (Appleton-Century-Crofts, New York, 1932).

experience was dubbed a *quale*.[32] The problem of explaining these phenomenal qualities, it is held, is the problem of explaining consciousness. For what characterizes *any* conscious experience are the distinctive *qualia* that accompany it.

(c) It is important to realize that the claim that 'there is something which it is like to have a given conscious experience' is not a statement of *similarity*. That is, to ask 'What is it like to walk fast?' is not a variant upon 'What is walking fast like, what does it resemble?' It is not to be answered by a comparison, such as 'Rather like running, only one foot is always on the ground'. The question is not 'What does it resemble?' but rather 'What is it like *for you*?' It concerns the subjective qualitative feel of the experience – what it feels like *for the subject*.

The depth of mystery or the depth of illusion   This conception of consciousness and of conscious experience captured the imagination of philosophers, psychologists and even cognitive neuroscientists in the USA. In due course, the confusions spread to Britain and continental Europe. It appeared to raise a whole battery of enticing and mysterious new questions for cognitive science and evolutionary theory to grapple with. What, it was wondered, is consciousness *for*? What is its evolutionary advantage? Could one not have creatures who behave just like us, only without any 'inner light' of consciousness – that is, without there being anything that it is like to be them? How could anything so mysterious as consciousness emerge from mere matter? Is consciousness compatible with our scientific understanding of the universe? And so forth. These are all either trivial questions or pseudo-questions.[33] But if one accepts this tempting account of the uniqueness and peculiarity of consciousness, then they seem anything but trivial or absurd – they seem deep questions at the frontiers of knowledge.

7. The dialectic of consciousness II

The 4 temptations on the road to illusion   Why is it evidently so tempting to agree to this analysis of consciousness? Four factors are in play.

---

[32] The term was borrowed from C. I. Lewis, *Mind and the World Order* (Scribner's, New York, 1929).

[33] See Bennett and Hacker, *Philosophical Foundations of Neuroscience*, ch. 11, for detailed deconstruction of these confused questions.

First is the persuasiveness of the claim that there isn't anything which it is like to be a brick or an ink-jet printer, but there is something it is like to be a bat or a dolphin and there is certainly something it is like to be a human being. Initially one is inclined to agree to this misconceived rhetorical statement. After all, you can ask someone what it was like for him to be a soldier, and you cannot ask an ink-jet printer what it is like for it to print a page.

The second factor to benumb our linguistic sensibility is the relative unfamiliarity of the phrase 'there is something which it is like to', which involves second-level quantification over properties coupled with an unrecognized misuse of the interrogative phrase 'what is it like'. I shall explain this below.

The third operative factor is the appeal of the idea of 'saving our humanity' – of providing a bulwark against the rising tides of reductionism and functionalism.

Finally, the appeal of mysteries, of facing the deepest and most difficult problem known to man, of being at the last frontier of knowledge, is well-nigh irresistible. In philosophy, *there are no mysteries* – only mystifications and mystery-mongering.

3 antidotes to the 4 temptations   The temptations must be resisted, and sober analysis should take their place. I shall briefly defend three antitheses.[34]

(1)   Experiences are not in general individuated by reference to what it feels like to have them but by reference to what they are experiences of. Most experiences have no qualitative character whatsoever – they are qualitatively neutral.

(2)   There is not *something which it is like* to have an experience.

(3)   There is not *something which it is like* to be a human being or, for that matter, a bat.

Let me explain.

The qualitative character of experiences   (1a) It is true that being in severe pain is awful, that smelling the scent of roses is pleasant, that the sight of mutilated bodies is horrifying. These are the qualitative characteristics of certain experiences.

---

[34] For more detailed treatment, see P. M. S. Hacker 'Is There Anything It is Like to be a Bat?' in *Philosophy*, 77 (2002), pp. 157–74. I shall use the term 'experience' in the broad and ill-defined sense in which it is currently employed by students of consciousness.

(1b) Every experience is a *possible* grammatical subject of attitudinal predicates, for example, of being pleasant or unpleasant, interesting or boring, attractive or repulsive. But it is false that every experience is *an actual* subject of such an attitudinal predicate. Hence it is mistaken to hold that every experience has a qualitative character. With respect to most experiences the question 'What did it feel like to . . . ?' or 'What was it like to . . . ? is correctly answered by 'It did not feel like anything in particular' and 'It was altogether indifferent'. To see the lamp-posts in the street or to hear the chatter in the bus feels neither pleasant nor unpleasant, and is neither repulsive nor attractive.

Experiences are identified by their object, not by their qualitative character

(1c) Experiences, which may indeed be the subject of the same attitudinal predicate, are not essentially distinguished by reference to it, but by their object. Smelling lilac may be just as pleasant as smelling roses, but the experiences differ despite sharing the same qualitative character. What distinguishes the experiences is not what it feels like to have them, but what they are experiences *of*.

Confusions of qualia

(1d) A persistent mistake among defenders of *qualia* is to confuse and conflate the qualities of *what* one experiences (e.g. the colour of the violets, the scent of the roses, the taste of the apple) with the qualities of the experiences (delightful, enjoyable, pleasant, revolting). *A perceptible quality is not a quality of a perception*. The colours of *visibilia* are not qualities of seeing them, but qualities of what one sees. The seeing of a red rose is not red, and the hearing of a bang is not loud, although it may be frightening.

(1e) It is altogether misguided to stretch the term 'experience' to include thinking. But be that as it may, what differentiates thinking that 2 + 2 = 4 from thinking that 3 + 3 = 6 is not what it feels like to think thus but rather is *what is thought*. Even if a binary whiff is associated with 2 + 2 = 4, and a tertiary whiff with 3 + 3 = 6, that is not what individuates the thinkings, as is obvious when one remembers that the tertiary whiff might become associated with the thought that 3 × 3 = 9.

The felt character of experiences and the confusions of existential quantification

(2) It is true that one can ask someone 'What was it like for you to V?' (where 'V' signifies an experience). This is not a request for a comparison, but for a description of the *felt character* of the experience. One may answer: 'It was quite agreeable

(unpleasant, charming, repulsive, fascinating or boring) to V'. Then, if we wish to indulge in second-level quantification, we may say 'There was something that it *was* for A (or for me) to V, namely: *quite agreeable* (unpleasant, charming, etc.)'. What we *cannot* intelligibly say is: 'There was something that *it was like* for A (or for me) to V, namely . . .'. That is, existential generalization requires the dropping of the 'like' – for the experience was not *like* quite agreeable, it *was* quite agreeable. This should be obvious from consideration of the answer to the question 'What is it like for you to V?' For the answer (save among the illiterati) is not 'To V *is like* wonderful', but 'To V *is* wonderful'. And the existential generalization of that is 'There is something that it is to V, namely wonderful'. It *cannot* yield the form 'There is something that it is like to V, namely wonderful'. The latter aberration is the result of a miscegenous crossing of the existential generalization of a judgement of similarity with an existential generalization of a judgement of the affective character of an experience. And the result is, strictly speaking, latent nonsense – which has now been rendered patent.

So, (i) It is simply ill-formed nonsense to suggest that a conscious experience is an experience such that *there is something it is like to have it*.

(ii) Most experiences are qualitatively (affectively) characterless – they have no 'qualitative (attitudinal) character' at all. (If anyone were to ask us such questions as 'What is it like to see the buttons on your shirt?', 'What is it like to hear Jack say "and"?' or 'What is it like to feel the arm of the armchair?', we should be very puzzled at the questions, since such perceptual experiences are obviously qualitatively neutral in normal circumstances.)

Logico-grammatical constraints on what it is like to be or to do

I now turn to the third antithesis. It makes perfectly good sense to ask 'What is it like to be a soldier (a mother, an old-aged pensioner, wealthy, unemployed)?'. This is a request for a description of the pros and cons of a certain social role, or of being a V-er, or of being in a certain condition. Such questions demand a specification of the qualitative character of the life of an X, of the typical career of a V-er, or of being in a given condition. That is precisely why this form of words was misguidedly chosen by modern consciousness students to explain what it is to be a conscious creature. Hence the statement: 'There is, presumably, something it is like to be a bat or a dolphin and there is certainly something it is like to be a human being.' But this statement is quite mistaken.

Specification of the subject of 'What is it like to be . . . ?' (3a) Let me explain why, from the point of view of English grammar and of the devices of second-level quantification, there isn't anything it is like to be a bat, or to be a dolphin, and there certainly isn't anything it is like to be human. Sometimes there is no need, in a question of the form 'What is it like to be an X?', to specify the subject class, that is, to specify what it is like *for whom* to be an X. For it is often evident from the context. 'What is it like to be a doctor?' is restricted to adult human beings, 'What is it like to be pregnant?' to women. But sometimes it *is* necessary, for example, 'What is it like *for a woman* (as opposed to a man) to be a soldier?' or 'What is it like *for a teenager* (as opposed to someone older) to be the champion at Wimbledon?' And often the question is personal, as in 'What was it like *for you* to be a soldier in the Second World War?'

Existential generalization again As in the previous cases of 'What is it like to V?', so too here the 'like' drops out in existential generalization. If one answers the question 'What is it like for a teenager to win at Wimbledon?' by saying 'It is quite overwhelming', then the existential generalization is not 'There is something which it *is like* for a teenager . . .', but rather 'There is something that it *is* for a teenager to win at Wimbledon, namely, quite overwhelming'. But this ineradicable flaw is not the worst of the ensuing nonsense.

Constraints on the subject and object terms of 'What is it like for a . . . to be a . . . ?' (3b) We can licitly ask 'What is it like for a Y – for a man, a woman, a soldier, a sailor, etc. – to be an X?' We can also licitly ask 'What is it like for you to be an X?' Note the general form of these questions. (i) The subject term 'Y' differs from the object term 'X'. (ii) Where the subject term is specified by a phrase of the form 'for a Y', then a principle of contrast is involved. We ask what it is like *for a Y*, as opposed to *a Z*, to be an X. (iii) There is a second principle of contrast involved in questions of the form 'What is it like for a Y to be an X?', namely with regard to the X. For we want to know what it is like for a Y *to be an X*, as opposed to *being a Z*.

The transgression of the 2 principles of contrast But the form of words that we are being offered is 'What is it like for an X to be an X?' The subject term is reiterated. But questions of the form 'What is it like for a doctor to be a doctor?' are awry. One cannot ask 'What is it like for a doctor to be a doctor *as opposed*

to someone else who is not a doctor being a doctor?' for that makes
no sense. Someone who is *not* a doctor cannot also *be* a doctor –
although he may *become* one. The interpolated phrase 'for a doctor'
is illicit here, and adds nothing to the simpler question 'What is it
like to be a doctor?' – which is a simple request for a description of
the role, hardships and satisfactions, typical experiences and episodes
in the life of a doctor. *A fortiori*, questions such as 'What is it like
for a human being to be a human being?', 'What is it like for a bat
to be a bat?' and 'What is it like for me to be me?' are nonsense. For
they violate the condition of non-reiteration, and they transgress the
two contrast principles. Gods and avatars apart, nothing other than
a human being can be a human being. A human being cannot be
anything other than a human being, for if a human being ceases
to be a human being he thereby ceases to exist. It makes no sense to
suppose that I might be someone else or that someone else might be
me. So the pivotal question 'What is it like for a human being to
be a human being (or for a bat to be a bat)?' collapses into the question 'What it is like to be a human being (or to be a bat)?'. But now
it is not clear what *this* question means – unless it amounts to no
more than 'What is human life like?'. If that *is* what it means – then
although it is nebulous, there is no difficulty in answering it, for
example, 'Nasty, brutish and short' or 'Full of hope and fear'. Nor
is there any difficulty in answering the question 'What is the life of
a bat like?' – any decent zoologist who studies bats can readily tell
us. It is even more obvious that the supposition that there is something it is like for me to be me is nonsense, for it is logically impossible
(there is no such thing) for me to be anyone other than myself. Not
only do *I* not know what it is like for me to be me – *there is nothing
to know*. I do not know what it is like for me to be a human being
either – for this is a form of words without any sense. But I can, of
course, tell you what my life has been like.

Reducing mountains to molehills   So, does anything come out of the mystification?
Well, yes. What comes out is the following.
One can ask a human being what it is like for
him to fulfil the various roles he fulfils or to do the various things he
does – and he can normally tell one. One cannot ask a brick what it
is like for it to fill a hole in the wall or an ink-jet printer what it is
like for it to run off 20 copies of one's paper. *For only sentient creatures have social roles and experiences, enjoying some, disliking
others and being indifferent to most* – a meagre result for so much
noise.

8. The illusions of self-consciousness

The ordinary notions of self-consciousness It should be evident that the philosophical conception of self-consciousness not only deviates from the common or garden notions, but is also a product of philosophical confusions rooted in the notion of apperception transmitted from Locke to Leibniz and from Wolf to Kant. The ordinary notions are perfectly respectable: (a) excessive concern with one's own appearance, especially one's dress; (b) one's responses to the thought that others are looking at one; (c) deliberate, as opposed to spontaneous, creative processes.

What self-consciousness is not What self-consciousness is *not* is:

(i)   Consciousness of one's self – since there is no such thing as a 'self' thus understood.[35]
(ii) Apperception – since there is no such thing as perceiving one's perceptions; *a fortiori* it is not a matter of the *possibility* of perceiving one's perceptions.
(iii) Thinking about one's 'thoughts' or 'perceptions' – since although one may indeed think about one's thinking (e.g. how muddled it is) and think about one's perceptions (e.g. how vivid they are), to do so is not to be conscious of one's thoughts or perceptions. In general, to think about something (e.g. Julius Caesar) is not to be conscious of that which one is thinking about.
(iv) An 'I think' that is capable of accompanying all one's representations (as Kant supposed transcendental self-consciousness to be) – What may be said to be capable of accompanying all my representations is an 'I say'. But *to be able to say* does not imply being conscious of things being as one might describe them as being, only not being ignorant of one's 'representations'.

So much for philosophical confusions. Unfortunately, these have spread to the scientific domain. In psychology, self-consciousness is commonly identified with introspection traditionally construed (as in James). We need not dwell further on this. Among animal behaviourists, the idea has sprung up that the ability to recognize oneself in a

---

[35] For detailed examination of the matter, see my *Human Nature: the Categorial Framework* (Blackwell, Oxford, 2007), ch. 9, sections 1–2.

mirror is a mark of self-consciousness.[36] We shall discuss this misconception below (see pp. 396f.). For the moment note that this temptation is generated largely by the form of words in which this capacity that we share with chimpanzees, elephants and dolphins is described, namely 'recognizing *oneself* in a mirror'. For it is but one short step from 'recognizing oneself' to 'recognizing one's self'. The temptation is greatly lessened if the ability is described as 'recognizing one's reflection in a mirror', which is no more a siren's song than is 'recognizing one's hand in a mirror', or even just 'recognizing one's hand'.

Neuroscientific confusions about self-consciousness   Neuroscientists are subject to all these pressures, but add more of their own. Impressed by the thought that 'the human capacity of self-perception, self-reflection and consciousness development are among the unsolved mysteries of neuroscience', scientists in the Max Planck Institutes of Psychiatry in Munich and for Human Cognitive and Brain Sciences in Leipzig and from Charité in Berlin have been studying lucid dreams. Their supposition is that 'during wakefulness, we are always conscious of ourselves' – which makes it difficult to identify the 'seat of meta-consciousness in the brain'. But lucid dreamers, it is argued, unlike normal dreamers, are conscious of dreaming while they are asleep. By examining their brain activity during sleep, it is therefore possible to identify the parts of the brain that are associated with self-consciousness. Indeed, such fMRI investigation has 'made the neural networks of a conscious mental state visible for the first time'.[37]

This is conceptually incoherent. First, it is wrong to suppose that when conscious (i.e. awake) we are always conscious of ourselves. This confuses the ability to say what we are doing with being conscious of doing what we are doing, either *qua* agent or *qua* spectator. Secondly, a lucid dream is a dream in which the sleeper dreams that he is dreaming, not a dream in which he is conscious that he is. For there is no such thing as being conscious of anything when one is fast asleep and dreaming. Whatever one dreams *of* is an object of one's

---

[36] G. G. Gallop, Jr, J. R. Anderson and D. J. Shillito, 'The Mirror Test', repr. in M. Bekoff, C. Allen and G. M. Burghardt (eds), *The Cognitive Animal* (MIT Press, Cambridge, Mass., 2002), pp. 325–34.

[37] M. Dresler *et al.*, 'Neural Correlates of Dream Lucidity Obtained from Contrasting Lucid versus Non-Lucid REM Sleep: a Combined EEG/fMRI Case Study', *Sleep*, 35 (2012), pp. 1017–20. Reported in *ScienceDaily* (27 July 2012), at http://www.sciencedaily.com/releases/2012/07/120727095555.htm, accessed 1 Feb. 2013.

dream, not something that catches and holds one's attention. One does not attend to anything when one dreams – at most one might dream that one is attending to something (while in fact one is snoring away and fast asleep). Nor is anything one dreams a factor that one might take into account in one's deliberations and decisions in one's sleep, since one neither deliberates nor decides anything while one is fast asleep. Thirdly, as we have seen, self-consciousness is not consciousness of one's self, nor is it 'consciousness of one's consciousness' – for these are conceptual chimeras. They need a Theseus to answer their riddles and destroy them, not a team of neuroscientists to discover the locus of 'meta-consciousness'.

2

Intentionality as the Mark of the Mental

1. Intentionality

Source of the problems The problems of intentionality have exercised philosophers since the dawn of their subject. They originate in Parmenidean and post-Parmenidean reflections on the possibility of *thinking what is not the case*, or *thinking of* what does not exist. For if it is not the case, how can we think *it* – after all, there is nothing to think! If it does not exist, how can we think *of* it – after all, there is nothing *of which* to think! These curious seedlings of conceptual anxiety can be, and have been, made to grow to monstrous proportions. Much the same unclarities attend believing, imagining, hoping, fearing or suspecting *something that does not exist* or *something that is not the case*. Comparable puzzlement can be generated in connection with wanting something that does not exist, wanting or intending to do something (which one has not yet done and may never do), and expecting something (that has not yet occurred and may never occur).

Brentano on intentionality In the late nineteenth century, these, and associated, problems were brought afresh into the limelight by Franz Brentano (1838–1917), and reoriented. He reintroduced the medieval notion of intentionality, and he characterized the mental in terms of its intentionality, that is, in terms of its being, metaphori-

The Intellectual Powers: A Study of Human Nature, First Edition. P. M. S. Hacker.
© 2013 John Wiley & Sons, Ltd. Published 2013 by John Wiley & Sons, Ltd.

cally speaking, 'directed towards' something, which may or may not exist or may or may not be the case. He wrote:

> Every mental phenomenon is characterized by what the Scholastics of the Middle Ages called the intentional (or mental) in-existence of an object, and what we might call, though not wholly unambiguously, reference to a content, direction toward an object (which is not to be understood here as a thing), or immanent objectivity. Every mental phenomenon includes something as object within itself, although they do not all do so in the same way. In presentation something is presented, in judgement something is affirmed or denied, in love loved, in hate hated, in desire desired and so on.
>
> This intentional in-existence is characteristic exclusively of mental phenomena. No physical phenomenon exhibits anything like it. We can, therefore, define mental phenomena by saying that they are phenomena which contain an object intentionally within themselves.[1]

Two different claims concern us here.

Brentano's twofold characterization of intentionality   First, that it is the mark of mental phenomena that they are 'directed upon an object'. The term 'object' here is being invoked in a special sense. It does not signify *things* (as in 'Put those objects on the table!'), but rather is derived from the notion of the *grammatical object* of a transitive verb. This needs elaboration.

Secondly, the 'intentional objects' upon which mental phenomena are directed need not (i) *actually* exist, or (ii) be the case.[2] This is all seen through a glass darkly and requires analytic investigation. But it is true that *some* mental phenomena are, metaphorically speaking, 'directed upon an object' in one sense or another, and *some* of these involve 'objects' that need not actually exist or obtain.

Scholastic origins of the notion   The terminology of intentionality is indeed scholastic. The scholastics distinguished between natural and intentional existence (*esse naturale* and *esse intentionale*). In medieval writings, the term 'intentio' occurs first in a Latin

---

[1] F. Brentano, *Psychology from an Empirical Standpoint* [1874], ed. L. L. McAlister, trans. A. C. Rancurello, D. B. Terrell and L. L. McAlister (Routledge, London, 1995), pp. 88f.

[2] This is implicit in Brentano's notion of mental in-existence, as is made clear in his supplementary remarks §1: 'If someone thinks of something, the one who is thinking must certainly exist, but the object of his thinking need not exist at all' (ibid., p. 272).

translation of Avicenna's explanation of Aristotle's account of thought. It was a rendering of Al-Farabi's term *ma'qul* (his translation of the Greek *noema*) and Avicenna's term *ma'na* (which signified what is before the mind in thinking).[3] Aquinas employed the term 'intentio' to signify an 'idea' of the intellect, a likeness in thought of what one thinks. But ideas of the intellect are not mental images, and their likeness to what is thought or thought about is not the likeness of a picture to what it depicts, or of a portrait to what it portrays. Rather the characterization of the idea as the idea *that* such-and-such is thus-and-so, or as an idea *of* such-and-such, is at the same time a characterization of that of which the idea is an idea. If one thinks of a horse, Aristotle had taught, the form of a horse (what it is for something to be a horse) exists in one's mind (otherwise one would not be thinking *of* a horse). An actual horse is also informed by the form of a horse. In the actual horse, its form has *esse naturale* (it exists in nature). In one's thought of a horse, the form of a horse has *esse intentionale* (it exists intentionally). The object of thought, it was argued, exists intentionally in the intellect, whether or not it exists materially in reality. The being of an *intentio* consists simply in its being thought (*esse intentionis intellectae in ipso intelligi consistit*).[4] It was the existence of something as an object of thought which may or may not actually exist that interested Brentano.

Concern with intentionality after Brentano　　The topic of intentionality thus conceived exercised philosophers from the turn of the century, both Brentano's pupils, such as Alexius Meinong and Edmund Husserl, and writers in the phenomenological tradition stemming from Husserl, such as Heidegger, Merleau-Ponty and Sartre. Philosophers in the analytic tradition in the first couple of decades of the twentieth century, such as Moore, Russell and Wittgenstein were equally deeply involved with problems of intentionality. However, they focused primarily on *logical* issues, such as how one

---

[3] See P. Engelhardt, 'Intentio', in *Historisches Wörterbuch der Philosophie*, vol. 4 (Wissenschaftliche Buchgesellschaft, Darmstadt, 1976), pp. 466–74, and C. Knudsen, 'Intentions and Impositions', in N. Kretzmann, A. Kenny and J. Pinborg (eds), *The Cambridge History of Later Medieval Philosophy* (Cambridge University Press, Cambridge, 1982), pp. 479–95.

[4] Aquinas, *Summa Contra Gentiles* IV.11. See W. Kneale, 'Intentionality and Intensionality', *Proceedings of the Aristotelean Society*, suppl. vol. 42 (1968), pp. 73f.; A. J. P. Kenny, *Aquinas on Mind* (Routledge, London, 1993), pp. 101–10.

can think of what does not exist, how a proposition can be both false and meaningful, the clarification of the logical form of belief statements, the nature of judgement, and the relation between what we judge and the facts. The matter of intentionality thus conceived was of paramount importance to Wittgenstein, both in the *Tractatus* and in the *Investigations*, where the *Tractatus* account was repudiated and replaced by a fresh analysis. His concern, however, was not with a mark of the mind, but with what he called 'the harmony between thought and reality' (see section 3 below).[5] Later in the twentieth century, the problem of intentionality was brought upon the carpet afresh, especially in the writings of American philosophers such as Roderick Chisholm, and subsequently John Searle, Daniel Dennett and Donald Davidson.

Purpose of this chapter Our concern in this chapter is to shed light on the intentionality of thought. Our interest is not historical, but analytical. So we are not concerned with explaining the conceptions of Aquinas or Brentano, but with pinpointing and analysing a feature of some psychological verbs and their use. In the previous chapter, I argued that the mind is not to be characterized as the domain of consciousness. To show that neither the mind nor the mental are to be characterized by reference to intentionality either is more straightforward. But intentionality, understood as the possibility of intentional in-existence (existence as an object of thought) in the absence of actual existence (existence as a subject), *is* a feature of *some forms* of the cogitative powers of man, and it requires elucidation – above all so that chimeras will disappear.

Sensations are not intentional Intentionality is not the defining feature of the mental, even if the 'mental' is taken in the wide sense inherited from the Cartesians. Sensations such as pains, tickles, feelings of nausea or giddiness are sometimes (misleadingly) classified as mental. But they are not 'directed at an object' in the relevant sense. To have a headache is not, logically speaking, akin to expecting success or hoping that Jack will come. The latter can be said to have an 'intentional content', namely, *that one will succeed*, and *that Jack will come*. These are, respectively, what one expects and what one hopes, no matter whether one's expectation is satisfied or one's hope

---

[5] Wittgenstein, *The Big Typescript* (Blackwell, Oxford, 2005), p. 189. For an excellent discussion, see E. Ammareller, 'Wittgenstein on Intentionality', in H.-J. Glock (ed.), *Wittgenstein: A Reader* (Blackwell, Oxford, 2001).

fulfilled. But having a headache involves no 'intentional content' in that sense. Nor can one feel a headache if there is no headache, as one can expect success even though as things turn out, there is no success.

Brentano's counter-argument and a riposte

Brentano had an argument to the contrary. He argued that 'in sensation something is sensed', for example, a pain. So when one feels a pain, the mind *is* directed on an object, namely a pain. Therefore feeling pain is no exception to the claim that intentionality is the mark of the mental. But this is to conflate the grammar of a transitive verb with that of an intentional one. Moreover, it is also to abandon what is logically distinctive about intentionality. Although *to feel* is specified by its grammatical object in the phrase 'to feel pain', that no more makes it intentional than does the fact that *to polish* is specified by its grammatical object in the phrase 'to polish silver' makes it intentional. Furthermore, felt pains do not enjoy intentional inexistence in the mind. One does not feel a toothache *in one's mind*, but in one's tooth.

A further defence of Brentano and a riposte

It has been argued in Brentano's defence that since one may have two pains, one felt to be in one's left hand and the other felt to be in one's right hand, therefore one's mental state of feeling is directed on different things. But this is misleading. One's *attention* here is indeed directed upon two different pains. But an *intentional* object is not, as such, an *attentional* object. The fact that one can attend to one's pains does not show that pain is an intentional object of feeling. To feel a pain is no more than to have a pain. To have a pain in one's left hand is simply for one's left hand to hurt. If one's left hand does not hurt, it does not follow that one feels a pain in it nevertheless. By contrast, if one believes that it is raining, and unbeknown to one it is in fact not raining, one believes that it is nonetheless. In this sense, believing something to be so is intentional, whereas feeling a pain (or any other sensation) is not.[6]

Objectless moods are not intentional

Again, if we count moods such as cheerfulness, feeling depressed, or feeling gloomy as 'mental phenomena', then they can sometimes be objectless, for one can feel cheerful, depressed or gloomy, without feeling

---

[6] Even if one holds that phantom pains have an 'intentional location', that does not show that having a pain is an 'intentional phenomenon', for one *really does* have a pain – one does not merely *think* one has a pain. It is rather that the pain seems to the amputee to be in his leg. *That* is a hallucination, since he has no leg.

cheerful, depressed or gloomy *about* anything. It has been suggested that if one is anxious without being anxious about anything in particular, at any rate this anxiety is directed at oneself. But that seems wrong. One *can* be anxious about oneself – but that is not objectless anxiety. In cases of objectless anxiety one is not anxious about anything *or* about anyone.

Factive cognitive verbs do not involve mental in-existence The possibility of intentional in-existence without actual existence does not characterize all those psychological predicates which *are* 'directed towards an object or content'. Many important epistemic attributes that are so directed do not involve the possibility of *mere* intentional in-existence. Although there is someone, something or something which a person knows, remembers, recognizes or is acquainted with, there is no possibility of mere 'mental in-existence'. For one can know, recognize or be acquainted with something only if it exists (or existed), and one can know, recognize or remember that things are so only if they are. So too, if one notices, is aware of or is conscious of something, there must *be* something that one notices, is aware of or is conscious of. And if one notices, is aware or is conscious that things are so, then it follows that they are. Cognitive verbs ('know', 'remember', 'be conscious of', 'be aware of', etc.), unlike cogitative ones, are *factive*, and their objects exist or obtain 'in reality', not merely 'in thought'.

Perceptual verbs and intentionality Perceptual verbs occupy a curious halfway house. They have non-intentional uses such that 'V-ing something' or 'V-ing that things are so' entails that that thing exists and that it is the case that things are so. If one saw, looked at, glanced at, observed Jack, then Jack must have been there. And if one saw that Jack was angry or cheerful, then it follows that he was angry or cheerful. Used thus, verbs of perception have been called 'achievement verbs'. But they also have intentional uses, as in 'I see something blurred', 'He heard a buzzing sound in his ears'. For in these cases, there need be nothing blurred, and there may have been no buzzing noises. Similarly, 'I see an indefinite number of snowflakes' does not imply that there was not a definite number in view, and 'Now I can see the bird in the nest' (twiddling the knobs at the oculist) does not imply that there is (a picture of) a bird in a nest.

So we must clarify the notion of intentionality. For 'being directed upon an object' and the possibility of mere intentional in-existence are characteristic of *some* mental phenomena, and of *some uses* of *some* psychological verbs.

2. Intentional 'objects'

Material and intentional object-accusatives   We are, in effect, investigating the logical functions of expressions that occur as grammatical complements of some psychological verbs (represented in the sequel by V) or of some uses of psychological verbs. Of course, we are thereby also investigating the intentional features of appropriate psychological attributes. Our investigation is not concerned with defining the domain of psychology, but with explaining the nature of intentionality. We should first distinguish between *object-accusatives*, *sentential-* and *nominalization-accusatives*[7] and *infinitive-accusatives*. The object-accusative of one's V-ing is a grammatical object of the verb that specifies *what one V-s* (the 'what' here being a relative pronoun). We may, in this context, distinguish two kinds of object-accusative: (i) material and (ii) intentional object-accusatives. A material object-accusative (*not* a 'material-object accusative') is an object-accusative the denotation of which must exist for it to be true that one V-s it. For example, one may know Jill, believe the rumour, or suspect the butler. One cannot know Jill if there is no such person, one cannot believe a rumour if there is no rumour to believe, and one cannot suspect the butler if there is no butler.[8] An intentional object-accusative is an object-accusative the denotation of which need not exist for it to be true that one V-s it. Just as one can look for Eldorado although it does not exist, so too one may fear ghosts, expect Santa Claus, imagine fairies, trust in the gods.

Nominalization- and sentential- accusatives; contents of V-ing are answers, not objects   One may also know, believe, hope, expect or suspect *that p*. The phrase 'that *p*' ('that things are thus-and-so') is here a nominalization-accusative.[9] But it is also licit in these contexts for the verb to take a sentential-accusative – as when we know

---

[7] See A. R. White, *The Nature of Knowledge* (Rowman & Littlefield, Totowa, NJ, 1982), chs 2–3, and 'What We Believe', in N. Rescher (ed.), *Studies in the Philosophy of Mind*, APQ Monograph series no. 6 (Blackwell, Oxford, 1972), pp. 69–84. I am much indebted to these works.

[8] Of course, one may suspect the butler in the detective story, just as one may believe the hero and trust the heroine. But then, *in the detective story*, the butler exists (unlike, say, Bunbury in Wilde's play or Mrs Gamp in Dickens's novel).

[9] That is, attaching a 'that' to a sentence transforms it into a noun-clause. So the grammatical object of such verbs is often the nominalization of the sentence *p*. As in reported speech, what is V-ed is given in the form of a nominalized sentence 'that *p*'.

Jack is in town, believe Jill is at home and hope they will meet. Both kinds of accusative can be said to specify the *content* of one's knowledge, belief, hope, expectation or suspicion, inasmuch as they are given in response to the question of *what* one V-s (here the 'what' is not a relative pronoun). A content, one might say, is *an answer*, not *an object*. The phrase 'that *p*' does not signify any existent, non-existent, let alone necessary existent, object (e.g. a thought, a proposition, a sentence) denominated 'that *p*', which someone V-s. Nor does the sentence '*p*' in the same context. It gives us the terms in which a person's knowledge, belief, expectation or suspicion might be expressed. Of course, the content of one's knowledge, belief or hope that things are so can be said to be *expressed* by the proposition 'Things are thus-and-so'. But it does not follow that what is V-ed when one V-s that things are so is a proposition. That should be obvious from the fact that although one *can* know or believe the proposition that things are so, there is no such thing as hoping, expecting or suspecting the proposition that things are so. Moreover, to know the proposition that things are so is not the same as knowing that things are so, and believing the proposition that things are so is not the same as believing that things are so. For example, one may know the third proposition in Bentham's *Principles* without knowing whether things are as it says they are; and one's dog may believe that the cat is up the tree, but surely cannot believe the proposition that the cat is up the tree. So the content of one's V-ing that things are so is not the proposition that things are so.

Derivative forms of nominalization-accusatives   Further, one may believe in fairies, suspect treachery, fear failure, hope for success, expect a triumphant outcome and be aware of the difficulty.

Despite superficial appearances, these expressions are not object-accusatives, but nominalization-accusatives. For they are variations upon a 'that-nominalization', being equivalent to 'V-ing that there are fairies', '. . . that there is treachery', and so on.

Infinitive accusatives   A further grammatical form characteristic of certain psychological verbs is the infinitive-accusative. One may hope to go to Italy this summer, expect to be given a party for one's birthday, want to write a paper on intentionality, intend to see Jack for lunch next week. In all such cases, the prospective act or occurrence may not materialize, even though the ascription of the verbal clause is perfectly correct. So one may characterize the psychological attribute as intentional. Philosophers are prone to assimilate the infinitive-accusative ('to V . . .') to a nominalization-accusative ('that *p*'). To hope to go to Italy, it is suggested, is equivalent to hoping that one will go to Italy; to want to write a paper is wanting that one write a paper; to intend to see Jack is to intend that one will see Jack. This grammatical transformation, perhaps acceptable in the first example, grates sorely in the other two. It would be more appropriate to enquire after the rationale of the infinitive-accusative than to hijack it. This will not be done here.

Whether what is V-ed need exist or not depends upon the character of the V-ing

When the expression of one's V-ing has a nominalization- or sentential-accusative, then whether what is V-ed may not be so, or whether it may not exist, *depends upon the character of the V-ing*. In the case of *intentional verbs* with a nominalization-accusative, for example, 'believe', 'hope', 'fear', 'expect', 'suspect', 'doubt', one may V that things are so even though it is not the case that they are.[10] So too, one may believe in ghosts, suspect treachery, fear failure, hope for success, even though ghosts do not exist, there is no treachery, failure does not ensue, etc. By contrast, in the case of *non-intentional* verbs with a nominalization-accusative, for example, 'know', 'aware', 'recognize', 'remember', what is V-ed must be so (i.e. it follows from its being V-ed that it is so), even though knowing, being aware of or recognizing treachery, i.e. that there is treachery, is not at all like knowing, being aware of, or recognizing the traitor (see fig. 2.1).

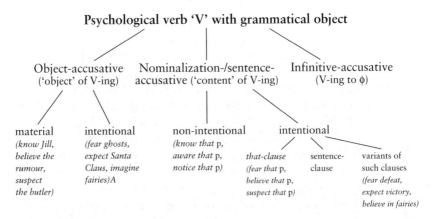

Figure 2.1 *Grammatical complements of psychological verbs*

[10] I shall henceforth disregard the sentential-accusative form, except in cases where it displays different logical characteristics from the nominalization-accusative.

Existence and in-existence What is signified by a material object-accusative of V-ing must exist if it is V-ed. The nominalization-accusative of V-ing, however, need not signify something that must exist, occur or be the case if it is V-ed. The material object-accusative signifies a relatum; the nominalization-accusative, irrespective of whether V is an intentional verb or not, does not. For all that, it is tempting to suppose that a nominalization-accusative denotes something that must 'exist' *in some sense* – if not actually, then intentionally. For, among other things, if it did not enjoy mental in-existence, how would we know what it is that we V when we V that things are, and things are not so? How could we read off our minds what it is that we believe, hope or fear if it were not in some sense *present in our mind* (if it did not enjoy 'immanent existence', as Brentano put it)? We shall examine this worry in section 6 below.

What one V-es when one V-es truly that p does not differ from what one V-es when one V-es falsely that p Finally, we must hang on to the simple truth that what we believe when we believe truly that things are thus-and-so is no different from what we believe when we believe falsely that things are thus and so. Equally, what we know, when we know that things are so, is precisely what we believe, when we believe that things are so. If Jack knows that things are so, and Jill believes (suspects, fears) that things are so, then what Jill believes (suspects, fears) to be so is precisely what Jack knows to be so.

An orrery of intentionality A variety of puzzles clusters around the 'phenomenon of intentionality'. These puzzles are interwoven, and the proposed solution to any one of them affects (or infects) the solution to others. They will be surveyed in this chapter. A clear picture of the problems serves to rule out many proposed solutions. The battery of puzzles can be presented in the form of a series of concentric circles centred on the focal point of a cluster which I shall refer to as the problems of *the relation of thought to reality*. This cluster may be viewed as the central sun, around which related problems orbit like the planets of an antique orrery (see fig. 2.2). As we shall see, some of the planets carry further epicyclical satellites.

3. The central sun: the relation of thought to reality

The relation of thought to reality The central sun of problems, around which the others orbit, can be epitomized by the question: What is the relationship between thought and reality? (The

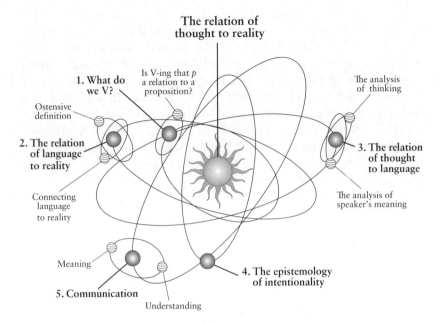

Figure 2.2   *The orrery of intentionality*

question, which has obsessed philosophers from Plato onwards, should be viewed with suspicion.) How must thought (belief, doubt, hope, expectation and indeed desire) be related to reality in order for it to be possible that it be true or false, correct or incorrect, fulfilled or unfulfilled, satisfied or unsatisfied? When we believe truly that things are so, then *what* we believe *is* what is the case – it does not fall short of it. Our thought, as it were, *reaches right up to reality*. But how can that be? What must thought be like, and what must reality be like, for this to be possible?[11]

Distinguish what   (i) *Ambiguities disambiguated.* To shed some light on
one has from   these murky questions, further distinctions must be
what one V-es   drawn. We may think, believe, hope, fear, expect or

---

[11] This is the problem of the pictoriality of the proposition, to which Wittgenstein's picture theory of meaning in the *Tractatus* provided a sublime metaphysical answer. In the *Investigations*, this sublime answer was revealed to be an illusion, and the pictoriality of the proposition was given a grammatical, rather than metaphysical, resolution.

suspect that things are so. For ease of reference, our language provides us here with pairs of homonymical nominals: 'belief', 'hope', 'fear', 'expectation', 'suspicion'.[12] On the one hand, a belief is something we *have* when we believe something to be the case. The belief we have may be firm, tentative, passionate or typical, if we believe firmly, tentatively or passionately, or if it is typical of us to believe thus. To 'have a belief', in this sense, is simply a matter of believing something to be so.

On the other hand, *what* we V, namely *that things are so*, is also called 'belief', 'hope', 'fear', 'expectation' or 'suspicion' – as in sentences of the form '*That things are so* is A's belief (hope, fear, expectation, suspicion)'. But *qua* what is believed (as opposed to the believing of it), A's belief cannot be firm, tentative, etc., although it may be likely, improbable or certain.

One's belief is essentially individuated by reference to what one believes
A person's belief, that is: his *believing* whatever he believes, is essentially individuated by *what* he believes, namely *that things are so*. A's belief (his believing what he believes) may or may not lead to his success or downfall, may be acquired on Monday or on Tuesday, may be firm or tentative. These are external, inessential, properties of his belief. By contrast, that the belief he has is the belief that things are so rather than the belief that things are otherwise is an essential characterization of his belief. Whatever, *if anything*, it may be like for someone to believe that things are so (e.g. uplifting, consoling, heart-breaking), it is irrelevant to the individuation of the belief.

Internal relations and the harmony between thought and reality
(ii) *Internal relations – what fits what?* One's belief is *internally related* to what is the case if it is true. For it is inconceivable that one might believe truly that *p* and yet it not be the case that *p*. Moreover, if one believes that *p* and one's belief *is false*, then what follows is not that *q* or *r* or *s* (i.e. something wholly unrelated to what one believes) but rather, *that it is not the case that p*. It seems as if thought fully describes reality, 'give or take a yes or no' (as Wittgenstein remarked). What must thought be like, what must

---

[12] So too for 'statement', 'assertion' and 'order': just as 'my belief' may signify either my believing (having the belief) or what I believe, so too 'my statement' may signify my making a statement or the statement I make. This is no coincidence, since such speech-act verbs likewise take nominalization-accusatives in *oratio obliqua*, and what is said may or may not be so.

reality be like, and how must thought and reality be related for this agreement-or-disagreement, this 'harmony between thought and reality', to be possible? It is tempting to suppose that thought (and the logic of our language – what it *makes sense* to say or think) must reflect *the objective, language-independent, metaphysical possibilities* available to reality. The world then determines which possibilities are realized. Such a *modal realism* inspired the vision of the *Tractatus*.

A thought and what makes it true seem to fit each other

It seems as if thought and what makes it true *fit* each other like cylinder and piston.[13] It is natural to conceive of thought, belief, expectation, etc. as mental states. They are commonly conceived to obtain in the mind, or, if the mental is thought to be identical with the neural, in the head. It is equally natural to think of facts or states of affairs as worldly denizens. So it seems as if, when a thought, belief or expectation is true, correct or right, two distinct items are matched: namely *how things are in the mind*, and *how things are in reality*. The state of affairs that obtains in reality exactly matches the true thought, as a cylinder matches the piston that fits it. What is the nature of this perfect fit between two ostensibly existence-independent items? One might think that just as the formula which describes the inner wall of a cylinder also describes the outer wall of the piston which fits into it, so too the intrinsic description of a thought as the thought *that things are so* is also a description of the fact *that things are so* that makes it true – that is why they 'fit'. But tempting as this is, it is misconceived.

1st objection: 'that things are so' is not a description

First, 'that things are so' is unhappily characterized as a *description* of the thought (expectation, fear, suspicion) one has when one thinks (etc.) that things are so (which may be described as lucid, coherent or plausible (eager, paralysing, neurotic)). It is better characterized as a *specification* of the thought (expectation, fear, suspicion). It specifies *what* we V, and does not describe what our V-ing *is like*. Moreover, 'it is a fact that things are so' is not a *description* of a fact either, but a *statement* of a fact (which fact may be described as fortunate or deplorable). So we are not here confronted with two descriptions.

[13] The simile is derived from Wittgenstein; see *Philosophical Investigations* [1953], 4th edn (Wiley-Blackwell, Oxford, 2009), §439.

2nd objection: it is an illusion that there is a mental item and a worldly item that fit Secondly, it is an illusion, generated by the Janus-faced character of nouns such as 'belief', 'thought', 'hope', 'fear', 'expectation', 'desire', that what *seem* to fit are, on the one hand, *some mental item* (the belief that *p*) and, on the other, *something worldly* (such as the fact that *p*). But if we look closely at these supposed items, such metaphysical fantasies crumble to dust.

The believing does not 'fit', and the belief fits too well If we bear in mind the Janus faces of 'belief', 'hope', 'fear' or 'expectation', we must first ask what precisely is meant to 'fit' some corresponding fact or state of affairs? Is it the believing, or is it what is believed? It seems that what is believed, when one believes truly, fits – as it were – *all too well*. For what we believe (when we believe truly) *is* what is the case – it does not *fit* it. Similarly, what we do, when we do what we were ordered to do, does not *fit* what we were ordered to do, it *is* what we were ordered to do. (But we must be on our guard here, for although this earmarks an internal relation, it is not an identity. This will be explained below.) Moreover, it is evident that this is not what is in question, since *what is believed*, namely *that things are so*, has no claim at all to being something 'mental' or 'psychological', something in the mind or in the head, that reaches out to reality. So what must 'fit' how things are in the world must be *the believing*. But where, in A's believing that things are so, can one find something that will fit a fact or state of affairs that things are so? Not in anything A *does*. If he believes that it is raining, he may take an umbrella and go for a walk, stay at home and read a book, cancel a picnic, and so forth. But nothing he does *fits* with merciless exactitude what makes his belief true, namely *that it is raining*. Is it then something in A's mind? No; for believing is not something that takes place or obtains in the mind (see chapter 5, section 8). One might suggest that believing *has a content*, and it is this that fits how things are in the world when one's belief is true. But the *that p*, which is the content of one's belief that *p* is not some *thing* that is *in* one's believing, let alone in one's mind or brain. To say that it enjoys 'intentional in-existence' in the mind is merely a misleading way of saying that it is what individuates or specifies one's belief irrespective of its truth. It is given *as an answer to the question* 'What do you believe?' – namely 'that *p*'. Here we have a candidate for fitting – not an item in the mind, but *a linguistic expression with a certain use*.

Facts are not worldly items with a spatio-temporal location

What now of the worldly item in this alleged fitting-relation? Facts can be dismissed, since facts are not 'in' the world, they have no spatio-temporal location, they do not come into existence and then cease to be, and the world does not consist of facts (rather, a true description of (some aspect) of the world consists of a statement of facts).

3rd objection: a thought and the fact that makes it true cannot 'fit' as piston and cylinder

Thirdly, neither thoughts nor facts can fit or fail to fit each other *on the model of a piston and cylinder.* A piston and cylinder are independent objects which may or may not stand in the relation of being fitted one into the other. The identity of each is independent of whether they fit (the piston may expand yet be the same piston). But the thought that *p* and the fact that *p* cannot 'exist' without 'fitting', and cannot cease to 'fit' without losing their identity. Their relation is *internal*, whereas the relation of piston to cylinder is *external*.

Fact and thought are internally related in a word–word relation rather than a word–world one

There is a kernel of truth in the conception of 'fit'. But it is misconstrued. It is true that *there is an internal relation between thought and fact.* It is true that the intrinsic individuation of thought and fact alike employ the same form of words 'that *p*'.

But this is not a matter of two objects or structures (thought and fact) matching each other, like a piston and cylinder. For the indisputable internal relation is forged *within language*, not by a relation *between thought and reality* or *mind and world*. It is forged by the grammatical equivalence of the phrases

the thought that *p*

and

the thought that is made true by the fact that *p*

as well as

the thought made false by the fact that not *p*.

These are simply different ways of characterizing one and the same thought. So too, the expectation that *e* (e.g. that he will come) is satisfied by the occurrence of the event *e* (e.g. of his coming). For the pair of expressions:

the expectation that *e*

and

the expectation that is satisfied by the occurrence of the event *e*

as well as

the expectation that is disappointed by the non-occurrence of the event *e*

are simply different ways of referring to the same expectation. So *of course* it looks as if we are dealing with a metalogical agreement between thought and reality[14] – a harmony that obtains irrespective of the truth of the thought, belief or expectation. For, of course, even if I believe falsely that *a* is black, then what *a* is *not* is black. The possibilities that can be represented in thought are the very same possibilities that are available to reality. As Wittgenstein noted, there appears to be a pre-established harmony between thought and reality.[15]

The illusion of a pre-established harmony between thought and reality They seem to share the same logico-metaphysical form. But that is an illusion! For it is evident that what appears to be a metalogical relation between mind and world is in fact a mere grammatical substitution rule. *Thought and reality make contact in language.* The 'harmony between thought and reality' is orchestrated *within* language, *not between thought and reality*. We *individuate* thought (belief, expectation, hope, fear, suspicion and so forth) by its content, specified in the *expression* or *statement* of what is thought by an intentional nominalization-accusative. Thought is said

[14] I borrow here Wittgenstein's idiosyncratic use of the expression 'metalogical' to signify something (apparently) presupposed by the very possibility of logic and representation.

[15] L. Wittgenstein, MS 114, pp. 139, 143.

to be right, correct or true if things in reality are as they are thought to be ('The thought that p' = 'The thought that is true if and only if it is the case that p'). It is all done *in language!*[16]

The apparent 'fit' between thought and reality, when what one thinks is so, between a belief and the fact that makes it true, or between a hope and the state of affairs that fulfils it, gives one the illusion of a relation of agreement or congruence bridging mind and world. But the correspondence theory of intentionality is as misconceived as the correspondence theory of truth. In both cases a mundane grammatical molehill is mistaken for a golden metaphysical mountain.

The grammar of the Wh-pronoun: what is V-ed is what is so, but is not the same as what is so

That this diagnosis is correct is confirmed by the grammar of the Wh-pronoun here. We do not say that what A believes (namely, that things are so) is *the same* as what is (in fact) the case. That is precisely what would be appropriate if there *were* two congruent items that fit or agree, or if there were a genuine identity here. Moreover, one could then also elaborate: same what? But we say that what A believes *is* what is the case, not *is the same as* what is the case. Similarly, if A is ordered to V, and he obeys, one would not say that A did *the same* as he was ordered to do, but rather that he did *what* he was ordered to do. By contrast, where there is genuine congruence, as when A and B are severally ordered to V and they both obey, *then* it is correct to say that what A did was *the same* as what B did, that A and B did the same. (Same what? Same action – such as guarding the gate, saluting, coming to attention.)

Deflationary analysis

It should be stressed that the views just advanced are not a form of scepticism. It is not that this 'connection' is too difficult to grasp. Nor is it being suggested that this 'gulf'

[16] It might seem that this is not so. For one may obey the order to leave the room by jumping out of the window, just as one's expectation that the postman may bring the mail today may be satisfied by Mr Smith's delivering a birthday parcel. That is true, but unproblematic. There is no internal relation between the order to V and X-ing, unless we add that X-ing is a way of V-ing. There is no internal relation between the expectation that p and q, unless q is subsumed by p. Nevertheless, that order and compliance, like expectation and its satisfaction, make contact in language remains true. For the order to leave the room is indeed the order that is satisfied by leaving the room, namely *by jumping out of the window* – which is one way of leaving the room. So too, the expectation that the postman, who is Mr Smith, will deliver the mail, which is a birthday parcel, is satisfied by Mr Smith's delivering the birthday parcel.

is too wide to bridge. Rather, *there is no such thing* as making this supposed 'connection' and no such 'gap' to bridge. What is being rejected is not a need that cannot be met, but a chimerical fiction generated by grammatical or conceptual misunderstandings. To be sure, the analysis is *deflationary* – but after a century of rampant analytic inflation, this is what is needed to ward off intellectual bankruptcy.

Direction of fit

(iii) *Directions of fit*. If there are no paired items to fit, but only an illusion of fitting, then this sheds light upon an associated philosophical doctrine concerning *directions of fit*. It has been suggested that where there is a fitting relation between mind and world (belief and fact, desire and fulfilment), then we must distinguish two different directions of fit.[17] The suggestion is that if an 'intentional mental state' is not *satisfied* (if there is no congruent fact, or condition-in-the-world), if the nominalization-accusative enjoys *only* mental in-existence, then the question arises of what is answerable for this non-satisfaction. In the case of belief and like cogitative states, if one believes that things are so and one's belief is false, then it is one's belief that is faulty and it must be changed to fit the world. This is a Mind-to-World direction of fit. In the case of desire and like volitional states, if one desires to bring it about that things are so, and it is not the case that they are, then it is the world that is faulty and one must change the world – one must *act* – to bring things into line with one's will. This is a World-to-Mind direction of fit.[18] This looks neat – but perhaps too neat to be true. The question 'Which is to be blamed (is at fault, or is responsible), the mental state or the world?' is misleading.

Belief and desire: what is at fault when they don't match the world?

A's belief may be false. If so, that is a fault inasmuch as falsehood is a fault. But it makes no sense to say that it is the fault of A's belief that it is at fault (i.e. false). It may be A's fault that he falsely

---

[17] The idea of a 'direction of fit' was advanced by J. L. Austin, in his papers 'Truth' and 'Unfair to Facts', repr. in *Philosophical Papers* (Clarendon Press, Oxford, 1961). It was inherited by his pupil J. R. Searle, who developed it in *Intentionality* (Cambridge University Press, Cambridge, 1983). It was borrowed by G. E. M. Anscombe, and inherited by her pupil A. J. P. Kenny, who developed it in *Will, Freedom and Power* (Blackwell, Oxford, 1975). B. O. A. Williams made much of the idea in his *Ethics and the Limits of Philosophy* (Fontana, London, 1985).

[18] See Searle, *Intentionality*, ch. 1. For detailed refutation, see P. M. S. Hacker, 'Malcolm and Searle on Intentional Mental States', *Philosophical Investigations*, 15 (1992), pp. 245–75.

believes that things are so, if, for example, he failed to examine the evidence, or jumped to the conclusion that things are so. But it may be the fault of A's informant. Or it may be no one's fault, since everything spoke in favour of its being the case that things are so. But there is no question of 'holding responsible' either the 'mental state' or 'the world' for the so called lack of fit between the false belief and what is actually the case. Nor is it correct to suggest that where there is a Mind-to-World direction of fit, one rectifies the lack of fit by changing the mental partner. For, first, if one finds out that it is not the case that things are so, then one's belief that they are will *already have changed*, and there is nothing further for one to rectify. Furthermore, if one believes that things are so, and they aren't, one may sometimes be able to 'rectify matters' by bringing it about that they are.

If A wants to V and his desire is not satisfied, is it 'the world' that is to be faulted, blamed or held responsible? Not obviously. A's desire may be at fault in various ways. It may be foolish, over-ambitious, unrealistic, shabby or shameful. If his desire (intention, plan or project) is not realized, we may blame it for being over-ambitious or unrealistic. But, as with false belief, to blame the unsatisfied desire is to blame A for having such a faulty desire – he should have known better. And, of course, we may hold A responsible for the non-satisfaction of his desire because he did not try hard enough, or forgot to V. On the other hand, it may be B's fault for negligently having forgotten to do something necessary for A to V. Or it may be no one's fault. Nor is it correct that in cases of World-to-Mind direction of fit, one can always 'rectify matters' by changing the world. If the opportunity has passed, no 'rectification' may be possible.

Is there then *no* truth in the idea of two different

The truth in the idea of directions of fit directions of fit? Indeed there is – but the truths are grammatical truisms definitive of belief and desire, not metalogical profundities linking Mind and World. Schematically speaking, beliefs are beliefs *that things are so*, and are true if things are indeed so. They are verified by finding out how things are. Desires are *desires for goals* and *for action to achieve goals*. They are satisfied by successful action. By definition, the belief that p is made true by the fact that p.[19] For 'the belief that p' = df.

---

[19] As men are made bachelors by being unmarried, but *not* as women are made widows by war.

'the belief that is made true by the fact that *p*'. By definition, the desire to V is satisfied by V-ing. For 'the desire to V' = df. 'the desire that is satisfied by V-ing'. The theory of direction of fit, far from demonstrating a bi-directional metaphysical agreement between Mind and World, is merely the distorted shadow of these and similar grammatical truisms.

What a thought is about

(iv) *What one thinks about*. One's thought, that is, one's thinking that things are so, does not merely have a content, which is given by the answer to the question 'What do you think?', but it also has an object or objects, in yet a further sense of this protean term. For a thought may be *about* something or other.[20] In the case of singular thoughts, one's thought may be about a person, thing, location and so forth. When one thinks that *a* is F, one thinks *of a*, who or which may be distant, long since dead or destroyed. One's thought, as it were, reaches right out to *a* and no other – one, so to speak, pinpoints *a* with one's thought. But how is it possible for thought to effect this? What mechanism guides one's thought so unerringly on to its target? What *makes* my thought that *a* is F a thought about *a*? Various answers have been essayed. One may hold that one's thought consists of images, which represent their object by similarity (i.e. that the mental image, like a picture, represents *a* inasmuch as it is a likeness or copy *of a*). Or one may hold, as Locke did for simple ideas, that the mental image is *of a* because it was originally *caused* by *a*. Or one may hold that a thought is an abstract entity – a Fregean *Gedanke* – which is composed of 'senses' which are modes of presentation. Accordingly, one's thought that *a* is F consists *inter alia* of a sense that is a mode of presentation of *a* – that is what makes it a thought about *a*. Or one may claim that thought too is a kind of language, consisting of thought-constituents which stand to reality in much the same way as the words of a natural language (as the author of the *Tractatus* supposed, and later definitively refuted). History, in ignorance of its past, has repeated itself in the current suggestion that there is a Language of Thought (Fodor). We shall discuss these familiar answers in chapter 10.

---

[20] It would, however, be wrong to suggest that thoughts *refer* to something or other. Thoughts may be *about* things, but containing no expressions, they do not *refer* to what they are *about*. It is speakers and the words they use that refer to things.

Contrast: What makes one's thought a thought about a? And what are the criteria for one's thought to be a thought about a? The temptation to answer, rather than to dissolve, these misbegotten questions is great, but should be resisted. One should rather reject the question. For the only thing that *makes* one's thought that *a* is F a thought *of a* is that it is a thought that is made true by the fact that *a* is F. To be sure, that evident grammatical nexus does not dissolve one's puzzlement. What must be done is to elaborate the *criteria* for a person's thought *being* a thought of *a*, while denying that the criteria are *features* of the thought. So, for example, if I think that I must write to Jack, my old friend who lives in New York, then what shows that my thought is about Jack is that it is Jack in New York of whom we were speaking before I sat down to write, that I then address my letter to Jack in New York (and not to a different Jack in London), that if I am asked to whom I am about to write, I explain that it is to my old friend Jack who lives in New York, and so forth. In short, it is the *circumstances* of my thought and my *behaviour* in the circumstances, it is what I do and say, or would do and would say, that determine what my thought is about. So, what, *non-trivially*, 'makes it true' that my thought is about my New York friend, are the circumstances, coupled with what I do or would do if . . .

In what sense do thoughts have a structure? (v) *Of the structure of thought.* The final problem in the central cluster stems directly from the previous reflections. Precisely because thinking not only has a content but is commonly also directed at, or is about, something or other, indeed, has the content it has *because* it is directed at, or is about, something or other, it seems that thoughts, beliefs, hopes, fears and suspicions, unlike mere sensations such as pain, cannot be amorphous. They must have an internal structure, must consist of elements (ideas, concepts, senses or thought-constituents in the language of thought) arranged in a certain way in order for the thought to be the very thought it is. Those elements, it seems, must be related to whatever objects in reality are thought of or about. If so, then thoughts, beliefs, etc. are representations – either by way of similarity, by projection or by causal generation. This is a tempting picture. But before succumbing to it, we must investigate whether it makes sense to conceive of thoughts as representations (as the British empiricists Frege and Russell and the *Tractatus* did, and as many contemporary philosophers do).

Thoughts are not representations Intentional *mental states* (such as eagerly expecting something, feeling pleased that things are thus-and-so, feeling frightened of something) are not representations. Thoughts, that is, what one has when one thinks (and, *mutatis mutandis*, believes, hopes, fears, suspects, etc.) are *not* representations either. A historical painting may be said to be a representation – of the historical event it depicts. A genre painting may be said to be a representation – of the imaginary scene it depicts. A proposition (an assertoric sentence in use) may be said to be a representation – of what it can be used to assert to be so. If something is a representation, it must have both representational features (its pictorial features in the case of the painting, its semantic features in the case of the proposition) and non-representational features in virtue of which it *can* represent and be perceived to represent, what it represents. The non-representational features are characteristics of the medium of representation. In the case of a drawing, the colour and character of the pencil, the ink, chalk or charcoal, the texture and colour of the paper are such features. In the case of a painting, the non-representational characteristics in virtue of which it can be perceived to be the representation it is are such features as the specific paint medium (oil, gouache, acrylic, watercolour, tempera), the canvas and its texture, the gesso, plaster or panel, and so forth. It is the non-representational features of a representation that enable one to perceive or apprehend the representation. But our thoughts are not representations at all. They are not perceptible objects. They involve no medium of representation. One cannot identify or misidentify, interpret or misinterpret one's own thoughts in order to find out what one thinks as one may identify or misidentify, interpret or misinterpret a representation in determining what it represents. Indeed, when one thinks that *p*, one does not *find out* that one thinks so. Thoughts, unlike representations, *are all message and no medium*.

So thoughts, beliefs, hopes, expectations, suspicions
It is the expression and doubts are neither amorphous nor structured.
of a thought that Holmes's suspicion that Moriarty was guilty of the
is a representation murder does not consist of a subject and predicate, or of the sense of a proper name and the sense of a function name. Nor does it consist of the concept of being guilty of murder. Thoughts do not *consist* of anything. *What we think* is not made, or made up, of anything. It is the *expression* of a thought that is a 'representation'. For the expression of our thoughts in speech or script has non-representational characteristics in virtue of which it is perceptible as a representation – the loudness and timbre of the spoken voice, the colour of the ink with which one writes, the characteristics of the handwriting and so forth. It is the *sentences* we use to express our thoughts, beliefs, hopes or expectations in speech or script that can

be said to have a logico-grammatical structure. For it is those sentences that have constituents (words) arranged in a certain rule-governed way. We shall explore this further in chapter 10.

So much then for the problems of the central sun (see fig. 2.3).

Figure 2.3 *The central sun of intentionality*

4. The first circle: what do we believe (hope, suspect, etc.)?

What is it we believe If we V truly (rightly or correctly), then what we
when we believe V to be the case is what is the case. If we V falsely
truly and what when (wrongly or incorrectly), then what we V is pre-
we believe falsely? cisely what is *not* the case. This pair of logical
requirements may seem problematic for two reasons:

(i)   If we rightly insist that when we believe truly that things are so, what we believe is what is the case, then it seems to follow that when we believe falsely that things are so, then what we believe is not what is the case, there is not anything that is so – that is to say: we believe nothing.

But, as Socrates already pointed out in the *Theaetetus*, even if our belief is false, we believe *something*, not *nothing*.

(ii) If our belief is incorrect, then what we believe is not what is the case. But how can what we believe both *be* what is the case when our belief is true and yet *not be* what is the case when our belief is false, and yet *be the very same thing*? For we surely believe *the very same thing*, namely *that things are so*, no matter whether our belief is right or wrong! ('The same thing' is the rat one should now be able to smell.)

So the first orbital question revolving around the core problems of the relation of thought and reality is: *what is it* that we believe (expect, fear, hope, etc.) when we believe that things are so?

Attempts to answer the question of what we believe — To ensure that there is something for us to believe, irrespective of whether our belief is true or false, it is tempting to suggest that what we believe, when we believe that things are so, is a Fregean thought (*Gedanke*), a Moorean or Russellian proposition (which, if our belief is true, is a fact 'in the world'), or – with a Tarskian or Quinean preference for austerity – a sentence. An immediate subsidiary question, as it were an epicycle on the question of what is believed, is whether, if what we believe when we believe that things are so is one of these items, belief is *a relation* between a person and an object of the preferred type. Russell's question-begging terminology of 'propositional attitude' disposed many philosophers to think that intentionally occurring verbs signify *attitudes* towards something (or indeed, towards some *thing*). Philosophers who argue that what one V-s when one V-s that things are so is a *Gedanke*, a proposition or a sentence, typically hold that V-ing that p is *a relation* between a person and an object. The object in question is then conceived to be signified (or even named) by the noun-phrase 'that p'. This, according to Frege, refers to the customary sense of the sentence p, which is a *Gedanke* or thought. Tarski held the nominal clause to name a class of inscriptions (or sounds) of similar form. Quine (and Prior) held (contrary to English grammar) that the *that* in 'A V-s that things are so' belongs to the V ('V-s that' being a predicate-forming operator on a sentence) so that what one V-s *that* is an utterance-sentence (Quine).[21]

Believing something to be so, and believing something to be true

For *some* verbs (e.g. 'believe') it makes perfectly good *sense* to say that one V-s propositions (but not sentences or classes of sentences). In this sense, propositions, even if true, are not facts 'in the world' (as the early Russell had supposed). They are what can be said or asserted to be true. There is an important difference between V-ing that *p* (e.g. believing that *p*) and V-ing the proposition that *p* (believing the proposition that *p*). In the case of belief, it is the difference between *believing something to be so* and *believing something to be true*.[22] In the first case, the focus of one's belief is on how things are, and one's belief is true or correct if things are as one believes them to be. In the second case, the focus of one's belief is on how things have been, or might be, *said to be*. For some verbs (e.g. 'expect', 'suspect', 'fear', 'hope') it makes no sense to V propositions, even though one may V that a certain proposition is true or false. And for others (e.g. 'understand', 'consider') it makes sense for one to V that things are so and it makes sense to V the proposition that things are so, but there is a distinctive *shift in meaning* between 'V-ing that things are so' and 'V-ing the proposition that things are so'. In the case of 'understand', for example, it is the difference between 'I take it that' or 'I gather' ('I understand that things are so'), on the one hand, and 'I comprehend' ('I understand the proposition that things are so'), on the other.

---

[21] Appealing though this suggestion may initially seem to be, it is mistaken. 'V-s that' is not a unified operator on a sentence that produces a predicate from it. If it were, then it would be ungrammatical to say 'That *p* is what he believes' – rather we should say '*p* is what he believes-that'. Nor could we employ the verb parenthetically, as in 'Global warming, he rightly believes, is immanent', as opposed to 'Global warming, he rightly believes that, is immanent'.

[22] For an illuminating discussion of the grammatical complexities, see B. Rundle, *Grammar in Philosophy* (Clarendon Press, Oxford, 1979), ch. 7, and 'Objects and Attitudes' in *Language and Communication*, 21 (2001), pp. 143–56.

4 reasons why it is mistaken to introduce Fregean thoughts, or propositions, as what we V when we V that p Introducing Fregean thoughts (senses of sentences), propositions, classes of sentences, or utterance-sentences to fill the role of what we V when we V that things are so ensures that we V something, indeed some *thing*, when we V falsely. This provides an answer to Socrates in the *Theaetetus*. It also ensures that what we V when we V truly is no different from what we V when we V falsely. But the consequences are unacceptable.

First, the proposals immediately conflict with the requirement that when we V truly that things are so, what we V *is* what is the case – the requirement that our thought should not fall short of reality. For if what we V is a sense, a proposition or a sentence, then what is V-ed is not what is the case, but something else which is related in some further way to what is the case. Similarly, what we V, when we falsely or wrongly V that things are so, does not clash directly with what is the case, but only indirectly, via the intermediary of the putative object introduced.

Secondly, if what we V when we V that things are so is a Fregean *Gedanke*, a proposition, a class of sentences or a sentence, then the intrinsic individuation condition is distorted. For if what we V is one of these items, then what we V is not an intentional nominalization-accusative at all, but an object-accusative (we V an O, so to speak). To believe that things are so is not the same as believing a proposition, any more than believing that Jill is having an affair with Jack is the same as believing a rumour. Of course, the content of one's belief may be *that the proposition that things are so is true* (or that the rumour that Jill is having an affair with Jack is true). But to believe that things are so is not the same as believing that the proposition that things are so is true.

Thirdly, it is misguided to hold that whenever we V that things are so, we V the proposition that things are so (let alone the sentence 'Things are so'), since *it makes no sense* to expect, fear, hope or suspect propositions (let alone sentences). It is equally wrong to suppose that whenever we *believe* that things are so, what we believe is the proposition that things are so. It is, of course, possible to believe the proposition that things are so, as one may believe the declaration, allegation, story or rumour that things are so. But the *content* of one's belief (given by a nominalization-accusative) when one believes the proposition (declaration, story or rumour) that things are so, is not the proposition (etc.) that things are so, but rather *that the proposition (declaration, story or rumour) that things are so is true.*

Fourthly, the proposal that what we V when we V that things are so is a proposition, Fregean *Gedanke*, or a sentence immediately clashes with the requirement that it must be possible for what A believes to be what B fears and what C suspects (as when A believes that war is about to break out, B fears that war is about to break out and C suspects that war is about to break out). For while one may believe the proposition that war is about to break out, it makes no sense to speak of fearing or suspecting the proposition that war is about to break out.

Why Russell's idea that what we believe when we believe truly is a fact is mistaken

An alternative strategy to pursue was the early Russell's idea that what we believe is a proposition, and that when we believe truly, the proposition we believe is a fact. Facts are not, as Frege had supposed, true thoughts; rather, according to Russell, they *constitute* the world. What our true belief is *about* are constituents of the fact that we believe. This, unlike the Fregean solution, ensures that what we believe when we believe truly 'reaches right up to reality'. But again, the price is unacceptable. For there is no fact to believe when we believe falsely. So what we believe, when we believe falsely, is different from what we believe when we believe truly.[23] Moreover, as we have already noted, facts are not 'in the world', or anywhere else. The world does not consist of facts.

Believing something to be so is not a relation

The truth of the matter is that believing something to be so is not a relation, and *that things are so* is not a relatum. Believing is not a relation between a person and a thought, or between a person and a fact, or between a person and a proposition, or between a person and a sentence.

When one believes truly and when one believes falsely, what one believes is the same, but not the same thing

The second problem cited above (p. 83, (ii)) can now be handled easily. The problem was how can what we believe both *be* what is the case when our belief is true and yet *not be* what is the case when our belief is false, and yet *be the very same thing*? The confusion is generated by the tacit assumption

---

[23] Russell rapidly came to realize that this won't do, and eliminated propositions from his analysis of judgement and belief. Instead he advanced his 'multiple relation' theory of belief, according to which belief is not a dual relation between believer and a proposition, but a multiple relation between a believer and the terms of the belief. The young Wittgenstein duly torpedoed this account (*Tractatus* 5.5422).

that what is believed is *some thing*. It is correct, and unproblematic, that when one believes truly that things are so and when one believes falsely that things are so, one has the very same belief. It is also true that when one believes truly that things are so, then what one believes is what is the case. But *what* one believes is not *the same* as what is the case, any more than when one does *what* one is told to do, one does *the same* as one is told to do. Of course, when one believes truly that things are so, the question 'What do you believe?' and the question 'What is the case?' *both receive the same answer*. It is a remarkable fact that we can be so misled by 'whats' and 'sames', and by wrongly taking 'what' to be a relative, rather than an interrogative, pronoun here.

The question 'What does one believe, when one believes that things are so?' is misleading   The conclusion is not that the answer to the question 'What does one V when one V-s that *p*?' is singularly elusive and mysterious, but rather that the question is misleading. For it calls out for an answer that gives the name of a thing – and that is precisely what cannot be given. Taken one way, the question contains its own answer, namely, one V-s that things are so. Taken another way, the answer consists in rejecting the question, for although there is *something* one V-s, given by the nominalization-accusative, there is no *thing* that one V-s. Taken yet a third way, one could also answer trivially, 'All manner of things'.

Once one realizes that there is no thing one V-s when one V-s that things are so, it becomes easier to see that to think, believe, hope, fear, suspect or doubt that *p* is not to have an *attitude* towards any thing, or indeed, towards anything. For these intentional verbs, or the intentional uses of these verbs, do not signify attitudes. We shall discuss this matter in chapter 4.

5. The second circle: the relation of language to reality

The intentionality of language   We use sentences of our language to represent things. We describe, in words, how we take things to be. But words and sentences are sounds and inscriptions – parts of the material world, as it were. How *can* a sound or mark on paper represent, stand for or mean something beyond itself? What makes a sound or mark the name of a particular thing? How can a string of sounds or marks represent a state of affairs – indeed represent one *which may not even exist*? In short, what might be called *the intentionality of language* calls out for explanation no less than the intentionality of thought. (Talk of the 'intentionality of language' moves away from Brentano's concerns, but the problems are related.)

The temptation to explain how signs can represent by the idea of a connection between language and reality   It is platitudinous that signs represent whatever they represent only in the use which living creatures, language-users, make of them. This truism by itself does nothing to explain how it is that a mere sound or mark, used by a living creature, *can* represent anything beyond itself. It is overwhelmingly tempting to ask how the signs of a language thus used must be *connected* to reality in order for them to be capable of representing what they represent. It seems plausible to hold (with Carnap and model-theorists) that the signs of language must be mapped onto entities in reality, that simple referring expressions must be correlated with individual things, predicates with properties, relation-terms with relations, and so forth. The combinatorial rules of the syntax of the language must then ensure that the combinatorial possibilities of signs coincide with the combinatorial possibilities of the corresponding entities in reality, to ensure that what makes sense neither exceeds nor falls short of what is possible in reality. So it seems that the *logico-syntactical forms* of language must coincide with the *forms* of what is represented by means of language. How this can be ensured is problematic. Hylomorphism and transcendentalism are indirect routes to an answer; the picture theory of meaning is a direct route.

How is the putative connection forged?   Given isomorphism, how are the forms of language given a material content? How is the *connection* between language and reality forged? Various possibilities have been explored. One may conceive of the connection causally, trying to explain the intentionality of the signs of language by reference to the causal genesis of the mastery of their use by a speaker. This in turn may be construed immediately or mediately. Philosophers of language attracted to behaviourist learning theory, such as Quine or Davidson, construed the connection as immediate. Quine held that 'words mean only as their use in sentences is conditioned to sensory stimuli, verbal and otherwise'.[24] Davidson argued that we learn our first words

---

[24] W. V. O. Quine, *Word and Object* (MIT Press, Cambridge, Mass., 1960), p. 17.

through a conditioning of sounds or verbal behaviour to appropriate bits of matter in the public domain. . . . This is not just a story about how we learn to use words: it must also be an essential part of an adequate account of what words refer to and what they mean. . . . it is hard to believe that this sort of interaction between language users and public events and objects is not a basic part of the whole story, the part that, directly or indirectly, largely determines how words are related to things. . . . in the simplest and most basic cases, words and sentences derive their meanings from the objects and circumstances in which they were learned.[25]

Thinking thus, it seems attractive to invoke ostensive *training* as a fundamental part of the process whereby the connection between word and object is instilled in the language-learner. One will then be prone to regard an ostensive *explanation*, which postdates the brute training, as a true predication – as Quine did.[26] The logical character of ostensive explanation and definition is a satellite moving epicyclically on the orbit of the relation between language and reality.

Ostensive explanation is often construed as the primary device *connecting language and reality*.[27] Thus conceived, the definables of language are ultimately analysable into combinations of indefinables. The indefinables (the 'primitive terms' of *Principia Mathematica* *1) are explained by reference to their connection with reality. Ostensive explanation is *the point of exit* from language. Words are 'pinned' to reality by ostensive explanation, *conceived as true descriptions* (Russell, Quine). But this is fundamentally mistaken.[28]

Ostensive explanations are norms for description   It is perfectly correct to distinguish between ostensive training and ostensive teaching. Ostensive training may indeed be conceived more or less behaviouristically. Ostensive teaching, however, is

[25] D. Davidson, 'The Myth of the Subjective', repr. in M. Krausz (ed.), *Relativism: Interpretation and Confrontation* (University of Notre Dame Press, Notre Dame, Ind., 1989), pp. 163f.

[26] W. V. O. Quine, 'Ontological Relativity', repr. in *Ontological Relativity and Other Essays* (Columbia University Press, New York, 1969), p. 39.

[27] See e.g. M. Schlick, 'Meaning and Verification', repr. in *Gesammelte Aufsätze* (Georg Olms Verlag, Hildesheim, 1969), p. 341, and 'The Future of Philosophy', ibid., pp. 129f., and F. Waismann, 'Theses', in *Ludwig Wittgenstein and the Vienna Circle* (Blackwell, Oxford, 1979), pp. 246ff.

[28] As Wittgenstein showed in *Philosophical Investigations*, §§28–64.

normative, for it involves explaining what words mean – giving *rules* for their correct use. Ostensive explanations (definitions) of the use of words, for example 'This ☞ ■ is black' or 'This ☞ ■ is square', are not descriptions, but norms for descriptions. They provide standards of correctness for the application of words. They are rules for the use of their definienda, connecting a word with an ostensive gesture, an indexical (which may be combined with a categorial term – as in 'This *colour* ☞ ■ is black' or 'This ☞ *shape* ■ is square') and a sample (e.g. a piece of paper, or a building block). They bear a kinship to substitution rules (such as analytic definitions). For the ostensive gesture, the indexical and the sample can also fulfil the role of the definiendum in a sentence expressing a true or false proposition (for example, instead of saying 'The curtains are black', one may say 'The curtains are *this* ☞ ■ colour'). That ostensive explanations (definitions) are rules is patent in the fact that the sample constitutes a standard for the correct application of the definiendum: if the curtains are *this* ☞ ■ colour, then they may be said to be black. But the sample employed in an ostensive definition is not thereby *described*. It belongs (at least *pro tempore*) to the means of representation, not to what is represented. In this sense, it is an instrument of the language. There is a *logical* difference ('all the difference in the world') between the two sentences 'This colour ☞ ■ is black' and 'This ☞ ■ square patch is black'. *Only the former is a rule for the use of the colour-word 'black'*. It is an ostensive definition of the word 'black'. By contrast 'This ☞ ■ square patch is black' is a contingently true description, which presupposes the meaning of the word 'black'.

There is no meaning-endowing connection between language and reality

There is no *meaning-endowing* connection between language and reality (no matter whether ideal or real) *in the sense that concerns us*. We do not 'connect language (what represents) with reality (what is represented)' by pinning simple names to simple ideas (Locke) or to simple objects or properties (Russell; the *Tractatus*). Rather, we connect one element that belongs to our means of representation (e.g. a colour-word) with another element that belongs to our means of representation – namely, a sample that functions as a standard of correct use. (Remember that what makes something a sample – and hence what represents or measures rather than what is represented – is nothing intrinsic, but rather the use we make of it.) We explain what symbols mean by connecting them to *other symbols*, not only words, but also gestures and samples.[29] In this sense too, there is no 'exit from language'. Consequently, the received distinction between syntactical rules and semantic rules (Morris, Tarski, Carnap) is misconceived. For it is confused to suppose that there is a distinction between intra-linguistic combinatorial rules, on the one hand, and rules 'connecting language with reality' (giving the syntactical forms of language an 'interpretation'), on the other. For in *this* sense, there *are* no rules 'connecting language with reality'.

6. The third circle: the relation of thought to language

Relation between intentionality of thought and of language   What is the relationship between thought and the 'intentionality of language' – the capacity of language to stand for things (that may or may not exist) and to represent states of affairs (that may or may not obtain)? Is the intentionality of language *derived* from the original intentionality of thought, or is the intentionality of thought *parasitic* on the intentionality of language? It is tempting to suppose that the intentionality of language is derived from the intentionality of thought. Thought, we may be prone to suppose, is *by its intrinsic nature* intentional. One's belief that things are so just does have an intentional content, and what is thus believed may or may not be the case. That may seem to be a fact of nature. The intentionality of language, one may then argue, is derived from the *original* intentionality of the mental.

Problems consequent to assigning priority to the intentionality of thought   Far from clarifying things, this makes matters even murkier. First, how is it effected? And secondly, what makes thought intentional? If it is a brute fact of nature, how does nature do it? Let us distinguish the following questions.

(i) Does the ascription of intentional attributes to a being presuppose that the creature is a concept-exercising animal, a language user? For example, does the ascription of belief to a creature presuppose that the creature possesses the concepts of truth and falsehood

---

[29] Consequently even if 'Mummy' or 'Daddy' are explained ostensively, nevertheless this is not an explanation by reference to a sample, since no one is a sample of themselves. Nor is Mother the meaning of the name 'Mummy'. So this kind of ostensive explanation does not make a *semantic* connection between language and reality either.

(Davidson)? If so, then non-language-using animals (and small children) cannot be said to believe (expect, fear) that things are so.

(ii) Is the intentionality of sentences of language to be explained by reference to the intrinsic intentionality of the mental (Searle)? If so, how? Is it to be explained by reference to a special mental act or activity of *projecting* the signs of language onto reality – for example, by reference to a mental act of *meaning* (the *Tractatus*) or intending (Grice, Searle)? Or, conversely, is the intentionality of the mental to be explained by reference to the intentionality of language? Or is this whole approach misconceived?

I shall discuss (i) here. Some of the questions of (ii) will be discussed in section 7 below, some in chapter 3. Others will be deferred until the examination of the concepts of believing and thinking in Part II.

Criteria for ascription of intentional attributes We must first reflect on ascribing intentional attributes to a creature. Clearly, we do so on the grounds of what the creature does and says in the circumstances of life. If someone says that things are so, and qualifies his assertion with an 'as far as I know', with a 'probably' or, of course, with an 'I think', then we may say 'He believes that things are so'. If someone explains his thought, feeling or action by reference to things being so, and we know that they aren't, then too we may say that he believes that things are so. If someone patently takes preventive action on the assumption that things are so, then even though he says nothing, we may ascribe to him the belief that things are so. And so on for other intentional verbs.

Coincidence of horizon of thought and horizon of its linguistic expression What then is the connection between intentional attribute and speech? It is not that an intentional attribute V is *truly ascribable* to a being only in so far as the creature expresses its V-ing in speech. For one need not voice one's beliefs, expectations, hopes and fears. To grasp the relationship, we must modalize the connection, and specify not a *condition of truth*, but a *condition of sense*. Is it then that it *makes sense* to say (truly or falsely, correctly or incorrectly) of a being that it V-s only in so far as it *could* express its V-ing in speech? That is still not quite right. For we do say that our dog believes it is going to be taken for a walk when, on hearing us take its leash off the peg, it rushes excitedly to the door, barking and wagging its tail. The fact that it cannot *say* that it is about to be taken for a walk, let alone that it cannot say that it *believes* it is about to be taken for a walk, is immaterial. Its behaviour warrants ascription of belief or expectation to it. The fact that it lacks the concepts, in particular the concepts of truth and falsehood, is also immaterial, as long as it *can discriminate* between things being as it believes or expects them to be, and things not being so – and *can exhibit* its so distinguishing in its behaviour. On the other hand, we could not intelligibly ascribe to the animal the belief that it is going to be taken for a walk next week, or next Christmas day. The fact that it cannot say so *is* crucial – for the *only* behaviour that could express such a belief or expectation is verbal behaviour utilizing a vocabulary with appropriate devices for temporal reference. And such behaviour does not lie within the behavioural repertoire of a non-language-using animal. That is why it is not false to ascribe *such* beliefs to an animal, but senseless – for nothing would *count* as a manifestation of its harbouring such a belief. So, we can *intelligibly* ascribe intentional attributes to a creature only in so far as its behavioural repertoire includes such forms of action and response as would warrant the ascription of the intentional attribute were the creature so to behave. *The horizon of possible thought is fixed by the limits of the possible behavioural expression of thought – in speech or action.* We shall explore animal thought further in chapter 10.

We are now on the brink of the general question of the relationship between thought (in all its variety) and language. For it is very tempting to suppose that what gives life to 'dead signs' are mental processes of intending or meaning. It seems to be the mind that animates dead signs by projecting them onto reality, and one plausible candidate for the method of projection seems to be *mental acts of meaning*, meaning *by* one's words *such-and-such states of affairs*. We shall discuss this in section 7 below and in chapter 3.

7. The fourth circle: the epistemology of intentionality

The immediacy condition and the cognitive assumption Any mature language-user who V-s that things are thus-and-so can say so. A person's avowal that he V-s that things are so is *immediate*. It does not rest on evidence and is not justified by reference to evidence. We may call this *the immediacy condition*. Any account of intentionality must elucidate how this is possible. It seems that in order to be able to say what one V-s one must *know* both that one V-s something, and what one V-s. We may call this *the cognitive assumption*. If one makes this assumption, one must explain how it is that one knows this. (Here we make contact with the illusions of consciousness discussed in chapter 1.)

1st-/3rd-person epistemic asymmetry There is an epistemic asymmetry between the first- and third-person cases. When it comes to knowing whether another person V-s that things are so, our knowledge rests on familiar kinds of evidence of what he experiences, says and does in the circumstances. Our assertions concerning the beliefs, thoughts, fears and hopes of others enjoy no epistemic privilege. They are often not *inferred* from evidence, but made as a consequence of our exercise of our recognitional capacities – we can *see* the joy on her face or the grief in her eyes. But if our claims are challenged, they can be justified by reference to such familiar kinds of evidence as the agent's behaviour, expression, demeanour and tone of voice, as manifest in the complex stream of human life.

The first-person case, however, is different. If I believe or expect that things are so, then I cannot rightly say that I am *ignorant* of the fact that I do. Nor can I say that I don't know *whether* I do, as I can say of another that either he believes that things are so or he does not, but I don't know which of these alternatives is correct.[30] These asymmetries reflect the immediacy condition, and seem to confirm the cognitive assumption. For they suggest that the reason for these epistemic asymmetries is that when one V-s that things are so, one knows immediately that one does.

Apparent 1st-person authority Corresponding to the epistemic asymmetry is *apparent first-person authority in utterance.* While my word carries no special weight independently of the weight of the evidence I might have in support of the claim that A V-s that things are so, my avowal or averral that *I* V that things are so does carry special weight. If a person avows that he V-s that things are so, then, other things being equal, we take his word for it. We do not ask him how he knows that he does, as we might ask someone, who asserts that A V-s that things are so, how he knows this. Of course, such an avowal or averral may be insincere. So first-person authority is defeasible. Indeed, there are other grounds for

---

[30] There are, of course, forms of subjective uncertainty. I can be unsure whether I (really) believe that things are so, or uncertain whether I (really do) expect a certain event to occur. But these are not cases of either believing (or not believing) that things are so, expecting (or not expecting) that a given event will occur, but being uncertain which. They are cases of being unsure whether *to believe* that things are so, or whether *to expect* such-and-such an event. What is called for here is scrutiny of the evidence for and against its being the case that things are so or for and against the occurrence of the event, and *a decision* as to *what* to believe or expect – not examination of evidence for *my believing* that things are so or for *my expecting* the event.

defeat than insincerity – such as slips of the tongue and self-deception. But if not defeated, the speaker's word goes. An explanation of this asymmetry too is necessary.

It seems that one can say that one V-s that things are so only if V-ing that things are so is something 'present to the mind', something of which one is conscious. Otherwise how could one's avowal be immediate? Indeed, how could one know what one V-s if V-ing that things are so were not a mental *phenomenon* with an intentional content possessing *mental in-existence*. For it seems that only then could one can read off the fact that one V-s that things are so by introspection.

Invoking the cognitive assumption to explain 1st-person authority The traditional strategy is to cleave to the cognitive assumption in order to explain the epistemic asymmetry. The cognitive assumption also offers an explanation of first-person authority in utterance. For if, when one V-s that things are so, one knows that one does, then one's word will carry special weight – the weight of the word of someone who is uniquely well informed about something accessible directly to him but not to others. The temptation to accept the cognitive assumption is great. To deny that when one V-s that things are so one *knows* immediately that one does seems tantamount to saying that when one, for example, believes that things are so, one is *ignorant* of one's so believing. But that cannot be right. Taking introspection to be a faculty of inner sense, one will therefore argue that our knowledge of our own 'intentional mental states' is immediate, for they are evident to the mind. As we saw in the previous chapter, the classical version of this conception presents such knowledge as indubitable and incorrigible. If a person V-s that things are so, then he knows that he does. This Cartesian *transparency thesis* was defended by Brentano.[31]

Modifying the cognitive assumption to budget for self-deception and hypocrisy Others, noting the defeasibility of first-person authority in cases of hypocrisy or lip-service, and self-deception, defended a modified version of the cognitive assumption, namely, that when a person V-s that things are so, he *normally* knows, corrigibly and dubitably, that he does. The corrigibility

---

[31] In Brentano's view we apprehend psychological phenomena by inner perception, and 'inner perception possesses another distinguishing characteristic: its immediate, infallible self-evidence' (*Psychology from an Empirical Standpoint*, p. 91).

and dubitability can, it seemed, be explained either by faulting the faculty of inner sense or by reference to the possibility of the object of inner sense being concealed. William James, Francis Galton and Herbert Spencer retained the perceptual model of introspection, but rejected the idea that it is superior, in terms of infallibility or indubitability, to outer sense. Alternatively, inspired by the Freudian conception of the unconscious, one might argue that objects of inner sense may not always be evident, since they may be hidden in the unconscious. (This, to be sure, involves a misconception. For an unconscious X does not stand to a conscious X as an occluded object to a visible one. Unconscious beliefs and desires are not just like conscious ones, only unconscious.)

Denying the cognitive assumption As we have seen in chapter 1, the correct line to take is not to modify the cognitive assumption, but to deny it altogether. To do so is not to argue, absurdly, that when one V-s that things are so, one is ignorant of the fact that one does. Rather, one must deny epistemic sense both to 'knowing', *and* to 'being ignorant' here. Accordingly, the epistemic asymmetries are not explained by doubt and ignorance being excluded by one's *knowing* that one V-s that things are so. Rather they are excluded *by grammar* – by the formation rules of our language. Or, to put the same point in more elevated terms – they are *logically* or *conceptually* excluded. If it makes no *sense* to say of a person that he is ignorant of the fact that he V-s that things are so when he does, then it also makes no sense to speak of his knowing that he does. Self-deception and unconscious beliefs and desires must, of course, be explained other than in terms of the cognitive assumption. As we shall see in chapter 6, where we shall explore all these matters further, this can be done.

8. The fifth circle: meaning and understanding

The final circle consists of a pair of interdependent issues concerning linguistic communication: meaning and understanding (as it were two satellites circling a common planet moving on an orbit). These will be discussed in detail in chapter 3. Here I wish merely to link them with the questions of intentionality that we have been examining, and to bring to light the pressures that generate the characteristic questions and misunderstandings in this domain.

Do meaning and intending breath 'life' into bare signs?

We communicate our thoughts, expectations and intentions to each other by using language. But the signs of language are surely just sounds or inscriptions. By themselves, they are lifeless – mere marks and noises. What breathes life into them? The most plausible reply seems to be that it is the mental activities that accompany the utterances of such signs – in particular the activities of meaning or intending by one's utterance such-and-such a state of affairs. It is the intentionality of one's mental act of meaning or intending that projects the sentence, and hence too the words of the sentence, onto reality. So semantic meaning is derived from the intentionality of meaning and intending.

Meaning and intending are not mental acts; we can't make words mean what we want

Although this looks promising, our suspicions should be aroused by the reflection that meaning and intending are not mental acts or activities at all. One cannot mean something quickly or slowly, and one cannot be interrupted in the middle of intending something. One cannot remember to mean something by an utterance or forget to intend something by a word one utters. It is evident that, unlike Humpty Dumpty, we cannot make words mean what we want. One cannot utter 'There's glory for you' and mean 'There's a nice knock-down argument'. Why not? What is the nature of the constraints on a speaker's meaning? To shed light on these matters, we need to clarify the concept of meaning something by one's words. This will be done in the next chapter.

Telementational conception of communication

The correlate of the questions related to the intentionality of language is an array of problems concerning the hearer's understanding that is the upshot of successful communication. How can the hearing of 'mere sounds' yield understanding of what is meant by an utterance? A *telementational conception of communication* pervades philosophers' and linguists' reflections on discourse.[32] If one conceives of words as standing immediately for ideas in the mind and only mediately for the objects of which the ideas are ideas, then one will follow the classical empiricists in thinking that

---

[32] Roy Harris, *The Language Machine* (Duckworth, London, 1987), pp. 7f., 29–36.

because the scene of ideas that makes one man's thoughts cannot be laid open to the immediate view of another . . . therefore to communicate our thoughts to one another . . . signs of our ideas are also necessary; those which men have found most convenient, and therefore generally make use of, are *articulate sounds*.[33]

Successful communication ensues when the words uttered 'excite in the hearer, exactly the same idea they stand for in the mind of the speaker'.[34] The same telementational conception was enshrined in the work of the founding father of modern theoretical linguistics, in de Saussure's famous 'speech-circuit' elaborated in his lectures (1906–11),[35] but with ideas replaced by concepts linked to representations of sound patterns (see fig. 2.4).

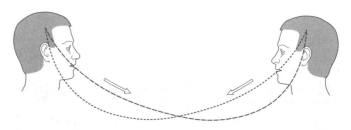

Figure 2.4   *Saussure's first speech-circuit, from* Course in General Linguistics

Understanding as computational interpretation More recently (1980), Chomsky argued that to know or understand a language 'is to be in a certain mental state, which persists as a relatively steady component of transitory mental states. . . . to have a certain mental structure consisting of a system of rules and principles that generate and relate mental representations of various types'.[36] To understand an utterance 'the mind/brain must determine its phonetic form and its words and then use the principles of universal

[33] Locke, An *Essay concerning Human Understanding*, 4th edn [1700], IV. xxi. 4.

[34] Ibid., III. ix. 6.

[35] F. de Saussure, *Course in General Linguistics* (Duckworth, London, 1983), pp. 11f.

[36] N. Chomsky, *Rules and Representations* (Blackwell, Oxford, 1980), p. 48.

grammar . . . to project a structured representation of this expression and determine how its parts are associated'.[37] To understand the sentence is then to interpret it 'by a computational process of unconscious inference' (ibid., p.55) which takes place virtually instantaneously (ibid., p. 90). Contemporary philosophers of language are similarly possessed by the telementational conception. If the 'input' in discourse (for the hearer) consists of sound waves impinging upon nerve endings (Quine) or of mere sounds (Davidson), how can the 'output' be understanding what was said, namely, that such-and-such is the case? The favoured answer is that understanding must be the upshot of interpreting. Davidson argued that 'speaker and hearer must repeatedly, intentionally, and with mutual agreement, interpret relevantly similar sound patterns of the speaker in the same way', and 'a theory of interpretation . . . allows us to redescribe certain events in a revealing way. . . . a method of interpretation can lead to redescribing the utterance of certain sounds as an act of saying that snow is white'.[38] The theory is a model of the interpreter's linguistic competence, but 'some mechanism in the interpreter must correspond to the theory'.[39]

The myth of the given in linguistic theory   Again, our suspicions should be aroused by a little reflection. It is a mistake to suppose that what we are given in intelligible discourse is mere sounds, let alone auditory stimulation of nerve endings. That is a dogma of empiricism, akin to the empiricist dogma that what is given in visual experience is mere patches of colour and shapes, or visual stimulation of retinae. What is given in discourse are significant utterances, not mere sounds, let alone the sound waves that impinge on our ear drums. What is given in perceptual experience, including what is given in discourse, is not *given* in the sense in which influenza is given – the given is what can be argued from, and need not be

---

[37] N. Chomsky, *Language and the Problems of Knowledge* (MIT Press, Cambridge, Mass., 1988), p. 136.

[38] D. Davidson, 'Communication and Convention', p. 277, and 'Thought and Talk', p. 161, both repr. in *Inquiries into Truth and Interpretation* (Clarendon Press, Oxford, 1984).

[39] D. Davidson, 'A Nice Derangement of Epitaphs', in E. Lepore (ed.), *Truth and Interpretation: Perspectives on the Philosophy of Donald Davidson* (Blackwell, Oxford, 1986), pp. 437f.

argued to. What we hear in our communicative transactions is meaningful discourse, and we cannot hear such discourse as mere sounds, even if we wanted to. So something seems awry.

Whether the telementational conception of linguistic communication makes sense will only become clear in the light of an investigation of the concepts of understanding and interpreting. If it is misguided to construe understanding a language as a state or to conceive of understanding an utterance as a process or activity of interpreting, then it must be rejected. So too, if it is mistaken (as it surely is) to take first-order model theory as an elucidation of what understanding a natural language consists in, then this conception of interpretation and understanding must be rejected. We shall examine the concept of understanding in the next chapter.

We have sketched out a wide range of interwoven problems, presenting them in the form of an orrery. The clear presentation of the problems, as we have seen, already serves to rule out many of the traditionally proposed answers. We have resolved some of the problems. Others have been deferred until later. The structure of the orrery is complex. The patterns of relations of the problems that revolve around the central core of questions concerning the relation of thought and reality are subtle. The problems ramify widely, reaching deep into questions in philosophy of language. It should be evident that mistaken answers to questions on one orbit affect the whole model, distorting the metal bands and jamming the cogs. The orrery will work only if all the pieces are put into their correct places. Only then can one hope to hear the music of the spheres.

3

Mastery of a Language as the Mark of a Mind

1. A language-using animal

Aristotelian conception of the rational psuchē is the superior framework

Consciousness was introduced into philosophy as the mark of the mind by Descartes. This was misguided. Intentionality was proposed as the mark of the mind by Brentano. This too was misguided. In *Human Nature: the Categorial Framework*, I suggested that the Aristotelian conception of the rational *psuchē* provides a far better framework for reflection on the nature of the mind and offers a far superior characterization of what is distinctive of mankind than the Cartesian conception, in the shadow of which we still linger.[1] To have a mind is to have a distinctive array of rational powers of intellect and will. A creature that has a mind is a creature that can reason, and hence is sensitive, in thought, affection and action, to reasons. Sensitivity to reasons and the ability to reason (to make inferences) are the prerogative of language-using animals.[2]

---

[1] See *Human Nature: the Categorial Framework*, in particular, ch. 8.

[2] This is sometimes contested on the grounds of Chrysippus' notorious dog, who, chasing a rabbit, comes to a trifurcation of the path, sniffs the first two paths, and then races down the third without even sniffing. This is held to indicate reasoning by elimination. To which there are two replies. First, ancient anecdotes are not evidence, and modern experiments with animals do not confirm the tale. Secondly, as was

---

The Intellectual Powers: A Study of Human Nature, First Edition. P. M. S. Hacker.
© 2013 John Wiley & Sons, Ltd. Published 2013 by John Wiley & Sons, Ltd.

To complete the prolegomenon to our investigations of the intellectual powers of mankind, we still need to add further lighting to the stage-set of *Human Nature: the Categorial Framework*. We must clarify the web of concepts that surround the notions of a language-using being, of meaning and understanding something by the words we use and of understanding the words of others.

Homo loquens: mastery of a language is a mark of the mind

We are born with the second-order ability to learn to speak a language. This is exercised in the early years of our lives, and we acquire mastery of a language. As noted in *Human Nature*, from our animal nature coupled to mastery of a language, all else flows. We are above all language-using animals – *homo loquens*, and only therefore (if at all) *homo sapiens*. Mastery of a language, exhibited in the stream of life, is a mark of having a mind.[3] Without having

pointed out by Kenelm Digby, in *Two Treatises* (Paris, 1644), pp. 312f.: 'But this needeth no other cause, than that their eagernesse of hunting having made them ouershoote the sent, (which for a while remayneth in their noses, after they are parted from the object that caused it) they cast backe againe . . . and with their noses they try the ground all the way they goe; till coming neere where the chace went indeede, the sent striketh their noses (that by this time are growne empty of it) before they come at the place: and then they runne amaine in pursuit of it, with their heads held up, (which is their convenientest posture for running) and all the way, the sent filleth them at that distance without their needing to smell upon the earth, to fetch it from thence.' (I am indebted to Hanoch Ben-Yami for this reference.)

Still, suppose a dog *did* sniff two paths and then dashed down the third path *without* scenting its prey. Would this provide sufficient grounds for the ascription of reasoning to a non-language-using animal? No. A creature can no more reason just once in a lifetime than a creature can follow a rule just once in a lifetime. To exhibit a capacity to reason, a being must manifest it not only (i) on a multiplicity of occasions, but also (ii) in a diversity of contexts (not just trifurcating pathways) with (iii) a variety of inference patterns (not just in a disjunctive syllogism).

[3] Strikingly, Descartes too argued for this connection – but for quite different reasons. He held that the stimulus-free character of human speech made it highly unlikely that the use of language could be explained along mechanistic lines. He argued that the use of language was the only reliable evidence for holding a creature to be conscious of anything, and hence to have thoughts (*cogitationes*). He did not, however, link mastery of a language with the powers of thought in any other way, let alone link the limits of thought with the limits of language. It is ironic that were the calculus conceptions of language, advanced by both philosophers and theoretical linguists such as Chomsky (who considers himself a Cartesian linguist) correct, then mastery of a language *would be* explicable in mechanistic terms. Knowledge of a language, Chomsky wrote, is 'represented somehow in our minds, ultimately in our brains, in structures that we can hope to characterize abstractly, and in principle quite concretely, *in terms of physical mechanisms*' (*Rules and Representations* (Blackwell, Oxford, 1980), p. 5; emphasis added). What Chomsky proposed, far from being Cartesian linguistics, as he claimed it to be, is a form of anti-Cartesian linguistics.

learnt to speak and to engage in the endless activities of language-using creatures, we would not be rational animals, would not reason, think, feel and act for reasons, and would not possess the distinctive powers of intellect and rational will that are constitutive of having a mind. Nor would our experience, perceptual, affective and active alike, be concept-saturated as it is.

To master a language is to learn new forms of behaviour, not to learn a meaning-calculus   To have mastered a language is to have learnt a vast range of *forms of action and activity* and of *reaction and response to speech* (and, in literate societies, *to writing*) and of *response to circumstance* which are constitutive of a human form of life. It is to be able to communicate by the use of language and to respond to the use of language by others. It is to be able to reason and deliberate. But, notwithstanding the claims of theoretical linguists and philosophers of language, it is not to know *a calculus of language* or a *generative grammar*. Nor is it to learn how to derive the meaning of a sentence from the meanings of its constituent words and their mode of combination, let alone to 'cognize' the depth-grammatical structures and how to map them onto surface grammar.

In this chapter, we shall examine the salient notions that form the conceptual framework for reflection on language-users, their linguistic powers and activities. Our concern is with the *connective analysis* of the concepts of linguistic meaning, understanding words, sentences and utterances, meaning something by one's words, and associated concepts in this semantic field. This will further our understanding of what it is to have a mind, and illuminate the nature of our cogitative and cognitive powers.

2. Linguistic communication

Learning a language is learning to do things with words   To learn a language is to learn an open-ended array of forms of action, the performance of which is integrated with the general forms of behaviour of the linguistic community to which one belongs. Language is an anthropological phenomenon, a language an ethnological one – an integral part of the form of life (the culture) of a human community. A language is a means of *communication*, and only secondarily a means of *representation* (not all linguistic communication involves representation). To learn a language is to learn to talk, to speak – and to respond to the speech of others. It is to learn to do things with words, symbols and gestures. It is to learn to request, entreat and plead, to comply and to refuse, to express and ascribe affections, attitudes, desires, intentions, aversions, to ask and answer questions, to guess and hypothesize, to thank others, to tell them things, to get them to do things and so on and so forth through myriad forms of action and response (both verbal and non-verbal) that the young learn at their parents' knee. The activities thus learnt are intelligible only as strands within the tapestry of human life. For one has to learn the 'language-games' in which these manifold forms of behaviour are embedded.[4] In short, to learn a language is to become a participating member of a culture.

Learning a language-game is learning to make moves in the game

To achieve mastery of a language is to learn to engage in the language-games that are part of the form of life of the culture into which one is born. To learn a language-game is to learn to make moves in the game. To use a sentence is to make such a move – it is to effect an *act of speech*. A large, if indeterminate, amount of common background knowledge, shared background presuppositions concerning regularities in nature and constancies in our own nature, common discriminatory powers and shared primitive responses, provide the framework for human beings to engage in language-games. In the absence of this framework, no communication by means of language would ever take place. A given language-game is played only in appropriate communicative contexts in the stream of life.[5] So too a given move in a language-game occurs only in a certain context within the game.

The instruments of language-games incorporate more than words and sentences

A language-game is played with more communicative instruments than spoken words and sentences. Words are uttered with intonation contour, and are accompanied by facial expressions and hand gestures. These are an integral part of the

---

[4] The term 'language-game' was introduced by Wittgenstein. The analogy between linguistic activities and playing games serves, among other things, to emphasize the integration of speech with context and action, to compare the normativity of language use with the normativity of playing games, and to highlight the fact that both *game* and *language* are family-resemblance concepts. Of course, speaking is not playing a game and a language is not a game.

[5] Although, of course, just as there are games one plays by oneself (e.g. patience), so too there are language-games one plays by oneself (e.g. writing reminders for oneself in one's diary, as well as reflexive language-games such as encouraging oneself, castigating oneself, ordering oneself).

communicative act. Indeed, gesturing alone (shaking or nodding one's head, thumbs up or down) may constitute a fully fledged act of communication. In highly literate cultures such as ours, the characteristic features and conventions of writing and reading should not be overlooked. The introduction of script has transformed human civilizations – but not because it maps the sounds of speech onto script (it commonly doesn't) – but rather because it introduces a wide spectrum of novel linguistic possibilities and activities. It has made it possible to make and keep a record of events, to engage in correspondence, to make inventories, to keep accounts, to signpost, to label, to codify laws, to record trials, to produce and transmit texts, to write commentaries on and annotate texts, to create and apply sophisticated mathematics and so on and so forth. It would be mistaken to restrict our concept of a language to word-language alone, for the very *symbols* that are involved in human communication incorporate more than just words. Samples, for example, are a part of our means of representation. We often explain words by ostensive explanations that make use of samples (as when we explain what colour-words or measure-words mean). Such an explanation is akin to a substitution-rule (e.g. anything that is *this* ☞ ■ colour can be said to be black). We make use of samples in our actual assertions and orders (as when we tell someone to bring 28 inches [i.e. *this* ☞ — length] of *this* ☞ □ material, in this colour ☞ ■, from the drapers). So too, iconic symbols are an (increasingly) important part of our communicative activities. Any attempt to describe the mastery and use of language, and to theorize about language and linguistic meaning that overlooks these facts will be defective (for elaboration, see section 4).

Consequences of conceiving of thought as antecedent to language

It is surprising that mainstream reflection by philosophers and linguists on the nature of language did not conceive of language as behaviour. Not 'In the beginning was the deed', but 'In the beginning was the thought' was the principal guideline for all too many.

Thought was generally held to be independent of language. It was an operation with ideas or concepts. The result of thinking was commonly conceived to be the generation of language-independent thoughts and judgements. Thoughts or judgements were conceived to be *representations* of how things are. These *ideational* or *conceptual* representations could then be 'translated' into the medium of language for purposes of communication. As noted in chapter 2, the primary use of language was considered to be *telementation*. What others do with the thoughts thus transmitted or induced is a further question.

This natural misconception has characterized philosophical reflection since antiquity. If one begins one's investigations into the nature of language from the primacy of thought, then all one's reflections are likely to be distorted. For thoughts – what we think – are typically *either true or false*, and are expressed by *assertoric sentences*. So one will be prone to assign analytic primacy (primacy in the order of analysis) to *representation* and hence to *truth* and *assertion*, and functional primacy to *naming* (the essential function of words is to name or stand for things) and *describing* (the essential function of sentences is to describe how things stand).[6] This is patent in the seventeenth century, in the Port Royal *Logic* and *Grammar* and in Locke's *Essay concerning Human Understanding*, Book III, which moulded reflection about language for the next two centuries. It is equally patent in Frege's *Begriffsschrift* and *Basic Laws of Arithmetic* in the late nineteenth century, in Russell's *Principia* and in Wittgenstein's *Tractatus*. It continues to flourish today among many theorists of language.

3. Knowing a language

Knowing a language contrasted with knowing a subject of study   Children learn their mother tongue at their parents' knee. Strikingly, we ask 'Has Thomas already started to talk?' not 'Is he already learning English?' It is when he goes to school and starts learning a second language that we may ask whether he is already learning French or German. A well-educated adult may know French, Italian and German, some Latin and a little Greek. To know a language is very different from knowing history, physics or chemistry. The latter involve coming to know a body of well-established facts and explanations, and, in the sciences, also well-confirmed theories. This includes learning what counts as, and what constitutes, evidence for factual, explanatory and theoretical claims in the relevant disciplines. Someone who knows *a great deal* of English history or physics can

---

[6] The essence of language thus conceived is the subject of withering criticism by Wittgenstein in *Philosophical Investigations* [1953], 4th edn (Wiley-Blackwell, Oxford, 2009), §§1–108.

answer a substantial range of questions about the subjects. The criteria for whether he possesses the relevant information lie in the behaviour that manifests knowledge: telling others appropriate facts and explanations, correcting the errors of others, solving problems that presuppose such knowledge for their solution and so forth. We also speak of knowing a little, or a fair amount of arithmetic or geometry. Here what is known are calculi, and methods of calculation and proof. What is learnt is not a body of empirical fact and explanatory theory, but the rules and operations of a calculus. To be good at arithmetic (as opposed to being a good mathematician) is to be able to calculate correctly and to apply arithmetical propositions to empirical reasoning in measuring and calculating magnitudes, quantities, and velocities of things. The criteria for someone's knowing such things consist in his correct performances, his spotting errors and correcting them, his explanations of how to arrive at a certain result and so forth.

To know a language is to be able to speak and understand it To know a language differs from both these groups of paradigms. Some of the differences come into view when one reflects on answers to the question 'How much X do you know?'. It makes little sense to ask a native English speaker how much English he knows. But that is not because a native speaker by definition knows a lot. One can ask an Englishman how much French he knows, and the answer may be 'A little', but not 'A great deal'. Amplification of the first answer may be 'Enough to get by with when shopping, but not enough to give a lecture in French'. The favoured alternative to knowing a little French is not knowing a lot of French, but knowing French well, that is, being fluent in French. (But a schoolboy may know a lot of French grammar (e.g. irregular verbs), yet nevertheless not know French at all well, i.e. not be able to speak or understand very much.) By contrast, to ask someone how much English history he knows, invites such answers as 'I know the Tudor period in great detail, but the Stuart only in rough outline'. But one cannot know French in great detail or Italian only in rough outline. To know a living language is to be able to *speak* and *understand* the language.

Knowing a language is not a state Knowing English, knowing English history, and knowing mathematics are all different kinds of complex *abilities* – not *states* of a person, let alone states of a person's mind or brain. Like all abilities, the abilities constitutive of knowing (being able to speak and understand) a language are exhibited in behaviour – in how a person reacts and responds to the speech of others, in what a person says and does. The appropriate forms of behaviour and reaction in context are criteria, logically adequate grounds, for ascribing to a person knowledge of the language. However, the ability to articulate the linguist's grammar of the language is *not* constitutive of knowing a language. We do not deny that a person can speak English because he cannot parse English sentences, cannot specify rules for Wh-nominalization, or specify rules for transforming declarative sentences into interrogative ones, or imperative sentences into declarative ones. Nor would we grant that someone can speak Latin on the grounds that he has mastered Latin syntax and has a decent Latin vocabulary – as many school-children do. Never mind *implicit* knowledge of depth-grammar or of a theory of meaning – even to have *explicit* knowledge of a theory of meaning for a language (if there is such a thing) would still leave one a communicational cripple.

3 objections to classifying knowing a language as an ability

It has been objected that knowing a language cannot be an ability.[7] For (i) two people may have the same knowledge of English, yet differ widely in their ability to use it, for example, an ordinary speaker and a great poet. (ii) The ability to use language can improve without any increase in knowledge – for example, if one takes a course in creative writing or public speaking. But such a person's knowledge of English need not increase at all – he need not learn any new words or new forms of sentence construction. (iii) An ability may be impaired or lost without any loss of knowledge. A person may suffer aphasia as a result of brain injury, losing all ability to speak and understand. But as his injury heals, he might regain these abilities without any new learning. So plainly something was retained throughout the period of aphasia and loss of ability to speak and understand. That surely was 'a system of knowledge, a cognitive system of the mind/brain'.

These objections display inadequate reflection on the *concepts* of knowing a language and of an ability:

(i) The fact that one person may be a great writer and the other writes journalese, even though both command the same vocabulary and syntax does not show that *knowing English* (mastery of the language) is not a complex ability. Nor does it show that both *know*

---

[7] N. Chomsky, *Language and the Problems of Knowledge* (MIT Press, Cambridge, Mass., 1988), p. 10.

English equally well. The confusion underlying the objection is the supposition that knowing a language is just a matter of knowing its vocabulary and rules of syntax (i.e. 'propositional knowledge' or 'knowing-that'), and that any increase in one's knowledge of a language is an increase in one's vocabulary and knowledge of syntactical forms. But that is mistaken. It is also a matter of how well one *uses* the vocabulary and syntactical forms in producing (and understanding) sentences in use. That is patent in the fact that as one's knowledge of English (or any other language) improves, one comes to speak and write better English, and becomes more aware of excellences and subtleties of expression in the speech and writing of others. Knowing a language, being able to speak and understand a language, is not reducible to knowing-that.

(ii) One can take courses in public speaking and creative writing. That may improve one's rhetorical and literary skills. Does it *not* contribute to one's knowledge of English? *Ex hypothesi*, it does not increase one's vocabulary or improve one's knowledge of syntax. But knowing the vocabulary and syntax of a language is *not* tantamount to knowing the language. Nor is knowledge of a language propositional knowledge of the meanings of indefinitely many sentences of the language. In taking lessons in rhetoric and creative writing, one comes to speak and write *better* English. But this *is* to know English better, to improve one's English. One will come to speak and write more lucidly and elegantly. One's *mastery* of English will improve. Far from showing that knowledge of a language is not a complex of abilities, this shows that it is.

(iii) Aphasia, unlike drunkenness, is not *an inner constraint* on a retained ability, but, like blindness, is the *loss* of an ability. To suffer from total aphasia is *to be unable to speak or understand one's language*, just as to be blind is *to be unable to see*. Amnesia is not forgetfulness. One cannot *remind* an amnesiac of some fact that he cannot recall. Amnesia is loss of memory. Aphasia is loss of the ability to speak and understand a language. There are cases of recovery from both. But it is mistaken to suppose that in these cases the knowledge was *retained* – in cold storage, as it were. For none of the criteria for knowledge (of one's past, and of one's language respectively) are satisfied in cases of amnesia and aphasia. Surely, *something* is retained in aphasia, since the patient's ability to speak his native language is *restored* without being learnt afresh! Certainly; but not a 'system of knowledge' or 'cognitive system in the brain'. What is retained are certain (as yet poorly understood) neural configurations and synaptic connections, which are causally necessary for being able to speak a language. But neuroscientific research into Broca's and Wernicke's areas of the cortex will never discover any *system of knowledge* or *cognitive system*. Neither what one knows (facts, truths, rules, explanations, theories), nor abilities to say, show or tell what one knows can, logically, be found in the brain. Abilities may be retained, but not stored – for there is no such thing as *storing* an ability. Facts and truths, rules and explanations, although they can be recorded on paper or on a computer disk, cannot be recorded on or in the brain. For whereas we record facts by means of a symbolism – a language – and write information down in a notebook or store it on a computer, there is no such thing as using one's brain as a repository for written records. Nor does it make sense to speak of the brain's knowing anything, let alone of its knowing the grammar and vocabulary of one's language. To say that facts, truths or rules are stored, filed away or retained *in one's mind* is just a picturesque way of saying that they are known and not forgotten. But that is precisely what one cannot say of the aphasic – who no longer knows his native language. If the aphasic recovers his mastery of the language, one cannot say 'Well, you see, he actually knew English all along – he just couldn't speak or understand it'.[8]

So, we may safely consider mastery of a language as a complex of abilities, exhibited in acts of speech and writing, in manifestations of understanding what was said or written, and in engaging in language-presupposing activities. One may perhaps say that the vehicle of these abilities is cortical, but the vehicle of an ability is not the ability.[9]

---

[8] Where does this newly restored ability *come from*? The question is misguided. A car may be unable to move because of the loss of a widget. Restore the widget, and the car can again go at a 120 mph. Where did this newly restored ability *come from*? It did not *come from* anywhere. Its restoration is *due to* the replacement of a widget. But for all that, the widget is not the store of the car's ability to do 120 mph. For more detailed refutation of Chomsky's arguments, see P. M. S. Hacker, 'Chomsky's Problems', *Language and Communication*, 10 (1990), pp. 127–48.

[9] The distinction between an ability and its vehicle is Anthony Kenny's in *Will, Freedom and Power* (Blackwell, Oxford, 1975), ch. 1. For close examination of powers, abilities and their vehicles, see also *Human Nature: the Categorial Framework*, ch. 4.

4. Meaning something

Meaning: natural, expressive, conventional, lexical and non-lexical

To shed light on the concepts of meaning, word- and sentence-meaning, meaning something by what one says and meaning what one says, we need to examine the weave of this conceptual network. The general concept of meaning is linked in different ways with those of sign, of signifying and of significance. Rain clouds mean rain inasmuch as they are inductive signs of rain – one can reasonably reliably infer rain from the presence of rain clouds. A different case is natural expressive behaviour – of pain, anger, fright, surprise and so forth. The expressive nexus between the behaviour and what it means is non-inductive. The behaviour *manifests* what it signifies (whereas rain clouds do not manifest, let alone express, rain). Conventional meaning is different again. Here one thing signifies another *by convention*. This may be verbal (lexical) or non-verbal. Non-verbal conventional meaning may be iconic, iconographic or gestural. Iconic signs may be signs *for* something (e.g. shop signs, icons on one's computer), insignia *of* something or someone (coats of arms), or signs (permitting, forbidding or requiring one) to *do* something (e.g. stop at the red lights). Iconographic symbolism, as in Renaissance painting, means what it does by convention *and* association. A female figure holding a palm leaf conventionally means that she is a martyr. A man holding a fish conventionally signifies that he is Tobias; if he is holding the hand of an angel, that associatively means that the angel is Raphael. Gestures, such as nodding or shaking one's head, thumbs up or down, likewise signify by convention. With respect to lexical meaning, we can distinguish the meaning of words (often signs *for* something), the meaning of sentences and the meaning of utterances. Quite differently, we also speak of what something, someone or some event or action means to us – of its axiological significance in our lives. In these ways (and many others too), meaning is linked with sign, signifying and significance (see fig. 3.1).

Lexical meaning and speaker's meaning

What a word, sentence or utterance means, what a speaker means by a word, what he means by the sentence he utters and what he means by uttering it are linked. Being derived from the Old High German 'meinunga' (from which the modern German 'meinen') and Old English 'mænan' ('to intend'), the English 'meaning' (a person's meaning something)

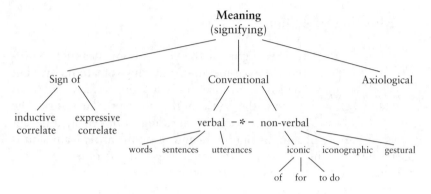

* Many forms of lexical communication include both words and gestures, written words and icons.

Figure 3.1   *Varieties of meaning (signifying)*

is interwoven with the psychological concepts of *intending* or *having in mind*, and hence with the *purpose* a person may have in word and deed. A person may mean something by an intentional gesture, wink or grimace. One may mean something by an agreed sign or icon (a chalk mark, a repositioning of an object, etc.). A speaker means such-and-such by an expression he uses (by 'You there!' he meant Jill, by 'the Canterbury Quad' he meant the back quadrangle at St John's College, Oxford and by 'Let's have a pre-prandial drink' he meant: Let's have an aperitif before lunch). We explain what a speaker meant by the sentence he uttered by paraphrasing it (perhaps spelling out any anaphoric references and indexicals). We may further explain what he meant by what he said by elaborating the implications he had in mind. We also speak of what someone meant (intended) to say, but didn't. But if he said what he meant to say, we may add that he also meant what he said, that is, that he was serious, and not jesting.

It is not the meaning of a sentence that is true or false, but what is said by using the sentence

Note that the meaning of a sentence cannot be true or false. It is what is said by the use of a sentence – that is, the statement or assertion made – that can be true or false. One cannot sensibly say that the *meaning* of the sentence 'Schnee ist weiss' is true. It is the statement made by uttering that sentence, namely the statement that snow is white, that is true. It is equally mistaken to suppose that an assertoric utterance *means* the state of affairs that it presents. Neither the sentence 'It is raining' nor its utterance *means that it is raining*. The sentence 'It is raining' *means the same as* 'Es regnet', 'Il pleut' or 'Rain is falling'. What may mean that it is raining is the drumming sound on the window panes. And, of course, what the speaker means by his utterance of the sentence 'Es regnet' is that it is raining – that's what he said, and he means exactly what he said (no jokes or litotes).

Speaker's meaning   Our first concern is with speaker's meaning. Although the verb 'to mean' has the superficial appearance of a verb of action or activity-verb, that is deceptive. To say something and to mean something by what one said is not to perform two actions, saying and meaning, but only one. (Try doing what you did when you meant something by your words but without saying anything!) To remember having meant such-and-such by an expression is not to remember a further action over and above saying what one said. Unlike what is signified by typical action- and activity-verbs, one cannot intend or decide to mean something by a word or sentence, one cannot be ordered to mean something and then agree or refuse to mean what one was ordered to mean, one cannot try to mean something by a word and then succeed or fail. There is no such thing as beginning to mean something, being interrupted in the middle of meaning it and later to resume meaning it. One may say something quickly or slowly, but there is no such thing as meaning something quickly or slowly. One may forget to mention someone, but not to mean someone. One does not learn how to mean things by the words one uses, and there is no such thing as being skilled at meaning things. In short, *meaning something by an expression is not accompanying one's utterance by a mental act or activity of any kind*. In what follows, we must bear in mind the varieties of speaker's meaning, and take care not to confuse what words mean with what speakers mean by them (see fig. 3.2).

Constraints on   What one *can* mean by a word is constrained by what
speaker's meaning   the word means, unless one is operating a code. In one's utterance 'I met him last week', one may mean by 'him' Tom, Dick or Harry. By 'I'll see you there', one may mean that one will see the addressee at dinner in St John's, at the British Museum or in Paris. By 'I'll meet you by the bank' one may mean Barclays Bank, National Westminster Bank or the bank of the Isis. And so on. But unless there is a pre-established code, one cannot mean by 'I should like a glass of hot water' that one would like a glass of cold water (although one may *have meant to say* that one

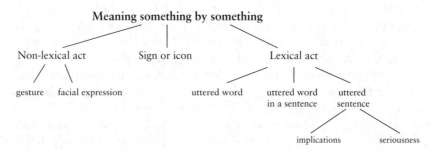

Figure 3.2   *Varieties of speaker's meaning*

would like a glass of cold water). One cannot mean by 'twelve' thirty-five or by 'red' blue. And so on. For what one means by an expression is constrained by what the expression means in the language. So it is mistaken to suppose that it is a mental act or activity of meaning something by one's words that projects one's words onto reality and thereby makes them represent what they represent. Meaning such-and-such by one's words is not a mental act or activity of any kind. Contrary to what Humpty Dumpty averred, the matter is not just a question of who is to be master. Rather, as Alice rightly retorted, the question is whether one *can* make words mean so many different things. In fact, it is the conventional meaning of the words that one uses that is the master. By 'There's glory for you' one cannot mean that there's a nice knock-down argument. In short, what one *can* mean by a word one utters *presupposes* its conventional meaning and cannot be invoked to explain it.

Attempts to explain lexical meaning by speaker's meaning or intentions
      The young Wittgenstein, and much later Paul Grice, mistakenly tried to elucidate the generation of linguistic meaning by reference to speakers' intentions. Wittgenstein, when writing the *Tractatus*, thought of mental acts of meaning ('meinen') as the method of projection by which words reach right up to reality and make contact with their meanings ('Bedeutungen'). Grice developed a fully fledged account of linguistic meaning in terms of speakers' communicative intentions.[10]

---

[10] H. P. Grice, *Studies in the Way of Words* (Harvard University Press, Cambridge, Mass., 1989), essays 5, 6, 14, 18. I have restricted consideration to the account of assertoric sentences.

The Tractatus The thought (implicit in the *Tractatus*) that mental acts of meaning something by one's words are the method of projection whereby language is connected to reality is defective. Meaning something by one's words is not a mental act. What one *can* mean by a word or sentence is constrained by what the word or sentence means, and cannot serve to explain what it means. In general, meaning something by an expression one uses presupposes that the expression has the meaning it has, and cannot serve to explain its meaning, save in cases of ambivalence. What gives the sounds and signs of a language the meaning they have is the normative practice of using them.

Grice's explanation of conventional meaning in terms of speaker's intentions According to Grice, the expression 'in uttering an assertoric sentence "s", a speaker means that p' is to be analysed thus: the speaker intends his utterance of 's' to induce in his addressee the belief that p by means of the addressee's recognition of that intention, and intends the intention recognized to be part of the addressee's reason for believing that p.[11] Consequently, a given sentence 's' non-naturally means what it does (means the same as 'p') in a speaker's idiolect if and only if in the speaker's behavioural repertoire there is the following procedure: to utter 's' if he intends his addressee to believe that p. This is duly generalized for a sociolect, and offered as a reduction of linguistic meaning to speakers' meaning something by their words.

3 objections to Grice's explanation There are three reasons for rejecting this. First, the communicative intentions suggested are complex. They involve the intention that one's utterance of a sentence 's' should induce the belief that p in the addressee, the intention that the desired belief be produced as a result of the addressee is recognizing one's primary intention in uttering 's', and the intention that part of the addressee's reason for believing that p should be his recognition of one's intention. But in order to have the intention to induce in the hearer the belief, for example, that the sun is setting, by uttering the sentence 'The sun is setting', one must already know what that sentence means. For one intends one's addressee to understand the words one utters *as one understands them oneself*. Otherwise one could not intelligibly be said to intend to induce in him the belief that the sun is setting by means of his recognizing one's

---

[11] This schematic account underwent much refinement, which, for present purposes, is irrelevant.

intention in uttering just those words, and for him to take one's utterance of those words as part of his reason for believing what one said.[12]

Secondly, this reductive analysis of meaning in terms of speakers' communication-intentions is flawed by failure to address the question of the conditions under which it makes sense to ascribe certain intentions to someone. To intend by one's utterance 's' to induce in an addressee a belief that *p* by means of his recognition of one's intention to do so, and to intend this to be part of his reason for believing what one intends him to believe, one must already be a mature language-user in possession of such concepts as belief, recognition, intention and reason for belief, as well as the huge range of expressions with which they are essentially bound up. So the communicative intentions suggested in order to explain what it is for expressions to have a meaning already presuppose, and so cannot explain, mastery of a very sophisticated segment of a language. It requires that one know what a wide range of words mean. It is not obvious that 'bootstrapping' one's way up from primitive cases can circumvent this difficulty.[13]

Thirdly, according to Grice's account, to mean by one's utterance that things are thus-and-so entails intending to induce in one's addressee the belief that they are (or the belief that one believes that they are). But that is mistaken. One may utter the sentence 's' and mean by it that *p*, while being absolutely certain that one's hearer will not believe that *p*. Or one may know that he already knows that *p*. Or one may be indifferent as to whether he believes thus or not, caring only to take a stand. What is crucial for communication is not that the addressee *believe* what one says in making an assertion by the use of a declarative sentence, but that he *understand* what one said. However, that presupposes the conventional linguistic meaning of the words one uttered.[14]

[12] See B. Rundle, *Grammar in Philosophy* (Clarendon Press, Oxford, 1979), pp. 406f.

[13] As was suggested by P. F. Strawson, 'Meaning and Truth', repr. in *Logico-Linguistic Papers* (Methuen, London, 1971), p. 174.

[14] See I. Rumfitt, 'Meaning and Understanding', in F. Jackson, and M. Smith (eds), *The Oxford Handbook of Contemporary Philosophy* (Oxford University Press, Oxford, 2005), pp. 427–53.

5. Understanding and interpreting

Understanding as a mental process of deriving meanings It is tempting to suppose that understanding an utterance is a *mental act* or *experience*. After all, we typically understand what someone says to us immediately; and we have all experienced eureka moments – the flash of understanding as we 'twig it' or 'cotton on'. It can be made tempting to think that understanding an utterance is *an interpretative process* or *activity* of deriving the meaning of the utterance from the known meanings of the constituent words and their mode of combination. According to Dummett, 'a process of derivation of some kind is involved in the understanding of a sentence'.[15] According to Chomsky, understanding is a computational process of unconscious inference. For a person to understand a linguistic expression, he contended, 'the mind/brain must determine its phonetic form and its words, and then use the principles of universal grammar and the values of the parameters to project a structured representation of the expression and determine how its parts are associated'. The 'structured representation', he claimed, is 'visible to the mechanisms of the mind'. To be sure,

> the computations involved may be fairly intricate . . . But since they rely on principles of universal grammar that are part of the fixed structure of the mind/brain, it is fair to suppose that they take place virtually instantaneously and of course with no conscious awareness and beyond the level of possible introspection.[16]

This conception of understanding the words of another belongs to the telementational conception of communication (see fig. 3.3). We saw in the last chapter how it was enshrined in Saussure's famous 'speech-circuit'.

Accordingly, what understanding the speech of another *must* consist in is interpreting the sounds one hears so that one will come to understand what thought was being communicated to one. The sounds have to be translated into ideas, concepts or senses the combination of which corresponds to the message the speaker means to

---

[15] M. A. E. Dummett, 'What is a Theory of Meaning', in *Mind and Language*, ed. S. Guttenplan (Clarendon Press, Oxford, 1975), p. 112.

[16] N. Chomsky, *Language and the Problems of Knowledge*, pp. 55, 81, 90, 136.

transmit to his addressee's mind. Note that nothing has been said in this tale about how the speaker understands the words *he* utters – how *he* 'translates' his wordless thoughts into words. We shall revert to this concern below.

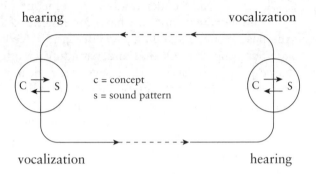

hearing   vocalization

c = concept
s = sound pattern

vocalization   hearing

Figure 3.3   *Saussure's second telementational speech-circuit. It should be noted that, according to Saussure, what occurs in the brain of the speaker is that 'facts of consciousness', which Saussure calls 'concepts', are associated with representations of sound patterns, which then cause phonation. According to the classical empiricists, ideas were associated with representations of sound patterns. According to Frege, senses are associated with representations of sound patterns*

Misconceptions of understanding as a dispositional, and as an occurrent, state

Though it is tempting to take understanding to be an instantaneous act or a rapid process of interpretation, it also seems plausible to take understanding to be *a state*. The termination of the interpretative or computational process is not, after all, the terminus of understanding. If I have to interpret an utterance, I don't cease to understand it as soon as I have finished interpreting. On the contrary, understanding seems to be the upshot of *coming to understand*. So must we not further distinguish understanding, construed as a *dispositional state* of the mind/brain (understanding or knowing a language),[17] from understanding as an *occurrent state* of the mind/brain (the upshot of interpreting the speech of another)? It is

---

[17] Again, Chomsky may serve as an example: 'To know a language, I am assuming, is to be in a certain mental state, which persists as a relatively steady component of transitory mental states. What kind of mental state? I assume further that to be in such a mental state is to have a certain mental structure consisting of a system of rules and principles that generate and relate mental representations of various types' (*Rules and Representations*, p. 48).

from the latter that behaviour *manifesting* understanding a particular utterance flows. For surely we behave in such-and-such ways in response to the utterances of others *because* we understand what they say?

All these categorial classifications are mistaken. Understanding a language is not a state of the mind/brain, since there is no such thing as a *mind/brain* – just as there is no such thing as a *sight/eye*. Understanding a language is a general *ability* to speak coherently in that language and to understand the utterances of others. Understanding a particular utterance is neither a mental act or interpretative process, nor a mental or neural state. It consists of being able to explain what the uttered sentence meant and what was said by its utterance, and to respond cogently to it. The mis-categorization of understanding as an act, process, disposition or state is anything but a matter of trivial detail. It misconstrues the concept and distorts the phenomena. That in turn leads to confused empirical theories of linguistic understanding and language learning.

Experiences of sudden understanding   Although normally there is no *experience* of understanding when one understands the speech of others, there is such a thing as the experience of *suddenly understanding* an utterance. However, even when one does have such an *Aha*-experience, the experience is not the understanding, and a description of such an experience is not the description of understanding. What happens when the penny drops (changes in breathing rhythm, lighting up of one's face, feelings of relief) is neither necessary nor sufficient for understanding. Indeed, the criteria for understanding are not criteria for experiences. And, of course, to understand what one says oneself, to speak with understanding, is not to have an experience of any kind.

Understanding is not a process   Although processes of reflection may lead to understanding, understanding is not a process. Processes go on; they take time. They consist of a sequence of events or actions, sometimes of ordered phases. They are clockable, may be interrupted, and sometimes can be resumed. Of course, there are mental processes. Humming a tune *sotto voce*, reciting a poem to oneself in the imagination, silently counting one's steps, can be said to be mental processes.[18] Understanding another's utterance, *a*

---

[18] But, of course, so can growing up, adjusting to a new country, coming to terms with the loss of one's parents, and so forth. The category of mental process is just as slippery as that of mental state.

fortiori understanding one's own words, are not. What one attends to with understanding may go on for a time, for example, a lecture. But understanding the lecture is not a process concurrent with hearing it. One may indeed begin to understand something, just as one may begin a process. But when one has fully understood, one has not finished understanding. Processes can be interrupted and often later resumed. But although what one is listening to may be interrupted, and one's listening may be interrupted, one's understanding of what one is listening to cannot be *interrupted*. Of course, there is such a thing as the dawning of understanding, but the dawning of understanding is not the beginning of a process – it marks the terminus of not understanding an utterance and hence of *being able to do* those things that are constitutive of understanding it.

Understanding is not interpreting   Understanding is not interpreting. First, interpreting may well be a process or activity one engages in when one interprets an utterance, but understanding is no process. One can begin interpreting an utterance, but one cannot begin understanding it – although one may begin to understand it. One can be halfway through interpreting an utterance, but not halfway through understanding it – although one may understand half of it, or half-understand it. One can break off interpreting an utterance in the middle and later resume, but one cannot break off understanding it in the middle and later resume understanding it. Secondly, if every sentence we heard required an interpretation, and an interpretation is given by another sentence, then we would never understand any sentence. Typical utterances in their context need no interpretation at all, for they are perfectly clear. Thirdly, interpretation presupposes understanding and cannot explain it. One cannot interpret a sequence of signs that is opaque to one (e.g. 'Abo gol tiftu ineas'), but only ask for it to be translated or deciphered. Then, when the translation is before one, one may interpret it – if it stands in need of an interpretation. Interpreting an utterance is clarifying what it means by giving a perspicuous paraphrase of it. The need for interpretation arises when an utterance is obscure and stands in need of clarification, or when it may be understood in more ways than one. A good interpretation is one that makes clear what was meant or that offers the better way of understanding what was meant.

Understanding is not a mental state   Understanding the utterance of another is not being in any kind of mental state. Why can it seem that it is? First, understanding a sentence seems to be the reservoir from which behaviour manifesting understanding flows. For surely, it is *because* one understood what was said that one proceeded to act intelligently on it. But this is confused. Linguistic understanding is a complex of *abilities*, and *to be able to* . . . is a power not a state. The behaviour that exhibits understanding is constitutive *evidence* for possession of a certain array of abilities, not for being in a state of mind. To say that one acted as one did *because* one understood what was said is akin to saying that one solved the problem because one had the skill. One may insist that understanding must have a vehicle, but the vehicle of an ability is not the ability.

A second reason for thinking that understanding is a state is that the verb 'to understand' is a static verb.[19] Philosophers are prone to justify their classification of mental attributes by reference to syntactical categories. But, as will be shown in chapter 4, our concept of a state is *not* a syntactical category. Moreover, our concept of a *mental state* (e.g. of feeling angry, of being in pain, of concentrating hard, of feeling cheerful) is characterized by the peculiar forms of duration and degree that are ascribable to mental states. These cannot be ascribed to understanding.

Understanding is not a brain state Materialists may hold that understanding is a state of the brain from which behaviour exhibiting understanding flows. But that too is wrong. For if it were so, then one criterion of understanding would be the persistence of that neural state. But, as we have seen, we do not grant that someone may understand an utterance despite the fact that given an opportunity, and being in command of his faculties, he cannot say what it means and cannot respond to it with understanding. Conversely, if someone manifests understanding in his behaviour, then no matter what the state of his brain, he understands. No doubt complex neural connections have to persist if a person is to be able to do those things characteristic of understanding. But these are not the understanding, just as the neural connections that make it possible for someone to be able to ride a bicycle are not the ability to cycle.

6. Meaning and use

Meaning and truth It has been characteristic of philosophical semantics over the last half a century to focus on the

[19] The syntactical category of static verbs is characterized by (i) lack of progressive form, (ii) lack of imperative form, (iii) absence of pseudo-cleft sentences with a Do pro-form ('what he did was to V').

connection between *meaning* and *truth*, arguing that the meaning of a sentence is given by specification of its truth-conditions and that the meaning of a word consists in its contribution to the determination of the truth-conditions of any sentence in which it may occur. This assigns analytic priority to truth and to declarative sentences – and hence to representation and description. It is noteworthy that the inspiration for truth-oriented calculus theories of meaning did not arise from reflection upon the roles of the concepts of word-, sentence- and utterance-meaning and their manifold connections within the web of words associated with linguistic meaning in our conceptual scheme. Nor was our ordinary concept of explaining the meaning of a word, sentence or utterance explored. It was taken for granted that specification of truth-conditions *counts* as an explanation of meaning. But this requires investigation.

The inspiration for truth-theoretic explanations of meaning
The inspiration for the idea of a theory of meaning for a natural language lay in the systems of mathematical logic invented for the purpose of the logicist project of reducing arithmetic to pure logic. A driving force behind subsequent reflections upon theories of meaning in the 1960s was the perceived need to answer the question of how we can understand sentences we have never heard before (see section 7). This truth-theoretic route is not the *connective-analytic* route followed here. I shall not give any analytic priority to the connection between meaning and truth. Instead, I shall describe the warp and weft of meaning, explanation of meaning and understanding.

Meaning and connective analysis
There are many aspects of language and linguistic meaning that give rise to conceptual confusion. Conceptual confusion results from unclarity about the use, and from the misuse, of the problematic words at hand – in the current instance words such as 'meaning', 'having meaning', 'having a meaning', 'meaningless', 'meaning the same as', 'meaning something different from' and so forth. To clarify conceptual problems in this domain, what is needed is not a compositional theory of meaning that will deliver for any well-formed sentence of the language a specification of its meaning in the form of a statement of its truth-conditions. What is needed is an overview of the conceptual field of semantic discourse. For what has to be brought into view is the web of connections between the concept of meaning and

related concepts.[20] When this has been done, we shall see whether any deductive, axiomatic, *theory of meaning* is necessary or even possible.

The concept of word-meaning is linked to a group of adjacent notions: to what a word *applies to*, to what it *signifies*, to what it *names*, to what it *stands for*, to what it *refers to* and to what it is a word *for*. There can be no presumption that these are the same. Each requires separate scrutiny. This will not be done here.

Meanings are not attachments and are neither inside nor outside the head
We distinguish, with respect to words in a language, between those that have meaning and those that are meaningless – such as 'Hey diddle diddle' or 'Fee-fi-fo-fum'. Among words that have meaning, we can distinguish those that have meaning, but do not have *a* meaning (like 'Tallyho' or 'Hello'), and those that have *a* meaning. The phrase 'having a meaning' can be misleading inasmuch as it invites reification. It has led some theorists of language (e.g. Dummett) to speak of *attaching a meaning* to a word, of the meaning of a sentence being *composed* of the meanings of its constituent words, of meanings being *inside* or *outside* the head (Putnam). This should be avoided. We must bear in mind the fact that the question 'What is the meaning of 'W'?' means the same as 'What does "W" mean?', and neither involve a relative Wh-pronoun, but an interrogative one. It is a request for an explanation of what 'W' means – not an explanation of what 'the-meaning-of-"W"' signifies. It is answered by giving an explanation – not by identifying a meaning. It is more akin to 'What is the purchasing power of that coin?' than to 'What did you buy with that coin?'.

Meaning is given by an explanation of meaning
The notion of the meaning of a word or phrase is linked to that of an explanation of meaning. For the meaning of a word (or phrase) is given by an explanation of what it means. Explanations of meaning may take many different forms. The one that has most attracted philosophers ever since Socrates is analytic definition, in which the necessary and sufficient conditions for the application of a word are spelled out (and hence too, the essence of what is signified). The most familiar kind of analytic definition is by genus and differentia. But

---

[20] See B. Rundle, 'Meaning and Understanding', in H.-J. Glock (ed.), *Wittgenstein: A Critical Reader* (Blackwell, Oxford, 2001), and *Wittgenstein and Contemporary Philosophy of Language* (Blackwell, Oxford, 1990), ch. 1.

there are yet other kinds, such as contextual definition, recursive definition and so forth. A quite different form of explanation of meaning is ostensive definition or explanation. The most familiar kind of ostensive definition involves the use of an ostensive gesture and a sample, as in explanations of colour-names, names of lengths or weights. But there are yet other kinds, such as explanations of names of tastes and smells (no ostensive gesture) or names of directions of the compass (no sample). Requests for explanations of word-meaning typically arise with respect to a particular phrasal or sentential context. So it is unsurprising that a common form of explanation of what a word means is by phrasal or sentential *paraphrase*. An alternative is *contrastive paraphrase*. Some words (family-resemblance terms) are explained by means of a series of examples together with a similarity-rider: *these*, and other things like these, are Ws (or are called 'Ws'). And so on.

Explanations of meaning are normative   Explanations of what words mean are not akin to explanations of empirical phenomena. They are *normative*, for they provide standards (norms) for the correct use of the word they explain. 'A vixen', we may explain, 'is a female fox'[21] – so any animal that is a female fox is correctly described as a vixen. 'This ☞ ■ colour is black,' we may explain, 'so anything that is *this* ☞ ■ colour is correctly characterized as being black.' Explanations of meaning are, in a perfectly ordinary and down-to-earth sense, *rules* for the use of the words they explain. They explain how the word or phrase *is to be used*, and hence, of course, how it *is* generally used. It is important to bear in mind that explanations are typically called for when there is a failure of understanding or a misunderstanding. An explanation is adequate if it averts some misunderstanding and enables the questioner to go on to use the word correctly. It is *not* required of an explanation of meaning that it specify *for every possible object* in *every possible circumstance* whether the word applies to it or not. That Fregean demand for determinacy of sense is incoherent.[22] For it seeks to elimi-

---

[21] This is no less an explanation of what the word 'vixen' means than 'The word "vixen" means a female fox', or '"Vixen" and "female fox" mean the same'.

[22] See Frege, *The Basic Laws of Arithmetic*, vol. ii, §56. For criticism, see Wittgenstein, *Philosophical Investigations*, §§71, 80, 84–7; for interpretation, see G. P. Baker and P. M. S. Hacker, *Wittgenstein: Understanding and Meaning*, vol. 1 of *An Analytic Commentary on the Philosophical Investigations*, part 2, *Exegesis*, §§1–184, 2nd, rev. edn (Wiley-Blackwell, Oxford, 2009).

nate not merely vagueness, but the very possibility of vagueness. This presupposes that there is such thing as circumscribing *all possible circumstances*. But there is no such thing. The assertion that vague concepts are *unsuitable* for the purposes of logic is one (debatable) thing; the Fregean suggestion that *there are no vague concepts* is another. It is an unwarranted stipulation rooted in the misguided idea that concepts are functions, coupled with the idea that a function must be defined for every admissible argument. Moreover, the idea that vague concepts are *intrinsically* defective is itself misconceived – for often that is just what is needed. (As Wittgenstein ironically remarked, 'I asked him for a bread-knife and he gives me a razor-blade because it is sharper!')

Explanations of meaning are rules; the concepts of a rule and of a practice are linked

The concept of a rule for the use of a word, given by an explanation of meaning, is in turn linked to the concept of a *practice*. For a rule is internally related to those acts that *count* as being in accordance with it. The rule to do so-and-so in such-and-such circumstances *is* the rule that is complied with by doing so-and-so in those circumstances. But this internal relation is not forged in nature. It forged by the practice of going by the rule. That the signpost **T** (which for present purposes may be considered a guiding rule) means 'Turn right!', that the traffic sign ⊖ means 'Stop' is determined by the practice of its use. Turning right is what we *call* 'following the signpost'; and stopping at the sign ⊖ is what we call 'complying with the stop-sign'. *Rules are alive only in practices*, in the context of the activities of being guided by them, of justifying or being willing to justify what is done by reference to them, of correcting and criticizing or being willing to criticize deviant behaviour by reference to them and so forth. (This is but one of many reasons why linguists' and neuroscientists' talk of there being rules *in the brain* is incoherent.)

Explanations of meaning remain within language

Explanations of meaning are given in words, gestures and samples – all of which belong (in so far as they are so used) to *the means of representation*, not to what is represented. Despite the deceptive appearance of ostensive definitions (e.g. in pointing at samples), of family-resemblance explanations in terms of a series of examples plus a similarity-rider, and despite the relatively recent conventions about the use of quotation marks apparently indicative of metalinguistic descent connecting words and world, explanations of meaning *remain within language*. We explain what words, phrases and sentences mean by other words, phrases and sentences (as well as samples and gestures). The explanations we give are not descriptions of how things are, but *expressions of rules* for the use of the expression explained. It is an illusion that we must 'exit' from language in order to correlate words with the things that are their meanings. For things aren't meanings of words despite the fact that they are sometimes pointed at in explaining what a certain word means. The meanings of words are no more *correlated* with words than uses are correlated with tools.

Meaning and use   It was Wittgenstein who drew our attention to the link between the concept of the meaning of a word and the concept of the use of a word. For a large class of cases, he wrote, *though not for all*, we can explain the phrase 'the meaning of a word' as having the same meaning as 'the use of the word'.[23] To ask what a word means is to ask how it is (to be) used. To explain what it means is to explain how it is (to be) used. To know what it means is to know how it is (to be) used. Once one has been reminded of this nexus between meaning and use, it becomes clear that much theoretical talk of meanings is misconceived – for example, that the meanings of words are ideas in the mind (British empiricists), or that they are objects, properties and relations in the world (*Tractatus* on the meaning of names), or that they are abstract entities that the mind can mysteriously 'grasp' (Frege on 'senses' of words). What a word means, how it is used, is not a kind of thing. Meanings are not attached to words, and they are not constituents of thoughts, propositions or meanings of sentences. The concept of the meaning of a word is at home in requests for explanations of word-meaning, in statements that such-and-such an expression is meaningless (e.g. 'Fee-fi-fo-fum', 'round square' or 'transparent white glass'), or that this expression *means the same* as, or *means something different* from, that one. So the concept of word-meaning is bound up with the concepts of sameness and difference of meaning, with ambiguity and polysemy. One should note that lexical synonymy is not an all-or-nothing, context-free business. One expression may mean the same as another in one sentential context, but not in a different one. Ambiguity or polysemy of type-sentence (both lexical and syntactic) commonly disappears in context of use – ambiguity is not as ubiquitous in the actual use of language as some linguists have suggested.

[23] Wittgenstein, *Philosophical Investigations*, §43. For reflections on the exceptions that he may have had in mind, see G. P. Baker and P. M. S. Hacker, *Wittgenstein: Understanding and Meaning*, part 1: *Essays*, pp. 152–8, and part 2: *Exegesis*, §43.

The meaning of a word is its place in grammar   Explanations of meaning, we have noted, are in effect rules for the use of the explananda. But many of the rules for the use of a given word are taken for granted in explanations of meaning inasmuch as the *general category* of the explanandum is understood. Someone who asks what *colour* eau de nil is already knows that what it is predicable of is extended (or just a flash of coloured light) and is detectable by sight, that being that colour all over excludes being any other colour all over at the same time, that eau de nil admits of different intensities, that it may be matt or glossy and so on. These features are partly constitutive of the concept of colour. These statements are in effect expressions of a range of rules for the use of colour-words – for they determine what it makes sense to say in using colour-words (and also what makes no sense). So if one knows that 'eau de nil' is a colour-word but not *which* colour it signifies, one at any rate knows its location in the web of words. This is why Wittgenstein remarked that the meaning of a word is 'its place in grammar'.[24] And, of course, that is why so much philosophical (conceptual) clarification involves *reminding us* of different strands and nodes in the network of conceptually associated words.

Links between meaning, grounds, criteria and verification   The concept of word-meaning is linked in various different ways with such concepts as grounds of application, criteria and verification. The logical positivists in the interwar years were mistaken to advance the principle that the meaning of a sentence is given by its verification conditions. Nevertheless, it would be a serious error to overlook the manifold conceptual connections between meaning, grounds of application, criteria and verification. To be sure, many predicates are applied to a subject without any grounds of application at all. (One does not say that one is in pain on the basis of any evidence; one does not judge something to be red on any grounds – one does not need grounds, one can *see* that it is red; and one does not have *evidence* for judging 25^2 to be 625 – a calculation is not evidence; and so on.) Nevertheless, there are many expressions that *are*

---

[24] Wittgenstein, *Philosophical Investigations*, §§29–31; cp. *Philosophical Grammar*, section 8, entitled 'Meaning, the position of the word in grammatical space'. This is not to say that words that belong to a given category have exactly the same grammar. The lights may flash red, green, white but not black; one can divide the playground into four or three or two parts, but not into one part. Nevertheless, the category (number, colour) gives one the location of a word in the web of words.

applied on grounds, that have *criteria* for their application and that are conceptually bound up with the manner in which the correctness of their application is *verified*. The word 'pain' does not *mean* pain-behaviour. We can typically recognize people to be in pain without making any *inference* from evidence – we can see the pain on their face. Nevertheless, someone who has *not* grasped that such-and-such behaviour is a justifying criterion for ascribing pain to another person has not grasped the concept of pain, and does not know how to use it. Someone who has no idea how to measure with a ruler cannot know what the words '1 inch' and '1 foot' mean, even if he knows that one foot is twelve inches. Someone who has not grasped that the *ability to perform some act* is verified by the subject's doing it or doing it recurrently in appropriate circumstances, does not understand what the word 'ability' means. And so on. The manner in which the application of a word is verified is *sometimes* partly constitutive of its meaning. So too are the constitutive grounds (criteria) for its application.

Concept and meaning Of course, we speak not only of the *meaning* of a word in a given language, but also of the *concept* expressed by a word. What is the relationship between them? And why do we need to have both notions? Our need for the idea of *having a concept* arises primarily in order to be able to speak of speakers' *linguistic* powers independently of alluding to any particular language in which those powers are exhibited. They may be common to speakers of different languages. Our need for the idea of *a concept* arises primarily in order for us to be able to speak of the *logical* powers of expressions. The notion of a concept is bound up with that of the inferential powers associated with more or less synonymous expressions in sentences in the same or in different languages. 'Square' means the same as 'equilateral rectangle', and expresses the same concept. 'Red' means the same as 'rot', 'rouge', and 'rosso'. These are different words in different languages. They all have the same meaning, and express the same concept. But the meaning of the word 'red' is not the concept of redness (or the concept of being red). *Words have a meaning,* and *express concepts.* Objects *fall under* concepts, but not under meanings. What a word 'W' in a given language means is by definition a language-relative enquiry. But the concept of W is what is common to expressions that are more or less synonymous with 'W'. To possess a concept is to be master of the technique of using of some word or phrase expressing that concept (but one does not *possess* the meanings of words – one knows them). To possess the concept of red, for example, is not the same as knowing the meaning of 'red' in English, since knowing the meaning of 'rosso' in Italian, or the meaning of 'rot' in German, are also sufficient for possessing the concept of red. Concept-possession inherits the normativity associated with linguistic meaning. There can be abuses and misuses of concepts, as there can be of words. However, it is cut free from dependence upon a *particular* language – as long as the concept possessed by a person is one that is expressed by some expression or combination of expressions in a language he has mastered.

Recognitional ability is insufficient for concept-possession

To possess a concept is to possess a linguistic ability. Possession of a mere recognitional ability is *never* sufficient for ascribing mastery of a concept to a being. That a bird can be trained to peck at red buttons (or red things in general) and not at things that are not red does not show that it has the concept of redness. What is required is a grasp of the conceptual links embedded in the grammar (the rules for the use) of the relevant concept-word or phrase. Furthermore, possession of a recognitional ability is commonly not even necessary for possession of a concept. Mastery of colour concepts does indeed require recognitional abilities, but to possess the concept of being old it is not necessary that one be able to recognize a rock from the pre-Cambrian era or an Old Master painting (as opposed to a new reproduction), any more than grasp of the concept of a fake requires one to be able to recognize fake paintings.

Concepts are not linguistic abilities

Nevertheless, concepts are not linguistic abilities. Unlike abilities, concepts are applied to items that fall under them, have an extension, are instantiated by objects they subsume, are introduced by definition or explanation of word-meaning. One might say that to know the meaning of a word 'W' is akin to knowing the powers of a chess-piece with a certain shape and colour. To possess the concept of a W is then akin to knowing the powers of a given chess-piece, irrespective of its shape or colour. The meaning of a word is its use in the language to which it belongs. To know what a word means in one's own language is to have mastered its use. To possess the concept expressed by a word is to have mastered *the technique of use* that is common to all expressions, in the same or different languages, that have the same meaning – that have the relevantly equivalent use.

The point and purpose of a word

Words are not only meaningful, have a meaning and express concepts, they also have a point. It always *makes sense* to ask of a given word (and so too of the concept it expresses) what its point is, what purpose it fulfils in our talk and thought. For philosophical clarification, this question is often important. Its answer makes clear what needs called forth the concept thus expressed. So it makes clear crucial features of the role of the problematic expression in the lives of members of the linguistic community in question. For our concepts lay down paths for our thought, determine transitions of thought and mould our behaviour. If we are puzzled, as we are, by the concept of knowledge, it is helpful – as we shall see in chapter 4 – to ask what the point of the concept of knowledge is, why we have an expression in our language which has these very peculiar features, what needs it meets. If we labour under the illusion that arithmetic is the science of numbers – a description of timeless truths about a domain of abstract objects, it is helpful to reflect on the point of number-words and concepts of number, and of their role in a numerate culture.

The context principle   We have focused thus far on the notion of word-meaning, while conceding that words fulfil their role (primarily) in sentences, since the sentence (including the one-word sentence) is, for the most part, the minimal unit for the performance of acts of speech. It has been customary, over the last decades, to aver that words have a meaning only in the context of a sentence,[25] that the meaning of a sentence is given by specification of its truth-conditions, and hence that the meaning of a word is its contribution to the determination of the truth-conditions of any sentence in which it occurs. This is not the place to confront truth-conditional semantics. All I wish to do is to suggest qualms, and point out that there is no *need*, for someone who is puzzled about one aspect or another of word-, sentence-, and utterance-meaning, to go down this route.

Falsity of the context-principle   *It is not true that words have a meaning only in the context of a sentence.* They do not lose their meaning when they occur in lists (e.g. of words beginning with Z, of synonyms, of antonyms, of shopping, of animal names), in crossword puzzles, in word games (Scrabble), on labels (on bottles,

---

[25] For an examination of the history of this polysemic Fregean dictum and an investigation into the various ways in which it has been understood, see Baker and Hacker, 'Contextual dicta and contextual principles', in *Wittgenstein: Understanding and Meaning*, part 1: *Essays*, pp. 159–88. See also H.-J. Glock, 'All Kinds of Nonsense', in E. Ammereller and E. Fischer (eds), *Wittgenstein at Work* (Routledge, London 2004), pp. 221–45.

clothes, tools, wine decanters) or on notices (on houses, shops, pubs, street signs).

The sentence is not   It is not true that only by the use of a sentence
the minimum unit   (including one-word sentences) can one perform an
for a speech-act   act of speech. Exceptions are expletives, many greetings and various forms of exclamation.[26]

5 reasons why the   It is not true that the meaning of a sentence is given
meaning of a   by specifying its truth-conditions. The concept of
sentence is not given   the meaning of an empirical, assertoric, utterance
by truth-conditions   is indeed bound up with the concept of truth. For
      to understand what was said by the use of such a sentence is to know what is the case if what was said is true and what is the case if it is false. But the concept of truth does not give one any purchase on the concepts of word-, sentence-, and utterance-meaning.

(i) Sentences have a meaning, but they are not bearers of truth-values. So they cannot be said to have truth-conditions. It is what is said by the use of appropriate declarative sentences, the statement made or proposition expressed, that can be true or false.

(ii) The interrogative and imperative discourse forms are defeasible markers of questioning and ordering (requesting, etc.). What is expressed by their use (questions and orders) bears no truth-values. Nor does any proper part of them. But the words that occur in them have exactly the same meaning as they do in declarative sentences being used to assert something to be the case.[27]

(iii) Explicit performative sentences such as 'I promise to go to the lawyer with you' are not used to make a true or false assertion at all (in this case, it is used to make a promise, and a promise is neither

---

[26] For an amusing example, see Leo Rosten's description, in *The Joys of Yiddish* (Penguin, Harmondsworth, 1968), of the manifold speech-acts that can be performed by the utterance of 'Oy', 'Oy yoi' and 'Oy yoi yoi' in Yiddish.

[27] Of course, with ingenuity things can be gerrymandered. Sentence-questions (*but not Wh-questions*) can be represented in the form 'Is it the case // that *p*?', imperatives can be recast in the form 'Make it the case // that *p*!', just as declarative sentences can be rephrased in the form 'It is the case // that *p*'. This is alleged to show that every sentence, no matter whether declarative, interrogative or imperative, has, on analysis (in its depth-grammar) a truth-value bearing element, 'that *p*'. So the words that occur in sentence-questions and imperative sentences do after all have a meaning that consists in their contribution to the truth-conditions of the sentences in which they occur. The possibility of such general paraphrase can, but need not, be contested. What is questionable is whether this mapping of one form of representation onto

true nor false). But the words in an explicit performative use of a sentence have the same meaning as they do in the corresponding third-person or past-tense declarative sentence used assertorically.

(iv) The very concept of a *truth-condition* is problematic. If the truth-condition of a conjunction 'p & q' is that both conjuncts be true, then a truth-condition is *a condition that the complex (molecular) sentence must satisfy* in order to be true.[28] It is a condition *on* the sentence.[29] And, of course, it presupposes that the meanings of the constituent conjuncts is given (otherwise *they* could not be said to be true or false). But the modern post-Tarskian idea of a truth-condition is held to apply to elementary sentences too, in the form of a so-called T-sentence: 'p' is true if and only if p'. But this is no longer a condition *on the sentence*, for its being the case that p is not a condition that the sentence can intelligibly be said to satisfy. (One cannot say that the condition which *the sentence* 'Snow is white' must satisfy in order for it to be true is that snow be white.) It is a circumstance in the domain of what is represented ('the world'). Hence the alleged truth-condition of an elementary proposition is *unlike* that of molecular propositions such as 'p & q', '$p \supset q$', 'p v q', where the truth-conditions are conditions the constituent elementary propositions have to satisfy. So advocates of truth-conditional accounts of meaning must decide which claim they are advancing – that the meaning of a sentence is given by specifying the condition that *the sentence must satisfy* to be true, or that the meaning of a sentence is given by specifying how things must be in reality for the sentence to be true. In the former case, one might say that the meaning of the molecular sentence is indeed explained, *on the assumption that the*

----

another shows what it is meant to show. After all, by parity of reasoning, every declarative sentence contains a question (Wittgenstein: *Philosophical Investigations*, §22), since it can be represented as a question plus an affirmation: 'It is raining' = 'Is it raining? Yes.' But that is no reason for claiming that declarative sentences are, on analysis (in their depth-grammar), really questions. For detailed discussion of the sense/force distinction required for truth-conditional semantics, see G. P. Baker and P. M. S. Hacker, *Language, Sense and Nonsense* (Blackwell, Oxford, 1984), chs 2–3.

[28] For ease of exposition, I disregard point (i) above. But one could just as well say that it is a condition on the proposition expressed by the sentence on an occasion of its use.

[29] This is patent in Frege's *Basic Laws of Arithmetic*, vol. 1, §§31–2, and in the *Tractatus*.

constituent sentences have a meaning and a truth-value. (In effect all that has been explained is the meaning, the use, of the truth-functional connective involved.) In the latter case, it is not at all clear that an explanation of the meaning of the sentence is being offered at all. For what is being given is an explanation of *what it is for the sentence* (or *proposition it expresses*) *to be true*, namely that things be as it describes them as being (i.e. 'It is true that *p* if and only if *p*'). But that presupposes, and does not explain, the meaning of the sentence.

(v) It seems patent that outside philosophy, we do not (and indeed could not) explain the meaning of sentences in terms of something called their truth-conditions. 'Species become differentiated by natural selection', 'The Second World War was caused by the Versailles Treaty', 'It is debatable whether Hamlet can be said to be suffering from an Oedipal complex' are sentences which one may well not understand. But one's understanding is not going to be furthered by specification of truth-conditions, but by quite different kinds of explanations of meaning.

The meaning of a word is not its contribution to the truth-conditions of a sentence

It is not true that the meaning of a word is given by specifying its contribution to the determination of the truth-conditions of any sentence in which it may occur. It is, of course, true that the meaning of a sentence (declarative, interrogative or imperative) *depends* upon what its constituent words mean. That does not mean that it is literally *a function* of the meanings of its constituent words and their mode of combination – that one can *calculate* the meaning of the sentence from the meanings of the words. What the constituent words in a sentence mean is given by contextual explanations of meaning, not by reference to truth-condition determination. Such explanations may take very varied forms (ostensive explanation, paraphrase, contrastive paraphrase, explanation by examples) tailored to the sentential context of the word and circumstantial context of the utterance, and to the misunderstanding or failure of understanding in question. Given the meaning of a word in an utterance, and if necessary, what is meant by its use in that utterance, *then* one can go on to specify what must be the case for the declarative sentence in which the word occurs to be used to say something true. But that is not an explanation of the *conditions* under which what is said is true, it is an explanation of *what it is* for it to be true. (Eating the right food and taking exercise are conditions one must fulfil in order to be healthy, but being in good health is not a condition for being healthy – it is what it is for a creature to be healthy.)

Sentence-meaning, utterance-meaning and what is meant It should be noted that what a sentence means, what the utterance of the sentence on an occasion means and what is meant by its use on a given occasion need not be the same. This is obvious in the case of type-sentences containing proper names and indexicals. 'Jack went from here to there' has, in one sense, a uniform meaning that is understood by any English speaker. It is equally obvious in the case of sentences that display syntactic ambiguity, such as 'They are flying planes'. To know what the utterance of a sentence means on a given occasion depends on disambiguating both lexical and syntactical ambiguities, and elucidating the references of indexicals and names.

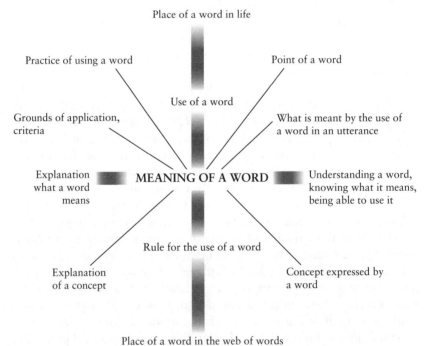

Figure 3.4 *Salient nodes in the web of the concept of word-meaning*

But it may still be unclear what the speaker was doing in uttering the sentence – and, in one perfectly decent sense of 'understanding what was said', one will not have fully understood what was said unless one grasps what was done by saying it. To bring sentence-meaning into connection with what the speaker meant, not only by *what* he said but also by *saying* what he said, one needs to grasp the contextual implications of his saying what he did.

Figure 3.4 sketches the major nodes in the network of concepts interwoven with the concept of the meaning of a word.

'Meaning' is not a refined technical term of a science A final point: the concept of meaning that we employ in talking about words, sentences and utterances is not a refined, precise, technical term of a science. It is a common or garden, unrefined and by no means precise, non-technical term of humdrum talk of words and utterances.

- The meaning of a word is its use in the language.
- The meaning of a word is given by an explanation of what it means.
- An explanation of meaning is a rule for the use of the word.
- The meaning of a word (or phrase) is what is known (or understood) when one knows (or understands) what the word (or phrase) means.
- The meaning of a word is its place in the web of words.
- Knowing what a word means is being able to use it in accordance with accepted explanations of what it means, i.e. in accordance with rules for its use.

List 3.1 *Strands in the conceptual network of word-meaning*

What belongs to meaning and what does not is not always clear or determined (is it part of the meaning of the word 'cat' that cats don't grow on trees?). What counts as the same meaning and what as a difference in meaning is often indeterminate, calling for a decision rather than an investigation (does 'however' mean the same as 'but'?). Although it is illuminating to be reminded of the nexus of meaning and use, it is obvious that not *every* difference in use is a difference in meaning. The difference has to be a significant one, and what counts as significant is both indeterminate and context-relative.

List 3.1 shows the primary conceptual links that we have surveyed.

Description of conceptual links is not a theory
These are not axioms or principles of a theory. They are conceptual truisms that Wittgenstein brought into view to contribute to the logical geography of the concept of word-meaning. They serve to dispel illusions and confusions, for example, that meanings are kinds of things; that words are attached to meanings; that meanings can combine together to form thoughts or propositions; that propositions consist of word-meanings (that thoughts consist of senses, and judgements of concepts); that the meaning of a word is its contribution to the truth-conditions of any sentence in which it occurs; that meanings of words can be stored in neural modules in the brain and associated with words (also stored in the brain in a separate module) to form a mental lexicon (Treisman, Levelt, Coltheart); and so on.

7. The dialectic of understanding: the 'mystery' of understanding new sentences

The alleged master-problem of linguistic theory
Our overview of the conceptual field of *meaning* will help us to find our way through one of the great confusions at the heart of philosophy of language and linguistic theory. Since the 1960s, philosophers and linguists have taken the fact that we can understand sentences we have never heard before to be the master-problem of linguistic studies.[30] It was conceived to have deep implications about the nature of the mind, the brain and even the human genome. 'Empirical linguistics', it was said, 'takes the most general problem of the study of language to be that of accounting for the fluent speaker's ability to produce freely and understand readily all the utterances of his language, including wholly novel ones'.[31] The question of how 'finite

---

[30] The point was first made in print by Wittgenstein in 1921 in the *Tractatus* 4.02–4.03 (derived from his 'Notes on Logic' of 1913), followed by Frege's discussion of 'thought-building blocks' in his 1923 article 'Compound Thoughts' (*Collected Papers* (Blackwell, Oxford, 1984), p. 390; it appears in Frege's *Nachlass* in his 1914 'Logic in Mathematics', *Posthumous Writings* (Blackwell, Oxford, 1979), p. 225, after lengthy conversations with the young Wittgenstein in December 1913). It was given prominence by Chomsky in the 1950s and later, and by Dummett and Davidson in the 1960s and 1970s. It is not a coincidence that the idea does not even surface in Wittgenstein's later writings.

[31] J. Fodor and J. J. Katz, 'What's Wrong with the Philosophy of Language?', in C. Lyas (ed.), *Philosophy and Linguistics* (Macmillan, London, 1971), p. 281.

minds' can grasp an 'infinity of sentences' became the drive shaft of theoretical linguistics.

The received   It was widely held that the only way in which
explanation of the   the ability to understand new sentences could be
ability to understand explained was by reference to speakers' *cognizing*
new sentences   the depth-grammar for the language and *calculating* the meanings of sentences from the meanings of their constituents and their depth-grammatical mode of combination.[32] Philosophers of language took much the same route.

> The fact that anyone who has a mastery of any given language is able to understand an infinity of sentences of that language, an infinity which is, of course, principally composed of sentences which he has never heard before . . . can hardly be explained otherwise than by supposing that each speaker has an implicit grasp of a number of general principles governing the use in sentences of the words of the language . . . [A]n explicit statement of those principles an implicit grasp of which constitutes the mastery of a language would be, precisely, a complete theory of meaning for the language.[33]

Such a theory of meaning was conceived to be a deductive theory that contains for each sentence of an object-language a theorem that states its meaning. Each such theorem is derived by canonical procedures from axioms characterizing the elementary constituents of which the sentences of the object-language are composed. A speaker was assumed to have *tacit knowledge* of such a compositional theory, and was held to 'derive his understanding of a sentence from the meanings of the component words' and to 'assign interpretations to sentences on the basis of his knowledge of the meanings of their parts' (ibid.).

It is common in philosophy for the deepest mistakes to be made before the answer has even been broached. For the root of the trouble often lies in the presuppositions of the question. So it is here. This

---

[32] To cognize, Chomsky explained (*Rules and Representations*, pp. 70, 72, 82f.), is just the same as *to know*, except that one need not be able to say what one cognizes, that one cannot recollect what one cognizes and cannot forget it either, and that one would not be able to understand what one cognizes if one were told. This leaves the notion of cognizing wholly indeterminate.

[33] M. A. E. Dummett, 'Can Analytic Philosophy be Systematic and Ought It to Be?', in *Truth and Other Enigmas* (Duckworth, London, 1978), p. 451.

question, which has mesmerized two generations of theoretical linguists and philosophers of language, is misleading. It requires no answer, just dismantling.

Presuppositions of the question

The question 'How is it possible for finite minds to understand a potential infinity of sentences of a language, the vast majority of which are novel?' presupposes:

(1)   That a natural language consists of an infinity of sentences.
(2)   That our minds are finite (infinite minds, it was implied, would have no problem).
(3)   That if we understood only sentences we *had* heard before, the puzzlement about the possibility of understanding would not arise.
(4)   That knowing what a sentence means or understanding an utterance-sentence is a distinct piece of propositional knowledge that has to be separately acquired for each sentence or utterance.
(5)   That understanding (or coming to understand) an utterance is something that hearers *do* – that understanding (or coming to understand) is an act, process or performance of some kind.

The answers to the question, both those given by linguists and those advanced by philosophers, hold:

(6)   That in order for speakers to be able to perform these acts of understanding, they must have *tacit knowledge* of a theory of meaning for their language, or *cognize* universal grammar and the depth-grammar of their language, as well as having a lexicon of their language in the mind/brain.
(7)   That the rules of depth-grammar guide speakers and hearers in their speech and understanding, and determine the meaning of their utterances.
(8)   That understanding the speech of others consists in or results from *computing*, *calculating* or *deriving* (unconsciously, and as quick as a flash) the meanings of their utterances from the meanings of the constituent words and their mode of combination.

These presuppositions and principles need challenging.

A language is not a set of sentences

(1) Is a language *a set of sentences*? English is no more a set of sentences than chess is a set of chess moves or tennis a set of strokes. Chess may allow

for indefinitely many possible sequences of moves, but it is not itself any such sequence. No more so is a human language. If a language is an anything, it is a practice embedded in a culture.

It makes even less sense to suppose that a language consists of an *infinity* of sentences.[34] No doubt indefinitely many English sentences can be formulated – but there is no need to drag infinity in, since a language is not a set of sentences anyway. 'Infinite sentences' is a red herring.

Do we have finite minds? (2) So too is 'finite minds'. Is the suggestion that to understand how an infinite mind could understand an infinity of sentences is dead easy? Does the problem arise only because our minds are finite? What exactly *is* an infinite mind? Since to have a mind is to have an intellect and will, perhaps an infinite mind is a mind that has the intellectual ability to do an infinite number of things. But if so, then we *do* have infinite minds! For since we have learnt to multiply, we have the ability to do $\aleph_0$ multiplications! Surely this too is a red herring. It makes little sense to speak of the finitude or infinity of a mind, and to do so engenders unnecessary confusion. No doubt, we can understand an *indefinite* number of sentences. That suffices for the problem. And it also suffices for the dissolution of the problem.

Novelty of a sentence is a red herring (3) The problem concerning understanding *new* sentences arose largely as a response to behaviourist linguistic theory. For it was alleged by critics of behaviourism (such as Chomsky) that behaviourism could not explain the possibility of understanding sentences one has never heard before. The assumption was that behaviourist linguistic theory *could* explain the possibility of understanding sentences one *has* heard before. But that is wrong. Stimulus–response theories are just as defective with regard to the understanding of familiar sentences as they are with respect to novel ones. In fact, the criteria of understanding an utterance are the same *irrespective of the novelty or familiarity of the sentence uttered*. The criteria encompass three kinds of grounds: using the sentence cogently in an appropriate context, explaining what an utterance of it on some occasion means, and acting intelligently in response to what was said by its use. Such behaviour does not lend itself to stimulus–response analysis. The correct use of a

---

[34] Except in the trivial sense in which one can insert *any* numeral or number-word into an appropriately formed sentence. But that is obviously not what theorists have in mind.

sentence must be relatively stimulus-free to count as a criterion of understanding at all – otherwise it would be parrot-like repetition indicative of incomprehension. Correct explanations of the meaning of an utterance, even if it is of a familiar sentence, may vary from occasion to occasion. How one explains the meaning of a word that is a sentence constituent ('maroon' for example) may depend on the range of optional samples in view: a maroon rose, a maroon dress, a maroon book cover. It also depends upon what the questioner already knows or understands. Similarly, what counts as an intelligent response to a familiar utterance depends upon the circumstances. One may show one's understanding of the utterance 'It's raining' by not going out, by going out with a raincoat, by taking an umbrella, by bringing in the washing from the line, by ringing up a friend to postpone a picnic and so on and so forth. If there is a problem about how it is possible to understand sentences, then it is as much a problem for familiar sentences as it is for novel ones. In this sense, novelty is a red herring.

Knowing a language is not reducible to propositional knowledge

(4) It is a consequence of misunderstanding what knowing a language consists in that theorists of meaning presuppose that knowing what a sentence of a language means is always a distinct item of propositional knowledge. They hold that such knowledge is *represented* by means of a Tarskian T-sentence. But this is mistaken. To know what a sentence means is to be able to use it cogently, to be able to respond to its use intelligently and to be able to explain what it means in a manner tailored to someone's incomprehension in a given context. *These* abilities are not given a 'theoretical representation' by T-sentences. So the very idea that 'a language-machine', that is, a generative compositional theory of meaning for a natural language, is a theoretical representation of a practical ability is wholly misconceived.[35]

Why the question 'How can one understand new sentences?' is misleading

(5) The very question 'How can one understand sentences one has never heard before?' or 'How is it possible for one to understand sentences one has never heard before?' is misleading. For it is modelled on the form of questions that enquire *how something is done* – like 'How can one open a locked door

---

[35] For helpful discussion, see E. Fischer, 'Bogus Mystery about Linguistic Competence', *Synthese*, 135 (2003), pp. 49–75.

without a key?' or 'How is it possible to crack a code?' So the question misleadingly suggests that understanding an utterance is something one does or the upshot of something one does. And it enquires after a means or method of doing it. Unsurprisingly, the answer is shaped to the form of the question. For the answer is: by calculating – as quick as a flash – the meaning of the utterance from its depth-grammatical form, the meanings of the words, and the context of utterance, by means of the theory of meaning for the language. But, as we have seen, *understanding an utterance* is to be able to do something, not something one does. *It is not an act or activity one performs,* nor is it a mental or neural *state* that is the upshot of such an act or activity. There are ways and means of explaining what an utterance means, ways and means of helping someone to come to understand what someone said or wrote, but no ways and means of *doing abilities* or of *doing being able to do something*.

The confusions of 'cognizing' and 'tacit knowledge'   (6) The suggestion that speakers of a language have *tacit knowledge* of, or *cognize*, a theory of meaning for their language is misconceived. Chomsky's notion of *cognizing* is unintelligible. There is such a thing as tacit knowledge, but the various forms it may take do not include *any* form such that someone who has tacit knowledge of something would be unable to recognize or even understand an explicit statement of what he is alleged to know tacitly. Furthermore, there must be some criteria for tacitly knowing a theory of meaning other than correct speech and comprehension. Otherwise explaining correct speech and understanding by reference to such tacit knowledge would be akin to explaining the effect of opium by reference to its dormitive powers.

Why there is no such thing as being guided by unknown rules   (7) There is no such thing as being guided by rules with which one is totally unfamiliar. A rule is a standard for correct behaviour. It is both a measure against which behaviour can be judged to be correct or incorrect, and a guide to action. But there is no such thing as *being guided* by unknown rules, or as judging conduct to be *correct or incorrect* by reference to rules one has never heard of. There is no such thing as being guided by rules buried deep in the mind/brain beyond the reach of consciousness, not only because there is no such thing as a mind/brain and no such thing as rules being buried in the brain or in the mind, but also because unknown rules *cannot be used.* Just as something is a ruler only if it is used as a ruler, so too something that cannot be (and so is not) used as a rule cannot be a rule.

Behaviour counts as acting in accordance with a rule only to the extent that there is a practice of following the rule and using it as a standard of correctness. For the internal relation between a rule and what counts as accord with it is forged by the practice of its employment. But there can be no practice of following hidden rules of language.

Coming to understand an utterance is not a computational process   (8) Coming to understand is not a process of derivation, calculation or computation the upshot of which is a state of understanding. We do not *calculate* the truth-value of an empirical proposition from our knowledge of a concept (a function from an object to a truth-value) and its argument. Nor do we *calculate a proposition* from our knowledge of a propositional function and an argument. Once the conceptual link between the meaning of a word and its use was grasped, it should have been obvious that it makes no sense to speak of the meaning of a sentence as being *composed* of the meanings, that is uses, of its constituent words. Of course, the meaning of a sentence or utterance obviously *depends* upon what its constituent words and phrases mean – but that does not even suggest that it can be *calculated* from the meanings or uses of its constituent words (as the value of a function for a given object as argument can be calculated).

The incoherence of explaining understanding new sentences by reference to a theory of meaning that we cannot understand   The putative explanation of how it is possible for us to understand novel sentences involves our tacitly knowing the theory of meaning for our language and computing the meanings of new sentences (or their utterance) from their syntactical form and the meanings of their constituent words with the aid of this theory. Explicit fragments of such a theory which philosophers have come up with (e.g. Davidson's analysis of the logical form of action-sentences, or belief-sentences) are not likely to be intelligible to normal speakers of a language. So the putative explanation of understanding presupposes that ordinary speakers of a language can compute sentence-meanings from a theory of meaning the explicit statement of which they are incapable of understanding. But that is not intelligible.

Of course, no speaker is aware of computing sentence-meanings. The language theorist (e.g. Chomsky) suggests that this is because the calculation is virtually instantaneous and non-conscious. This is supposed to be an empirical claim. But we have been given no *empirical* reason why understanding sentences of a language involves calculating in the first place. The claim that understanding utterances is a high-speed, unconscious computational process should be treated with the gravest suspicion.

Why we do not A deeper criticism lies in a misconceived presupposi-
have to calculate tion, namely that it makes sense to suppose that
the meanings of normal speakers of a language in normal circum-
sentences stances confronted with standard kinds of sentences
may know what the constituent words of an utterance mean and grasp the syntactical form of the sentence uttered, but still have to *calculate* the meaning of the utterance. But this supposition is questionable. For to know what a word means *is* to know the combinatorial possibilities that its literal use allows. To know what the word 'red' means is to know that red is a colour, that if any object is red it is extended, that red is darker than pink, that nothing can simultaneously be red all over and green all over, that red is seen and not heard, and so forth. For these are in effect rules for the use of the word 'red' that determine its meaning. No extra step, in particular no calculation, *could* be needed, even though semi-productive formations (e.g. 'white coffee', 'white Christmas', 'white rhinoceros') have to be learnt one by one. So too, to know what '2' and '+' mean is *already* to know what '2 + 2' means.[36] For if someone knows what '2' means and what '+' means, then he knows (can explain) what '2 + 2' means (can use the expression, etc.).

Compositionalism is The compositional conception of sentence-meaning
rooted in a mistaken is bewitched by a mistaken analogy, namely, be-
analogy tween knowing the meaning of a sentence such as
'Emeralds are green' and knowing the *answer* to a calculation such as '25 × 24'. But if there is any comparison to be made here, it is between knowing the meaning of 'Emeralds are green' and knowing the meaning of '25 × 24'. If one knows what the constituent words and phrases of an ordinary sentence mean, and has mastered the ordinary grammar of the language, then one *ipso facto* knows what the sentence means and what is meant by its utterance. For if one knows what the words and phrases mean, is familiar with the grammatical form of the sentence and grasps the context of speech, then one is able to respond sensibly to the utterance, to explain what was meant and to use it oneself. One does not have to *calculate* anything, but only to be *able* to do various other things.

---

[36] For elaboration, see E. Fischer, ' "Dissolving" the "Problem of Linguistic Creativity" ', *Philosophical Investigations*, 20 (1997), 290–314.

The novelty of sentences is a red herring   It is an illusion that there is anything extraordinary or surprising about understanding *novel* sentences. 'Thomas's green teddy bear is in the fridge' is immediately understood. The only thing surprising about it is that Thomas should have a green teddy, which is unusual, and that someone should have put it in the fridge, which is odd. What *would be* surprising is if someone were able to explain what the constituent words and phrases in an ordinary sentence mean, were familiar with the grammatical form of their combination, and yet *not know* what the sentence means. We would not know what to say in such a case. For his not knowing would, other things being equal, be a criterion for his *not* knowing what one or other of the constituent words or phrases means or of *not* grasping the syntax of the sentence.

There is no more of a problem about utterances of others than about one's own   Scepticism about this pivotal question and incredulity about its answers are increased when it is noted that the whole focus of debate over the last decades has been on understanding the utterances of others. All understanding has been held to be interpretation, and interpretation has been construed as computation. But the question of how it is possible for a speaker to understand what *he says*, to know what *he* means by the sentences he utters, has by and large been bypassed. Had it been squarely confronted it should have given theorists of language pause. *For there is no deep problem, and no deep conceptual puzzle, about how we can understand what we ourselves say.*[37] And if that is no problem, then there is no problem about how we can understand what others say. The only question is what led so many people to think that there is a problem and that it is the deepest problem in philosophy of language and theoretical linguistics.

---

[37] Chomsky holds that this is in fact the deepest problem of all, and declares it to be a mystery beyond the reach of human intelligence. But it is only a mystery given the truth of his theories, and there is no reason whatsoever for taking his theories to be true.

PART I

The Cognitive and Doxastic Powers

4

Knowledge

1. The value of knowledge

We exercise our intellectual powers in judging things to be so or not to be so. The use of the power of judgement, Aristotle observed, is a characteristic activity of man.[1] It is an aspect of our rational nature. In judgement we aim at how things are. If things are as we judge them to be, then we judge truly. If we judge falsely, we miss our aim. True judgements may be expressions of opinion or belief, guesses or hunches, hypotheses or suppositions – or they may be manifestations of knowledge.

All higher forms of animal life can know things — All higher animals achieve various forms and degrees of knowledge. Non-human animals learn to recognize things and clues of things, learn where to find food or prey, learn to distinguish things of a kind and to discriminate between things of different kinds. They come to know what foods to eat and what to shun. They know their way to waterholes, and the way back to their lair or burrow. Generally, they know what to fear, when to freeze and where to hide. Their behaviour patterns are plastic, and sensitive to their knowledge of their environment. They learn and come to know how to do a variety of things – how to hunt and kill, to dig for roots, to crack shells and, in the case of some kinds of apes and Corvidae, how to make and

---

[1] Aristotle, *Nicomachean Ethics*, 1139ª29.

The Intellectual Powers: A Study of Human Nature, First Edition. P. M. S. Hacker.
© 2013 John Wiley & Sons, Ltd. Published 2013 by John Wiley & Sons, Ltd.

use rudimentary tools. They also know to do various things, such as to take cover or to flee when apt. But the limits of animal knowledge are incomparably narrower than the broad horizon of human knowledge.

The limitations of non-human animal knowledge   Non-human animals can know things to be so, but cannot know things to be true. For it is sayables, such as propositions, statements, declarations, stories and rumours, that may be true. Such bearers of truth and falsehood can be understood only by language-users, and only language-users can know whether they are true or false. Both my dog and I may know that the cat it was chasing is in the tree, but only I can know that the proposition that the cat is in the tree is true. Animal knowledge goes but little beyond acquired cognitive skills, recognitional capacities and limited forms of knowing *that, where, what, when, which* and *to* that can be exhibited in non-linguistic behaviour. It makes no sense to ascribe to a non-language-user knowledge of generalities, temporalities or apriorities.

The value of knowledge   Being sons of Adam and daughters of Eve, we value knowledge. We compare knowledge with light and ignorance with darkness. Those who act in ignorance are benighted – and know not what they do. According to the book of Genesis, knowledge of good and evil (and what more important knowledge could there be?) was bought at a high price and against the will of God.[2] It is not absurd to cry:

> Give me the storm and tempest of Thought and Action, rather than the dead calm of Ignorance and Faith. Banish me from Eden when you will, but first let me eat of the fruit of the tree of knowledge.[3]

Of course, this does not mean that *every* item of knowledge is valuable. Nor does it mean that there may not be some things better left unknown. It does not mean that knowledge may not have fell consequences. Nor, alas, does it mean that we do not sometimes cleave

---

[2] For an insightful interpretation of the creation myth of Genesis, see David Daube, 'Prophets and Philosophers', in his *Civil Disobedience in Antiquity* (Edinburgh University Press, Edinburgh, 1972), pp. 60f. Stripped of later Jewish and Christian interpretation, it is, like the Greek Prometheus myth, the tale of the Rise of man, not of the Fall.

[3] Robert E. Ingersoll, epigram to *The Gods and Other Lectures* (D. M. Bennett, New York, 1876).

to our prejudices and reject what is known. Nevertheless, we do in general value knowledge, and not merely because knowledge is power. We value it because we value truth and understanding. When we are ignorant of some matter of moment, we often seek information – not mere belief or opinion – from others. Does it not suffice that they have *true* belief? Only if we *know* that their belief is true – but if we know *that*, we know what is the case. If we possess knowledge, we can conform our lives, our thoughts, our passions and purposes to how things are, and not merely to how they seem to be. Some human beings crave to understand why things are as they are – to make sense of the world we live in and of our place within it. To achieve such understanding, one rests on what one knows (or thinks one knows) of how things are, and tries to advance to explanations of why things are so. Some human beings, sometimes, crave to understand both themselves and others. Knowledge of our fellow human beings is a prerequisite for mutual understanding. Self-knowledge is a prerequisite for self-understanding.

2. The grammatical groundwork

Philosophical problems about knowledge

Many problems and unclarities surround the concept of knowledge. Some are categorial: is knowing something to be so a mental act or activity, a disposition, a mental state or a rational ability? Is knowing that something is so a propositional attitude, as Russell supposed? Other problems concern the analysis of knowledge. Is knowing something to be so analysable? Does it amount to belief that is both true and certain? Or to belief that is both true and justified? Or to some other conjunction of conditions? Other problems cluster around the relationship between knowing something to be so, knowing someone or something by acquaintance and from experience, knowing how to do something and knowing to do something. We distinguish between empirical knowledge of many logically different kinds (observational, psychological, scientific-theoretic, historical, etc.), mathematical knowledge, moral and aesthetic knowledge. Are these simply knowledge of different things, or are they different kinds of knowledge? These latter questions will be deferred for discussion in *The Moral Powers: a Study of Human Nature*. Finally, there are numerous questions concerning the relation of knowledge to adjacent concepts, such as belief, understanding, certainty, indubitability, justification, memory, sources of knowledge, modes of knowledge acquisition. Is knowing something to be so compatible with doubting whether it is so? If one knows whether things are so, does one also opine that they are, think that they are or believe that they are? These are philosophical questions we shall be occupied with in this chapter and the next two.

Objects of knowledge   Philosophical concern with knowledge aims to achieve an overview of its nature. To do this, we must clarify the concept of knowledge. The only way to do so is to examine the uses of the verb 'to know' and its cognates (or equivalents in other languages). We shall start by looking at some straightforward grammatical and syntactical features, which will be useful in the subsequent connective analysis.[4] 'A knows . . .' is a sentence-forming operator on a variety of linguistic forms. Examining them will shed light upon the objects of knowledge (see table 4.1).

It is important not to confuse the fact that what is known, when it is known that things are so, is *expressed* by a proposition, with the non-fact that what is known when it is known that things are so *is* a proposition. Whereas to believe the proposition that so-and-so advanced is to believe that what he said is true, to know the proposition that he advanced is not to know that it is true – but rather, to be familiar with it, to have heard it before. One may know many propositions without knowing whether they are true or false, and one may know many propositions that are false (schoolteachers often collect the plums from their pupils' essays).[5]

Wh-nominalizations   Wh-nominalizations (knowing where, who, when, etc.) and hence too noun-phrases that are variants on an interrogative ('knowing the colour, length, weight of') are systematically related to *knowing-that*. Roughly speaking, the Wh-nominalization states what it is to which one knows the answer, and the that-nominalization states the answer one knows.[6] To know who did such-and-such is to know that so-and-so did it; to know where he did it is to know that he did it there; to know where

---

[4] See A. R. White, *The Nature of Knowledge* (Rowman & Littlefield, Totowa, NJ, 1982), ch. 2. I am much indebted to this little-known but brilliant monograph.

[5] Similarly, to understand (gather) that p is not the same as to understand (comprehend, be able to explain) the proposition that p.

[6] 'Roughly speaking', because, among other things, this account must (and can) be modified to embrace non-language-using animals' knowing where, who, which and when.

Bases	Examples
Declarative sentences	'A knows Jack is in town'
That-nominalizations	'A knows that Jack is in town'
Wh-nominalizations involving a Wh-interrogative These may be followed either by: • a verb in the indicative	'A knows whether Jack is at home', 'A knows where Jill is and when Jack will be home', 'A knows who is in the room'
• a verb in the infinitive	'A knows whether to take the car', 'A knows when and where to plant the roses', 'A knows what to do', 'A knows which book to take', 'A knows whom to ask'
Wh-nominalizations involving a relative Wh-clause	'A already knew what you said'
How-nominalizations, followed by a verb in the infinitive	'A knows how to V'
Noun-phrases that are variants on an interrogative	'A knows the colour (weight, height) of . . .' (to know the colour and weight of the chair is to know what colour the chair is and what its weight is)
Nouns signifying something that has been learnt or learnt by heart, and can be used, spoken, recited or rehearsed	'A knows Latin (physics, the alphabet, 'Ozymandias')'
Verbs in the infinitive	'A knows to V', 'A knows better than to V'
Nouns indicating an object of acquaintance or experience	'Tom knows Jill', 'Dick knows Paris', 'Harry has known sorrow'

Table 4.1 *Bases for the sentence-forming operator 'A knows'*

to go is to know that one should go there; and so forth. To know the colour of the cloth is to know what colour the cloth is, that is, to know that it is such-and-such colour. To know the length of the carpet is to know how long the carpet is, that is, to know that it is *thus* long. That one knows is shown by what one says and does.

Is practical knowledge autonomous?
Whether *knowing how to do something* is reducible to *knowing-that* is disputed. Ryle argued that these are two different kinds of knowledge – that *knowing-how* is not reducible to *knowing-that*. White disagreed, holding that these are not two kinds of knowledge, but knowledge of two kinds of thing.[7] He claimed that to know how to V is, in the case of task-verbs (e.g. 'to look for', 'listen', 'investigate'), a matter of knowing *the manner* in which to V, that is, the way of carrying out the task, and in the case of achievement-verbs (e.g. 'to prove', 'solve', 'ascertain'), it is knowing the *means* by which to V, that is, the means to bring off the achievement. The question of the autonomy of practical knowledge will be examined below.

Acquaintance, familiarity and experience
We speak of knowing things, of being acquainted, for example, with Jack and Jill.[8] But to know a person well is more, often much more, than just being acquainted with them. *A fortiori* it is not merely knowing numerous truths about them. We also speak of knowing – being familiar with (knowing one's way around) places, such as London and Paris, as well as of knowing works of art, music and literature. Finally, we also talk of knowing – having experienced – joy and sorrow. Other European languages employ two different verbs here to do the service of the English 'to know': Latin has 'cognoscere' and 'scio', French 'connaître' and 'savoir', German 'kennen' and 'wissen'.

Etymological clues
How is one to find a conceptually illuminating order in this diversity? Etymology is suggestive. 'To know' is etymologically connected with the archaic 'to can' (Old English *cnáwan*) and 'to ken' (Old High German *knāen* and Middle High German *-kennen*) and is unrelated to *wit* and *wiss*. The former

---

[7] G. Ryle, 'Knowing How and Knowing That', *Proceedings of the Aristotelian Society*, 46 (1945), pp. 1–16, and *The Concept of Mind* (Hutchinson, London, 1949), ch. 2; White, *The Nature of Knowledge*, pp. 14–29.

[8] Note that *to be acquainted with*, in the ordinary sense of the phrase, is *not* what Russell meant by 'knowledge by acquaintance'. For scrutiny of the varieties of objectual knowledge, see T. Chappell, 'Varieties of Knowledge in Plato and Aristotle', *Topoi*, 31 (2012), pp. 175–90.

have the same Indo-European base as archaic Latin *gnō* (as in *gnōscere* – to know, and *gnōtus* – known), and ancient Greek γνω- (*gno-*) The Old English *gecnáwan* and Middle English *cnowe* overlapped semantically with 'to can', 'to ken' and 'to wit'. The verb 'to can' meant to know or be acquainted with a person, to know or to have learnt a thing, to have practical knowledge of a language or art ('to can by heart', 'to can one's good'). 'To can some (no small, good) skill of' meant to have skill in, to be skilled. In due course, it came to mean 'to have knowledge', 'to know of', 'to have learned how', 'to know how' and subsequently 'to be able to', until it finally cut its moorings and evolved into the current modal auxiliary verb 'can'. This gives us an important clue, namely to look for conceptual links between the family of cognitive verbs and the notion of being able to do something (see below, section 7).

Stative verbs and uses of verbs   'To know' is generally held by grammarians to be a 'stative' verb. Stative verbs, they commonly contend, signify states. Such verbs are characterized by lack of a continuous tense, absence of a Do pro-form, and absence of an imperative form. One cannot licitly say 'I am knowing' or 'While I was knowing . . .'. One cannot say 'What I did was to know that it was raining'. One cannot say 'Know that Caesar was murdered in 44 BC'. To this one may object: one can say 'Know this: there will be no excuses!', 'Know thyself!' or 'Know this poem by next week!'. One may respond that these imperatives are non-stative *uses* of the verb 'to know' that modulate its meaning – that they mean 'bear in mind', 'get to know' and 'make sure that you know'. That is correct. But that means that one and the same verb can have both stative *and* non-stative uses. This suggests that the distinction between states and other such general categories may be semantic rather than syntactic. Evidently we shall have to investigate the relationship between stative verbs and states, and between cognitive stative verbs and mental states. For we aim to resolve the question of whether knowing something to be so is a special kind of mental state.

Transitivity   One final grammatical point: 'to know' followed by a declarative sentence or a that-nominalization appears transitive, given the permissibility of transforming 'A knows that things are so' into 'That things are so is known by A' (e.g. 'That the euro is in danger of collapse is well known to the Cabinet'). It is noteworthy that when the 'that' is omitted, any appearance of transitivity vanishes (*'It is raining is known by A'). This is not surprising. Despite Frege's insistence that sentences are names of one or another of two objects, namely The True and The False, sentences are not names, and, contrary to what he held, the sentence-nominalization 'that things are thus-and-so' is not a name of the sense of a sentence. Lack of genuine transitivity is further shown by the parenthetical use of 'know', as in 'The struggle, Jack knew, had to continue', as well as by the legitimacy of moving the operator to the end of the sentence, as in 'The struggle had to continue, Jack knew'. This grammatical datum will be important when we consider whether knowing is a 'propositional attitude'.[9]

3. The semantic field

The concept of knowledge links the concepts of *information* and *skill*. The connection is via their nexus with 'have', 'can', 'is able to'. Knowledge, as Aristotle pointed out, is also linked to *understanding*, *insight* and *wisdom*.[10]

Possession is the representational form of knowledge

The general representational form of knowledge is *possession*. Knowledge is something sought, acquired, possessed, retained, kept to oneself, shared, given to others – that is how we present it. What is possessed in the case of our *knowing-that* is *information*. Such information may be before one's mind – as when one is conscious *that things are so*. It may be readily brought to mind – as when one is already aware *that things are so* and does not need to be told. Or it may have slipped out of mind, and one needs to call it to mind, or, in some cases, to be reminded *that things are so*. This is the picture we use. The general form of information is 'things are so' – the general propositional form. It is by means of propositions (sentences with a sense) that information is expressed and conveyed.[11]

[9] See B. Rundle, *Mind in Action* (Clarendon Press, Oxford, 1997), pp. 53f., for illumination on this.

[10] Aristotle, *Nichomachean Ethics*, 1139^b16–17. *Techne* (skill), *episteme* (science), *phronēsis* (wisdom), *sophia* (understanding) and *nous* (insight) are the five intellectual excellences the successful exercise of which produces true judgement.

[11] It is striking that although we rightly describe animals as knowing things to be so and as knowing how to do things, we baulk at saying that they have acquired, and are in possession of, information. This is paralleled by our willingness to say that an animal thinks things to be so, and our reluctance to say that it has the thought that things are so. This is no coincidence. Possession of information is restricted to those who can express it and transmit it, who can inform others and be informed by them – in short, to language-using beings.

Knowing that things are so; general expertise Unsurprisingly, we distinguish between possessing single items of information and general expertise in a given field of knowledge. We may be aware that something is so, be cognizant of, or apprised of something's being so. Here we can be said to know what we know *perfectly well* or *for certain* (but not 'perfectly', 'thoroughly', 'poorly' or 'in detail'). But we may be knowledgeable – conversant with some branch or other of study. Then we can be said to know what we know *thoroughly*, *in detail*, and to have *extensive* or *profound* knowledge. One may know a little or a lot of history and a great deal of physics. By contrast, in the case of knowing a language, one may know it *well* or *poorly*; one may know a little Greek but not a lot of Greek; one may have extensive, but not profound or detailed, knowledge of Greek. To know a language is to possess a multifaceted skill.

Possessing information If one possesses information, one can inform others, answer the question of whether things are so, act or respond to the information, make use of it in one's plans and projects, explain and come to understand phenomena by reference to what one knows to be so. To perceive things to be so is to acquire (come to possess) information at first hand. To be informed and to be kept well informed is to acquire information from others. If one is well informed, one can speak with authority on the subject and supply information to others. If one has mastered a subject, has professional competence, one is able to answer questions, explain phenomena and apply the knowledge in professional activities (of doctor, lawyer, economist). Here the application converges on mastery of an art.

Varieties of know-how What is possessed when one has achieved mastery of an art or craft is *practical knowledge* or *know-how*. We may distinguish, in Aristotelian spirit,[12] between the know-how of *making* (mastery of a craft) the successful exercise of which produces an artefact that is good of its kind, the know-how of *educating* (of cultivating analytic powers, teaching intellectual and practical skills, inculcating virtues), and the know-how of *doing* (e.g. mastery of the art of medicine, the arts of politics or of war, the performing arts). All involve acquisition of information and principles to a greater or lesser degree. But neither information nor maxims suffice for mastery of a craft or art. To know the mysteries of an art,

[12] Aristotle, *Nicomachean Ethics*, 1140^{a}1–24.

a craft, or of a profession is to have informed practical *skill* – resulting from learning, training and practice, good *judgement* – resulting from experience, and *flair* or *knack* – which are native.

Knowledge may also take the form of *recognitional ability* ('I'd know her voice anywhere', 'I know that gait – it's Jill!'). This may involve possession of factual knowledge, but is not reducible to it. For it involves the ability to identify the relevant object of knowledge on encountering it.

Our perceptual faculties are cognitive but also fallible

Our perceptual faculties are cognitive ones. It is by their use that we achieve or are given information about our immediate environment. They are fallible and sometimes dubitable. Nevertheless, the mere possibility of doubt and error does not exclude knowing. The senses are sources of knowledge, as is patent in the logical connections characteristic of perceptual verbs. Perceptual verbs operating on that-nominalizations are (save in intentional uses previously mentioned) cognitive verbs: to see that things are so is to know that they are, to hear that it is raining is to learn something about the weather, and to smell that the dinner is burning is to acquire information, and so to be able to inform others, about the dinner.

Knowledge and understanding

Knowledge is a fountainhead of understanding and hence linked to being both able to explain and to deal with phenomena. Nevertheless, knowledge (cognition) is not the same as understanding (comprehension), even though the two concepts make tangential contact with each other at various points. Like 'to know', 'to understand' takes names, sentences and that-nominalizations as grammatical objects. However, it is more restricted in the Wh-nominalizations it takes, namely 'what', 'why' and 'how', but not 'whether', 'when' or 'where'. Even where there is grammatical convergence, there are often striking semantic differences. To understand that things are so is *to have gathered*, to have learnt from others, that they are so; but, of course, one may know that things are so without having gathered it. One may know what someone said without understanding it, one may understand what he said without knowing whether it is true, and one may know that what he said is true even though one does not understand it. To understand how to do something is to have grasped the principles, maxims or rules guiding the action and so to be able to explain how to do it. But it is narrower in scope than knowing-how to do something, and more closely tied to knowing that a certain action is done in such-and-such a way (see section 8 below).

There are further differences, which do not pertain to Wh-formations. One may know something by heart, that is, be able to recite it, but that is not the same as understanding it. One may know one's way home, but there is no such thing as understanding one's way home. One may know (be acquainted with) a person without understanding him, and understand a person (e.g. Napoleon) without knowing him. One may understand a sentence or utterance of a sentence, that is, know what it means – which is not the same as knowing a sentence, let alone knowing whether what is said by its utterance is true.

Figure 4.1 schematically represents a part of the web of cognitive concepts.

Innateness   What is possessed, if not possessed by nature, must be acquired. We possess cognitive capacities (second-order abilities) by nature, for we are born with a variety of innate learning abilities. But we possess no innate knowledge, only innate pronenesses, tendencies and reactive propensities without which we would not be able to learn what we can learn.[13] Our actual knowledge is acquired.

Modes of knowledge acquisition   What is known is what it generally makes sense for someone to learn, be taught, find out for himself, discover or detect, experience or be aware of. The knowledge that things are so may be gained in many different ways, by many different means and methods. One may acquire knowledge by perception, observation, motivated scrutiny and investigation, engaging in an activity or practice. It may be acquired by inference from information already available. Knowledge may be transmitted to one by others, who teach or inform one. Or it may be received by noticing, recognizing, becoming aware, becoming conscious or realizing that things are so.

Result, task and achievement verbs   Modes of knowledge-acquisition may be active or passive. Active forms of gaining knowledge are signified by such cognitive verbs as 'detect', 'discover', 'find out', 'ascertain', 'prove', 'solve', 'perceive' (and factive perceptual verbs).[14] One may detect something by sheer luck, discover something by accident or find something out serendipitously – in

---

[13] The revival of innatist accounts of linguistic abilities in the hands of Chomsky and his followers has no evidential basis. The evidence supports no more than the claim that humans possess extensive innate propensities to cotton on to patterns of regularity that facilitate language acquisition and recognition of linguistic norms.

[14] See Ryle, *The Concept of Mind*, pp. 149–52.

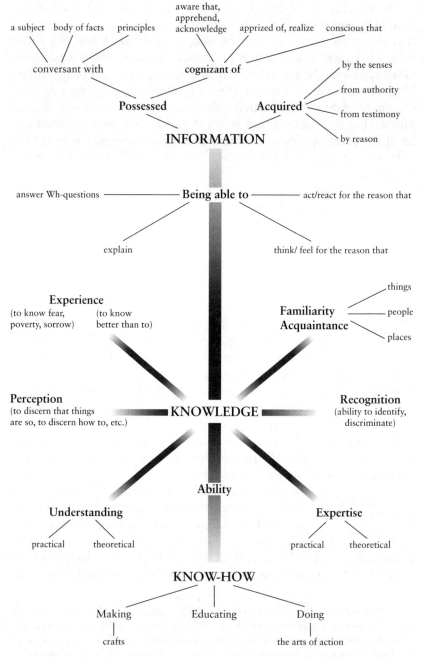

Figure 4.1 *A representation of a part of the cognitive conceptual network*

which cases 'detect', 'discover' and 'find out' are *result-verbs*, signifying the cognitive upshot of the fortuitous event. But even in the case of these verbs, *a fortiori* in the case of such verbs as 'prove' and 'ascertain', which are *achievement-verbs*, it makes sense to speak of *trying* – trying to find out, discover, ascertain or prove. And to succeed here is to achieve knowledge of one form or another. The attempt to achieve knowledge may involve such tasks as looking, observing, scrutinizing, listening, experimenting, consulting, looking up, all of which may be done voluntarily and intentionally. These can be described by the corresponding *task-verbs* (see list 4.1).

Verbs of cognitive endeavour and acquisition	
task-verbs	looking, observing, scrutinizing, listening for, experimenting, consulting, looking up, checking
achievement-verbs	prove, ascertain, discern, detect, solve
result- or achievement-verbs	learn, discover, find out
Verbs of cognitive receptivity	conscious of, aware of, recognize, notice, realize

List 4.1 *Kinds of cognitive verb*

Modes of cognitive receptivity

Verbs of *cognitive achievement* may be contrasted with verbs of *cognitive receptivity*, such as 'To become (and then to be) conscious of', 'to become (and then to be) aware of', 'to notice' and 'to realize', which were discussed in chapter 1. Here knowledge is not achieved or attained by voluntary acts or activities. One cannot voluntarily become conscious or aware of something, or intentionally notice or realize something to be so. These verbs do not signify activities at all. One cannot be engaged in being conscious of something, *or* in realizing something, *or* in being conscious or aware that something is so. Nor are there methods of becoming conscious or aware of something or of noticing or realizing something – only ways of sharpening one's receptivity by practice and experience. These forms of knowledge acquisition are not things we do, but things that happen to us. We are in passive receipt of knowledge.

Knowledge and validation

There are many different ways of acquiring information. Hence the question 'How do you know?' can arise. So *knowing how things are* is linked to *validation*. What is known is generally what it *makes sense* to confirm, verify or otherwise validate. If one knows that things are so, then it makes sense for one to *satisfy oneself* that they are – should a doubt arise or a challenge need to be met. The concept of validation is in turn linked to that of sources of knowledge (see list 4.2).

- Experience – the senses are cognitive faculties, even though fallible.

- Practice – we not only learn how to do many things in practice, but we also often learn that things are so or are to be done thus-and-so by practice.

- Testimony – we are eyes and ears to each other.

- Authority – the common fund of knowledge of culture and science.

- Reason – exercised in deductive, inductive and analogical reasoning.

List 4.2 *Sources of knowledge*

It is noteworthy that certain propositions of our 'world-picture', such as 'the world has existed for a long time', are not attained from a cognitive source, and do not rest on evidence. Any evidence for them would be less certain than what it would allegedly support. Hence Wittgenstein's interest in such propositions in his last notes *On Certainty*.

Retention, loss and retrieval of knowledge

Knowledge, once attained, must be retained, or it will be lost to one (see fig. 4.2). Since knowledge is *possessed*, we speak metaphorically of having a *store* of knowledge. That leads us into conceiving of memory (as Aristotle, Aquinas and Locke did) as a 'storehouse of ideas', and we wonder (as some neuroscientists do) where in the brain the knowledge is stored and in what form it is 'encoded'. We shall discuss such misconceptions concerning memory in chapter 9. Being possessed, knowledge is associated with cognitive *retention*, with *being aware that* things are so, *bearing in mind* that they are, *learning* and *not forgetting* things to be so, *being knowledgeable* or *possessing expertise* in a given subject of learning or craft. It is equally closely associated with cognitive retrieval, with *recalling, recollecting* and *remembering*. What is acquired may be lost. Loss of knowledge may be inability to recollect information once possessed, general failure of memory or loss of skill or knack. Lack of knowledge may be ignorance, lack of competence, unfamiliarity or lack of first-hand experience.

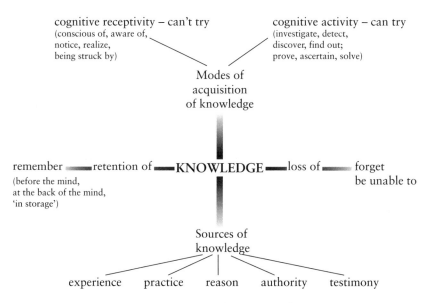

cognitive receptivity – can't try
(conscious of, aware of, notice, realize, being struck by)

cognitive activity – can try
(investigate, detect, discover, find out; prove, ascertain, solve)

Modes of
acquisition
of knowledge

remember ▬▬ retention of ▬ **KNOWLEDGE** ▬ loss of ▬▬ forget
(before the mind, at the back of the mind, 'in storage')

be unable to

Sources of
knowledge

experience   practice   reason   authority   testimony

Figure 4.2 *Acquisition and retention of knowledge*

Knowledge, certainty and doubt

Finally, to complete our sketch of the semantic field, knowledge is linked to *certainty* (see section 5 below). One can know *for certain* that something is so, and know that *it is certainly so*. One may *make certain* that something is so, and if one has made certain, then one does indeed know that it is so. Whether *being certain* (subjective certainty) is a necessary condition of knowing something to be so, and whether what is known must *be certain* (objective certainty), as Descartes and others supposed,[15] is contentious. Knowledge has similarly been connected, by exclusion, with doubt – and that in two different ways. It has been argued that knowledge is incompatible with *actually* doubting (and commonly it has been held to require certainty). It has also been argued that knowledge is incompatible with the very *possibility* of doubting. Only what is *indubitable*, it has been thought (by Descartes), amounts to genuine knowledge (*scientia*).

Knowledge is likewise connected with belief – a connection which has been the source of much puzzlement throughout the ages. Since antiquity it has been widely supposed that knowing-that is a species of true belief or at least that the proposition that A knows that things are so is dependent on the truth of 'A believes that things are so'. We shall examine the matter below and in chapter 5.

4. What knowledge is not

We can gain a distinct idea of knowledge, although not yet a clear idea, by investigating the category to which it belongs. Knowing things to be so has been variously categorized as an act, an achievement, a disposition, a mental state and an attitude. Showing why it is none of these will distinguish knowledge from things with which it is liable to be confused.

To know is not an act or action
    Acquiring knowledge may involve performing an act or engaging in an activity, namely: whatever acts or activities are involved in trying to find out, discover or detect how things are, for example, observing, investigating, experimenting. But to know something is not an act. What one *did* may have been to observe, prove or detect, but not to know. Whereas ascertaining something to be so may take time, knowing something to be so cannot take time. One may be interrupted in the middle of solving a problem, but one cannot be interrupted in the middle of

---

[15] For example, 'We ought to concern ourselves only with objects which admit of as much certainty as the demonstrations of arithmetic and geometry' ('Rules for the Direction of the Mind', AT X, 366). He never changed his mind on this. In the *Discourse* he wrote: 'But since I now wished to devote myself to the search for truth, I thought it necessary to . . . reject as if absolutely false everything in which I could imagine the least doubt, in order to see whether I was left believing anything that was entirely indubitable' (AT VI, 31). (See also Fifth Meditation (AT VII, 69–71), and *Principles of Philosophy*, part 4, 206 (AT IXB, 328f.).)

knowing the answer to the problem. One cannot know, but only come to know or learn something, quickly or slowly, and one cannot know something, but only do something, voluntarily or intentionally, carefully or carelessly. So knowing is not a mental act.

Knowing something need not be an achievement
If knowing something is not an act, is it an achievement? We have seen that 'solve', 'prove', 'ascertain', 'discover', 'detect', 'find out' are verbs of cognitive achievement. If one proves something to be so, one has proved it, if one ascertains that something is so, one has ascertained that it is, and if one discovers something, one has discovered it. But if one knows something, it does not follow that one has known it. As noted, knowing something need not be the successful upshot of endeavour – one may have been a passive recipient. Although if one knows things to be so and says that they are, one is right, being right is not necessarily an achievement.

Knowing is not a disposition
Is knowing something a disposition? This thought is tempting.[16] Like habits and dispositions, knowledge is acquired, possessed, retained and lost. Like habits (a drink before, and a nap after, lunch) and dispositions (cheerfulness, credulity, irritability), knowing something has no location and cannot be stored, but only retained. Nevertheless, 'to know' is not a tendency-verb, and knowing is no disposition. One may know something without any corresponding tendency to do anything. One may know a secret without being in the slightest bit inclined to reveal it. More knowledge does not imply more pronenesses. One may know something trivial for a moment or two and then forget it, but one cannot have a habit or disposition for a moment or two. One can know something and never act on what one knows, but one cannot have a habit and never exemplify it, or a disposition and never display it. The criteria for whether someone knows something to be so are not criteria for having a disposition to do anything.

Is knowing a mental state?
Is knowing something a mental state or state of mind? This idea has, in recent years, become popular.[17] It is

---

[16] See G. Ryle, *The Concept of Mind*, p. 44.

[17] See e.g. T. Williamson, *Knowledge and its Limits* (Oxford University Press, Oxford, 2000): 'Knowing is a state of mind . . . A state of mind is a mental state of a subject. Paradigmatic mental states include love, hate, pleasure and pain' (p. 21). 'To call knowing a mental state is to assimilate it, in certain respects, to paradigmatic mental states such as believing, desiring and being in pain' (p. 27). See also C.

superficially tempting. As noted above, grammarians classify the verb 'to know' as a stative verb, and take it to signify a state. In general (with various qualifications) they mark stative verbs by an array of negative grammatical features specified in list 4.3.[18] 'To know' certainly fits the bill.

Lack of a progressive form	*'He is knowing p'
Inadmissibility of a Do pro-form	*'What he did was to know p'
Absence of an imperative form	*'Know Crécy was in 1346'
Absence of 'for . . . sake' construction	*'I know p for her sake'
Absence of volitional manner adverbs	*'He knows p reluctantly'

List 4.3 *Marks of stative verbs applied to 'to know'*

Knowing has often been linked with being or feeling sure or certain, and these at least *seem* to be mental states. And since ignorance is a state (although not a mental one) inasmuch as one may be in a state of blissful ignorance, it may seem that knowledge must be a state too. Nevertheless, to know something to be so is not a state of any kind, let alone a mental one.[19]

Not all stative verbs signify states

The verbs grammarians characterize as stative include 'to be', 'to consist of', 'contain', 'cost', 'fit', 'have', 'lack', 'include', 'seem', 'sound', 'tend', 'to

---

Peacocke, *Being Known* (Clarendon Press, Oxford, 1999), pp. 52–5; J. H. McDowell, 'Knowledge and the Internal', *Philosophy and Phenomenological Research*, 55 (1995), 877–93. An earlier adherent to this view was H. A. Prichard, 'Knowing and Believing', in his *Knowledge and Perception* (Clarendon Press, Oxford, 1950), pp. 85–91.

[18] R. Quirk, S. Greenbaum, G. Leech and J. Svartvik, *A Comprehensive Grammar of the English Language* (Longman, London, 1985).

[19] For an explanation of why ignorance is a state even though knowing is not, see p. 185 below.

be disposed' and 'to be able'. Although grammarians are prone to say that all stative verbs signify states, this is mistaken. Many do not. The key that *fits* a lock is not in a state of fitting; *including* the 'Moonlight' Sonata is not a state of a concert programme; and *to be able* to play the piano is not to be in a state of any kind. There is no such thing as being in a state of *consisting of* flour and water, or in a state of *containing* flour. *Costing* 99 pence a pound is not a state of cabbages, any more than *rising* in price is an activity of butter. The verbs 'to intend', 'to mean', 'to mind', 'to understand' are all psychological stative verbs, but none of them signify mental states or states of mind that people may be in. I may *intend* to go, but I cannot be in an intending state of mind; I may *mean something* by what I say, but I cannot be in a mental state of meaning something; I may *mind* being insulted, but I cannot be in a state of minding. Syntax here is a poor guide to semantics. The concepts of a state in general and of a mental state in particular are not syntactical categories, but semantic ones.

Stipulating that a state is what is signified by a stative verb multiplies confusion

It might be supposed that one may simply *stipulate* that a state is what is signified by a verb lacking a progressive form, and that mental states are whatever is signified by a psychological verb of such a kind. One may, of course, stipulate as one pleases. But one is ill-advised to stipulate a novel use for an existing expression (such as 'mental state'). For then one will be prone to draw inferences from the new use which can be drawn only from the old one, and to assimilate things that are categorially quite different (such as knowing something to be so and being in pain). More importantly, what illumination can be derived from a stipulation that rides rough-shod over distinctions between the actual and the potential, between being and being able to, between what one is in and what one can do?

We have a vague and elastic concept of a mental state. It has its uses, which are not Linnaean. Pain is not a mental state, but a sensation (one may have a pain in one's leg, but not a mental state in one's leg). Love is not a mental state but a complex disposition. *Being* in pain, however, is a mental state, as are feeling cheerful or sad, depressed or joyous, concentrating hard or feeling relaxed and dreamy (in a dreamy state of mind). One may be in a state of indecision (but not in a state of decision), in a state of anxiety or of contentment. Believing, far from being a paradigmatic mental state, is not a mental state at all (see chapter 5), and although feeling lustful is a mental state, desiring to go to Naples before one dies is not.

What a mental state is
So what is a mental state? Mental states are states of consciousness, that is, they are characterized by obtaining only while one is awake and conscious, and ceasing when one falls asleep or loses consciousness.[20] They can be interrupted by distraction of attention, and subsequently resumed. They are roughly or accurately clockable, with beginnings and endings. They admit of degrees of intensity, so one may be *very* joyous, angry or pleased, or *quite* tired, contented or cheerful. They may wax and wane. Names of mental states generally lend themselves to the form of words 'in a state of . . .' – as when we speak of being in a state of intense concentration, of rising excitement, of blissful contentment, of acute anxiety. Mental states are manifest in expression, mien and tone of voice (see list 4.4).

- One can be *in* them, but one cannot acquire or possess them.
- They obtain during periods of waking.
- They are states of consciousness, hence cease with loss of consciousness.
- They are interruptible by distraction of attention.
- They can resume or be resumed after interruption.
- They have more or less determinable beginnings and termini – are roughly clockable.
- They admit of degrees of intensity.
- They may wax and wane.
- They have distinctive forms of facial expression, mien, and tone of voice.
- If a noun signifies a mental state, there is commonly a corresponding adjective which goes with the verb 'feel' ('feels depressed, cheerful, anxious'). Hence someone who is in a mental state is commonly describable by the use of the continuous or imperfect tense: 'is feeling depressed', 'has been feeling anxious ever since . . .'.

List 4.4 *Ten marks of mental states*

[20] The first to identify the marks of a mental state was Wittgenstein. He introduced the quasi-technical term 'genuine duration' (as opposed to mere duration) to demarcate mental states (see *Zettel*, §§472–89).

Why knowing is not a mental state Clearly knowing that something is so is not a mental state. We ask why – not how – someone is so cheerful, but how – not why[21] – someone knows that things are so. One is not '*in* a state of knowing' as one may be in a state of eager anticipation; and learning something new does not put one into a fresh state of knowledge, even though it may put one into a state of dreadful anxiety or acute excitement. One *possesses* knowledge, but one is *in* mental states and states of mind.[22] One *acquires* knowledge, one *finds oneself in* a mental state – but does not acquire it. One may *work oneself up* into a state of dreadful anxiety, but one cannot work oneself up into a state of knowing that things are so. One does not cease to know the date of the battle of Hastings when one falls asleep, and one's knowing the date cannot be interrupted by a telephone call as can one's state of concentration. One may be in an excited state of mind from the time one heard that Jill was coming until her arrival, but one cannot be in a state of knowing that Harald Hardrada died in 1066 from the time one learns until one forgets. One cannot know something intensely, as one may be intensely excited – or mildly, as one can be mildly interested. One may be in a very cheerful state of mind or in a slightly irritable one, but one cannot very know or even quite know that the battle of Stamford Bridge was fought in 1066 – only know it or know it very well. One's knowledge that Bannockburn was fought in 1314 and Agincourt in 1415 cannot wax and wane, as one's indignation can, and one cannot be in a state of knowing as one can be in a state of anxiety. One may look anxious, have an expression of contentment or delight on one's face, or frown with intense concentration. One may speak in joyous tones, or in an anxious voice, but there is no facial expression of knowing something to be so, nor a cognitive tone of voice. There is, of course, such a thing as a 'knowing look', but a knowing look is not an *expression* of knowledge as a cheerful smile or laugh is an expression of feeling cheerful. Someone may look as if he knows what he is doing, but that is not because he has a knowing look on his face, but because he is going about a task efficiently and confidently.

[21] To be sure, one may ask of someone who is not supposed to know some confidential piece of information 'Why does he know?' – meaning 'How come he knows?'. But this is not a request for grounds.

[22] One should not assume that the concept of a mental state is no different from that of a state of mind. States of mind converge on frames of mind; mental states do not.

Dispositional mental states   We also use mental state predicates to signify *dispositional mental states*. One may feel depressed all day, but mercifully cease from feeling so when one falls asleep. But one may suffer from depression, and be in a thoroughly depressed state for some months. What this means is that for this period one is prone to feel depressed in the course of the day. One may feel anxious this afternoon, but be in a prolonged state of anxiety for many months – if one has a tendency to feel anxious during one's waking hours over a long period of time.

Why knowing is not a dispositional mental state   Of course, one may have known all the time that things were so. Nevertheless, knowing something to be so is not a dispositional mental state. For if it were, there would have to be some mental state that actualizes the dispositional state, as *feeling depressed* actualizes the dispositional state of *being in a depression*. But feeling that one knows is not knowing, and there is no other candidate for actualizing the putative dispositional state of knowing.

Why knowing is not a propositional attitude   A further categorial candidate, originating with Russell and currently much canvassed, is that to know something to be so is an attitude. In particular, it is held to be an attitude towards a proposition.[23] Knowledge that something is so is commonly referred to as 'propositional knowledge'. But this is quite mistaken.

One may hope, fear, or suspect that things are thus-and-so, but there is no such thing as hoping, fearing or suspecting the proposition that things are thus-and-so. One may know that things are so, and one may know the proposition that things are so. But what A hopes,

---

[23] For example, T. Williamson, '[paradigmatic mental states] include attitudes to propositions: believing that something is so, conceiving that something is so, wondering whether it is so, intending or desiring it to be so. One can also know that something is so . . . the claim is that knowing itself is a mental relation such that, for every proposition *p*, having that relation to *p* is a mental state. . . . Our initial presumption should be that knowing is a mental state. Prior to philosophical theory-building, we learn the concept of the mental by examples. Our paradigms should include propositional attitudes such as believing or desiring, if our conception of the mental is not to be radically impoverished' (*Knowledge and its Limits*, p. 21).

The notion and terminology of a 'propositional attitude' originates with Russell, 'Meinong's Theory of Complexes and Assumptions', *Mind*, 13 (1904), pp. 339, 523, and 'The Philosophy of Logical Atomism' (1918–19), in R. C. Marsh (ed.), *Logic and Knowledge* (Allen & Unwin, London, 1956), p. 218. It is noteworthy that paradigmatic attitudes, such as liking/disliking, approving/disapproving, are not mental states.

B fears and C suspects to be so may be precisely what D knows to be so. So what D knows when he knows that things are so cannot be the proposition that things are so. We must distinguish:

(i)   knowing that things are so;
(ii) knowing the proposition that things are so;
(iii) knowing that the proposition that things are so is true.

None of these, *pace* Russell and his followers, signify attitudes towards anything. 'To know the proposition that *p*' signifies no attitude towards the proposition, any more than to know the Treaty of Lisbon signifies an attitude to the treaty, or 'to know London' signifies an attitude towards London. As we have seen, 'knows' in 'A knows that things are thus so' is not transitive, and 'that things are so', unlike 'the Pythagorean Theorem', is not the name of a proposition. So for A to know that things are so is not for A to stand in a relation to an object called 'that things are so'.

Genuine verbs of propositional attitude   Strikingly, if a verb *requires* a proposition-like object (such as a claim, rumour, story, announcement, declaration) towards which an attitude *can* be taken, then a that-clause is not generally licit.[24] One can *endorse* the proposition or the claim that things are so, *ridicule* and *dismiss* the rumour that things are so, be *amused by* the story that things are so and *approve* of the declaration or announcement that things are so. But one cannot endorse, ridicule, dismiss, be amused by or approve *that things are so*. One can take up an attitude towards declarations and statements, but not towards *that things are so*. It was mistaken of Russell to suppose that such verbs as 'to know', 'to believe', 'to fear', 'to hope', 'to suspect', 'to desire', 'to want' and so forth signify propositional attitudes. (He even went so far as to suppose that to want a cup of tea is an attitude towards a proposition.[25]) The use of the term of art 'propositional attitude' should be

---

[24] Rundle, *Mind in Action*, p. 53.

[25] Just how confused he was can be seen in A. R. White, 'Propositions and Sentences', and his 'Belief as a Propositional Attitude', in G. W. Roberts (ed.), *Bertrand Russell Memorial Volume* (Allen & Unwin, London, 1979), pp. 22–33, 242–51. Quine went even further than Russell: 'Taking the objects of propositional attitudes as sentences does not require the subject to speak the language of the object sentence or any. The mouse's fear of a cat is counted as his fearing true a certain English sentence' (*Word and Object* (MIT Press, Cambridge, Mass., 1960), p. 213).

restricted to such verbs as 'endorse', 'approve', 'ridicule', when they take proposition-like objects. Knowing that something is so is neither an attitude towards a proposition nor towards anything else.

5. Certainty

Knowledge has traditionally been associated with both certainty and indubitability. Inasmuch as scepticism threatened the very possibility of knowledge, certainty or even indubitability seemed to be the weapon with which to combat it. Whether either is indeed necessary for knowledge will be examined in section 6 below. But the concepts of objective and subjective certainty – the certainty of things and the certainty of people – are problematic and have been little examined in the last four decades. It is well worth mapping the contours of the concept of certainty in order to shed further light upon that of knowledge.[26] First we must shed some light on the relationships between certainty, necessity and probability.

Possibility for things to be otherwise and possibility that they are otherwise — We distinguish between the question of whether it is possible *for* things to be otherwise (the actuality of a possibility), and the question of whether it is possible *that* they are otherwise (the possibility of an actuality). The first possibility (which can be logical, physical, technical, psychological, etc.) concerns whether things *can* (or *could*) be otherwise, and is contrasted with necessity. The second (which can be none of these) concerns whether things *may* (or *might*) be thus-and-so, and is contrasted with certainty.[27] Two principles must be kept in mind here:

> *If it is necessary that things are so, then it is not possible* FOR *them to be otherwise.*

[26] The best guide is A. R. White, *Modal Thinking* (Blackwell, Oxford, 1975), ch. 5; *The Nature of Knowledge*, pp. 66–72, 75–8; 'Certainty', *Proceedings of the Aristotelian Society*, 72 (1972), pp. 1–18. I am much indebted to these discussions.

[27] It is noteworthy that if this is correct, then the idea of *epistemic possibility* is a confused blend of the question of whether it is possible *for* things to be thus-and-so, and the question of whether it is possible *that* things are thus-and-so. But the question of whether, *relative to what one knows*, it is possible that things are thus-and-so is patently a question concerning the possibility of an actuality, rather than the actuality of a possibility. Hence it does not belong together with logical, physical, technical or psychological possibility.

If it is certain that things are so, then it is not possible THAT *they are otherwise.*

'It is certain that things are so' is equivalent to 'the possibility that things are not so (or, the possibility of things not being so) is excluded'. What excludes alternative possibilities may be circumstances (events, actions, states of affairs) that *make* it certain that things *are* so, or evidence that *shows* it to be certain that things *are* so.

Certainty and necessity
Certainty does not imply necessity. Many things are certainly true without being necessarily true; for example, the fact that in present economic circumstances inflation is certain does not mean that it is necessary. But if something *is* necessarily so, then it is certainly so, for whatever makes it necessarily so also makes it certain that it is so. Both the possibility *for* its being otherwise *and* the possibility *that* it is otherwise are excluded. 'It is necessary that things are so' is equivalent to 'It is not possible *for* things not to be so // that things *should* not be so //'.

The possible, the probable and the certain form a continuum. Something may be probable but not certain, and possible but not probable. If it is certain that something is so, then it is certainly so. It *could* have been different (unless it was inevitable), but it is not possible that it *is* different. Things can be made probable or possible no less than they can be made certain.

The certainty of things
'Certain' (from *certus*) signifies something settled, fixed, determined, which – if known – is therefore to be trusted, relied or depended on. Things are certain when it is settled that they are, were or will be so – when alternative possibilities are excluded by circumstances or action, or are shown to be excluded by evidence. The certainty of things is distinct from the certainty of people. *It is certain* that the melting of the ice-caps increases global warming; the sun *will certainly* turn into a red giant before collapsing into a white dwarf star; the prime minister faces *certain defeat* in the House. These are objective *certainties* – made certain by foreclosing circumstances (e.g. the increase in carbon dioxide in the atmosphere), or by evidence (e.g. of the evolution of stars) or by people foreclosing possibilities through their actions (e.g. party pacts). Something can be, and can be made, possible, probable, and more or less, or absolutely, certain. Something can be revealed to be certain by evidence. For evidence may *show* that it is certain that things are so inasmuch as it *shows* that all other

possibilities are, for one reason or another, not realized. *That it is certain* that things are so does not imply that anyone *is certain* that they are. For whatever makes it possible, probable or certain that things are so need not be known to anyone. Something is or becomes certain (e.g. the demise of the dinosaurs, the occurrence of tsunamis) if and when alternative possibilities are foreclosed (e.g. by the impact of a giant meteor, by movement of tectonic plates) – not if, or indeed when, they become known to be foreclosed. Similarly, the evidence that shows it certain that things are so need not be recognized as such until some time after it is known (as any reader of the tales of Sherlock Holmes must realize).

The certainty of people   Someone may *be* certain that things are so – or be uncertain, doubtful or unsure.[28] Both the certainty of things and the certainty of people admit of degrees. Something or someone may be absolutely, nearly, reasonably, fairly or not at all certain (but not 'a little certain'). Someone who is certain that things are so is convinced that they are. He has ruled out the possibility of things not being so, and harbours no doubts about whether they are (he is quite sure). This may be because he thinks (rightly or wrongly) that *it is certain* that they are so. It may be because he has *made certain* (ascertained) that they are so, or because he has *made it certain* (ensured) that things are or are going to be so by taking appropriate measures. But it may also be because he has a hunch, intuition or premonition.

Being sure and being certain   The relationship between *being certain* and *being sure* is subtle. The two concepts run for a while along parallel tracks, but then diverge. If one is sure that things are so, one is certain that they are, and if one is certain that things are so, then one is sure that they are. But whereas it may be certain that things are so, it cannot be sure that they are. One can make sure, as one can make certain, that something is so, but one cannot *make it sure* that something will be so as one can make it certain that it will. Certainty is related to the exclusion of

---

[28] But subjective certainty is not a mental state. To have excluded alternative possibilities from one's mind is not to be in a mental state. It should therefore be unsurprising that someone's being certain does not satisfy the requirements of 'genuine duration'. One cannot be interrupted in one's certainty and later resume it (loss of conviction and the subsequent recovery of certainty is not an *interruption* of certainty). One's conviction or certainty does not cease when one falls asleep.

possibilities, being sure (from *securus*) is related to the exclusion of doubts. One can be sure of oneself (free from doubts), but not certain of oneself. Something is said to be sure (a foothold, an income or a refuge) if it allows someone to be sure about it – to be free of doubts or worry.

Objective and subjective certainty are independent

It is evident that something's being certain and someone's being certain about it are independent. Someone may be certain that things are so without it being at all certain that they are, since other possibilities obtain. It may be certain that things are or will be thus-and-so without anyone being certain that they are or will be – for no one may know that all alternative possibilities have been fore-closed or recognize the evidence that shows it to be certain that things are so.

Being certain, thinking it certain and feeling certain

Someone may *be* certain that things are so without thinking that it *is* certain – as when a gambler is and feels certain that his next throw of the die will be a six (but he knows enough about probability to know that the chances are one in six). One may feel certain that things will turn out well (one has faith, believes in one's luck, has a premonition), while realizing that it is by no means certain they will – nothing makes it certain and other possibilities are still open. One cannot be certain without also feeling certain, or feel certain without being certain. But being certain is subject to standards of rationality in a way in which feeling certain is not. It would be inappropriate to *say* 'I feel certain' rather than 'I am certain' when one knows for certain that things are so.

List 4.5 makes surveyable the central distinctions we draw.

Certainty and inevitability

Just as it is important not to confuse what is certain with what is necessary, so too it is important not to confuse the certainty of things with the inevitability of things. If something is inevitable, then it is certain to happen – for whatever makes it inevitable also makes it certain. But there are many things that are certain to happen without it being inevitable that they should happen, since although they *will not* be avoided, they are *avoidable*. (Inflation is certain to rise, but it is not unavoidable. A decline in academic standards in Britain is certain, but not inevitable.) Circumstances may make it certain that things will be so without making them inevitable, just as evidence may *show* it to be certain that things are so, without showing that they are *inevitably* so – only that they certainly are so.

The certainty of things	*It* is certain that things are so (but it may be only more or less certain, probable or possible that they are). If it is certain that things are so, then the possibility of their not being so is excluded. This may *be* excluded by prevailing circumstances, events or actions, or *shown* to be excluded by evidence. Something may be certain without anyone either knowing it to be certain, or being certain that it is so.
Making it certain	Something *makes it certain* (ensures) that things *will be* so by foreclosing alternative possibilities. Someone makes something certain by taking preventive or productive action that ensures it. Something or someone makes it *more or less* certain that things will be so (or makes it more or less *probable*). Only what has not yet happened can be made certain. If something is (or has been) made certain, then it is certain that it will happen.
The certainty of people	*Someone* is certain that things are so. One may be certain that things are so without its being certain that they are. Similarly to belief, but unlike knowledge, one can ask 'Why are you certain?' but not 'How are you certain?' (only 'How certain are you?'). When one is certain that things are so, then alternative possibilities are excluded from one's mind. (One is *sure* if all doubts are excluded.)
Feeling certain	Someone *feels certain* (confident, sure) if and only if he is certain (confident, sure) that things are so. Neither feeling certain nor being certain, unlike knowing, imply being right. There are criteria of rationality for someone's being certain, but feeling certain does not *require* a warrant. *Feeling/being certain* approximate *feeling/being sure* (having no doubts).
Making certain	Someone *makes certain* that something is, was or will be so by *ascertaining* that alternative possibilities are excluded (but one cannot make more or less certain that something is, was or will be so – just as one cannot more or less find out). If one makes certain that things are so, then one knows for certain that they are.
Knowing for certain	To know for certain that things are so is not the same as to know and be certain that they are so. If someone knows for certain that things are so, then it is certain that they are. But if someone merely knows and is certain that things are so, it does not follow that it is certain that they are. If one knows for certain that things are so, then the possibility of one's being mistaken is excluded.

List 4.5   *Certainties*

6. Analyses of knowledge

'Know-that'
is factive
It is clear that 'A knows that things are so' implies that things are as A knows them to be. If things are so, then it is true (to say) that they are, and the proposition that they are is true. One might say that such knowledge is only of truth, as long as that does not lead one to suppose that its formal objects are propositions, and that the uniform content of knowledge is that a given proposition is true. What is correct is that the phrase 'to know that', like 'to detect that', 'to discover that' or 'to discern that', is factive. This does not mean that facts are the formal objects of knowledge rather than propositions, but rather that what is known to be so is in fact so.

It has commonly, but by no means uniformly, been thought that knowledge implies belief. There are various reasons why philosophers have assumed this. None are wholly convincing.

3 inconclusive reasons
why knowledge has
been thought to
imply belief
First, it would be decidedly odd to say 'I know that things are so, but I don't believe it'. It would be almost as odd to say 'He knows things to be so, but he doesn't believe it', although we might well say 'I've told him, but he doesn't believe it'. On the other hand, it does not *follow* that the oddity stems from a contradiction of the form 'Abp & p & . . . & ~ Abp'.

Secondly, if someone sincerely asserts that things are so or says that he knows that things are so – and he is mistaken, then we would correctly characterize him as having believed (falsely) or thought (wrongly) that things are so. So believing seems the 'default position' when knowledge fails, just as trying is the default position when action fails. So if believing is knowledge minus something, knowledge seems to be belief plus something. On the other hand, this conceptual arithmetic does *not* show that knowing something to be so is truly believing it to be so plus some further condition, any more than acting is trying to do something plus some further condition – namely succeeding (although that too has been argued).[29]

Thirdly, someone may believe things to be so, because he has a premonition or hunch. If he acquires decisive evidence, *then* he will

[29] For refutation of this idea, see P. M. S. Hacker, *Wittgenstein: Mind and Will* (Blackwell, Oxford, 1996), 'Willing and the nature of voluntary action', section 6(b); also S. Schroeder, *Wittgenstein: the Way out of the Fly-Bottle* (Polity, Cambridge, 2006), pp. 221–4.

know that what he previously believed to be so is so. Consequently knowledge seems to be true belief together with good evidence, or justification, or a right to be sure. – On the other hand, there seem innumerable cases of knowledge that things are so which are not supported by evidence (e.g. that the world has existed for many years), that have no justification (e.g. that one's arm is bent) and where no question of having a right to be sure arises (e.g. that 'Edinburgh' is spelled 'E-d-i-n-b-u-r-g-h').

Note that the attempt to explain knowing in terms of believing is not necessarily to claim that knowledge is a *species* of belief, for something may be a necessary condition of another thing without demarcating a species – just as travelling is a necessary condition of arriving, but arriving is not a species of travelling.[30] The moot question is whether believing is a necessary condition of knowing, not whether knowing is a certain kind of believing.

The relationship between knowledge and belief will be discussed in chapter 6. In the meantime, we shall keep any doubts in abeyance, and examine analyses of knowledge that things are so. We shall scrutinize three proposals that explore and exploit the nexus between knowledge, indubitability, certainty and justified true belief.

Defining knowledge in terms of indubitability   Descartes and his early modern followers held that if we *cannot* doubt something to be so, then it is metaphysically certain. Only what is metaphysically certain qualifies as *scientia* – genuine knowledge of truth. The mark of truth, as Descartes claimed to have discovered from scrutiny of the *cogito*, is clear and distinct perception (apprehension). Whatever is clearly and distinctly perceived is certain. The mark of certainty is indubitability.[31] Genuine knowledge must be completely certain and resistant to all forms of doubt.

1st objection: logical exclusion of doubt excludes certainty   It is wrong to suppose that if we *cannot* (logically or 'metaphysically') doubt something to be so, then it *follows* that we know for certain that it is

[30] R. Chisholm, *Perceiving* (Cornell University Press, Ithaca, NY, 1957), pp. 17f.

[31] To be sure, according to Descartes, we must also know for certain that God exists. Atheists, he held, cannot achieve *scientia*. 'I see plainly that the certainty and truth of all knowledge depends uniquely on my knowledge of the true God, to such an extent that I was incapable of perfect knowledge about anything else until I knew him. And now it is possible for me to achieve full and certain knowledge of countless matters' (Fifth Meditation (AT VII, 71)).

so. As we saw in chapter 1, if doubt is *logically* or *grammatically* excluded, as it is in the case of Cartesian *cogitationes* such as 'I think', 'I am in pain', 'I seem to see' or indeed 'I doubt', *then so too is certainty*. In such cases, the very indubitability of such *cogitationes* also excludes any possibility of knowing *for certain* that things are so, just as the logical exclusion of ignorance excludes the intelligibility of knowing. If 'I don't know whether' and 'I doubt whether . . .' *make no sense*, then 'I know that . . .' as well as 'I am certain that . . .' make no sense either. For there is nothing for knowledge or certainty to exclude.

2nd objection: inability to doubt is not sufficient for knowing

Secondly, that one *does not*, and perhaps *in fact* cannot, doubt something to be so is not a mark of its indubitability but only of one's subjective certainty or faith. Nor is it a mark of one's knowing for certain that things are so. For most of human history, people did not and could not bring themselves to doubt the existence of a god or gods. They were quite certain that a god exists. It was not possible *for them* to doubt this. But that does not mean that they *knew for certain* that a god exists or that the existence of a god was *indubitable*.

3rd objection: absence of doubt is not necessary for knowing

Thirdly, it is perfectly possible for someone to know something and yet to doubt whether his answers are right – as in the case of the hesitant examination candidate, who despite his trepidation does the calculation correctly or gets the proof right. What shows that he knows is not his inability to doubt the answer he produces, but the fact that he produces the right answer.

Absence of doubt is necessary for claiming to know

Nevertheless, there is a truth lurking in the background here. If one doubts whether things are thus-and-so, one *should* not claim to know they are so. Absence of doubt (which is not the same as presence of certainty) is a normative condition for *claiming* to know something to be so. But it is *not* a condition for knowing something to be so. It is evident why it is a condition for claiming to know. To *say* 'Things are so, but I doubt whether they are' or 'I know that things are so, but I'm not sure' is a solecism. For to assert things to be so is to give others to know that they are. It is to tell them what they may rely on. But to add 'but I'm not sure' or 'but I doubt it' is precisely to deny that they may rely on what one has told them. So it is akin to 'Take my word for it, but I wouldn't'.

Defining knowledge in terms of certainty The endeavour to explain the nature of knowledge that things are thus-and-so by reference to certainty has been popular throughout the centuries. Such accounts may take at least two different forms: one doxastic and the other not. Locke spoke of 'the certainty of true knowledge'.[32] Kant held (in his lectures) that 'to know is to judge something and hold it to be true with certainty' or, again, that 'to know means to hold something to be true with sufficient certainty that no doubt remains or can remain'.[33] Knowing something to be so is accordingly true belief coupled with certainty. This idea was revived and elaborated, in terms of being sure, by Ayer in the mid twentieth century. He argued that the conditions for knowing that something is the case is 'first, that what one is said to know be true, secondly that one be sure of it, and thirdly that one should have the right to be sure'.[34] Earlier in the twentieth century, Cook-Wilson and Prichard denied that to know something to be so is to believe it, holding rather that it is a *sui generis* self-certifying mental state characterized by certainty, which is distinct from merely thinking without question that things are so.[35]

The concepts of knowledge and of certainty are independent Both accounts are wrong, irrespective of their differences concerning belief. For both misconstrue the relation between knowledge and certainty through lack of an overview of the concept of certainty. Reverting to our survey of certainty, it should be evident that one can know something to be so without *knowing for certain* that it is so. One can know something to be so without *being certain* that it is so. And one can know something to be so without *its being certain* that it is so. Conversely, one may hold

---

[32] Locke, *An Essay concerning Human Understanding,* 4th edn [1700], IV. xiv. 1; see also chs xv–xvii. 'True knowledge' is being contrasted with what is wrongly taken to be knowledge, but which is in fact mere opinion.

[33] Kant, 'The Blomberg Logic' (1770s), in *Lectures on Logic* (Cambridge University Press, Cambridge, 1992), pp. 116, 180; see also 'The Jäsche Logic' (1800), ibid., p. 574.

[34] A. J. Ayer, *The Problem of Knowledge* (Penguin, Harmondsworth, 1956), p. 35.

[35] Prichard, 'To know is not to have a belief of a special kind, differing from beliefs of other kinds; and no improvement in a belief and no increase in the feeling of conviction which it implies will convert it into knowledge' ('Knowing and Believing', p. 87). Moreover, he claimed, knowing is transparent: 'When we know something, we either do, or can, directly know that we are knowing it [*sic*]' (ibid., p. 96).

something to be so with complete certainty, without its being certain that it is so, without knowing it to be so and without its being so. The concepts of knowledge and certainty are, in this sense, mutually independent.

Certainty is not necessary for knowledge

So, contrary to Kant, it is evident that believing that something is so, its being so and one's being certain that it is so are not sufficient for knowing that something is so. Contrary to Cook-Wilson, it is clear that being certain that things are so is not necessary for knowing things to be so. One may know the answer without being at all certain about it. Equally, one may know that things are so (someone told one the tale going round) without knowing for certain that they are so, since one has not made certain (ascertained) that they are. Contrary to Prichard, knowing something to be so is not transparent and self-certifying, for in some circumstances one may know something to be so without realizing that one does or without being sure that one does.

Defining knowledge in terms of justified true belief

The final analysis of knowledge that we shall examine is the proposal that to know things to be so is a conjunction of three conditions:

(i)   believing things to be so;
(ii) things being so;
(iii) having a justification for one's belief.

This has been a common view throughout the last half-century. But there are objections.

4 objections to defining knowledge in terms of justified true belief

First, the normal contextual understanding of the negation of 'A knows that things are so' does not suggest that it is a disjunction of negations, that is, that either A does not believe things to be so, or that things are not so, or that A is not justified in believing things to be so. 'Jack doesn't know that today is my birthday' would, in typical contexts, be taken to imply that he lacks the information – not that either it is not my birthday, *or* that he lacks justification for thinking it to be, *or* that he does not believe it is. (Indeed, 'He doesn't believe that she is forty today' would normally be taken to imply that he has been given the information, but would not credit it.) In general, 'A doesn't know that things are so' defeasibly presupposes that things are so. 'A doesn't know *whether* things are so' is normally rightly taken to mean that he cannot answer the question 'Are things so?'. However, in some contexts one may continue 'but that is his best guess', which normally defeats the factive presupposition.

Secondly, one may have good answers to the question 'Why do you believe that?' which by no means establish that one knows what one is justified in believing. Justified true belief often needs *clinching* evidence before one can be said to know (there are very good reasons for thinking that due to global warming, this century will end in global catastrophe, but no one knows this to be so yet). So justification is often not sufficient for knowledge.

Thirdly, there are indefinitely many things we know to be so, even though we could give no justification for believing them to be so, for example that we dreamt of so-and-so last night, that when you interrupted me yesterday I was about to say such-and-such. One may know the correct way to address the head of one's College, how to spell 'queen', who composed the 'Moonlight' Sonata – but one is unlikely to have *evidence* for such things, only the ability to give the right answer to the corresponding question.[36] So justification is often not necessary for knowledge.

Finally, we must bear in mind qualms about whether knowledge necessarily involves belief at all. For if that is wrong, then *a fortiori* the claim that knowledge is justified true belief is wrong. This will be examined in chapter 6.

7. Knowledge and ability

An alternative account of *knowing-that* suggested by a minority of philosophers explores the relation between knowledge and ability. The idea originates in Plato and Aristotle, was mooted by Ryle in *The Concept of Mind*, suggested by Wittgenstein in the *Philosophical Investigations*, and advanced by White in *The Nature of Knowledge*.

Knowing-that and ability   The proximity of *knowing-how* to *ability* is patent, and will be examined in section 8 below. But the categorial similarity between *knowing-that* and *ability*, though latent, is no less striking. Both knowledge that something is so and an ability to do something can be acquired, possessed and

---

[36] Similar considerations apply to Wittgenstein's 'propositions of the world-picture'.

lost. Neither knowing that things are so nor an ability can be stored anywhere, but they are retained without storage. Like knowledge, abilities are neither acts or activities, nor achievements or dispositions. The ability to do something – even a mental ability like calculating in one's head – is not a state one is in, let alone a mental state, and neither is knowing something. Similarly, the ability to do something, like knowing something to be so, is not a disposition, tendency or proneness. One may have abilities one never uses, just as one may have knowledge one never makes use of or reveals.

Is knowing-that an ability to answer questions? White suggested that the ability in which knowledge consists is the ability to produce a correct answer to a possible question or a solution to a possible problem.[37] This nexus, he argued, is patent in cases in which knowledge is expressed by 'know', followed by a Wh-pronoun. To know what, where, when, which, who, is to be able to produce the correct answers to questions introduced by the corresponding interrogatives. To know that something is so is to be able to answer the question of whether it is so. Furthermore, to know people and places is to be able to answer questions about them based on one's familiarity with them. To know physics or biology is to be able to answer questions concerning the subject and to explain matters by reference to the facts and theories of physics or biology. And so on.

Knowing-that is not identical with the ability to answer a question It may be objected that this implies that non-language-using animals cannot know anything, since they cannot answer questions. One may try to meet this objection by stretching the notion of *manifesting the ability to produce the right answer*. So White suggested that animals exhibit their ability to produce the right answer to a given question in their non-linguistic behaviour – by finding the bone they buried, recognizing their master's footsteps, barking at a cat hiding up a tree, finding their way home. No doubt such behaviour does indeed show that the dog knows where it buried the bone, knows that the cat ran up the tree and knows its way home. But it is not easy to see why this should be thought to be a matter of *an ability to answer questions*. More generally, White argued, the ability to answer a given question is manifested in indefinitely many ways 'by showing or telling it, by deed or word, directly or indirectly'.[38] But now what was a clear and determinate ability (namely, to answer a Wh-question) has become

---

[37] White, *The Nature of Knowledge*, pp. 115–21.

[38] Ibid., p. 120.

so diffuse that it is no longer clear why the ability to produce an answer should be given pride of place over all the other kinds of things one can do if one knows something to be so. If one knows that things are so, then one can not only answer the question of whether they are so, one can also tell someone that things are so without being asked, teach one's pupils that things are so, correct someone who thinks they are not so, draw conclusions from things being so, adjust one's plans, projects and behaviour to things being as one knows they are, and so forth. The link between *knowing* and *being able to* is surely right, but the prominence given to *having the ability to answer the question of whether . . .* is not.

Is knowing-that the ability to be guided by reasons that are facts? An important alternative explanation of knowledge as a kind of ability has recently been advanced by John Hyman.[39] Knowledge that things are so, he argued, is the ability to be guided by reasons that are facts. The facts one is guided by are one's reasons for acting, and also for thinking and feeling. To know that things are so is to have the ability to do things for the reason that they are so. (If one does not know that things are so, then the fact that things are so cannot be one's reason for doing anything.) This connects knowledge with rationality, with the ability to reason, and with reasons for thinking, feeling and doing. It draws an important construction line (as in geometry) between things being so, things being known to be so and doing something for the reason that things are so. But as an analysis of knowledge it is mistaken.

4 reasons why there is no such thing as the ability to act for the reason that It is true that if I know that things are so, then I can act, react or respond in or to circumstances for the reason that things are so. I can also cite the fact that things are so as my reason for having acted, reacted or responded as I did. But to know that things are so is not *to have the ability to act for the reason that things are so* since there is no such ability.

(i) A person may have the ability to read or write, run or swim, cook or bake. But no one has the ability to read-*War-and-Peace*-for-the-reason-that-it-is-a-famous-novel, and Tolstoy did not have the ability to write-a-novel-for-the-reason-that-he-would-become-famous-by-doing-so. No athlete has the ability to run-for-the-reason-that-it-is-sunny, even though the fact that it is sunny may be his

[39] J. Hyman, 'How Knowledge Works', *Philosophical Quarterly*, 49 (1999), pp. 433–51.

reason for going for a run. Reasons for acting do not individuate abilities that are exercised in acting for a reason. Neither does the possession of the information which is one's rationale for doing what one does. Let me explain further.

Abilities are generic. Cooking and baking are two different act-categories. The ability to cook is different from the ability to bake. But the ability to cook dinner for the reason that it will please Daisy does not differ from the ability to cook dinner for the reason that it will please Maisy. It is one and the same culinary art that is exercised. Abilities are abilities to do things, and abilities are individuated by reference to what counts as their successful exercise. 'To Φ', one might say, is the general form of an *act-description*. But 'to V for the reason that *p*' is no more an act-description distinct from 'to V for the reason that *q*' than 'to V for A's sake' is a different act-description from 'to V for B's sake'. 'Is able to V for the reason that *p*' *does not describe a kind of ability*. *A fortiori*, it does not describe a different ability from 'is able to V for the reason that *q*'. So to know that things are so is not the ability to act for the reason that things are so. Indeed, this is what one should expect, given that there is no limit to the *different* abilities that one may exercise in doing something for the reason that things are so. So *being able* to do something for the reason that things are so is not *a kind of ability*.

(ii) With respect to a host of act-categories, one may *learn* and often *has to learn* to perform acts of the category. Only by learning can one acquire these abilities. One may learn to bake cakes, but there is no such thing as learning to bake a cake for the reason that it will please Daisy. One may be more or less skilful at baking cakes, but not more or less skilful at baking cakes for the reason that Daisy is coming to tea. One may forget how to V (and so lose the ability to V), but one cannot forget how to V for the reason that *p*, let alone forget how to V for the reason that *p* as opposed to forgetting how to V for the reason that *q*.

(iii) If one knows that it is raining, one has a good reason for using one's umbrella to keep off the rain. If one sees that it has stopped raining, one no longer has a reason for using one's umbrella. Nevertheless, the cessation of rain has not deprived one of the ability to open-one's-umbrella-for-the-reason-that-it-is-raining – only of the opportunity to use one's umbrella in the rain.

(iv) If one knows that things are so, one can forget that they are. But to forget that things are so is not to lose an ability, namely the ability to act-for-the-reason-that-things-are-so. To forget that Daisy is coming to tea is not to forget how to bake cakes for the reason that Daisy is coming to tea. Nor is there any such thing as remembering how to V for the reason that things are so, only remembering *how to V*, and remembering *to V* for the reason that things are so (e.g. to lock the door because no one is home, to turn the light on because it is getting dark).

Why knowledge is not the ability to be guided by the facts

Can one say that knowledge in general is the ability to be guided by the facts? Can one argue that 'since the facts that we are guided by are the facts that are our reasons, this means that knowledge is the ability to do things, or refrain from doing things, for reasons that are facts'.[40] I think not. It is true that if one possesses factual knowledge, that is, knowledge that things are in fact thus-and-so, then that things are thus-and-so *may* provide one with a reason for doing something or other. It does not follow that knowledge, like rationality, is an ability to do things for reasons. In addition, to say that reasons are facts is not like saying that Coxes are apples, or even like saying that substances are material objects. To say that we are guided by the facts is not akin to saying that we are guided by the white lines. 'Reasons are facts' amounts to this: that if A's reason for V-ing is that things are so, then it is a fact that things are so. What that means is that it is *in fact* the case that things are so; that, *as a matter of fact*, things are so; and equally, that it is *actually* the case that things are so – or simply, that things are so. To say that something is a fact is not to classify it or predicate something of it.

Rationality is the ability to do and respond to things for reasons

A rational creature is a creature that has the ability to reason and to do things for reasons – not merely to make inferences, but also to think, feel and act for reasons. That ability is *rationality* – not knowledge. Knowledge is indeed connected to rationality. For what one knows to be so can be taken into account in one's reasonings, in one's plans and projects, thoughts, feelings and attitudes. One can reason from what one knows, cite what one knows as a reason for thinking, feeling or doing something or other, as well as give it as one's reason. What another person knows may be a reason for him to do something. This may enable one to predict his future action on the basis of his current knowledge, or explain his past action by reference to his knowing what he knew. But a

---

[40] J. Hyman, 'Knowledge and Evidence', *Mind*, 115 (2006), p. 893.

construction-line is not a theorem. Knowing something to be so is not an ability to do something for the reason that things are so.

Knowledge has a kinship with ability
Is knowledge that things are so an ability? It surely seems ability-like – this is the right area on the conceptual map in which to locate the concept. On the other hand, there seems no act-category that answers to such a description. It is right to connect knowledge in all its forms to potentiality rather than to actuality, but questionable whether to squeeze it into the category of ability.[41] Wittgenstein exhibited characteristic insight in his remark 'The grammar of the word "know" is evidently closely related to the grammar of the words "can", "is able to".'[42] This appropriately removes knowing from the categories of mental act, activity, achievement, state and disposition – but nevertheless displays due caution in avoiding its straightforward assimilation to an ability.

Why one can be in a state of ignorance but not in a state of knowing
As earlier noted, we speak of someone being in a state of (e.g. blissful) ignorance, but not in a state of knowing or of knowledge. It should now be clear why that is so. It is because being able to do something is a potentiality, not a state (no one speaks of being in a state of being able to). But to lack the ability to do something, and equally to be unable to do something, *may well be* a state of a thing, animal or person. One may be in a state of paralysis (mental or physical) – when one cannot move. One may be in a state of confusion – when one does not know what to do or think. And one may be in a state of ignorance with respect to some piece of information that one should or might be expected to have. One's state of ignorance will persist – until one learns, is told or taught how things are. But one does not then make a transition from a state of ignorance to a state of knowledge, any more than when one terminates one's dithering by making up one's mind, one makes a transition from a state of indecision to a state of decision – for there is no such thing as a state of decision. So the fact that ignorance can be a state (though not a mental one), is perfectly compatible with the fact that knowledge is not a state.

[41] This modifies what I wrote in *Human Nature: the Categorial Framework*, p. 109, where I suggested that knowledge is an ability even though not rigidly tied to any single act-category. That qualification now seems to me too weak.

[42] Wittgenstein, *Philosophical Investigations* [1953], 4th edn (Wiley-Blackwell, Oxford, 2009), §150.

Links between knowing and being able to The rationale for dissociating knowing something to be so from the category of mental state, and of locating it in the domain of potentialities rather than actualities has become clear. Although it is incorrect to character-ize knowing something to be so as an ability without more ado, it is correct to link it with being able to do a variety of things. A non-language-using animal can modify its behaviour and change its goals in virtue of what it knows, even though it cannot reason from what it knows or cite what it knows as a justifying or explanatory reason.[43] Human beings can transmit what they know to others, inform them how things are, advise them what to do, think or feel in the light of the information they have. They can also turn to their fellow men to find out how things are, to find out who can tell them how things are and to find out who needs to be told how things are. They can explain or justify their thoughts, feelings and deeds by reference to their knowledge of how things are. And they can predict, explain, justify and criticize the deeds of others by reference to the information the others are known to possess or to lack.

8. Knowing-how

The Concept of Mind emphasized the irreducibly practical nature of some fundamental, as well as some sophisticated, forms of knowing how to do things. Ryle remonstrated against the over-intellectualizing of human cognitive powers, reminding us that there is more to intel-ligence than intellect. Knowing-how, he held, is an autonomous form of knowledge. As he put it, 'intelligent behaviour is not piloted by the intellectual grasp of true propositions'.[44]

Similarities between knowing-how and knowing-that Knowing how to do something and knowing that things are so share common features. One can learn how to do something as well as learning that things are so. One can find out how to do some-thing, as one can find out whether things are so. One may wonder *how* as well as wondering *whether*. One can forget *how* as well as forgetting *that*, and one can be reminded how to do something as one can be reminded that things are so. Similarly, one can ask whether

---

[43] See *Human Nature: the Categorial Framework*, ch. 7.

[44] Ryle, *The Concept of Mind*, p. 26.

someone knows *how* to do something just as one can ask whether he knows *that* or *whether* things are so. Nevertheless, Ryle insisted, knowing-how is not merely another form of knowing-that. Moreover, he claimed, 'knowledge-how cannot be defined in terms of knowing-that', and 'knowing-how is not reducible to any sandwich of knowing-that'.[45]

For this he was criticized.[46] It was argued that to know how to do something is to know the way to do it. To know the way to do something subsumes both knowing *the manner* in which to perform a task and knowing *the means* and *method* by which to succeed. To know these, like knowing *why, when, who, which*, etc. is to know *that*. It is to know that it is done *so* – which may be demonstrated or described. The prominence of demonstration in the analysis of knowing-how was emphasized in the claim that to know how to V is to know, of some way *w* of V-ing, that *this way* is a way to do it. On both analyses, knowing how to do something is no more than a form of knowing-that – and practical knowledge is not a special kind of knowledge, but only knowledge of a special kind of thing. But it is far from obvious that all skills can be represented in the form of *knowledge-that*. We must be careful not to conflate knowing how something is done with knowing how to do it.

Being able to, having an ability to and knowing how to

A first step towards clarity is to disentangle the concepts of *being able to, having an ability to* and *knowing-how to*.[47] To be able to do something does not imply having the ability to do it, and having the ability to do something does not imply knowing how to do it. Conversely, one may know how to do something, but lack the ability to do it, just as one may have the ability to do something, but be unable to do it (one may not have an opportunity, or an instrument, or one may be prevented, or one may just fail despite one's best efforts on the occasion).

---

[45] Ryle, 'Knowing How and Knowing That' (1946), repr. in *Collected Papers*, vol. 2 (Hutchinson, London, 1971), pp. 213, 224. See also *The Concept of Mind*, p. 32. For a spirited defence of Ryle and Aristotle, see David Wiggins, 'Practical Knowledge: Knowing How and Knowing That', *Mind*, 121 (2012), pp. 97–130, to which I am indebted.

[46] First by White, *The Nature of Knowledge*, pp. 14–29, later by J. Stanley and T. Williamson, 'Knowing How', *Journal of Philosophy*, 98 (2001), pp. 411–44.

[47] For elaboration of the concept of human powers, see *Human Nature: the Categorial Framework*, ch. 4, section 7.

Being able to without an ability   A beginner may hit the bull's-eye with his first shot. He was able to hit the bull the first time he tried (he succeeded in hitting it), but could not do so again. It was a fluke, and he lacks the marksman's ability. (We distinguish the 'can' of success from the 'can' of ability.) Abilities are inherently general. Having the generic ability to V is compatible with occasional failure. In such cases, one may say: 'I couldn't do it' (I failed). But one may equally say: 'I could have done it' (I have the ability). If one has the ability to V, then when one sets oneself to V in favourable circumstances, one *normally* succeeds.

Having an ability to without knowing how to   One may have the ability to do things with regard to which there can be no question of knowing *how* to do them. A normal human being has the ability to blink, breathe, move his limbs – but cannot be said to know how to do such things. Those with sharp senses have the ability to see distant things, hear faint noises, smell the faintest whiff of a scent; others can fall asleep at will, or go without sleep for twenty-four hours at a stretch – but no knowledge and so no knowing-how is involved. Such abilities may be innate or acquired, but if acquired, then through application (one learns *in* and *by* trying). So one may learn to sleep in the saddle, or to hold one's drink. Such abilities may be improved, not by acquiring information but by practice. One may lose the ability to see or to walk, to fall asleep immediately or to hold one's drink – but one cannot *forget* how to see or walk, to sleep at will or to hold one's drink.

Learning how to and knowing how to; skills and mastery of techniques   By and large, one can be said to *know how to V* only where there are means and methods of V-ing.[48] Here to learn how to V is a matter of learning the way to V, and one's knowledge of how to V may improve over time and with practice. Where the means and methods are of sufficient complexity to amount to a technique or techniques, the ability is a skill. To possess a skill is to have mastered a technique. Mastery of a technique is not *reducible* to knowledge of a set of instructions and precepts, even though it involves knowledge of maxims, principles and precepts, and the

---

[48] 'By and large', since the boundary lines are blurred. One may say indifferently 'He can hold his drink' and 'He knows how to hold his drink' – even though there are no means, methods and techniques of holding one's drink. Similarly, one may say 'Jerry knew how to mimic Isaiah Berlin to perfection', even though there are no rules for such mimicry. But if one wants a clear boundary line, this is where to draw it.

'mysteries' of a craft involve extensive knowledge of materials and procedures. To know the rules and principles of a practice is not the same as knowing how to engage in the practice.

Knowing how to without the ability to

Nevertheless, knowing how to do something does not always imply being able to do it, or having the ability to do it. Having learnt how to do something, having mastered a certain technique for doing something, one may – *in certain kinds of case* – cease to be able to do what one thus learnt to do, even though one still knows how to do it. The aged tennis coach may no longer have the ability to play, because of rheumatism or lack of strength. But that does not mean that he no longer knows how to play. He may still be an excellent instructor, even though he cannot play himself. Similarly, in cases where *no* skill is involved, someone may know perfectly well how to do something (e.g. to lose weight), know the method of doing it (to eat less and to take more exercise), but be unable to do so through lack of will-power.

The relationship between knowing-how and knowing-that

What then is the relationship between knowing-how and knowing-that? Ryle was mistaken to claim that knowing how to do something is *never* paraphrastically reducible to knowing-that. It often is. To know how to spell 'queen' is to know that it is spelled 'q-u-e-e-n'; to know how to address the Queen is to know that she is to be addressed as 'Ma'am'; to know how to pronounce 'C-h-o-l-m-o-n-d-e-l-e-y' is to know that it is pronounced 'Chumley'. On the other hand, his critics were mistaken to suppose that to know how to do something is *always* reducible to knowing that it is done *so*, or to knowing of some way that it is a way to do it. To know that *that* (pointing at someone in the swimming pool) is the way to swim is not to know how to swim at all. To know how to win battles is neither knowledge that can be *explained* demonstratively, nor is it knowledge possession of which is proven by pointing at another's successful exemplification of such military prowess. Reading Liddell-Hart's books on strategy may teach one the principles of warfare, but it does not follow that one will know how to win battles. Knowledge of the principles of warfare is unlike knowledge of an instruction book for assembling a mechanical device or for using an electronic gadget. Such knowledge will not enable one to go on and do it. One may know how baseball is played but not know how to play it, as one may know how battles are won, but not know how to win them. One may know the theory of the practice without knowing how to engage in the practice.

Reducible and   So some kinds of know-how can be spelled out in a
irreducible cases description or a straightforward set of instructions,
               such that grasping the description and instructions
suffices for knowing how to execute the task. Here one may say
that knowing-how is reducible to, or is equivalent to, knowing-that.
Other kinds of know-how are not, either (i) because there *are* no
maxims and principles to speak of, or (ii) because, although there
are, teaching them is not adequate to impart knowledge of how to
execute the task. Knowing how to ride a bicycle approximates (i),
knowing how to fly an aeroplane is of kind (ii). Ryle was right to
insist that finding out how to do many things, discovering new ways
and means of doing things, and learning to do many kinds of thing
are not, or not only, a matter of finding out, discovering or learning
facts. There is much that we unavoidably learn to do by doing and
by trying (swimming, riding a bicycle) – not by learning rules
or maxims. There is much that we learn *how to do* by learning *to
do*. Information is doubtless crucial, but so too are experience and
practice. There are many sophisticated skills knowledge of which
cannot possibly be transmitted *merely* by instructions – but only
acquired through experience and practice. To know the theory of a
practice is not necessarily to know how to put the theory into practice successfully.

Demonstrating how   There are some kinds of know-how that cannot
to and learning how be captured by an array of instructions, recipes
to by doing   and maxims, but have to be pedagogically dem-
               onstrated. That is why master-classes are so
helpful for acquiring the mysteries of an art. But one must not
confuse demonstration with exemplification, even though demonstrating a technique does involve exemplifying it. Rachmaninov's
performances (unlike his master-classes) did not show how to play.
Watching Picasso painting shows one how *he* does it, but one will
not have learnt how *to do* it – although one may pick up some
clues. Furthermore, there are many highly skilful activities (the arts
of politics, or of war) that *cannot* be ostensively demonstrated but
only exemplified, and hence can be learnt only from a combination
of knowledge of principles, observation of masters at work, practice
and experience.

Practical knowledge is not in general reducible to knowledge of
facts, maxims and principles. Knowing-*how* is not in general reducible to knowing-*that*. Both kinds of knowledge are indispensable for
all human forms of life and are woven into their woof and weft.

9. What is knowledge? The role of 'know' in human discourse

Traditional attempts to *analyse* the concept of knowledge failed; and we have replaced traditional *decompositional analysis* by systematic *connective analysis*. This proves far more illuminating. We can shed further light on the nature of knowledge by asking a new question: Why do we need this expression? What would we lack if we had no such word? What needs does it fulfil?[49]

Its negation can be used to signify inability to answer a question

We are eyes and ears to each other, and information which one person lacks may be available to others. So we ask others whether such-and-such is the case, hoping that they will be able to tell us. Our questions take various forms. We may use a sentence-question: 'Is it the case that . . . ?' – and our respondent may reply 'Yes' or 'No'. Or we may use a Wh-question: 'Where is X?', 'Who is NN?', 'When is *e*?', etc., and our respondent may tell us. These exchanges do not call for the verb 'to know'. It is *not* the role of the assertion 'I know that things are so' to supply the information that things are so – that is a role of an assertion of the declarative sentence *simpliciter*. But in many cases, the person we ask may not be able to answer the question – and, to make his position clear, he will naturally reply 'I don't know'.[50] So one core use of 'know', together with negation, is to indicate that one cannot answer a certain question – that one lacks the relevant information. It is used, typically in ellipsis, as an operator on a Wh-nominalization. In the same kinds of context, one may use the expression 'As far as I know' or 'To the best of my knowledge' to qualify the blunt assertion (knowledge-claim) that things are so. Like some uses of 'I think' and 'I believe', this serves to indicate that the grounds for asserting that things are so are less than optimal, and not beyond dispute.

Interrogative use to ask for credentials

A person may assert that things are so (no matter whether in answer to a question or not). The assertion may be surprising and unexpected, or it may conflict or

[49] It was Oswald Hanfling, in *Philosophy and Ordinary Language* (Routledge, London, 2000), ch. 6, who pioneered this route.

[50] Of course, he could also say 'I can't tell you', but the reason for not being able to tell someone something may be that the information is to be kept secret. 'I don't know' is more specific than 'I can't tell you'.

seem to conflict with what we ourselves have observed or been told. So we may doubt his word and question his credentials. Alternatively, we may not doubt his word (perhaps we are already aware of how things are), but may wonder how he could be in the position to assert what he averred. For it may be that the speaker could not or should not have been in a position to assert that things are so (e.g. if it was supposed to be kept secret from him). Epistemic operators have a role in these kinds of case. For we should naturally ask 'How do you know?' or 'Why do you believe that?'. 'How do you know?' may be a request for general credentials, that is, enquiring how the agent is able to judge of such things. Or it may be asking more specifically how the agent was in a position to assert that things are so – which might be answered by, for example, 'I saw it', or by explaining that he gained the information by inference from such-and-such evidence, or obtained it from testimony, or on the authority of an expert. Alternatively, the question may be a request for evidence in support of the assertion that things are so, which may take different forms, for example, 'How can you tell?' or 'What are the grounds for this claim?' The kinds of answer to the latter questions merge with responses to the question 'Why do you believe that?', which can be a challenge to the addressee's credulity and is a request for reasons. If the answer is in one way or another inadequate, then the questioner may be in a position to reply 'So you don't know', thus denying the reliability of the informant or of the information offered, either because the informant was not in a position to make an unqualified claim or because his supporting grounds are inadequate to the case at hand.

To find out who can tell one, or whether someone is informed Often, wondering how things are, we must find out whom to ask. Here too there is an obvious role for the word 'know'. For we may ask 'Do you know *whether* things are so?' or 'Does he know what (when, who, etc.) . . . ?' or just 'Who knows whether things are so?'. Here the verb 'know' is used to enquire who can tell us. Sometimes we may already possess the information in question, yet we may ask 'Does he know *that* things are so?' (which here presupposes that we know that they are), not in order to obtain the information, but in order to find out whether we need to tell him. So too, we may start telling someone something, and he may stop us by saying 'I already know', that is, there is no need to tell him. Differently, someone who is seeking information may preface his question with an 'I know that things are so, but . . .', in order to narrow down the range of information needed, as when one says 'I know that the next London train is at 12.30, but could you tell me from which platform it leaves?' Furthermore, there are other circumstances, for example of examinations, in which the question 'Does he know?' arises, even though we ourselves possess the requisite information. Here we want to find out whether a student, who ought to be similarly informed, can or cannot answer the relevant question. Here (and in some other contexts too) there is an obvious use for the response 'I think I know' or 'I believe I know' to express uncertainty as to whether one has got things right, remembered correctly what one was taught, worked out the answer correctly, etc. 'I think I know' here is tantamount to 'If I am right, then I know, although I may not be'.

To ward off objections; to indicate possession of information

There are other contexts that call for the use of this epistemic operator, for example to ward off an objection, as in 'I know that things are so, but nevertheless I am going to V'. The role of 'I know' is not to impart the information that things are so, but to make it clear that the speaker has already taken it into account or dismissed it. Differently, 'I know that things are so' has a role not to supply the addressee with the information that things are so, but to tell him that the speaker is in possession of it, information that functions as a background or condition for some further move in the language-game – as when one says 'I know that you told A about the matter, but I wish you had asked me before you did so'. Yet another familiar role for 'I know' is where there is a need to forestall or repress doubt, either for oneself or for another, as when one explains, while rummaging in a drawer, 'I know I put it here'.

Explaining, justifying and predicting

Since rational creatures act on, and reason from, information they possess, there are three further important roles the verb 'to know' and its negation fulfil, namely *explaining, justifying* (or *excusing*) one's own or others' behaviour and reactions, and *predicting* the behaviour and reactions of others. We may enquire whether another knows (or knew) that things are so (which defeasibly presupposes that we do) or whether he knows or knew whether things are so (which does not), in order to be able to understand, justify or excuse, or to predict his reasonings, his responses, actions and omissions. For if the information that things are so is available to him, then, given the context of his projects, it is plausible to suppose that he has reasoned or will reason thus, has or had reason for reacting so. Conversely, if he does *not* know, then certain courses of action and certain kinds of response to the situation will seem unreasonable to him. Given his plans and projects, that he knows (or does not know) that things are so will often render his responses and actions relatively predictable, and *ex post actu* intelligible, not on causal, but on rational grounds. For if a person possesses the information that things are so, then it is possible for him to take it into account in his reasoning and in his action. Similarly, 'I didn't know' or 'He didn't know' is often an excuse or explanation of an omission or impropriety. List 4.6 gives one an overview of some of the roles and functions of the verb 'to know'.

- To indicate inability to answer a question: 'I don't know.'
- To qualify an answer: 'As far as I know.'
- To ask for the source or grounds of another's information: 'How do you know?'
- To find out whom to ask: 'Who knows wh . . . ?', 'Do you know wh . . . ?', 'Does he know wh . . . ?'
- To find out whether another needs to be told or already has the information: 'Do you (Does he) know . . . ?'
- To indicate the redundancy of being told: 'I already know . . .'.
- To indicate that one has taken information into account: 'I know that . . . , so (or, 'but nevertheless . . .).'
- To forestall doubt: 'I know I left it here.'
- To explain and predict: 'He knew that . . . , so he . . .', 'He does not know . . . , so he won't . . .'.
- To justify or excuse: 'I V-ed because I knew . . .', 'He didn't know . . . , so he . . .'.

List 4.6   *Ten uses of 'to know' as an instrument*

General conclusions   From this schematic survey some general conclusions can be drawn. First, in accounting for the use of the phrase 'to know that' (and its various equivalent transforms), primacy should be given to the notion of possession of information, to being able (or unable) to say or tell how things are. Secondly, a large part of the rationale for the concept of knowledge turns on the fact that information is shareable and commonly shared, that most of our stock of knowledge is learnt not from personal experience but from others. Hence a large part of the point and purpose of the verb 'to know' and its cognates lies in the quest for information and sources of information. Thirdly, given the multiplicity of roles of this cognitive verb, and the variety of contexts in which it is called upon to fulfil one or another of its functions, it becomes obvious that what is presupposed by its use, and what is demanded of its user, will vary greatly from context to context, content to content, speaker to speaker and questioner to respondent. The evidential demands of the law courts, on the one hand, and of the scientific community, on the other, are quite different from the demands on answers to requests for humdrum information that is part of the stock of common cultural knowledge (e.g. 'Do you know the date of the battle of Waterloo?', 'Who was the inventor of the computer?', 'Is nitrogen heavier that oxygen?'), on the one hand, and for passing on information (e.g. 'Does Jack know he has got the job?', 'When is the next train to London?', 'What is that fellow's name?'), on the other. So too the requirements that have to be satisfied for someone rightly to be said to know vary further according to the information already possessed, and reciprocally known to be possessed, by speaker and hearer. Fourthly, given that we are rational creatures capable of acting for reasons, it is obvious that what another knows has a pivotal role in predicting, explaining and justifying his action, and what we know has an equally pivotal role in our plans and projects, and in explaining and justifying our behaviour. This too provides a shifting scale for the warranted application of the concept. For often the only relevant factor in making predictions and giving explanations is that the person whose behaviour is being predicted or explained has the right answer, and not whether he has the right warrant or justification.

It is noteworthy that the connection between knowledge and belief seems surprisingly slender. Far from knowledge looking like belief 'plus something', belief seems to be knowledge 'minus something'. We shall pursue this matter further in the next chapter.

5

Belief

1. The web of belief

The weave of belief   Rationality is bound up with reasoning. If one is rational, one is able to reason from premises one takes to be true to conclusions well supported by such premises, and to justify one's deeds by reference to (what one takes to be) the facts of the case that provide one with reasons for acting. In the absence of omniscience, some of the premises rational creatures reason *from* are bound to be false. In the absence of incorrigibility, some of the conclusions rational creatures reason *to* are bound to be mistaken. Often the available evidence makes it reasonable to believe that things are so, but does not warrant a knowledge claim. One may reason from what one knows to be so or from what one merely believes to be so, and one may know or merely believe the conclusions one derives. It is reasonable to believe what is adequately, even though not conclusively, supported by reasons, and it is reasonable to withhold belief from something one knows lacks adequate support. So the concept of belief is interwoven with the concepts of rationality, reasonableness and grounds of judgement.[1]

Belief is the default when knowledge fails   Belief is equally interwoven with the concept of knowledge. As we saw in the last chapter, many philosophers have argued that knowledge entails belief.

---

[1] For a discussion of rationality and reasonableness, see *Human Nature: the Categorial Framework*, ch. 7, section 1.

The Intellectual Powers: A Study of Human Nature, First Edition. P. M. S. Hacker.
© 2013 John Wiley & Sons, Ltd. Published 2013 by John Wiley & Sons, Ltd.

It has been held that to know something to be so is to believe truly, and to be certain that what one believes is so. An alternative view is that it is to believe truly, and to be justified in believing what one believes. Others, however, have argued that knowing is neither a form of, nor a function of, believing. This much, however, is clear: someone who takes himself to know that things are so when they are not, does not know, but only believes things to be so. So even if knowledge is not 'belief plus something', belief is the default position when knowledge claims fail. Moreover, one may believe that one knows, but be wrong – as when one mistakenly believes one has the right answer. And one may know without believing that one knows – as students sitting examinations often do. One may not know what one believes, but, as we noted in chapter 2, this is quite different from not knowing what another believes. The latter is a case of ignorance; the former is a matter of not knowing *what to* believe. The relationship between knowing and believing requires systematic scrutiny. We shall defer this until the next chapter.

Belief is directed at how things are

Our empirical beliefs are generally measured against the world and found adequate or wanting. If things are as one believes them to be, then one's belief can be said to be right or correct. If things are not as one believes them to be, then one's belief is wrong or incorrect. Belief is above all 'directed' at reality – at how things are in the world, and only secondarily at the truth of propositions.[2] *What* one believes is: *that things are so*. One's belief is correct if things are as they are believed to be. Being correct (right) or incorrect (wrong, mistaken) are the primary 'values' of believing something, as being true or false are the primary 'values' of propositions, statements, assertions, declarations, confessions, allegations, rumours, histories and tales. But, of course, beliefs too may be true or false – of which more anon.

---

[2] Cp. B. O. A. Williams: 'beliefs aim at truth . . . Truth and falsehood are a dimension of an assessment of belief as opposed to many other psychological states or dispositions . . . to believe that *p* is to believe that it is true that *p*' ('Deciding to Believe', repr. in *Problems of the Self* (Cambridge University Press, Cambridge, 1973), pp. 136f). This is mistaken. First, it is the expression of belief (namely, that things are so) that may be true or false, not the object of belief – unless what one believes is a proposition, statement, declaration, etc. (Similarly, what one sees is often reported by a proposition, but what one sees is not a proposition or the truth of a proposition.) Secondly, as we shall see, believing is not a psychological state, and psychological states are not true or false.

The virtues and vices of belief
Given that belief is bound up with rationality and reasonableness, and given the role of these in the optimal conduct of human life, belief is interwoven with a variety of intellectual and moral virtues and vices. Credulity and gullibility are intellectual vices of doxastic excess, the former involving an undue proneness to believe people and their stories, the latter a tendency to be taken in or fooled by the tales of others. Incredulity and scepticism are intellectual vices of doxastic deficiency – of reluctance to believe or an undue proneness to disbelieve. Superstition is the fault of wrongly believing in a causal nexus based on mere association (e.g. *post hoc, propter hoc*) or old wives' tales, or behaving as if one so believed (as when one walks around rather than under ladders even when one does not believe there to be any danger of something falling). Bigotry and dogmatism are the vices of closed minds. The bigot ascribes features allegedly characteristic of some members of a class to any member of the class. The dogmatist is unwilling to consider or reconsider countervailing evidence to his beliefs and opinions. Conversely, good judgement and open-mindedness are intellectual virtues – the former, among other things, providing a 'filter' for the latter (an open mind should not be like an open drain).

Etymology of 'believe'
Scrutiny of the etymology, the grammatical forms and the adverbial modifications of 'believe' will provide useful clues for further analysis. It is of interest to learn that 'believe' is a remote cousin of 'love'. Late Old English *belēfan* was derived from *gelēfan* which has been traced back to ancient West and North Germanic **galaubian* (the source of the German *glauben*). This meant 'to hold dear' or 'to love', and hence 'to trust in' and 'to believe'. It was formed on a base **laub*, meaning 'pleasure' or 'approval', from which *love* as well as *lief* (dear) are apparently derived. This ancestral connection is still evident in the patent nexus between belief and *trust*. For to believe a person is to trust his word, to take what he says on trust. If one takes a person's word for it, then one relies on what he affirms, depends upon it or counts upon the truth of his report. A number of the verbs related to belief are still at home in discourse concerning love. For we *hold* and *cleave to* our most *cherished* beliefs, and we *embrace*, *foster* or *nurture* new ideas.

Landmarks in the doxastic landscape
So: important proximate landmarks in the web of belief are *trust*, *dependency* and *reliance*. These are connected not only with believing a person and therefore trusting his word, but also with the notion of *faith*,

both in the sense of *religious belief* and in the sense of *believing in* a person, a political party or an ideal. The notions of trust, trusting *the word of another*, and taking *what another says* on trust provide pathways leading to the notion of believing something to be so. For much of the information we possess has been imparted to us by others, and we normally give credence to what they say and regard it as true. One may *gather* that things are so from what others say; one may *be given to understand* that things are so, be *persuaded* that they are; and one may *take it* from what has been said, that things are so. We also form our own beliefs, as a result of observation, scrutiny of evidence, inferences, guesses and hunches.

A group of related doxastic verbs and corresponding nouns nicely distinguishes differences here. We may *think* things to be so, or *feel* that they are so. We *opine* that they are so; it may *be our conviction* that they are; we may *judge* them to be so. And we may *take a stand* on their being so: *hold* or *maintain* that they are, and so on. A related range of verbs signify inclinations to believe: one may *suspect, presume, conjecture, surmise, fancy, guess*; one may have *a hunch, presentiment* or *impression* that things are so. Moving off in yet another direction that is related to, but falls short of, both believing and being inclined to believe, we have *assent* (for the sake of argument), *accept* (for the moment, or as an operative premise in reasoning), *acquiesce* and *go along with*. It is important to keep in mind this refined set of doxastic tools that is available to us (see fig. 5.1)

Modes of belief One may come to believe something for different kinds of reasons, and one's belief may be derived from different kinds of sources. We distinguish, by means of adverbs, the various *manners* in which one comes to believe what one believes, for example, *readily, hesitantly, reluctantly*. Since when one believes that things are thus-and-so, one has, holds or embraces a belief, idea or opinion, we similarly differentiate adverbially the various ways in which one may cleave to what one believes, for example, *whole-heartedly, passionately, firmly, fervently, unswervingly, obstinately, obtusely, fanatically, waveringly, tentatively*. Believing something, by and large, ought to be supported by adequate reasons. So we evaluate the reasonableness of believing adverbially, as when we speak of believing something *reasonably, sensibly, understandably, groundlessly* or *dogmatically*. What is believed is likewise evaluable in various dimensions, in particular truth and falsehood. So one may believe something *truly* or *falsely*. These two adverbs qualify what is believed rather than the believing of it (see pp. 204f.) But there is a

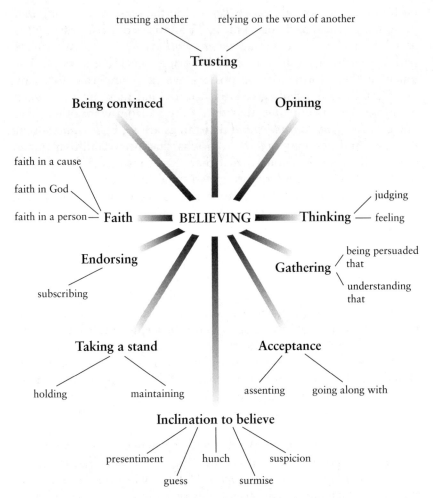

Figure 5.1 *The web of belief*

range of adverbs that qualify one's believing, which correspond to the dimensions of evaluation of what is believed, for example 'correctly', 'rightly' (if what one believes is true), and 'mistakenly', 'wrongly' (if what one believes is false). And since the various beliefs one has stand in logical relations to each other, this is reflected in adverbs of believing, for example 'logically' and 'consistently' (see fig. 5.2).

Degrees of belief Philosophers, psychologists, theologians and economists commonly speak of *degrees of belief*, differentiating a spectrum ranging from the total certainty of unshakeable conviction to the thinnest of suspicions. They have

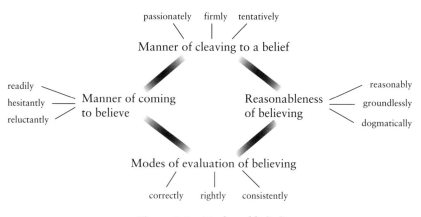

Figure 5.2 *Modes of belief*

associated degrees of belief with degrees of probability, on the one hand, and with degrees of feeling, on the other. But it is mistaken to suppose that to believe that something is possible, probable or certain is to enjoy different degrees of belief. To believe that it is possible that things are so is not to believe weakly that they are so, nor is it to have a lesser belief than if one believes it probable. If you believe that it is certain that My Love will win the 3.30 and I believe that it is only probable, you have more faith than I in the prowess of My Love, but you do not have *more belief* than I. Similarly, whereas one may feel sure, certain or convinced that things are so, one cannot *feel belief* that they are. While one may feel more convinced that things are so after further argument, one cannot *believe more* that things are so.

Degrees of conviction   What is true is that belief may vary in respects that do have degrees. A belief may be strong, firm, obstinate and passionate, or tentative, hesitant, wavering, half-hearted and faint. But these do not signify degrees of belief, but degrees of conviction, confidence or the tenacity with which one cleaves to a belief. It is also true that beliefs may be entrenched. But an entrenched belief is not *greater* than one that is not entrenched – only less readily surrendered. We shall investigate further below.

2. The grammatical groundwork

Before confronting the conceptual problems that concern us, we must demarcate the grammatical terrain. Table 5.1 lists grammatical forms on which 'A believes' can operate to form a sentence: Note that to believe things said or sayable is to believe them to be true; to believe people or institutions is to believe what they say, announce, declare, etc.; and to believe that what they say is true. This will be discussed below.

Bases on which 'A believes' operates	Results of the operation
sentences	'A believes things are so'
that-nominalizations	'A believes that things are so'
relative Wh-clauses	'A believes what he was told (read, heard)'
quantified Wh-clauses	'A believes whatever (everything, anything) the Pope says'
proper names signifying people	'A believes Jill'
associated quantified clauses	'A believes whoever last spoke to him'
definite descriptions signifying people or institutions	'A believes the author of *What is to be Done* (the government of the UK, the BBC)'
count-nouns signifying sayables	'A believes the statement (announcement, confession, allegation, declaration, as well as story told or rumour circulating)'[a]
propositions	'A believes the proposition that things are so'
count-nouns, signifying sense organs	'I believe//cannot believe//my eyes (couldn't believe my ears)'

[a] These must exist if they are to be believed – they must have been made, told, circulated and so forth.

Table 5.1 *Grammatical bases for the sentence-forming operator 'A believes'*

The varieties of believing in

In addition to the verb 'believe', we have the phrase 'believes in', the significance of which differs, depending on its sequel. In 'to believe in fairies (ghosts, gods, God)', the preposition is followed by an intentional accusative. Such intentional object-accusatives are equivalent to nominalization-accusatives. To believe thus is to believe *that there are* fairies, *that* ghosts or gods *exist* or that God *exists*. The existence of what is believed in is not necessary for the truth of the belief-ascription. But 'believe in' has other uses too. It may signify having faith or trust in someone or something – which may be God or a friend, a nation or a party. To believe, that is have faith, in God is to put one's trust in God (and then one *presupposes* that God exists). To believe in one's party is not to believe that one's party exists or to trust one's party but to subscribe to its principles and to support it. When attached to an abstract noun, as in 'I believe in kindness (mercy, justice)', 'believe in' signifies neither belief in the existence of anything, nor faith or trust in anything, but rather a moral commitment. All these admit of negation, that is 'A does not believe . . .' or 'A does not believe in . . .'. Curiously, the alternative negation, 'A *disbelieves* . . .' takes only proper names, count-nouns prefixed by an article (e.g. 'the story'), and relative Wh-clauses as grammatical objects. One can disbelieve Jack and his story, but one cannot disbelieve that Jack loves Jill. Unlike 'to know', 'to believe' cannot take Wh-interrogatives (one cannot believe whether, who, when, where, which, why or how) or variants on them (one can know the height, weight and colour of something, but one cannot believe the height, weight or colour of the thing). That is why although you may know what I believe, it does not follow that what I believe is what you know (see chapter 4, p. 150).[3]

Belief qua what one has and qua what one believes

As observed in chapter 2, it is important not to conflate *the believing* with *what is believed* – both of which are denominated 'belief'. Many psychological verbs that occur in the form 'A V-s that *p*', for example, 'believes', 'thinks', 'assumes', 'fears', 'hopes', 'suspects', 'expects', yield corresponding nominals: 'belief', 'thought', 'assumption', 'fear', 'hope', 'suspicion', 'expectation'. These abstract count-nouns make it possible for us to refer concisely to the belief that A and B have in common, to the thought they both share, or to the assumption that they both make. The nominals can collect such

---

[3] The grammar of 'believing the proposition that *p*' has affinities with, as well as differences from, 'believing the rumour (declaration, statement) that *p*' and also 'believing that *p*', despite the fact that believing that *p* is distinct from believing the proposition that *p* (although the latter implies the former). For meticulous examination of this delicate matter, see B. Rundle, 'Objects and Attitudes', *Language and Communication*, 21 (2001), pp. 143–56, to which I am indebted.

predicates as 'typical', 'fervent', 'reasonable' or 'irrational' to characterize what A and B have. They make it possible to avoid needless circumlocution in speaking of possible beliefs or expectations, even though no one actually has them, and to talk of suspicions that have not been raised, but might be, or of assumptions that might be, or might have been, made. The nominals are a convenient grammatical construction, but they introduce no new 'entities' and involve no fresh 'ontological commitments' that are not already involved in speaking of a person's believing, thinking, assuming, expecting or suspecting that things are so. However, these advantages are bought at the price of ambiguity in the nominal 'V' ('belief', 'fear', 'suspicion', etc.) between *what one V-s* when one V-s that things are so and *what one has* when one V-s that things are so. This ambiguity corresponds to two different foci of interest with respect to someone's V-ing that things are so, namely what is believed (suspected, feared), and the believing (suspecting, fearing) of it.

Modes of believing and modes of what is believed

This ambiguity must be borne in mind. For we distinguish the modes of believing from the modes of what is believed. 'True', 'possible', 'probable' characterize *what* is believed. For it may be true, possible or probable *that things are so*. By contrast, 'fanatical', 'passionate', 'whole-hearted', 'fervent', 'firm', 'tentative', 'hesitant' characterize the manner in which one cleaves to one's belief when one passionately, firmly, tentatively, etc. believes that things are so. So too, 'wisely', 'reasonably', 'foolishly' characterize the believing rather than what is believed. For they describe the wisdom, reasonableness or folly of believing what one believes. For it is wise, reasonable or foolish *of* one to believe what one believes. The adverb 'truly', however, is deceptive, for although we say of someone that he believes truly that things are so, what is true is not his believing, but what he believes. Unless one is aware of this, one may make the serious mistake of supposing that since believing is apparently something 'mental' (a mental state, for example), and that one can believe truly that things are so, therefore some mental states have the property of being true (or false). One may then be tempted to aver: 'Much of the point of the concept of belief is that it is the concept of a state of an organism which can be true or false, correct or incorrect.'[4] But what can be true or false is what can

---

[4] D. Davidson, 'Rational Animals', repr. in E. Lepore and B. P. McLaughlin (eds), *Actions and Events: Perspectives on the Philosophy of Donald Davidson* (Blackwell, Oxford, 1985), p. 479. See also Williams, 'Deciding to Believe'.

be advanced, asserted, stated, claimed, supposed or conjectured, that is, nothing mental or neural, in particular not a mental state or state of an organism.[5]

Belief is individuated by its content   Belief is *essentially individuated* by its content, that is by its nominalization-accusative. It is *externally individuated* by circumstances of the believing (the belief acquired on such-and-such an occasion, imparted by such a person, shared with so-and-so, etc.). It is *internally related* to what makes it true. This, as explained in chapter 2, is the shadow of a grammatical relation, not a meta-logical relation between words and world. For the belief that *p* just *is* the belief that is made true by the fact that *p* – these are simply two different ways of referring to one and the same belief. As we saw in chapter 2, the question 'What is it that one believes when one believes that *things are so?*' is misleading. One may answer that one does not believe any *thing*. But one may equally reply that one may believe all sorts of things – that Jack loves Jill, that oxygen is heavier that water, that the battle of Hastings was fought in 1068, and so forth. As we have seen, the traditional answers to this misbegotten question are either altogether mistaken (we do not believe *sentences*) or misleading (we *can* believe propositions, but to believe that things are so is not the same as believing the proposition that things are so).

Believing something to be so and believing something to be true   One must be careful not to jump to the conclusion that believing something to be so is the same as believing something to be true.[6] What one believes when one believes that something is so is precisely *that things are so*. What one believes when one believes something to be true is *a proposition, statement, assertion, declaration, allegation or announcement to the effect that things are so*. For it is propositions, statements, assertions, declarations, allegations and announcements that are true or false. These can be believed or disbelieved. But what is believed when it is believed that things are so is not what is believed when the statement, assertion, allegation or proposition that things are so is believed to be true. While one can disbelieve, misunderstand or mistrust the statement, declaration or allegation that things are so, one cannot disbelieve, misunderstand

---

[5] B. Rundle, *Mind in Action* (Clarendon Press, Oxford, 1997), p. 40.

[6] Cp. Williams: 'To believe that so-and-so is one and the same as to believe that that thing is true' ('Deciding to Believe', p. 137).

or mistrust that things are so. Belief is first and foremost *directed at what is so*, and only secondarily at what is true (i.e. at a proposition asserted, a statement, assertion or declaration made in saying that things are so). What is so is what is the case. What is true is the statement, assertion, declaration, etc. made in stating, asserting or declaring that such-and-such is the case. 'Is that true?' is a query about a statement; 'Is that so?' is a question about how things are. 'That is so', like 'That is already the case' or 'That is indeed a fact', confirms that things are so. 'That is true' confirms the statement that things are so. Similarly, 'I fear (suspect, hope, expect) that things are so' does not mean the same as 'I fear (suspect, hope, expect) that it is true that things are so'. The latter is appropriate only if it has been (or is envisaged as being) stated or mooted that things are so, and consequently alludes to how things have been (or might be) *said* to be.

Believing that it is true that . . .
It might be objected that one can believe that it is true that things are so no less than one can believe that things are so. So what one believes is indeed what is true (or false). Hence one's belief, when one believes that things are so, is directed at what is true no less than at what is so. But this is mistaken. To be sure, what one believes may be true or false, for if one believes that things are so and they are, then one's belief is true, and if it is not the case that things are so, then one's belief is false. But it does not follow that to believe that things are so is the same as to believe that it is true that things are so. What A believes when he believes that *p* is *that p*, but what he believes when he believes that it is true that *p* is not *that p* but *that q*, namely *that it is true that p*, just as what he believes when he believes that it is false that *p* is not *that p* but *that r*, namely *that it is false that p*.[7] 'I believe that *p*' is not used in the same way or circumstances as 'I believe that it is true that *p*', although, to be sure, the latter implies the former.

'That is true'
If someone utters the sentence 'It is raining' thereby making an assertion, one may respond: 'True; it is raining' or 'That is true; it is (indeed) raining', thereby reaffirming his assertion. 'It is true that it is raining' can be viewed as a variant upon these. It is noteworthy that this form of words can also be used

[7] See A. R. White, 'What We Believe', in N. Rescher (ed.), *Studies in the Philosophy of Mind*, APQ Monograph series no. 6 (Blackwell, Oxford, 1972), p. 75.

even when no one has actually asserted that it is raining, but the possibility of such an assertion is being envisaged. The form of words 'It is true that . . .' is an affirmation or concession which may be, and often is, employed as a prefix to a denial or qualification of consequences which might otherwise be drawn from the actual or possible assertion – as when one says 'It is true that things are so, but nevertheless . . .'. Of course, we also have the response 'That is so; it is indeed raining', which can be contrasted with 'That is true; it is indeed raining'. In the latter case, we focus upon what is said *qua* asserted, affirming the statement made. In the former case, we focus upon *what* is said to be so, upon *how* things have been said to be. So we can indeed say 'What A believes is true' by way of confirming the content of A's belief, conceived as assertable, as something that A may advance. But, again, we may shift the focus of our concern in saying 'What A believes is so', or 'What A believes is a fact' – signifying not that a fact (like a rumour) is what A believes, but rather by way of affirming that it is indeed a fact that things are so, that this is indeed how things are.

3. The surrounding landscape

'I believe', 'I think' and 'As far as I know' as qualifiers on assertions

The concept of believing borders on the concept of thinking something to be so. Both (English) verbs, in the first-person present tense, can fulfil the role of qualifying or modifying the strength of an assertion. If one recognizes that things may not be as one takes them to be, if one realizes that one is not in a position to refute the denial of what one says or is about to say, then it is proper to prefix to, or interpolate in, the assertion one makes, an 'I think'. 'I believe' can do the same service. Like 'as far as I know', and 'to the best of my knowledge', they indicate that one cannot give the addressee one's word for it. They signify the epistemic weight one assigns to the sequel, in particular indicating that it falls short of knowledge. This will be elaborated below.

It is easy to see why this function of 'I believe' and 'I think' should evolve into a different but familiar one. For both are used not only to qualify an assertion, but to soften the bluntness of an assertion for the sake of courtesy, as in 'I believe // think // these are your gloves' said to a lady who has dropped them, or 'I believe // think // that you may be exaggerating' said in a courteous argumentative exchange.

Differences between believing and thinking; believing and gathering   However, believing and thinking converge only over a short stretch. We can ask what someone is thinking, but not what he is believing. We can believe people and their statements, but cannot think people and their statements. One can think quickly or slowly, but one cannot believe quickly or slowly, and one can be interrupted in the middle of thinking, but not in the middle of believing. One can be sunk in thought, but not sunk in belief, and to be unable to believe something is not to be unable to think something. A further subtle difference already noted is that in some contexts 'I believe' is indicative of second-hand information, and hence converges on 'I gather'. By contrast, 'I think', in such contexts, is an expression of one's own judgement.[8] Note that here the qualifying role of 'believe' and 'think' is absent. One cannot say 'I believe (gather) your roses are spectacular this year, but I may be wrong', let alone 'I think you look beautiful, but I may be mistaken'.

Believing and opining   'Believe' (like 'think') shares a common boundary with 'opine'. The questions 'What do you think?' and 'What do you believe?' are closely related – and in such contexts, 'believe' does not mean 'gather'. 'Think' and 'believe' have a role in the expression of moral commitment, in those aesthetic judgements that are essentially contested, in the expression of opinion and in commenting on things that are by their nature matters of opinion. Hence their prominent role in predictions, in judgements about what policies should be adopted and about what one ought to do, and in giving advice. Again, this nexus is readily intelligible given the role of 'I believe' in qualifying a judgement. For opining falls short of knowing.

Belief, doubt and certainty   A quite different array of doxastic phenomena comes into view when we turn our attention in a different direction. The concept of belief is entwined with the concepts of certainty and doubt. Many of our beliefs are supported by reasons. The reasons one has for believing whatever one believes may make one certain that things are as one believes them to be. One may believe with certainty, or believe without being certain. But one cannot both believe things to be so and also at the same time doubt

---

[8] Cp. Rundle's example: 'I believe your roses are wonderful this year' – that is what I have been told, as opposed to 'I think your roses are wonderful this year' – I have just been looking at them.

or be *uncertain* whether they are. ('He believes that the next train is at 12.45, but he is not certain // sure' is in order. 'He believes that the next train is at 12.30, but he doubts // is uncertain // whether it is' is not.) The fact that one is *not* certain does not imply that one is *uncertain*. One may not have reasons that make one certain that things are as one believes them to be, but it does not follow that one therefore has reasons for doubting. To say that one believes that things are so is, among other things, to imply that not all doubt can rationally be excluded, *even though one has no doubts*. If one has doubts as to whether things are thus, then one does *not* believe them to be thus, although one may be *inclined* to believe, suspect or guess that they are or one may believe that things are *probably* thus. Knowledge, by contrast, is compatible with doubt (as is evident from successful examinees, who may have doubted whether they had got things right). It is *a claim to know* that is not compatible with acknowledgement of undefeated reasons for doubting (see chapter 4 above). Both believing and averring one's belief are compatible with acknowledging the *possibility* that things may not be so, but they are not compatible with doubting whether things are so.

Belief, subjective certainty, feeling convinced and feeling doubtful

Subjective certainty and conviction are closely associated with belief. To be certain and convinced that something is so is to place one's trust in its being so, and hence implies a willingness to rely on, or depend on, its being so. Being and feeling certain, as we have seen, admit of degrees. So one can believe something with complete certainty, with reasonable certainty, or one may believe without any kind of certainty. One may be convinced by someone, by what someone says, by something one perceived or experienced or by evidence one has. Although there is no such thing as feeling belief, one may feel convinced, sure, certain or doubtful. To feel convinced, sure or certain that things are so implies believing that they are. To feel doubtful whether something is so is to be *inclined* to believe that it is *not* so. That is why believing that things are so is compatible with absence of certainty, but not with presence of doubt.

Belief, expectation and surprise

Belief also infringes upon the boundaries of expectation and surprise. One can expect something only if one knows or believes it to be probable or certain, but not if one believes it to be improbable or impossible. Although one cannot feel belief, one *can* feel expectant, and one may excitedly, fearfully or hopefully expect that such-and-such will happen. So one can be in a state of excited expectation, but cannot be in a state of excited belief. So too, one may have been expecting, but not have been believing, all week that so-and-so would telephone one. Surprise admits of degrees and one may be very surprised or only a little surprised at what happened. One is surprised at those things one did not expect to be so or to happen, at things one thought to be improbable or even impossible. So 'I should be surprised if things were not so' implies that one believes or is inclined to believe that things are so. Surprise, like certainty, conviction, doubt and expectation, can be felt.

Belief and suspicion
Suspicion, contrary to what H. H. Price averred, is neither a weak belief nor a low degree of belief.[9] As we have seen, belief does not come in degrees. Nor can one's belief that things are so increase in amount. It is one's conviction or confidence that may wax or wane. Like confidence, suspicion may be strong or weak, may grow or diminish. It is not believing, but *an inclination to believe*. The strongest suspicion is still only an inclination to believe. Suspicion is felt (one may feel suspicious), whereas belief is not (one cannot feel doxastic or credal). What makes one suspect that things are so are whatever reasons there are for feeling *inclined* to believe that things are so, for thinking not that things *are* so but that they *may* be so. Suspicions, like inclinations, but unlike beliefs, can be aroused or calmed. Like beliefs, suspicions can be right or wrong, reasonable or irrational, well founded or groundless. Suspecting things to be so is linked to behaviour, inasmuch as one who suspects things to be so will tend to behave, tentatively, like someone who believes things to be so. His behaviour will be informed by the thought that things may be so.

Belief and hope
To hope that things are so is not a form of belief. But one can hope that things are so only if one believes that it is possible or probable that they are, and if one believes that their being so is good. The greater one believes the possibility to be, the more confidently one will hope. One can 'hope against hope' even if one thinks that the chances are low. However, if one is certain, convinced or knows for certain that things are so, one cannot hope either that they are so, or hope that they are not so. For in order to be able to hope that things are so, there must be some degree of subjective uncertainty or doubt whether they are. That is why it is

---

[9] H. H. Price, Belief (Clarendon Press, Oxford, 1969), *passim*. For the contrary view, see A. R. White, *Misleading Cases* (Clarendon Press, Oxford, 1991), pp. 131ff.

possible to harbour hopes about the past and present only as long as one is not certain how things were or are.

Belief and fear
Fear is similarly interwoven with belief. Fearing that things are or will be so is not the same as believing that they are or will be. But it does involve believing that it is possible or probable that they are, as well as believing that things being so is bad or detrimental in some way. If one knows for certain that things are not or will not be so, then one cannot also fear that they are or will be. Like hope, fear can be directed towards the past and present no less than towards the future, only as long as one is not certain how things are or were. However, unlike hope, if things come to be as one feared they would, then although one can no longer fear *that* they will, one's fear that things will be so may well be transformed into fear *of* things being so. For one can fear, but not hope, people, objects and events. One may fear Jack, but not hope Jill, fear dogs, but not hope cats, as one may fear operations, but not hope parties. Hence, as Price nicely noted, fear *of* something, unlike hoping or fearing *that* something is so, is not abolished by certainty. Unpleasant certitudes may well be what one fears most of all.[10] (See table 5.2.)

Certainty	not necessary for, but compatible with believing
Subjective doubt	excluded by believing
Expectation	excludes believing what is expected to be impossible
Surprise	implies believing its object to be improbable or impossible
Suspicion	implies an inclination to believe
Hope	implies believing that what one hopes is possible or probable, but excludes believing it certain
Fear	excludes believing that what one fears is impossible

Table 5.2 *Compatibilities and incompatibilities*

So much for *some* of the conceptual environs of belief. We now turn to the vexing question of what belief is. Is it an act or activity, a mental state or disposition, or a dispositional state or a feeling? Is

[10] Price, *Belief*, p. 273.

believing something we do, or something that happens to us? Is it something that obtains, and that has an onset and ending? What is the categorial form of belief?

4. Voluntariness and responsibility for belief

Is believing a mental act? Descartes held that to believe (affirm or deny) is an *act of will*: 'I assigned the act of judging itself, which consists simply in assenting (i.e. in affirmation or denial), to the determination of the will rather than to the perception of the intellect.'[11] Save in the case of clear and distinct perception (apprehension), Descartes held, one is at liberty to withhold assent. So believing, in his view, is something for which we can, and should, be held responsible, for it is within our power to believe or to refuse to believe. – We must grant that there are affinities between believing something to be so or believing a person and his story, on the one hand, and doing something, on the other. These affinities encourage the idea that believing something is a mental act, that it is voluntary and therefore something for which one may be held responsible. But this is too quick.

5 reasons for thinking that belief is an act Certainly, we can ask a person to believe someone or his story, as we can ask someone to do something.[12] We can urge him to believe something and warn him not to believe someone. While we cannot ask a person to want, mean or intend something, since wanting, meaning and intending are not actions, we can and do say 'Believe me!', 'Please believe my story!'. Indeed, we occasionally order someone 'Don't believe him – he is an inveterate liar' or 'Don't trust a word she says!'.

Secondly, we speak of it being easy or difficult to believe something, just as we speak of it being easy or difficult to *do* something. 'It is hard to believe that he would do such a dreadful thing', we

---

[11] Descartes, *Comments on a Certain Broadsheet* [1648], in *The Philosophical Writings of Descartes*, trans. J. Cottingham, R. Stoothoff and D. Murdoch (Cambridge University Press, Cambridge, 1985), vol. I, p. 307 (AT VIIIB, 363). Rather surprisingly, Reid too conceived of belief as 'the act of believing' (*Essays on the Intellectual Powers of Man* [1785] (Edinburgh University Press, Edinburgh, 2002), p. 132).

[12] The following discussion of belief and mental act is indebted to J. F. M. Hunter, 'Believing', *Midwest Studies in Philosophy*, 5 (1980), pp. 239–60.

may say, or 'I find it difficult to believe that', as well as 'I can well believe it'.

Thirdly, it seems that believing can be voluntary or involuntary. For we say such things as 'I refuse to believe him', 'I couldn't help believing her', and 'I am unwilling to believe that'.[13]

Fourthly, we give reasons for believing, for refusing to believe and for being unable to believe something or someone, just as we give reasons for doing, refraining from doing or being unable to do something.

Finally, the idea that believing is an act is strengthened by noting that we hold people responsible for (some of) their beliefs. 'It is all your fault', we may say, 'you should not have believed him'. 'How could you believe him,' we may remonstrate, 'his report was full of holes', or 'You should know better than to believe such tosh!' But how could this be if believing were not an act that we can perform at will?

4 reasons why believing is not an act

That believing someone or something is *not* an act is easy to show.

(i) Although the imperative 'Believe this!' looks like an order or request to *do* something, it is not. For one cannot intelligibly reply, 'Not now, but I'll do it tomorrow'. Nor can the person entreating one to believe their story ask 'Well, have you done so?', but only 'Well, do you?'.

(ii) One cannot plan to believe something, or intend to believe something before breakfast. Nor can one excuse one's failure to believe something by saying that one forgot to do it. One cannot believe something or someone inadvertently or accidentally, on purpose or by mistake. One may wish one could believe something or someone, but one cannot try one's best to believe something or someone and then admit failure.

(iii) Although 'How could (can) you believe that?' looks like a request for an explanation of how one does something, it is not. For the possible answers do not include ways and means of believing, or descriptions of how to bring it off. Rather, we explain, for example,

---

[13] plato told
him: he couldn't
believe it (jesus
told him: he wouldn't believe
it)
e. e. cummings

that despite appearances to the contrary, what we believe is not all that implausible. We give reasons for believing, not methods of doing so. Or we explain that we did not know something that makes what we believed highly implausible.

(iv) Although we do say 'I find it hard to believe that', this does not mean that it is something too difficult for me to do. One cannot respond, as the White Queen would, by saying that one needs doxastic practice and then it will get easier. What it means is that the reasons against the proposal are weighty, and that one cannot explain them away.

Is believing something that happens to one? If believing something to be so is not an act, is it then something that happens to one? Hume held that belief 'consists merely in a certain feeling or sentiment; in something that depends not on our will, but must arise from certain determinate causes and principles, of which we are not masters'.[14] Certainly there are contexts in which 'believe' and 'feel' are interchangeable. 'I feel that we ought to V' and 'He feels very strongly that we ought to V' are respectively expression and description of belief. We shall examine the relation of believing and feeling below. Other turns of phrase suggest that believing is something that happens to one. We say such things as 'I found myself believing him // believing his story//', from which one might infer that 'beliefs are things we find we have'[15] – they come when they come. Many philosophers hold that perceptual beliefs are caused by perceptual experiences – that the visual experience of a tree in the quad is the cause of one's believing that there is a tree in the quad. Indeed, it is claimed, it is a fortunate fact that beliefs happen thus (a fact which is held to be readily explicable in evolutionary terms). Others speak of the 'onset' of belief.[16] Belief, they argue, is not an event, but the *onset* of belief is. So beliefs set in – like the weather!

Why believing is not something that happens to one This is confused. To say that one found oneself believing someone or someone's tale is not to remark on an event beyond one's control – namely,

---

[14] Hume, *Treatise of Human Nature* [1739] (Oxford University Press, Oxford, 1976), p. 624.

[15] Williams, 'Deciding to Believe', p. 147.

[16] D. Davidson, 'Actions, Reasons, and Causes', repr. in his *Essays on Actions and Events* (Clarendon Press, Oxford, 1980), p. 12.

that believing *happened*. It is to observe that although what one heard was more than a little implausible, nevertheless, one believed it – although one had no clear and specific reason for doing so.[17] When we read something in the paper, we generally believe it, but nothing *happens* that constitutes the believing of it. To assure someone that we believe his tale is not to report on something that happened to us. If believing were something that happened to one, then it would make sense to ask how many times it happened in the last ten minutes. To say that one believes what someone is saying is not to say that believing is happening.

Why there is no such thing as the onset of belief
Secondly, to remark that as soon as she started explaining her position, one believed her is not to say that believing *set in* as soon as she spoke. There is no such thing as the 'onset' of a belief, because, as we shall see, *belief is not a mental state with a beginning and ending* – even though one may have believed what one heard at the lecture at noon, and one may later, at three o'clock, realize that what one was told is quite wrong. One may indeed have believed that things are so ever since one spoke to NN, but one did not *start* to believe when one heard what he had to say and one did not *carry on believing*, although one may have continued to believe. Belief did not *set in* when one heard his explanation, and it did not then *persist* until it *lifted*. One is not *saddled* with a belief in the way in which one may be saddled with acrophobia. Beliefs are no more passions than they are actions.

Responsibility for one's beliefs
Recognizing that believing is not an *act* one performs leaves the idea of bearing responsibility for belief in the dark. We do hold people to be responsible for their beliefs, and we sometimes praise or blame them accordingly. We are, sometimes, ashamed of believing something that, on reflection, we should not have accepted, credited, endorsed or subscribed to. Is this irrational of us? No, not at all. We need to reflect on what is meant by 'being responsible for believing', on the contexts in which we hold someone responsible for his beliefs, and on the kinds of beliefs for which we hold someone responsible. The core of the family of notions of responsibility is the idea of *being answerable*. This idea is pivotal in explaining the sense in which we are

---

[17] Hunter, 'Believing', p. 246.

responsible for our beliefs, and in which we may be criticized for believing someone or something.

Belief and reasons for believing
To have a true belief concerning how things are is to be right; to have a false belief is to be wrong. One is right if things are as one believes them to be, wrong if they are not. If one *recognizes* that one is wrong, one *thereby* ceases to believe what one believed.[18] In avowing or averring a belief, one lays oneself open to the question 'Why do you believe that?' This is a demand for the reasons, grounds or source of one's belief. One can either satisfy this demand or not. If one can satisfy it, one's sincere answer may represent what one takes to be a reason. It may actually not be a reason, let alone a good reason, but the agent must take it to be one. *He* cannot view his beliefs as contrary to reason – *credo quia absurdum est* is dramatic but also absurd. His answer may explain his belief by citing the exercise of a cognitive faculty – 'I saw it happen', he may say. Of course, our cognitive faculties are not infallible. But one cannot believe something to be so because one saw things to be so, and simultaneously admit that one misperceived – if one knows *that*, then one does not believe at all. One's sincere answer may specify the source of one's belief – for example, the word of another – but one must view that source as trustworthy, or at least not untrustworthy. If one cannot answer the question 'Why do you believe that?' then one's belief is, as it were, free-floating. There are many beliefs we hold that do not rest on reasons, and are none the worse for that. There are many beliefs the reasons for which or the sources of which we have long forgotten. That does not make them unreasonable. However, irrational faith apart, an agent cannot intelligibly avow a belief that he himself admits to be *contrary* to reason.[19]

[18] In irrational cases, one may still be haunted by *thoughts* (as opposed to beliefs), fantasies and phobias that force themselves upon one. For to believe something to be so is to subscribe to its being so: one cannot say 'I believe things are so, but they aren't'. One can recognize the irrationality of an irrational desire, dissociate oneself from it and still be saddled with it. But to recognize the irrationality of a belief is already to abandon it. It may now be a haunting, obsessive thought – but not a belief. One cannot say, 'Nevertheless, I still believe that things are so', but only 'I cannot help thinking (imagining) that things are so'. Then one is in the grip of a delusion or fantasy, but not of a belief.

[19] For further elaboration, see S. N. Hampshire, *Freedom of the Individual* (Chatto & Windus, London, 1965), ch. 3, and J. Raz, 'When We are Ourselves: The Active and the Passive', repr. in *Engaging Reason* (Oxford University Press, Oxford, 1999), pp. 5–21.

Rationality and doxastic responsibility It is the rational powers of a language-using agent, his ability to reason and to give reasons, that renders him responsible for his beliefs. He is *subject to criticism* if the reasons he offers for his belief fail to support it, given that it is the kind of belief that requires support. He can be criticized if he holds his reasons for a belief to be adequate despite being apprised of overwhelming reasons to the contrary. He is equally open to criticism if his belief flies in the face of reason and he has no reasons for holding it. Such kinds of belief are not reasonable, and sometimes not rational. Harbouring such beliefs makes one less than altogether reasonable – which we all are from time to time. But more is required for one to be *responsible, blameworthy* or *culpable* for believing something. Here such criticisms as 'You should have known better', 'How could you believe that?', 'You ought to have believed what he said', 'You should have trusted her word' are in place.

One is answerable for one's belief when failure to believe what one *should* have believed is unworthy of one or has significant deleterious consequences. One is to blame for believing what one believed if one trusted someone one should not have trusted, or failed to trust someone one should have trusted. In some cases, one may have a moral obligation to trust the word of another (e.g. one's spouse, one's dearest friend) and one is blameworthy if one withheld trust. After all, whether one takes someone's word for something is, within the limits of reason, up to us. Similarly, one is held responsible for *consequential beliefs* that demand consideration and reflection, examination of grounds or evidence, and require a decision on the balance of reasons. This too is up to us. Hence, one is to blame if one does not exercise one's judgement in a manner appropriate to the seriousness of the matter at hand and to the quality of the evidence before one. Here one might be criticized for accepting, crediting or endorsing something without adequate reflection. One should have asked further probing questions, demanded further evidence. One may have negligently overlooked available evidence, been precipitate in judgement or allowed one's biases sway in coming to a conclusion that one unwarrantedly believed to be true.

Being responsible for one's beliefs is perfectly compatible with believing's being neither an act nor an event, and with its being neither voluntary or involuntary as acts may be, nor non-voluntary as things that happen to one are. It is an essential aspect of human rationality and autonomy. It is no coincidence that animals are not held responsible for thinking or believing something to be so.

5. Belief and feelings

As remarked, Hume held that belief is a special feeling, which happens when it happens, and is beyond the control of the will.

> When we are convinc'd of any matter of fact, we do nothing but conceive it, along with a certain feeling, different from what attends the mere *reveries* of the imagination. And when we express our incredulity concerning any matter of fact, we mean, that the arguments for the fact produce not that feeling.[20]

Why Hume held belief to be a feeling   Transposed into modern idiom, Hume's reasoning was straightforward. The difference between merely understanding something said or thinking or wondering about something's being so, on the one hand, and believing that things are so, on the other, cannot lie in any difference between what was said to be so and what is then believed. For it must be possible for A not to believe that things are so and for B to believe that they are, just as it must be possible for A to wonder whether, suppose or imagine that things are so, without believing them to be so. Nor can it lie in our voluntarily adding something to what is understood (or entertained). For then we could believe whatever we like. So, it seems, belief must be a non-voluntary feeling *associated with* what is believed. However, when it came to characterizing the feeling in question, Hume had difficulties:

> An idea assented to *feels* different from a fictitious idea, that the fancy alone presents to us: And this different feeling I endeavour to explain by calling it a superior *force*, or *vivacity*, or *solidity*, or *firmness*, or *steadiness*. This variety of terms, which may seem so unphilosophical, is intended only to express that act of the mind, which renders realities more present to us than fictions, causes them to weigh more in thought, and gives them a superior influence on the passions and the imagination. Provided we agree about the thing, 'tis needless to dispute about the terms. . . . I confess, that 'tis impossible to explain perfectly this feeling or manner of conception. We make use of words, that express something near it. But its true and proper name is *belief*, which is a term that everyone sufficiently understands in common life. And in philosophy we can go no further, than assert, that it is something *felt* by the mind, which distinguishes the ideas of the judgement from the fictions of the imagination.[21]

[20] Hume, *Treatise*, p. 624.

[21] Ibid., p. 629.

Later support for belief feelings: James, Russell, Ramsey The Humean account still commanded assent more than a century later. At the end of the nineteenth century, William James wrote 'As regards the analysis of belief, i.e. what it consists in, we cannot go very far. *In its inner nature, belief, or the sense of reality, is a sort of feeling more allied to the emotions than to anything else.*' What sort of feeling is it? Like Hume, James thought that here one hits bedrock. 'Belief, the sense of reality, feels like itself – that is about as much as we can say.' The belief feeling is a psychological attitude towards a proposition. 'This attitude is a state of consciousness *sui generis*, about which nothing more can be said in the way of internal analysis.'[22] Russell, in *The Analysis of Mind* (1921), argued that 'believing is an actual experienced feeling'.[23] What exactly is this feeling? Russell hesitated: 'I, personally, do not profess to be able to analyse the sensations . . . , but I am not prepared to say that they cannot be analysed.'[24] Ramsey, in 1927, wrote that 'The mental factors of . . . a belief [are] words spoken aloud or to oneself or merely imagined, connected together and accompanied by a feeling or feelings of belief or disbelief'.[25]

The difference between believing things to be so and feeling things to be so It is true that we speak of feeling that things are so, as we speak of believing that things are so. One may feel or believe very strongly that an injustice has been done. One may not be able to help feeling or help believing that the wrong should be righted. Credal feelings are not confined to moral concerns. One may feel that all will go well, or that one's party will win the election.[26] Nevertheless, to believe that things are so is not the same as to feel that they are. To feel that things are so is to have a hunch,

---

[22] W. James, *The Principles of Psychology* (Holt, New York, 1890), vol. 2, pp. 283–7.

[23] Russell, *The Analysis of Mind* (Allen & Unwin, London, 1921), p. 233.

[24] Ibid., p. 250.

[25] F. P. Ramsey, *The Foundations of Mathematics and Other Papers*, ed. R. B. Braithwaite (Routledge & Kegan Paul, London, 1931), p. 144. That he held belief to be a feeling no doubt made him think, wrongly, that it admits of degrees.

[26] It is noteworthy that one cannot feel that $2 + 2 = 4$ or that grass is green, for one cannot feel things to be so if one knows for certain that they are so. So if believing were a feeling it would be incompatible with knowing for certain.

intimation, intuition or presentiment. A vague feeling that things are so is not a vague belief, but a felt inclination to believe. A strong feeling that things are so may be tantamount to a belief that they are, but one for which there are no, or no adequate, grounds. Alternatively, a strong feeling that things are so may be taken to indicate a strong inclination to believe. To query 'Why do you believe that?' is to ask for the reasons or grounds for believing, but the question 'Why do you feel that?' asks what makes one feel so. One can feel inclined to believe that things are so, but one cannot feel inclined to feel that they are.

5 reasons why belief could not be a feeling

To believe that things are so is not to have a special kind of feeling, let alone an indefinable feeling with which all of us are acquainted. First, if it were, it would be unintelligible how anyone could learn the use of the verb 'to believe'. We do not teach the use of 'I believe . . .' by teaching children how to identify a special indefinable feeling, and one does not say that one believes something on the grounds that one has noted a special feeling that one associates with it.

Secondly, the supposition that belief is a feeling would imply that in order to know whether another person believes that things are so, we should have to establish that he has a special indefinable feeling associated with entertaining the proposition that things are so. But an interest in the beliefs of another is not an interest in his feelings, and the criteria for whether another believes something are not the criteria for his having a feeling.

Thirdly, as we have seen, there are degrees of feeling and sensation. One may have little, more or much pain – but one cannot have little, more or much belief that things are so. One may feel a little sad, quite pleased, very cheerful – but one cannot be or feel a little, quite or very belief-ful. So belief cannot be a feeling. Of course, one may firmly believe that things are so, but this does not indicate a degree of believing. It signifies the tenacity with which one cleaves to one's belief. It is the ease or difficulty of shaking the belief in question that has degrees. It makes sense to ask how convinced, doubtful, suspicious, confident, etc. someone is that things are so, but not to ask how much one believes that they are. The evidence one has in favour of what one believes may increase, but one's believing does not therefore *increase*. It is one's conviction, certainty or confidence that do so.

Fourthly, the difference, which puzzled Hume, between merely entertaining an idea or proposition without believing it and believing it does not turn on the absence of feeling in the first case and its presence in the second. To entertain the idea that things are so is to consider whether things are so, to wonder whether they are or to imagine that they are. But if one *believes* that things are so, then what one believes is something one acknowledges as a potential reason for one's reasoning, feeling or acting in a certain way if fitting circumstances arise. This is not so in the case of merely entertaining an idea. In entertaining an idea there is no question of whether one is either right or wrong. But when one believes something to be so, one *is* either right or wrong. In entertaining an idea, one is not committing oneself either way. But one cannot believe things to be so, and at the same time hold that, as far as one is concerned, the question of whether they are so is still open.

Fifthly, if having a belief were having a feeling associated with an idea, and if the putative feeling were a mere sensation, as Hume implicitly supposes and Russell explicitly avers, then it would be obscure why evidence should provide reasons for believing. For sensations can have causes but cannot be supported by grounds or reasons. On the other hand, if the feeling which one's believing is alleged to be is not a mere sensation but a doxastic feeling, such as feeling that things are so; feeling convinced, certain or sure that things are so; or hoping, fearing or expecting that things are so – that is, an 'intentional' feeling, then such feelings seem uniformly to presuppose the concept of belief and cannot be invoked to explain it. Far from such feelings being indefinable, primitive or unanalysable, they are all explicable partly in terms of believing.

6. Belief and dispositions

Belief conceived as a disposition

The idea that to believe that things are so is a disposition has been popular among philosophers since Ryle's *The Concept of Mind*.[27] Ryle argued that neither 'know' nor 'believe' signifies an occurrence. They are both what he

---

[27] He was anticipated by Alexander Bain, *The Emotions and the Will* (John W. Parker & Son, London, 1859), p. 568; see also R. B. Braithwaite, 'The Nature of Believing', *Proceedings of the Aristotelian Society*, 33 (1932–3), pp. 129–46.

called 'dispositional verbs', but of quite disparate types. 'Know' is a capacity-verb, whereas 'believe' is a tendency-verb, which, unlike 'know', does not signify an ability to get things right or bring things off. 'Belief', he noted, can be qualified by adjectives such as 'obstinate', 'wavering', 'unswerving', 'unconquerable', 'stupid', 'fanatical', 'whole-hearted', 'intermittent', 'passionate', 'childlike', some or all of which are appropriate to 'trust', 'loyalty', 'bent', 'aversion', 'habit', 'zeal' and 'addiction', which are perspicuously tendency-nouns. Beliefs, like habits, can be inveterate, slipped into or given up; like partisanships, devotions and hopes, they can be blind and obsessing; like aversions and phobias, they can be unacknowledged; like fashions and tastes, they can be contagious; and like loyalties and animosities, they can be induced by tricks.

The variety of dispositions that believing has been held to be

It has been suggested that to believe that things are so is a disposition to *act*.[28] If so, the character of the act which exhibits the disposition must be specified. It has been suggested that to believe that things are so is not a disposition to *do* anything, but rather a disposition to *feel* – in particular, a disposition to feel it true that things are so, irrespective of whether one is or is not willing to act, speak or reason accordingly.[29] Some philosophers have suggested that it is a disposition to bet on the truth of the proposition that things are so, others that it is a disposition to behave as if it were true that things are so, and yet others that it is a disposition to assent to the proposition that things are so.

The plausibility of these suggestions is increased when it is explicitly argued, as it was by Ryle, that belief is a *multi-track disposition*. 'To believe that the ice is dangerously thin', he wrote,

> is to be unhesitant in telling oneself and others that it is thin, in acquiescing in other people's assertions to that effect, in objecting to statements to the contrary, in drawing consequences from the original proposition, and so forth. But it is also to be prone to skate warily, to shudder, to dwell in the imagination on possible disasters and to warn other skaters.[30]

---

[28] P. T. Geach, *Mental Acts* (Routledge & Kegan Paul, London, 1957), p. 8.

[29] L. J. Cohen, *An Essay on Belief and Acceptance* (Clarendon Press, Oxford, 1992), ch. 1.

[30] Ryle, *The Concept of Mind* (Hutchinson, London, 1949), pp. 134f.

White argued that belief is a multi-track disposition to behave as if it were the case that things are so, where 'behave' includes both acting and reacting, in word and deed, in thought and action.[31]

Differences between human and inanimate dispositions

The debate is vitiated by lack of awareness of the differences between inanimate and human dispositions. Human dispositions (other than dispositions of health) are traits of temperament, character and personality. They are logically quite different from inanimate dispositions.[32] Inanimate substances may have a disposition to V, yet never manifest it, since the conditions for its actualization never arise (e.g. a fragile object that is never dropped). But a person cannot have a disposition (e.g. be indolent, pleasure-loving, thoughtful) and never exhibit it. An inanimate substance may have a disposition to V for only a few minutes in the course of its existence (e.g. a blob of sealing wax, as it congeals), but a human being cannot have a disposition (e.g. to be kind, generous or courageous) for only a few minutes. Dispositions are inherently general (one may be disposed, i.e. *inclined*, to go to the theatre tonight, but one cannot have such a *disposition*). The concept of a human disposition approximates tendency and frequency concepts (such as *habit*). Someone of an irascible disposition tends to become irritated by the slightest provocation, a person who has an indolent disposition tends to avoid work, and somebody with an affectionate disposition tends to display affection. There are indeed doxastic dispositions. Gullibility and credulity are traits of human personality. They are dispositions to *believe* (and are contrasted with *being of a sceptical disposition*, which is a disposition to withhold belief). One may say such things as 'I believe any bad news these days', and that, like 'I am very irritable these days', does specify a disposition – a credulity with respect to bad news. Nevertheless, believing something to be so is obviously not a disposition of character, personality or temperament.

[31] White, *Misleading Cases*, p. 131. See also W. V. O. Quine, *Quiddities* (Penguin Books, London, 1990), p. 20: 'A belief, in the best and clearest case, is a bundle of dispositions. It may include the disposition to lip service, a disposition to accept a wager, and various dispositions to take precautions, or to book a passage, or to tidy up the front room, or the like, depending on what particular belief it may be.'

[32] For detailed discussion, see *Human Nature: the Categorial Framework*, pp. 118–21.

Beliefs and tendencies   The term 'disposition', even in its application to human beings, also has a loose use to signify a tendency. Even in this use, human dispositions (save for dispositions of health) are unlike inanimate dispositions. Evidently, what is intended by the claim that belief is a disposition is that it is a *tendency* or *proneness*. So what is meant by the claim that the concept of belief is a dispositional concept is that it is a *tendency* or *frequency concept*. Let us examine this proposal. There are indeed affinities between belief and tendencies.

First, tendencies, unlike mental states but like beliefs, are not states of consciousness, although of course, one may have a tendency to be in a certain mental state that is frequently manifest – as when one is of a melancholic or cheerful disposition.

Secondly, belief, like behavioural tendencies (and dispositions of character and temperament), is conceptually connected to action in two general ways:

(a) The criteria for whether a person believes that things are so, like the criteria for whether a person has a tendency to V, are what the person does (and says) in certain circumstances. (But one must be careful not to confuse the fact that the criteria for believing something are multiple with the non-fact that believing something is a multi-track disposition.)

(b) An agent's V-ing is often explained by reference to what he believed or by reference to his believing it, as it is also commonly explained (or explained away) by reference to his having a disposition or tendency to V.

Thirdly, it is correct that many of the adjectival and adverbial modifiers appropriate to 'belief' and 'believes' are also appropriate to human dispositions, tendencies, pronenesses, habits, inclinations, liabilities and susceptibilities.

Nevertheless, as we shall now show, believing that things are so is no disposition. Nor is the concept of belief a tendency concept.

9 reasons why belief is not a disposition   (i) Dispositions and tendencies are essentially characterized by what they are dispositions or tendencies to do. Beliefs are essentially characterized by reference to what is believed to be so. Concepts of dispositions and tendencies are frequency concepts, and to characterize someone as having such-and-such a disposition or tendency (e.g. as irascible, credulous, amiable) is to indicate the kinds of things he is prone to do. But to say that someone believes that things are thus-and-so is not. To say that someone believes that things are so, unlike saying that he is amiable or irascible, is not to indicate any kind of act or activity that he is prone to do or engage in.

(ii) Different people may share the same belief. However, that does not imply that they have a common disposition to do anything. The rash person may respond by doing or thinking one thing, the more cautious person by doing or thinking something quite different. It depends upon their respective situations, goals and purposes, and their character and personality.

(iii) To *explain* behaviour by reference to a disposition is to explain it by reference to the nature, temperament or personality traits of a person, or, more generally, to explain it by reference to a proneness or tendency to act thus. We explain A's surprising response by pointing out that A is excitable, so tends to over-react, or that he is unflappable and dour, so is prone not to show his feelings, or that he is tactless, and so liable to drop clangers. But to explain A's V-ing by reference to his belief that things are so is to explain it in terms of what A took as his reason for V-ing. 'A V-ed because he believed that things are so' explains A's V-ing by reference to its rationale – not by reference to a behavioural tendency. To explain a specific act (going for a walk) by reference to a proneness (such as a habit of going for a walk at three o'clock every afternoon) is in effect to reject the need for any explanation of the act (that is what he always does, it is nothing unusual), although it leaves the habit unexplained. This is altogether unlike explaining an act by reference to believing or to what is believed.

(iv) Correspondingly, one can *justify* someone's V-ing, on a certain occasion, by reference to their belief. But to say that someone's act exemplifies his disposition, habit or proneness is not to justify it at all. What someone believes may give the rationale for his actions, which is precisely what his habits and dispositions do not do.

(v) One establishes that A has a certain disposition (e.g. that he is irascible, gentle, timid) or that he has a certain tendency (to become tired by ten o'clock in the evening) or habit (to go to the cinema every Friday evening) by observing regularities in his behaviour in recurrent circumstances. But to establish that another believes that things are so does not generally require observation of behavioural *regularities*.

Furthermore, I may come to know of my own tendencies, character and personality traits and dispositions by noting my own regular reactions and responses, but that is not how I am able confidently to say that I believe something to be so. If believing were a disposition (or mental state), then one could say such things as 'Judging by my behaviour, it is very probable that I believe that'. Indeed, 'I think I believe that' would be analogous to 'I think I have a tendency to V' – but it is not.

(vi) To know that someone has a disposition or tendency to V is to know that he is prone or liable to V in response to certain circumstances. But one may know that A believes that things are so without having any idea of what, if anything, he is prone to do. A may believe that it will rain this afternoon. So he may stay at home; he may go for a walk, with or without an umbrella; he may bring in the deck chairs, or leave them outside; he may tell someone that rain is likely, or not tell anyone; he may answer the question whether it will rain truthfully, or tell a lie; and so on. So whereas one specifies A's disposition by saying what it is a disposition to do, one cannot specify A's belief by reference to what he is going to do. One specifies a belief by saying what is believed.

(vii) One may believe something for a few moments, until one realizes that what one was told cannot be true or until the triviality one read in the newspaper slips from one's mind and is forgotten. But one cannot have a tendency or proneness to act for a few moments, any more than one can have a disposition (character trait, trait of personality) for a few moments.

(viii) 'I believe that things are so, but they are not' is a (kind of) contradiction. But 'I tend, am inclined or prone to V as if things were so, but they are not' is not a contradiction of any kind, even though it calls out for an explanation. (It is easy enough to imagine appropriate explanations. To be prone to behave as if it were the case that Stalin was a great and benevolent leader, even though he was not, was a dictate of self-preservation in Stalinist Russia.)

(ix) If A believes that things are so, then A is either right or wrong. But ascription of a tendency to A does not involve any such commitment.

We may safely conclude that believing something to be so is neither a human disposition as credulity and gullibility are, nor a proneness or tendency as habits are. Similarly, the concept of belief is not a dispositional concept, as the concepts of a habit, tendency or proneness are.

7. Belief and mental states

Believing is not a state of mind
It has become common over the last few decades to take it for granted that beliefs are mental states or states of mind.[33] This is surprising. As noted in chapter 4, it is cavalier to equate a mental state with *a state of mind*. It is obviously mistaken to hold that believing is a state of mind. 'What sort of state of mind did you find her in?' may be answered by 'She is calm now' or 'She is deeply depressed', but not by 'She believes that it is going to rain tomorrow' or 'She thinks that Jack is in London'. One can be in an enthusiastic, anxious, cheerful state of mind, but not in a believing-that-the-lawn-needs-watering state of mind.[34]

Why one might suppose believing to be a mental state
What are the grounds for holding belief to be *a mental state*? Sometimes it is held to be so by default: since believing is not a mental act or event, and not a process or activity either, it must be a mental state. Sometimes it is noted that the verb 'believe' is a stative verb, and it is taken for granted that all stative verbs signify states, and psychological stative verbs signify mental states. As we saw in chapter 4, that is altogether mistaken. It is also remarked (perfectly correctly) that one may come to believe something at a time, continue

[33] 'We think of our beliefs as states of mind that are normally responsive to truth' (L. J. Cohen, *An Essay on Belief and Acceptance* (Clarendon Press, Oxford, 1992), p. 22). 'The mental states in question are beliefs, desires, intentions, and so on, as ordinarily conceived' (D. Davidson, 'Knowing One's Own Mind', repr. in *Subjective, Intersubjective, Objective* (Clarendon Press, Oxford, 2001), p. 24); as well as 'states of mind like doubts, wishes, beliefs, and desires' in 'The Myth of the Subjective' (ibid., p. 51) and 'Having a belief is not like having a favourite cat, it is being in a state' ('Indeterminism and Antirealism', ibid., p. 74). 'I shall be talking about belief as a psychological state . . . the state of somebody who believes something' (Williams, 'Deciding to Believe', p. 136). 'Belief is a state which we are in throughout our waking lives, and often too when we are dreaming' (Price, *Belief*, p. 24). 'Intentionality is that property of many mental states and events by which they are directed at or about or of objects and states of affairs in the world. If, for example, I have a belief, it must be a belief that such-and-such is the case' (J. R. Searle, *Intentionality* (Cambridge University Press, Cambridge, 1983), p. 1). 'Paradigmatic mental states include love, hate, pleasure, and pain. Moreover, they include attitudes to propositions: believing that something is so, conceiving that it is so' (T. Williamson, *Knowledge and its Limits* (Oxford University Press, Oxford, 2000), p. 21).

[34] It is noteworthy that although there is no such thing as being in a state of belief or in a state of believing, one may be in a state of *disbelief* – just as one may be in a state of ignorance, although not in a state of knowledge or of knowing (see above, p. 185).

for a time to believe what one came to believe, and subsequently one may cease to believe it. It is then assumed that this suffices for allocating belief to the category of mental state. Further, many philosophers hold belief to be a 'propositional attitude', and they assume that attitudes are states. Two theoretical motives for holding beliefs to be mental states are prominent. First, it is held that to do something because one believes things to be thus-and-so is a causal explanation, and that beliefs are implicated in the aetiology of other mental states. It is assumed that if beliefs are states, that explains their causal powers inasmuch as states can be causes (cp. 'the state of the road was the cause of the crash'). Secondly, it is widely assumed that beliefs are identical with brain states.[35] But only if believing something to be so is itself a state (a mental one) can it be identical with a state of the brain.

6 reasons why beliefs are not mental states

However, it is mistaken to suppose that beliefs are mental states. Our concept of a mental state is far richer than that of a psychological attribute acquired at a time, possessed for a time and then no longer possessed. First, mental states are things one is *in*. One can be in a cheerful or depressed state, in a neurotic state or in a state of intense excitement or elated anticipation. But there is no such thing as being in a state of believing something, any more than there is such a thing as being in a state of knowing something. No one would answer the question 'What sort of mental state is Jack in today?' with sentences of the form 'He is in a state of believing that things are so'.

Secondly, if a noun signifies a mental state, there is commonly a corresponding adjective that goes with the verb 'to feel'. Hence, corresponding to depression, anxiety, joy, cheerfulness, excitement, elation, agitation, despondency, one may *feel* depressed, anxious, joyful, cheerful, excited, elated, agitated, despondent. A person's being in such a state is then describable by the use of the progressive or imperfect tense, as in 'A *is feeling* cheerful, anxious, despondent' or 'A *has been feeling* agitated, worried, depressed ever since hearing the bad news'. But although one may hear the good news and believe what one hears, and although the good news may make one cheerful, it cannot make one 'belief-ful' – since there is no such thing. *A fortiori* it cannot make one *feel* belief-ful either.

[35] For example, W. V. O. Quine, *The Pursuit of Truth* (Harvard University Press, Cambridge, Mass., 1990), p. 71: 'Perceptions are neural realities, and so are individual instances of beliefs.' See also his *From Stimulus to Science* (Harvard University Press, Cambridge, Mass., 1995), p. 87.

It is true that one may feel convinced that things are so. But a feeling of conviction is no more a mental state than is believing. Like belief, it lacks genuine duration – for one does not cease to be or feel convinced when one falls asleep, nor can one's conviction be interrupted by distraction of attention. The phrase '. . . feels (more or less) convinced that things are so' signifies the degree to which one embraces or cleaves to the belief that things are so, the extent to which one places one's trust or reliance upon the premise that things are so in one's reasoning. There is an aetiological difference between feeling conviction and being in a mental state. What makes one feel convinced that things are so, if anything, is the evidence for its being the case. But what makes one feel depressed that things are so is not the *evidence* for things being so but the fact that things *are* so (or are taken to be so).

One may indeed feel that things are so, for example have a presentiment. But to have a presentiment that things are so is not to believe that they are; rather, *that things are so* is what, without determinate grounds, one is inclined to believe.

Thirdly, mental states, because of their relation to feelings, which may be pleasant or unpleasant to endure, or their relation to attention, which may involve effort, can be exhausting or tiresome, innervating or enervating. One may be tired of being depressed, exhausted by long bouts of concentration or attention, weary from excitement. But one cannot be tired of believing that things are so or worn out as a result of believing them to be.

Fourthly, mental states are states of consciousness. They are characterized by 'genuine duration'. But believing that things are so is not a state of consciousness at all. One does not cease to believe all that one believes merely because one falls asleep.[36] Though one

---

[36] It has been suggested that we must distinguish between conscious and unconscious belief states. A conscious belief state is manifest only when one's belief is 'present to consciousness'. Most of one's beliefs are unconscious, no matter whether one is awake or asleep. A belief becomes conscious only if one is currently thinking about it or 'occurrently believing' that things are so (J. R. Searle, *The Rediscovery of the Mind* (MIT Press, Cambridge, Mass., 1992), p. 154). We can indeed distinguish between bearing in mind something one believes to be so, something one believes to be so crossing one's mind, and thinking about what one believes to be so. But these are not 'conscious beliefs'. If something one believes to be so does not cross one's mind and is not the subject of current reflection, that does not make it an 'unconscious belief', any more than all the things I know to be so but am not thinking about are 'unconscious knowledge'. An unconscious belief would be a belief that colours my emotional responses and informs my actions, but which I am *unwilling to acknowledge*, either to myself or to others, *as* something I believe (see below, chapter 6, section 4). Similar considerations apply to attempts to distinguish latent belief states from patent ones.

may have believed something for twenty years, one has not believed it intermittently – one's belief state being interrupted daily by sleep – nor continuously, any more than if one has learnt something and not forgotten it, one has known it continuously. There is such a thing as an intermittent belief, but it is not a belief that is interrupted by sleep or distraction. Rather it is a matter of first believing something, then ceasing to believe it, being convinced again and then again coming to think that one is mistaken. One's state of depression or elation may be interrupted by something that distracts one's attention and later be resumed. But distraction of attention cannot interrupt one's believing something any more than it can interrupt one's knowing something.

Fifthly, it may be hard to believe something, but that does not mean that it is hard to get oneself into a certain state of mind – as it is hard to be cheerful in the face of adversity. It means that it is difficult to explain away all the evidence that speaks against its being the case. Similarly, one sometimes cannot help believing something, but that is not at all like being unable to help feeling anxious, despondent or excited. It means that despite the absence of evidence or the thinness of the evidence for its being the case or despite the countervailing evidence, one still cleaves to the belief.

Sixthly, a mental state could not have the consequences of believing. If A believes that things are so, then it follows that A is either right about whether things are so or wrong. No such consequences flow from the fact that A is in a cheerful mental state or in a despondent one.

There are many other categorial dissimilarities. The subjective epistemology of mental states is wholly unlike the subjective epistemology of belief (see chapter 6). The indefinitely large number of beliefs one harbours is incongruous with the idea that one can be said to be in a single state of believing that indeterminate totality. We need not pursue the differences further. It is surely evident that to characterize believing something as being in a mental state is mistaken.

8. Why believing something cannot be a brain state

Modern philosophers are prone to embrace neural mythologies. One of these, cited above, is the idea that believing something is a brain state. This is a contingent identity claim. The identity was initially held to be a type-identity, subsequently a token-identity.

It is mistaken to embrace any such claim, not because it is false, but because it makes no sense, for the following reasons.

6 reasons why believing something is not a brain state First, if believing something to be so were contingently identical with a cortical state, then believing would have to be a mental *state* – but we have seen that it is not.

Secondly, a necessary condition for two different state-descriptions to be descriptions of one and the same state is that they be descriptions of the state of one and the same object. But 'A believes that such-and-such' is a description of a human being, whereas 'A's brain is in such-and-such a cortical state' is a description of a brain, and a human being is not a brain. So someone's believing something to be so cannot be identical with a state of his brain.

Thirdly, if a person's believing that things are so is in fact a neural state of his brain, then the question 'Where do you believe that it will rain tomorrow?' would be ambiguous. Taken one way it would be answered 'I believe it will rain in Oxford tomorrow', and taken another it would be answered 'In my brain, of course'. But it is not ambiguous, and the latter answer is nonsense. There is no such thing as 'believing in my brain that things are thus-and-so'. One might ask 'Where did you acquire that belief?' or 'Where did you come to believe that?'. To which the answer might be 'I came to believe it in America'. But it is not intelligible to say 'I came to believe it in my prefrontal cortex'.

Fourthly, believing something could not be a neural event or state, for a neural event or state could not have the consequences of believing something. If A believes things are so, then, as we have seen, it follows immediately that A is either right about whether they are or that he is wrong. Just as 'A knows that things are so' implies that they are (which exhibits the irreducible connection between knowledge and objective fact), so too belief is irreducibly connected with objective fact, albeit in a disjunctive way. But A's being in a certain neural state does not imply that A is either right or wrong about anything. No description of a neural state could *logically entail* that the person whose brain is in that state is right or wrong about whether things are or are not thus-and-so.

Finally, if believing something were a mental state which, as it happens, is identical with a brain state, then someone who says 'I believe that things are so' would be asserting that he is in a certain mental state, which, whether he knows it or not, is actually a state of his brain. However, if that were so, it would be intelligible for him to go on to assert 'but it is not the case that things are so' or 'but I take no stand on whether it is or is not the case'. For whether things are so or not is wholly independent of whether A is or is not in the relevant mental/neural state. So there could be no inconsistency in his specifying his state and then denying that things are so. But while one can assert that A believes that things are so, but in fact they aren't, *A* cannot assert that he believes that things are so but they aren't. For to say 'I believe that things are so' is, in many contexts, akin to saying 'Things are so, unless I am much mistaken' or 'Things are so, to the best of my inconclusive information' or, indeed, 'To the best of my knowledge, things are so'. But one cannot, without contradiction, assert 'To the best of my knowledge, things are so, but in fact they are not' or 'Unless I am much mistaken, things are so, but in fact things are not so'. However, there is no contradiction in asserting 'I am in mental state B, but things are not so', let alone 'My brain is in neural state N but things are not so'.

9. What is belief? The role of 'believe' in human discourse

Why the question 'What is belief?' is awry

The considerations thus far advanced make it clear what belief is not, but do not help us in answering the question of what it is. That is no coincidence. It should be obvious from controversies over the ages that the question itself is problematic. It points us in the wrong direction before we have even begun. For it demands an answer of the form 'Belief is a . . .' – and there is no such answer that satisfies our puzzlement. In the light of the connective analysis that we have been conducting, that should not be surprising. For belief does not fall under any illuminating categorial or structural concept. That is because it is a multi-focal concept, the structure of which is highly irregular and unique. Generic analysis and description of specific differentia are of no avail here. There is no substitute for attention to the particular.

What are the point and purpose of the verb 'to believe'?

We should think of the verb 'believe' as an instrument of language and ask after its role and function. We must enquire what we do with it, and why we need it – and not worry further about what kind of thing belief is – to which abstract category it belongs. We might think of the first-person present tense 'I believe' (and 'I don't believe') as a card we play in a game with sentences, and reflect on its role in the game. We place this card on another card (the expression of a judgement), and it reduces the value of the first card. Or it informs the other players of the value one places upon the first card. Or it tells them that one is willing to stake a bet on the first card. We might think of 'He believes' (as well as 'He doesn't believe') as a card we place on the card which another person has played. Placing our card on his informs others what we think of the value of his card (if we know it is false), or indicates what other card he is likely to play (given that he stands by it). And so on. Let us try to cash this simile.

'I believe' as a qualifier Being an operator on declarative sentences, the use of the first-person present tense 'I believe' presupposes mastery of the use of the declarative sentence on which it operates. How might one teach the use of this operator? In what circumstances is it appropriate to prefix an 'I believe' to a sentence? First, it is taught as a *qualifier* to the blunt assertion of the sentence to make a judgement. The latter, as noted in the previous chapter, is the typical form of a knowledge-claim. What is the role of the qualifier? Not, as has often been asserted, to indicate an element of doubt or hesitation, for then it would be incoherent to say 'I believe that things are so *with complete conviction* (certainty)'. But it is not. The primary role of 'I believe . . .' is to indicate that one's grounds are insufficient to *rule out* doubt, *even though one has no doubts oneself*. One's grounds are insufficient to exclude the possibility that things are not as one believes them to be. Hence the affinity of 'I believe that things are so' with 'As far as I know, things are so' and 'Unless I am much mistaken, things are so'. Hence also the prominence of its parenthetical occurrence, as in 'A is, I believe, F' (and 'A is, to the best of my knowledge // as far as I know // unless I am much mistaken //, F'. All these are not *assertions of hesitancy* (as 'I'm not sure' is) but rather *hesitant* (qualified) *assertions*. In this role, using 'I believe that things are so' is still, in effect, an assertion that they are – with a qualification. This is one reason why 'I believe things are so, but they aren't' is a kind of contradiction, whereas 'He believes that things are so, but they aren't' is not.

That 'I believe that things are so' has a use as a qualified assertion that things are so (and not as a piece of autobiography) is evident from the fact that it can be met with 'You're wrong (mistaken)'. This does not assert that you do *not* believe what you say you believe, but rather that you are wrong *to believe* what you believe. You are making a mistake, not about your believing, but about what you believe – about what you hesitantly assert to be so. In saying 'I believe that things are so' (as well as 'Things are so, as far as I know' and 'Things are so, unless I am much mistaken'), I am still asserting, albeit with qualification, that things are so. Hence it is that, if someone says 'I believe that Jack is in town' and another replies, 'No, I don't think he is', they *are* contradicting each other – which they would not be if the roles of 'I believe' and 'I think' were to describe or self-ascribe a mental state, a neural state, a disposition or dispositional state.[37]

Qualified assertions of belief are expressions of belief

'I believe that things are so' used as a qualified assertion and 'Things are, I believe, thus-and-so' are *expressions* (not statements) of belief, just as 'I wish you would go away' is an expression of a wish no less than 'Oh, do go away!'. If someone said 'I believe that things are so', we can perfectly correctly report this by saying 'He expressed the belief that things are so', just as we can report his utterance 'I wish that things were so' in the words 'He expressed the wish that things were so', and his utterance 'I fear that things are so' by 'He expressed his fear that things are so'. These doxastic first-person present-tense utterances are not *self-ascriptions* of belief in the sense in which 'He believes that things are so' is an ascription of belief. Their denial, 'You are mistaken', does not imply that you don't believe, but denies what is believed. Like the bare utterance 'Things are so', 'I believe that things are so', 'Things are so, I believe', 'As far as I know, things are so' and 'Things are so, unless I am much mistaken' all express the speaker's qualified *endorsement* of or *subscription* to the proposition that things are so. On the other hand, 'I don't believe things are so' is an *emphatic* (not a tentative) *denial* that things are so.

The endorsing role of 'I believe'

The step from *qualified endorsement* to *endorsement* is a small one. It is therefore unsurprising that 'I believe' should also be linked with endorsing, and perfectly intelligible that it should be, given the original connections between belief and trust or dependency. So a second important role that 'I believe' may fulfil is as an endorsement of the base on which it operates, or as an endorsement of what another

---

[37] See A. W. Collins, *The Nature of Mental Things* (University of Notre Dame Press, Notre Dame, Ind., 1987), ch. 2; 'Moore's Paradox and Epistemic Risk', *Philosophical Quarterly*, 46 (1996), pp. 308–19, and 'Behaviourism and Belief', *Annals of Pure and Applied Logic*, 96 (1999), pp. 75–88.

person has asserted to be so. 'I believe that too', one may say – in effect underwriting something another has said. Here, in this kind of use, the relative adequacy or inadequacy of one's reasons slips into the background (although it does not always fade from sight). Thus used, 'I believe' (unlike 'Unless I am much mistaken', or 'As far as I know') does not qualify an assertion but subscribes to one. This is another reason why 'I believe things are so, but they aren't' is a kind of contradiction, whereas 'Things are so, but he doesn't believe they are' is not.

Expression of opinion

'I believe that things are so' has a third role, namely, *to express one's opinion*. In cases where the judgement expressed is intrinsically a matter of opinion, the prefix 'I believe' does not function to earmark a tentative assertion that falls short of knowledge, but rather to indicate how one sees things. This is particularly apt in such moral deliberation that concerns essentially contested matters, and in practical reasoning concerning what ought to be done. Here, to ask another what he believes or thinks is not to ask for a qualified judgement, but to ask for his opinion – which may or may not be qualified or hesitant.

Taking a stand

It is easy to see how an instrument appropriate for expressing a personal judgement on something that is a matter of opinion, as well as apt for endorsing something that has been said to be so, should also evolve a use in *taking a stand* upon how things are. Sometimes we may ask 'Who believes such-and-such?' or 'Do you believe such-and-such?' in order to find out how people stand or how a given person stands on some matter. Here the answer 'I do', or 'Yes, I believe that things are so', is a confession, admission, declaration or statement that one believes thus. Its point is not to assert with qualification that things are so, but to take a stand, or to confess, admit or report how one stands on the matter. These uses of 'I believe' do not comfortably allow a parenthetical employment of the phrase. It is striking that to say 'I don't believe that things are so' is not merely a refusal to take a stand. On the contrary, it is to take a stand on things not being so. This too does not allow parenthetical occurrence.

Declarations of trust; gathering from others how things are

Since many of our opinions derive from the advice and observations of others whom we trust and whose word we are willing to take on trust, it is evident how some uses of this protean verb should signify trust in another and trust in the word of another. To say 'I believe what he said' is not used to signal that one accepts what he said with qualification and hesitation, but *to declare one's trust in his word*. Similarly, to believe a statement, an announcement, a declaration, story or rumour is to rely on it – to be willing to reason or act on the grounds of things being as they are said to be. As we have seen, there is a quite different use of 'I believe' that converges on 'I gather'. It serves not to *endorse* what I have gathered from others, but merely to report what others judge to be the case and to indicate one's *acceptance* of their word. It is akin to 'I have been given to understand that . . .'.

The role of 'believe' in rehearsing one's reasoning   Since we reason from what we know or take to be the case, 'I believe that things are so' also has a role in rehearsing our reasoning and our reasons for doing, feeling or thinking what we do, feel and think. 'I believe that it is going to rain, so we had better take an umbrella' and 'It is, I believe, going to rain, so the garden party will probably be cancelled' invoke the qualifying use of 'I believe' in spelling out a practical or theoretical inference. It differs from 'It is going to rain, so . . .' only in involving the qualified rather than the blunt assertion. (I am not drawing an inference from my mental state, let alone from the state of my brain, but from what I believe.) But one can also reason from the fact that one subscribes to a truth or principle, or from one's staking out one's position, as in '*I believe this, so I must stand up and be counted*'.

There are very different things one may do with this particular linguistic instrument (see fig. 5.3). That does not mean that 'believe' is polysemic – for it is no coincidence that all these are instances of

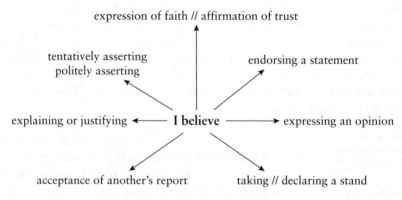

Figure 5.3 *The uses of 'I believe'*

believing something to be so. Moreover, the boundaries between the different functions are blurred, and more than one purpose may be served by a single application of the term.

1st-/3rd-person asymmetry The first-person present and the third-person uses (as well as the other-tensed first-person uses) differ. Whereas 'I believe that things are so' is an *expression* of belief, 'He believes that things are so' and 'I believed that things are so' are *ascriptions* of belief. In ascribing a belief to another or to himself in the past, the speaker neither endorses nor subscribes to the belief ascribed. There is no contradiction of any kind in asserting 'I believed that things were so, but they weren't // I was wrong //' or 'He believes that things are so, but they aren't // He is wrong //'. Nor are such utterances endorsements, tentative or otherwise, of the judgement that things are or were so. In many contexts, 'He believes that things are so' implies that he at any rate does not *know* that things are so, or even that he is *mistaken* in believing them to be so. Belief ascriptions to others have a prominent role in explaining or predicting their behaviour. This is not because what they believe, or their believing what they believe, is a *cause* of their behaviour, but because it may be a reason – as they see things – for them to behave in certain ways.[38]

Criterionless 1st-person use; criteria for 3rd-person use In expressing my belief by means of a doxastic utterance, I employ no criteria. But, of course, in ascribing belief to another, criteria are involved. If one says of another that he believes things to be so, one must be able to answer the question 'How do you know?' The criteria for the ascription of belief to another are multiple, and rendered even more complex by the multifaceted character of the concept of belief. For the criteria for whether someone tentatively judges things to be so, or adamantly takes a stand on how things are or should be, or gathers from others how things are, or expresses an opinion, or trusts the word of another, are obviously very different. They are all, of course, behavioural and circumstance-dependent. The criteria for whether someone believes things to be so are what he says and does in given circumstances.

---

[38] See *Human Nature: the Categorial Framework*, pp. 226–32.

6

Knowledge, Belief and the
Epistemology of Belief

1. Knowledge and belief

The conceptual environment of knowledge

As we saw in chapter 4, knowledge is connected with observing, finding out and discovering, since observing, finding out and discovering that things are so are coming to know that they are by one's efforts and activities. It is connected with becoming and being aware or conscious that things are so, and with realizing or noticing that they are – for these are ways of receiving knowledge. It is bound up with learning that things are so by hearing from trustworthy informants, or by reading in reliable sources, that they are so – for these are ways of acquiring knowledge from others. So too, it is linked with proof and conclusive argument. Acquisition of knowledge of how things are is acquisition of information. For a human being to know how things are is to possess the information that things are so. If one knows how things are, one can answer correctly the question of whether they are so, transmit the information that things are so, reason from things being so, and do or refrain from doing things for the reason that things are so. And so forth. Knowledge is linked with remembering, since knowledge retained is (roughly speaking) information previously possessed and not forgotten (see chapter 9). What is known *can* typically be forgotten, since to forget is, among other things, to fail to retain information once possessed. If one has forgotten that things are thus-and-so, one cannot plan on the basis of that

The Intellectual Powers: A Study of Human Nature, First Edition. P. M. S. Hacker.
© 2013 John Wiley & Sons, Ltd. Published 2013 by John Wiley & Sons, Ltd.

information, reason from it to conclusions it supports or invoke it as a reason for thinking, feeling or doing.

The conceptual environment of belief

Belief, by contrast, belongs to a very different circle of concepts, none of which exclude the possibility of things *not* being as they are held to be. Whereas to know something to be so is to be right, believing something to be so is to be *either* right *or* wrong. As we have seen in the previous chapter, believing something to be so belongs to the family which includes thinking something to be so and feeling that things are so. It is connected with opining and judging, with gathering, or taking it that things are so. It is associated with trusting another and with relying on his word. It is linked with subscribing to, and endorsing, the claim that things are so. It is bound up with taking a stand on how things are, holding or maintaining that they are so.

Problems concerning the relation of knowledge to belief

Our surveys can now be used to confront some vexed questions concerning the relationships between knowledge and belief. What is the difference between knowledge and belief? Indeed, *can* one both know *and* believe that things are so? If so, is belief a constituent element in knowledge? That is, is knowledge some form or other of true belief? If not, does knowing things to be so imply believing them to be so? That is, is believing an *accompanying condition* of knowing something to be so? If so, is that an empirical truth or a conceptual one? We sometimes say, 'I don't believe it, I know it'. But is this like 'It isn't large, its huge'? Or is it like 'I didn't remember it; he told me'?

Contrasts between knowing and believing

The contrasts between knowing and believing something to be so are striking.[1] One can try to acquire knowledge, but not belief (save in the case of faith). For to acquire knowledge is to acquire information. One may ask 'How *can* you believe that?' – if the reasons you have are flimsy or transparently inadequate. But if one

---

[1] Of course the differences between knowledge and belief *simpliciter* are even greater. One can have extensive knowledge of physics, but not extensive belief of physics; one can know French well, but not believe it well; one can know how to drive a car, but not believe how to drive a car; one can know Paris, but not believe Paris; and so on. But these deviations need not concern us here, since our considerations are those that bear on the questions of whether knowing that things are so implies believing that they are.

asks 'How can you know that?' that can only mean 'How come you know that?'. Conversely, one asks 'How do you know that?' but not 'How do you believe that?'. On the other hand, one asks 'Why do you believe that?' and not 'Why do you know that?'. One may have reasons for believing what one believes, but no reasons for knowing what one knows. 'Are there any reasons for me to know that?' is altogether unlike 'Are there any reasons for me to believe that?'. 'I believe that things are so' is an expression of belief, but 'I know things are so' is not an *expression*, but an admission or averral, of knowledge. Sincerely saying that I believe things are so is a *criterion* for my believing, but a sincere assertion that I know that things are so is not a criterion for my knowing. It is an admission or assertion that one is in possession of the relevant information. One can know for certain that things are so, but not believe for certain that they are, only be sure that they are. Normal loss of knowledge is a matter of forgetfulness. It can often be remedied by a reminder. Cessation of belief, however, is quite different. It is not produced by forgetfulness, but by counter-examples, or by reasons for doubting, by psychological pressures of one's peers or teachers. Belief, once lost, is not restored by reminders, but by further convincing reasons. Believing that things are so may be right or wrong, foolish or intelligent, reasonable, rational or neither, blameworthy or praiseworthy. But to know something to be so can be none of these. One can believe things to be so whole-heartedly, passionately, firmly, fervently, unswervingly, obstinately, obtusely, fanatically, hesitantly or tentatively. But one cannot know things to be so whole-heartedly, passionately, firmly, etc.

knowing/ believing and Wh-clauses The contrast between the uses of cognitive and doxastic questions and ascriptions is equally marked when it comes to Wh-clauses (see table 6.1). '*Who* knows whether (why, when, where, who, what) . . . ?' is typically an enquiry for a reliable source of information. It may also be an enquiry as to whether the addressees (e.g. pupils at school) have the information they should have. 'Do you know whether (why, when, where, who, what) . . . ?' is an enquiry as to whether the addressee can give one the information one seeks or whether the addressee knows something he is supposed to know. But one cannot ask 'Who believes whether (why, when, where) . . . ?'. The enquiry 'Do you believe that things are so?' is not a question about possession of information, but about the addressee's credulity, or his opinion, or the stand he takes – where, so to speak, he is placing his bets. 'Does he know whether things are so?' may be a query as to

	Knowledge//know// knowing//know that . . .	Belief//believe//believing// believe that . . .
Can one try to acquire?	✓	✗
'How can you . . .?'	✗	✓
'How do you . . .?'	✓	✗
'Why do you . . .?'	✗	✓
Reasons for . . . ing	= why one should	= grounds for
'I . . .' is an expression of . . .	✗	✓
'. . . for certain'	✓	✗
Loss of . . .	forgetting	ceasing to believe[a]
Restoration of . . .	reminder	further grounds for believing
'I don't . . . whether'	confession of ignorance	✗
'I don't . . . that'	denial of cognitive ascription	normally a denial of things being so
'Who . . . Wh-interrogative?	✓	✗
'Who . . . that *p*?'	who has the information	who takes a stand on or gives credence to
'He . . . that *p*'	implies that the speaker knows that *p*	does not imply that the speaker believes that *p*

[a] 'Loss of belief' normally signifies loss of faith. Here we are concerned solely with ceasing to believe something in contrast with ceasing to know something. This does not occur through forgetfulness, but, for example, as a result of being shown that what one believes is false or improbable.

Table 6.1   *Contrasts between knowing and believing that //*
Wh- // things are so

whether he has this information; 'Does he believe that things are so?' is not. 'He knows that things are so' typically implies that the speaker himself knows that they are. But 'He believes that things are so' does not imply that the speaker either knows or believes that they are. To know what he said is to know that he said that things are so, but to believe what he said is to believe that things are as he said they are.

Does belief accompany knowledge? These extensive logico-grammatical differences between knowledge and belief, and the differences in the roles that the verbs 'to know' and 'to believe' fulfil, suggest that knowledge is not a form of belief, that believing is not a constituent element of knowing something to be so. But the questions still remain: Is knowledge compatible with belief? Is belief a constant accompaniment of knowledge?

Many philosophers, from Plato onwards, have denied that what one knows can also be what one believes. But there is nothing awry with insisting that one believes what the witness says, since one was there too and *knows* that things were as he claims them to have been. If one were asked 'Do you believe what he says?', one would reply 'Yes, I was there, and I saw it (so I know it was so)'. So one is in a position to endorse what he says. But, of course, it does not *follow* that knowing something to be so *implies* believing it to be so. The matter must be handled with delicacy (and relative Wh-pronouns must not be confused with interrogative ones).

We have seen that the *expression* of belief, 'I believe that things are so', straddles:

- asserting something to be so with qualification;
- opining things to be so;
- gathering from others that things are so (being persuaded, taking things to be so);
- trusting another and so accepting his word and depending on it;
- subscribing to the proposition that things are so (endorsing, being convinced);
- taking a stand on things being so (maintaining, holding that things are so).

Each of these is surrounded by further subtly nuanced variations. Which use or uses of this multi-purpose instrument may be involved on any given occasion depends upon what is believed, what the believer and hearer know or assume, and the context of utterance.

Criteria for belief ascription

'He believes that things are so' *ascribes* belief to another. Depending on the context and on what is known or believed by speaker and hearer, this may imply (i) that he does not know, but believes (gathers, takes on trust) that things are so, (ii) that he falsely believes, (iii) that this is his opinion, (iv) that this is something on which he takes a stand. The *criteria* for whether he believes things to be so turn on what he says and does, as well as on the circumstance of whether things are so or not – since if things are not as he asserts them to be, he believes, but does not know, that they are.

3 reasons for thinking that knowing implies believing

Philosophers have been disagreeing for centuries over the question of whether knowing that things are so implies believing that they are. If someone claims that things are so, and they are not, then he believes falsely that things are so. So false belief appears to be knowledge minus truth. So knowledge seems to require belief plus truth (and whatever further conditions are deemed fit). But one may be sceptical about such conceptual arithmetic. A second reason for thinking that knowing implies believing is that if one knows things to be so, one would not wish to say that one does *not believe* them to be so. There is a use for 'I know it is so, but I can't believe it' – but not for 'I know it is so, but I don't believe it'. But that may be because in such cases one neither believes nor fails to believe (just as one neither recognizes nor fails to recognize one's wife at the breakfast table every time one looks up). A third reason for embracing the idea that knowledge implies belief is that it seems acceptable to say 'I not only believe it to be so – I know it to be so'. But we need to explain how this is compatible with the intelligibility of 'I don't believe it, I know it'.

When the question of believing does not arise

Clearly there are many things one knows with respect to which the question of whether one also believes them cannot arise. 'It is a sunny day', I may remark. Obviously I know it to be so – I just looked out of the window, and there was not a cloud to be seen. Do I believe what I just said? Well, my utterance was not a qualified assertion, it was an unqualified assertion expressing a knowledge-claim. Certainly it is not an opinion that I am voicing. It is not something I have gathered from others – I can *see* that it is a sunny day. Nor am I 'taking a stand' on such a matter. I can hardly be said to be endorsing anything said – I am just making a casual remark on what I see to be so. Of course, it would be misguided to say that I don't believe what I said, for that would suggest that I *disbelieve* my own statement. I certainly don't *disbelieve* it – I *know* it to be true. In this context, the question of believing or not believing cannot arise. Were someone to respond to my utterance by saying 'Do you believe that?', I should not understand what he meant. And it would be bizarre to say the least if someone in this context were to report of me 'He believes it is a sunny day' rather than 'He can see that it is a sunny day'. There are in fact indefinitely many contexts in which adding the belief-operator to an assertion that, in context, is a knowledge-claim would plainly be wrong (and clearly *not* for reasons concerning conversational implicature).

I don't believe it – I know it / I don't just believe it – I know it

It is striking that, on an appropriate occasion, we can say 'I don't *believe* it – I *know* it to be so', and, on another occasion, we can equally intelligibly say 'I don't just believe it – I know it to be so'. How can this be? Denial of belief in the first utterance is tantamount, above all, to denying that what follows is the expression of opinion or unconfirmed supposition. For obviously, if I know that things are so, then it is not an *opinion* of mine; it is not something that I merely *think* is so – rather I am in a position to confirm that things are so. What then of 'I don't just believe it – I know it to be so'? Evidently what this amounts to is that I not only take a stand on this, I do so advisedly – for I know that this is how things are. The different utterances focus on different facets of belief.

If I rightly assert that things are so, and am asked 'Do you believe that?', I would in most cases naturally say that I do, even though I *know* that things are so. For here the question 'Do you believe that?' is a request for me to *underwrite* what I said, and the answer 'Yes, I do' effects just that.

The 3rd-person case

Switching to the third person, we find the pattern to be similar. Given that he knows things to be so, does it follow that he believes that they are so? If the question, taken in a proper context, means 'Does he think it to be so – is this his opinion?', then the answer 'No, he knows it to be so' is correct. If the question 'Is this what he believes?', in context, amounts to 'Is this what he endorses?', 'Is this what he maintains?' or 'Is this what he stands by?' – then the answer would very often quite properly be 'Yes'. For if he knows things to be so, he will obviously endorse an assertion that they are so. To say 'No, this is what he knows to be so' would be frivolous pedantry. But, if in ignorance, one asks another a Wh-question, and he replies without qualification that things are thus-and-so, it would be wrong (and not merely an understatement) to report 'He believes things to be so' – for that would quite clearly imply that he does *not* know, and that one had better check his statement by asking someone else.

So, 'Does knowledge imply belief?' is not a good question. The answer is not 'yes' or 'no' – for either would be misleading. The better question is 'How is knowledge related to belief?' – and that question has now been thoroughly explored.

2. The epistemology of belief

Does one know that one believes what one believes?

It was a prominent part of Cartesian philosophy that *cogitationes* are known for certain by a person (otherwise they would not be suitable as premises for a *cogito* argument for one's own existence). We have called this the 'cognitive assumption'. That assumption was built into the empiricist conception of 'privileged access' to 'one's own consciousness'. Surely, it was argued, someone who believes that things are so *knows* that he believes this. He knows his own beliefs *by introspection*. He has privileged access to them, whereas others have to make do with what he says and does. It is this that explains so-called *first-person authority*. In chapter 1, section 5, I argued that this tempting conception is misconceived. It is time to dissolve the cognitive assumption and its corollaries.

8 conditions for using the cognitive operator

The first problem to confront is whether there is any use for sentences of the form 'I know I believe that things are so'. In particular, is there a use for such sentences that is akin in its epistemic import to 'I know that he believes that things are so'? There are eight requirements on the intelligible use of 'know' as an operator on common-or-garden empirical sentences.[2] These are itemized in list 6.1.

It should be clear that 'I believe that things are so' is not a legitimate base for the epistemic operator 'I know (that)' and its negation 'I don't know whether'.[3] But two caveats are in order.

---

[2] Hence excluding, as a matter for further scrutiny, such sentences as 'I exist', 'I am dreaming', as well as propositions belonging to what Wittgenstein called one's 'world-picture'. For detailed defence of the eight requirements, see P. M. S. Hacker, 'Of Knowledge and of Knowing that Someone is in Pain', in A. Pichler and S. Säätelä (eds), *Wittgenstein: the Philosopher and his Works* (Wittgenstein Archives at the University of Bergen, Bergen, 2005), pp. 123–56.

[3] And equally, is 'He believes that things are so' a base for the operator 'He knows that'? Note that there is no need for a restriction to the present tense – only to the same tense for both operator and base.

1. It must make sense for one not to know that . . . , or to be ignorant of whether . . . 'I know . . .' must exclude a genuine possibility, namely the possibility of my not knowing – otherwise it has no content. If 'I know' makes sense, then its negation makes sense too.[a]

2. It must make sense for one to believe, conjecture, suspect, surmise or guess that . . .

3. It must make sense for one to doubt whether . . . and for one to be certain that . . .

4. It must make sense for one to think one knows or for it to seem to one that . . ., but to be mistaken.

5. It must make sense for one to wonder whether . . . and to want to know whether . . .

6. It must make sense for one to satisfy oneself, to verify or confirm that . . .

7. There must be criteria for someone's knowing that . . . which are distinct from the criteria, grounds or evidence for . . .

8. Truthfulness in asserting that . . . should not guarantee truth.

[a] The principle underlying this is not a bare principle of contrast (which would after all be satisfied by 'He knows // He doesn't know // that I believe things are so'). It is rather that if an empirical proposition makes sense, then its negation also makes sense. 'I know that he believes things to be so' is an empirical proposition, so 'I do not know (am ignorant of) whether he believes things to be so' makes sense too. So too, if an empirical proposition makes sense, then it excludes an empirical possibility. But if 'I am ignorant . . .' is logically excluded in advance, then there is nothing for 'I know . . .' to exclude.

List 6.1 *Requirements on the use of 'knows that' as an operator on an empirical sentence*

2 caveats: uses for 'I know I believe'

First, we need not deny *any* use to the sentence 'I know that I believe that things are so' – what we are investigating is whether there is an *epistemic* use akin to 'I know that he believes that things are so'. We can happily concede that the sentence may be used as an *emphatic avowal of belief* – akin to 'I really do believe that things are so'. So too 'I know that I believe that things are so – you needn't keep on reminding me' is a *concessive response* to someone's insisting that I believe things are so – which is tantamount to 'Yes, I do indeed believe thus, don't keep on reminding me'. One can, of course, say 'I know what I believe, but I am not going to tell you' – that is tantamount to 'I have an opinion on the matter, but I am going to keep it to myself' or 'I have made up my mind (come to a verdict on the matter), but I will not tell you'. And one can say 'I know that I believe that things are so, but nevertheless I shall V', not to indicate one's possession of a piece of information that one might lack, but as equivalent to 'Granted that I believe that things are so, nevertheless . . .'. One may say 'Ask him whether he believes that things are so, he ought to know' as a joke – a grammatical joke, since *his* avowal of belief has a special weight. His word is a criterion for whether he so believes. All this may be granted without prejudicing the denial of the cognitive assumption and of the epistemic explanation of what is wrongly taken to be first-person *authority*.[4]

The second caveat concerns the import of the qualification on the guarantee that truthfulness gives to the truth of an avowal of belief. It is not absolute, but subject to a *ceteris paribus* clause. This is obvious in the case of slips of the tongue, malapropisms and similar misunderstandings of what one is saying – all of which are uninteresting in the present context. What *is* interesting in the case of avowals and averrals of belief is that self-deception is sometimes possible, and so are second thoughts. And room must be made for unconscious beliefs. But these are necessarily exceptions to the rule – deviations from a norm, not exceptions to a regularity. I shall therefore defer consideration of these until the standard cases have been investigated.

Not knowing here is indecision not ignorance

If 'I know I believe that things are so' makes sense, it must exclude my believing thus but *not knowing* that I do. But is there any such thing? Could someone intelligibly say (other than as a joke), 'Perhaps I believe that things are so, but if I do, I don't know it (or, I am ignorant of that fact)'? Self-deception and unconscious belief apart, would we understand someone who said of another, 'Actually, he believes that things are so, but he does not know that he does'? (But we might say

---

[4] One has no *authority* on whether and what one believes; rather one's word has a privileged, although defeasible, status.

'Actually, he believes things are so, but he won't admit it to himself'.)
Indeed, the force of the grammatical proposition 'You must know
what you believe' is precisely to emphasize that when a person
believes something, his ignorance that he so believes and his doubt
whether he so believes are, other things being equal, grammatically
excluded. This grammatical proposition emphasizes that *his avowal
of belief is a criterion for his believing*. To be sure, there *is* a use for
'I don't know whether I believe that things are so'. It is in place in
contexts where the question of whether things are so needs thinking
through, where there is evidence both for and against things being
so. But unlike 'I don't know whether he believes that things are so',
it is not an expression of ignorance but of uncertainty. And the
uncertainty involved is unlike 'I am not sure what he believes'. For
it is not an uncertainty regarding whether I do or do not believe that
things are so, but uncertainty regarding *what to believe*. What I need
here is not to investigate myself further to find out whether I believe
this. Rather, what I need is to investigate the evidence for and against
the supposition that things are so. And once that is clear, what I must
then do is *make up* my mind, not *peer into it*. I must *decide* what to
believe (i.e. what, on the balance of evidence, is really credible), not
discover what I believe. Hence in the third-person case, one can say
'I don't know whether he believes that things are so – I must find out
whether he does'. But one cannot say 'I don't know whether I believe
that things are so – I must find out whether I do'.

Can one suspect, surmise or guess one's own beliefs? Just as it makes no sense to be ignorant of one's
beliefs, so too it makes no sense to suspect, surmise
or guess that one believes something. I may think,
believe, opine, surmise, guess or suspect that A
believes that things are so, and it may seem to me that he does. But
'In my opinion, I believe that things are so' is surely nonsense, and
it is not easy to find any use for 'My guess (surmise, belief, suspicion)
is that I believe that things are so', or indeed for 'It seems to me that
I believe that things are so'. But it is noteworthy that 'I *think* that I
believe that things are so' might be used as a tentative expression of
an inclination to believe – when I am partly, but not wholly persuaded
that things are so. This contrasts with 'I think that he believes . . .'
– which is tantamount to 'As far as I know (or, in my opinion), he
believes that things are so'. Interestingly, 'He thinks that he believes
that things are so' does have a use, although an anomalous one. It
might be employed in imputing self-deception to a person, in which
case it would be followed by 'but he doesn't really'. It is noteworthy

that it would *not* be followed by 'and so indeed he does' or 'and, what is more, he is right'.

Believing and being sure/ unsure I may be unsure what to believe. But that it is not an expression of uncertainty over whether I do or do not believe that things are so. Second thoughts, self-deception and unconscious beliefs apart, there is no such thing as my believing something, but being uncertain whether I do. So, in the normal case, there is no such thing as my being certain that I believe that things are so. If someone were to say 'I am sure I believe that things are so', we would not understand him. So too, were someone to say 'It seems to me that I believe that things are so', we would not ordinarily know what to make of his words. And the supposition that someone might sincerely avow that he believes something and be *mistaken about his believing* (as opposed to being mistaken about what he believes) is not intelligible. He may indeed be deceiving himself, but, as we shall see, self-deception regarding one's beliefs is not a kind of mistake.

Can one verify that one believes? Just as there is no such thing as making *a mistake* about whether one believes something, so too there is no such thing as satisfying oneself, verifying or confirming that one believes that things are so. For having the belief that things are so is not like having a photograph of a state of affairs, the continued possession of which one might verify by checking to see whether it is still in the files. If it were, then saying 'I believe that things are so' would not be the qualified assertion that it commonly is – it would just be a report on what is in the file, and I could go on to say 'but as for whether it is or is not the case that things are so, that is still an open question as far as I am concerned'. It would be possible to say 'I believe that things are so, and my belief is trustworthy (the photograph is reliable), so presumably things are so' – which would be an absurdity akin to saying 'I believe thus, so I'll believe thus'.[5] One may satisfy oneself, verify or confirm that things are so; but one cannot satisfy oneself, verify or confirm that one believes thus. Rather, one may pause to *reconsider* one's position and satisfy oneself that one *still* believes it.

Are there criteria for someone's knowing that he believes? Another person needs criteria to assert of me that I believe something. But there are no additional criteria for another to assert of me that I *know*

---

[5] See Wittgenstein, *Remarks on the Philosophy of Psychology* (Blackwell, Oxford, 1980), vol. 1, §§481–3.

that I believe it. By contrast, I do not, in the normal case, say that I believe, think or opine that things are so on the basis of evidence that I so believe, but on the basis of evidence that things are so. Consequently, although one may say '*p*, and I know that I am right that *p* because *q*' and 'I believe that *p*, and I know I am right to believe that *p* because *q*', it would be a joke to say 'I believe that *p*, and I know that I am right *that I believe that p*'. Hence 'How do you know that you believe that *p*?' and 'Why do you believe that you believe that *p*?' are out of order. To be sure, there is a use for 'He knows what he believes' – it characterizes a person as doxastically decisive, and is akin to 'He knows his own mind'.

Truthfulness guarantees truth   Finally, while sincerity does not guarantee truth for third-person ascriptions of belief, the sincere utterance 'I believe that things are so', like the sincere confession of my thoughts or expression of my opinions, does (other things being equal) guarantee the truth of my avowal. Sincere avowals and confessions of belief are defeasible. But if not defeated by the very special circumstances that can undermine them, the truthfulness of an avowal of belief assures its truth.[6]

---

[6] It might be thought that the arguments of this section can be dismissed on Gricean grounds. For, it might be said, of course no one goes around *saying* 'I know that I believe that *p*'. But that is because it is too obvious to be worth saying. No one would say this, because normally, when someone believes that *p*, he knows that he does. So it is redundant to prefix an 'I know' to 'I believe that *p*', just as, in Grice's view, whenever one perceives an object, it seems to one that one perceives an object, even though we would not say this, since it is too obvious to be worth saying. Whether Grice was right about perception is debatable, although I shall not debate it here. But it is noteworthy that one conversational principle that he appealed to was that one should not make a weaker statement (e.g. 'It seems to me that I see an object') when one is in a position to make a stronger one (e.g. 'I see an object'), and that is why we would not say the former, even though it is true. But, by parity of reasoning, far from *not* saying 'I know that I believe that *p*', one should *always* say it in preference to the simple 'I believe that *p*', since, on the Gricean conception of 'strength', it is the stronger of the two (see O. Hanfling, *Philosophy and Ordinary Language* (Routledge, London, 2000), pp. 185–8).

Furthermore, if, normally, when A believes that *p*, he knows that he so believes, then although we don't, allegedly for Gricean reasons (e.g. 'No remark without remarkableness'), ordinarily say so, if we *were* to say so, what we say would be readily understood and no one would gainsay us. But if someone were to say 'I believe it is raining, and I know that I believe it', we would not know what he was driving at. And if someone were to say 'I believe that *p*', and we were to ask him 'Do you know that?', his reply would not be 'Of course I do', but rather 'I didn't say that I know that *p*, I said that I believe it'. Were we to persist, and say 'I mean, do you know that you believe that *p*?', he would not know what we wanted from him.

3. Non-standard cases: self-deception and unconscious beliefs

The defeasibility of avowals of belief

The authority or evidential weight of an avowal or averral of belief is defeasible. Most obviously, it is defeated by insincerity and dishonesty. It is defeated by slips of the tongue, saying something without properly understanding the words one uses, spoonerisms and malapropisms. These are unproblematic – roughly speaking, they are cases of a speaker either not meaning what he said or not saying what he meant. They do not call into question the non-cognitive account of avowals of belief or the deconstructive elucidation of 'first-person authority'.

4 problematic cases

Four kinds of case, however, are more puzzling. First, there are cases of a person's sincerely avowing a belief, but not matching his deeds to his beliefs. Secondly, there are cases of self-deception. Thirdly, a person may harbour unconscious beliefs. Fourthly, a person may avow a belief and when challenged, start to give his reasons for believing what he just avowed he believed, only to realize that they are defective. He might then say 'I thought I believed that, but perhaps I don't really believe it at all'. These are puzzling in so far as they appear to exemplify a person's being ignorant of, or making a mistake about, what he believes, just as he may be ignorant of, or make a mistake about, what another believes. If so, it seems that he does not know that he believes what he believes or does not know that he does not believe what he thinks he believes – just as he may not know what another believes. The alternative to explore, however, is that these kinds of fault are mischaracterized as mistakes, cognitive errors or ignorance *simpliciter*.

In short, the case is unlike both the Gricean examples of seeing/seeming to see (as well as V-ing/trying to V) and unlike the uncontroversial case of adding to every answer to the question 'What were you doing?' the phrase 'and I was breathing'. For in the latter case, we would reply, 'Well, of course'; but in the case of adding to the assertion 'I believe that it is raining' the supplement 'I know that I believe this', we would reply not 'Of course', but 'What *do* you mean?'. To be sure, we might be puzzled and respond, 'Could there be any doubt?'. But what that indicates is not that *of course* he knows, but rather that avowing a belief and simultaneously expressing doubt about whether one so believes is excluded. The grammatical exclusion of doubt does not imply the presence of certainty, let alone of knowledge.

Lip-service and self-deception are not mistakes (i) The lip-server and self-deceiver aver that they believe such-and-such. Knowing them full well, we wish to deny that they really believe what they say they believe. But their fault is not that they *mistakenly* believe that they believe that things are so, as they might mistakenly believe that another person does. In the case of doxastic judgements about others, one may mistakenly take something they say or do to betoken their believing that things are so, whereas in fact it only appeared to be so – they were lying or pretending. But in one's own case, one does not avow a belief on the basis of evidence that one so believes, but, if anything, on the basis of the evidence for what one believes. So one does not and cannot wrongly aver a belief as a result of mistakenly taking one's behaviour to betoken belief when it does not. And there is surely no such thing as mistaking the presence of a belief for its absence, or vice versa.

Mismatch between words and deeds A person's avowing a belief is a defeasible criterion for others' ascribing that belief to him. So too is the person's acting for the reason that (as far as he knows) things are so. But in exceptional circumstances, these two criteria may come apart. A person may aver a belief, but fail to match his deeds to his words. Other things being equal, we favour deeds over words. Here we *may* say that he *thinks* that he believes what he says that he believes, but that he does not *really*, since he fails to act accordingly. Yet his fault is not a mistaken second-order belief, but rather the fault of merely paying lip-service to some cause, unthinkingly averring something without really subscribing to what he says he believes. Alternatively, we may accept that he believes what he says he believes, but accuse him of hypocrisy – of failing to live up to the commitments of his belief. But that has no bearing on 'first-person authority'.

Motivated disregard of evidence (ii) Similarly, the self-deceiver has not made a *mistake* about what he believes. Rather, he avows a false belief in the face of overwhelming evidence to the contrary, *which he has a powerful motive for disregarding*. His faults are a lack of sense of reality, misguidedly succumbing to his own motivated bias, lack of courage in facing the facts. Karenin did not make a mistake at the racecourse about his beliefs, but about Anna's relations with Vronsky. He deceived himself by refusing to confront the evidence that stared him in the face and by invoking unwarranted excuses to defeat the evidence, which he would not have invoked in cases in which he was not emotionally involved. Here too we are inclined to say that despite his avowal he did not *really* believe what he said he believed – how could he, given what he knew? (The naturalness of the interpolation of a 'really' is striking.) What does that mean? That he made a mistake about whether he believed what he averred he believed? Surely not – he sincerely avowed that things are so, and indeed acted on the basis of what he avowed he believed. It means that he motivatedly failed to give the evidence against things being so the scrutiny and evaluation which he would give in other cases. It is not that he jumped to an unwarranted conclusion, for that is not a case of self-deception. It is rather that his failure properly to evaluate the evidence was *motivated* – and it is this that warrants the epithet 'self-deception'. Does he not believe that things are so? Yes, he does – but only because he is *unwilling* to give due weight to the evidence to the contrary. He does not need more evidence, but more candour. So we are inclined to say that he does not *really* believe that things are so – in his heart, we say metaphorically, he knows that he is fudging the evidence. And what that means is that were he honest with himself, he would *realize* this.

The problem of unconscious beliefs
(iii) We sometimes explain people's behaviour by reference to 'unconscious beliefs' (this form of explanation predates Freud (e.g. Schelling, Coleridge, Carus, James, not to mention Shakespeare). Unconscious beliefs may well seem to be beliefs which the agent has, but which he does not know that he has. And that suggests that an agent's ordinary beliefs are conscious ones, that is, ones which he *does* know that he has. But this is mistaken.

The first point to emphasize is that the Freudian conception of the unconscious is awry. For an unconscious belief does not stand to a belief that is not unconscious as an occluded chair stands to a visible one.[7] Introspection, as we have seen, is not a form of perception, but of reflection, and an unconscious belief is not a belief that is hidden from sight any more than a belief that is not unconscious (which is not to be denominated 'a conscious belief') is one that is in view. It is rather a belief only in an attenuated sense.

---

[7] Freud was confused by traditional philosophical misconceptions of introspection as a form of inner perception: 'In psycho-analysis there is no choice for us but to declare mental processes to be in themselves unconscious, and to compare the perception of them by consciousness with the perception of the outside world through the sense-organs' (Freud, 'The Unconscious' [1915], trans. J. Rivière, in J. Strachey (ed.), *Collected Papers of Sigmund Freud*, vol. 4 (New York, Basic Books, 1959), p. 104).

One kind of case in which the notion of unconscious belief is invoked is that in which we explain a person's puzzling behaviour pattern by reference to a belief which he had, but has 'repressed' (perhaps because it is, in one way or another, painful or shameful). Another kind of case is that in which a behavioural and emotional syndrome is explained by reference to an agent's 'unconscious beliefs' about himself which he may never have articulated, for example, a belief in his own worthlessness. He may, initially, sincerely deny that he harbours the belief that we impute to him. In the former kind of case, he has, to all intent and purpose, forgotten what he previously knew or believed (but can, under appropriate circumstances, retrieve it). In the latter, he may deny that he conceives of himself thus, for there may be no good reasons for him to do so (but perhaps the awakening of a childhood memory or trauma may disclose the irrational genesis of his self-image). What we allege he believes never features in his sincere avowals of belief, in the reasons he honestly gives for what he says and does, or in his own reflections. So he satisfies one criterion for *not* believing what we suppose him to believe. But his problematic and puzzling behaviour is rendered more intelligible by explaining it in terms of the so-called unconscious belief. We may say that the 'repressed' belief is, as it were, alive in his pattern of actions and reactions in certain recurrent circumstances, providing an intelligible reason or motive for his otherwise inexplicable behaviour. But the concept of an unconscious belief clearly deviates from our ordinary concept of belief. For unlike ordinary beliefs, its ascription need not be defeated by the agent's sincere denial that he believes thus or by the fact that it plays (and can play) no role in the sincere reasons he gives, both to himself and to others, for what he does, feels and thinks. Nevertheless, its imputation renders recurrent patterns of his behaviour and reactions intelligible.

Hermeneutic insight   It is important that the criterion for whether our explanatory hypothesis is correct is whether the agent, on reflection or under analysis, accepts it. Let us suppose that he is brought to recollect the belief he once harboured or the circumstances which may have given rise to the thought of his worthlessness. Suppose further, that he now *realizes* that coming to see his problematic behaviour and reactions in the light of this belief renders them intelligible. Moreover, he comes to *accept* the explanation, and acknowledges that the repressed or suppressed belief was 'alive' in his emotional and behavioural syndrome. This, we are inclined to say, confirms our explanatory hypothesis. But for the agent, this is not an explanatory hypothesis, it is a *hermeneutic insight*. If it were merely an explanatory hypothesis for him, it would be akin to a medical hypothesis concerning an illness, and the patient's consent would be irrelevant to its truth. But for the agent, it is an *interpretation* which effects a *change of aspect*. He does not become conscious of a belief of which he was previously unconscious, as he may become conscious of another person's belief of which he was previously ignorant. He does not *testify* to the truth of the hypothesis which explains his behaviour. Rather he makes sense of his behaviour in the light of an interpretation by reference to 'unconscious beliefs', and comes to a new understanding of himself, sees himself and his past in a fresh light. It is his acceptance of the interpretation, manifest in his current avowal that *this* belief is why he behaves or behaved thus-and-so, that constitutes the criterion for the truth of our explanatory hypothesis. Does it follow that all along he believed such-and-such, but did not know that he did? Not in the ordinary sense. An unconscious belief is not a belief that one has but of which one is ignorant, and explaining one's behaviour in terms of an unconscious belief is not akin to explaining another's behaviour in terms of his beliefs of which one was hitherto ignorant. It is noteworthy that in such cases, the agent would not say 'I believed that things were so, but I didn't know that I did', but rather 'I believed that things were so, but I didn't realize it' (or, '. . . but I could not admit it to myself'). Realization here is a form of pattern recognition or aspect-apprehension, and the confirmation of the pattern consists in the patient's coming to see his behaviour and feelings under a new aspect. Indeed, one might say that the pattern is partly *constituted* by its subjective recognition.

Second thoughts　　(iv) The case of second thoughts is similarly only apparently an objection to the analysis under consideration. It is not a case of making a *mistake* about what one believes. It is rather a case of having previously made a mistake about the force of the supporting evidence for the belief that things are so and now *bethinking* oneself, reconsidering the matter. When one previously asserted that things are so, one really did believe thus. But on unreflectively reaffirming one's belief, one suddenly realizes that one had been wrong to believe thus, that one had been credulous. So one reconsiders the matter, and accordingly withdraws one's avowal, refuses, as it were, to underwrite the supposition that things are so. But it would be misleading to characterize one's initial, unreflective or credulous avowal as mistaking the absence of a belief that things were so for its presence.

These anomalous cases do provide occasion for the use of such phrases as 'I thought I believed that' and 'He believes that he believes that' or 'I didn't realize that I believed that'. But these phrases are not akin to 'I thought he believed that', 'I didn't realize that he believed that' or 'He believes that A believes that'. They are cases that deviate from the *centres of variation* that characterize the language-game of expressions and ascriptions of belief. What they show is that the logic of epistemic terms is complex and subtle – like the complexities of human thought and life.

7

Sensation and Perception

1. The cognitive powers of the senses

Perceptual faculties are cognitive faculties

Sense-perception is the fundamental source of empirical knowledge. Our sense-faculties are exercised by the use of our sense-organs. The function of our sense-organs is to enable us to learn how things are in our environment, and how things are with us in respect of our body (we can see whether our hands are clean, feel whether our hair is dry, etc.). By the use of our sense-organs in looking, listening, feeling, smelling and tasting we can perceive things and can apprehend how things are. It is unsurprising that the dominant use of perceptual verbs is factive. There is a subordinate intentional use (paraphrasable by 'it (sensibly) seems (seemed) to me as if'), as when we say 'I saw a blur' (as a ball whizzed by), 'I hear a constant buzzing sound' (as sufferers from tinnitus report) or 'I felt two spherical surfaces' (when subjected to tactile illusion with crossed fingers). Such cases apart, if one sees something, then there is something one sees. If one sees that something is red, it follows that it is red. Otherwise one misperceived, was subject to illusion, and it merely struck one, or sensibly seemed to one, to be thus.

It is from the testimony of others (which we hear) and from the authority of books (which we read) that we learn the large part of the permanent, as opposed to the passing, knowledge we have of the world. To say that sense-perception is the fundamental or basic

The Intellectual Powers: A Study of Human Nature, First Edition. P. M. S. Hacker.
© 2013 John Wiley & Sons, Ltd. Published 2013 by John Wiley & Sons, Ltd.

source of empirical knowledge is not to suggest that the foundations of empirical knowledge lie in sense-perception – for it is not even to say that empirical knowledge *has* foundations (it doesn't). It is to say no more than that without the exercise of our sense-faculties we should not acquire the empirical knowledge we do acquire, nor indeed should we possess the concepts that we do possess and in terms of which we are able to say, and think about, what we perceive.

Etymology of 'perceive' The etymological source of the Anglo-Norman verb 'perceivre' – the Latin *percipere* – signifies *to take possession of, to lay hold of, to grasp* or *to understand*. It is not surprising that 'to perceive' came to mean 'to apprehend', that is, any form of cognitive receptivity. It is striking that the German *begreifen* (*to understand, conceive, comprehend, grasp*) and *Begriff* (*concept*) incorporates the very same picture. On the other hand, the German for 'perceive', *wahrnehmen*, embeds the image of *taking to be true*. Both verbal pictures intimate something important. We share our sense-faculties with other animals. But with us, and not with other animals, sense-perception is suffused with concepts. This does not imply that everything we perceive, we perceive *as* something (as if all perception were aspect-perception). What it means is that we cannot perceive something without being *able* to say, *in some form or other*, what we perceive (even if only 'What a strange taste'). Perceiving, *with us*, is indeed apprehension, a 'laying hold of' – a bringing within the compass of understanding and thought. And since we perceive *that* things are so, and can *say* that they are, we do indeed take the statement that they are to be true.

Sensation and perception amalgamated The noun 'sensation' and the cognate verb 'to sense' are latecomers on the English linguistic scene. They were introduced in the seventeenth century, and were employed (in one of their meanings) over the next two centuries more or less coextensively with 'sense-perception' and 'sensation' (such as pain, or cramp, or feeling tired). Dr Johnson defined 'sensation' as 'perception by means of the senses'. This presented perception in general as any form of apprehension, and blurred the distinction between sense-perception and sensations proper. This had already been patent in Locke:

> *Our senses*, conversant about particular sensible Objects, do *convey into the Mind*, several distinct *Perceptions* of things, according to those various ways, wherein those Objects do affect them: And thus we come

by those *Ideas*, we have of *Yellow, White, Heat, Cold, Soft, Hard, Bitter, Sweet*, and all those which we call sensible qualities, which when I say the senses convey into the mind, I mean, they from external Objects convey into the mind what produces there those *Perceptions*. This great Source, of most of the *Ideas* we have, depending upon our Senses, and derived by them to the Understanding, I call *SENSATION*.[1]

So too, Hume, writing fifty years later, divided all 'perceptions of the human mind' into two classes, those of impressions (which include impressions of pain no less than impressions of perceptual qualities (of colour, sound, smell, etc.) and those of ideas. Perceptions, 'which enter [the mind] with most force and violence', he named 'impressions', which include 'all our sensations, passions and emotions'.[2] So 'sensation', for Hume, encompassed both localized bodily sensations (e.g. pains, tickles and itches) and sense perceptions. Neither Boyle nor Newton felt any unease in conceiving of seeing as a form of having sensations, and of colours seen as 'sensations in the sensorium'. The consequence was widespread confusion. These confusions are with us to this day, especially in psychology and cognitive neuroscience, where, in the wake of Helmholtz, sensation is commonly held to be a constituent of every perception. To eradicate such confusions requires careful differentiation of sense-perception from sensation.

Sources of conceptual puzzlement: (i) the unity of experience Philosophical preoccupation with sense-perception is as old as philosophy itself. It has multiple sources. One has already been noted (chapter 1, pp. 34f.). It is the puzzlement over the unity of our perceptual experience despite the multiplicity of our sense-organs and faculties, and their proper objects. Given the different sense-organs and the differences in the kind of information we attain by their use, how can it be that we perceive a unified perceptual field of coloured, noisy, odorous material objects in a unified spatio-temporal framework. This difficulty was met by the Aristotelian idea of a general sense (*sensus communis*), the task of which is to synthesize the multiple data into a unified perception. This evolved into the high Kantian doctrine of transcendental synthesis of representations. In the twentieth century the very same problem gave rise to the so

[1] Locke, *An Essay concerning Human Understanding*, II. i. 3.

[2] Hume, *A Treatise of Human Nature*, I. i. 1.

called *binding problem* in cognitive neuroscience. The confusions involved here have already been discussed (see pp. 34–5).

(ii) Illusions, hallucinations and dreams

A second source of philosophical interest lies in the existence of illusions, hallucinations and dreams, which give rise both to conceptual concern and to sceptical worry. The conceptual concern is the distinction between illusion, hallucination and dreaming, on the one hand, and sense-perception, on the other. For someone subject to one of the former is, it seems, incapable of differentiating it from the latter. All four seem to involve the same subjective experience: namely *its sensibly seeming to one exactly as if one were perceiving that things are thus-and-so*. But how can *seeing*, for example, also be *seeming to see*? Is perception hallucination plus something? Or is hallucination perception minus something? Or should we abandon such conceptual arithmetic? Conceptual analysis is called for.

This concern in turn gives rise to a sceptical worry, namely how can we ever know that we are perceiving the real world at all? Maybe, for all our subjective experience can show us, life is but a dream rounded with a sleep. Or maybe any given current perceptual experience is illusory, since we cannot subjectively distinguish perceiving from hallucinating, having an illusion or dreaming? Scepticism will not be discussed here; but the idea that illusion, hallucination and perception have a common 'experiential content' will be examined.

(iii) The relation between scientific and philosophical investigation

A third source of philosophical puzzlement about perception lies in the relationship between the scientific enterprise of explaining the physical and physiological processes involved in perceiving something, and the philosophical enterprise of clarifying the concepts of perception. The scientific enterprise is concerned with explaining the processes whereby nerve-endings are irritated by contact with material things, with air and liquid solutions, and by the impact of air-waves or light-waves, and how the consequent stimulation is conveyed to, and processed in, the brain – without which we should not perceive what we perceive. Perception, it seems, is a causal process and the concept of perception seems to be a causal concept. That thought is enshrined in the *philosophical* causal theory of perception – both in its classical representational form (e.g. Descartes, Hobbes and Locke), its neo-classical representational form (e.g. Ayer, Mackie), and in its more recent non-representational form (e.g. Grice and Strawson).

(iv) Scientific world-view A fourth and closely related source of bafflement about perception lies in the emergence, in the seventeenth century, of the modern scientific world-view. From Galileo, Descartes, Hobbes, Boyle, Newton and Locke to the present day, it has been held to be one of the fundamental discoveries of science that the world, as it is independently of sentient creatures' perceptions of it, is dark, colourless, soundless, tasteless, odourless, neither hot nor cold, neither dry nor wet. The world as it is in itself, scientists inform us, is dramatically *unlike* how we perceive it to be. A recent Nobel laureate and his colleagues wrote as follows:

> We *receive* electromagnetic waves of different frequencies but we *perceive* colors: red, green, orange, blue or yellow. We receive pressure waves but we hear words and music. We come in contact with a myriad of chemical compounds dissolved in air or water but we experience smells and tastes.
>
> Colors, sounds, smells and tastes are mental constructions created in the brain by sensory processing. They do not exist, as such, outside the brain. Therefore, we can ask the traditional question raised by philosophers: Does a falling tree in the forest make a sound if no one is near enough to hear it? We can say with certainty that while the fall creates pressure waves in the air, it does not create a sound. Sound occurs only when pressure waves from the falling tree reach and are perceived by a living being.[3]

Psychologists of perception concur: 'Colors, tones, tastes and smells are mental constructions, created out of sensory stimulations. As such they do not exist outside living minds.'[4] Of course, this is not a new scientific discovery (as many scientists suppose it to be), nor is it an old scientific discovery – since it is not a scientific discovery at all. For no scientific experiment could possibly show that everything is colourless, that the world is dark and silent, that nothing has either taste or smell. This doctrine is a piece of questionable seventeenth-century metaphysics, with roots going back to the Greek atomists, such as Democritus. It opens an unbridgeable gulf between the world as it is in itself (according to the 'scientific world-image') and the world as we experience it as being. For if it is right, then we live in

[3] E. R. Kandel, J. H. Schwartz and T. M. Jessell, *Essentials of Neuroscience and Behaviour* (Appleton & Lange, Stamford, Conn., 1995), p. 370.

[4] I. Rock, *Perception* (Scientific American Books, New York, 1984), p. 4.

a world of false appearances. This thought forces reconsideration of sense-perception. Sense-perception can hardly be said to be the basic way of informing ourselves about the world if most of its deliverances are illusory and inform us not about objects in the world around us but about how they affect our sensibility. For what we perceive (or 'directly perceive') cannot be the world as it is in itself, but only the ideas, impressions or perceptions caused in us by agitation of our nerve-endings.

So, the concept of sensation needs to be clarified and differentiated from that of perception. The general concept of perception has to be anatomized. The concepts of the five perceptual senses require elucidation. The causal theory of perception needs critical examination. These are the tasks of this chapter and its sequel. Demonstration of the incoherence of the scientific world-picture inherited from the seventeenth century will not be undertaken.[5]

2. Sensation

Sensation and the mental

The concept of sensation subsumes various forms of awareness of one's body and disturbances to one's body. It is a constitutive element in our conception of many of the passions (appetites, emotions and moods), and of forms of tactile perception. Aristotle and the medieval Aristotelians allocated sensation to the sensitive *psuchē* possessed by all animals, rather than to the mind or rational *psuchē*. For susceptibility to bodily disturbances of pain, sensual pleasure, itches, giddiness and so forth are aspects of our animal nature. Since Descartes, however, it has become customary to characterize sensations as 'mental'. Descartes conceived of *having pains* (and all other sensations too) as kinds of 'thoughts', hence as modes of the mind. For, he held, a human being cannot have a pain and not be conscious of it. One cannot doubt that one has a pain. When one has a pain, one knows for certain that one does. So, *that one has a sensation* can fulfil the role of the premise in a 'cogito' proof of existence. Mere brutes, he held, do not have pain in the sense in which we do. Their apparent

---

[5] For critical examination of the doctrine, see P. M. S. Hacker, *Appearance and Reality* (Blackwell, Oxford, 1987).

pain-behaviour is no more than a mechanical reflex, involving no conscious experience. Animals do not have a mind, are not conscious and do not think.

In what sense sensations are physical

This Cartesian conception is confused. There is no distinction between being conscious of a pain, being aware of a pain and having a pain. Animals have pains no less than humans, and although some of their pain behaviour, like some of ours, may involve reflex actions (e.g. recoiling from a hot surface one has touched), much of it (e.g. assuaging the injury, favouring the injured limb) does not. It is true that when one has a pain, one cannot doubt that one does. But by the same token one cannot be certain that one does either. One cannot be ignorant of having a pain, and by the same token, one cannot know that one has a pain either. Once one rejects the Cartesian conception of the mind[6] and of consciousness (see chapter 1 above), it becomes unclear what is meant by the claim that sensations are 'mental' or that they are modes of the mind. For, in one perfectly decent sense, they are *physical*. It is *one's back* that aches when one has a backache, *one's hand* that hurts when one has cut it, *one's head* that throbs when one has migraine. Contrary to what Descartes averred, a living organism is not a senseless machine. *Living creatures have a sensitive body.* If they hurt their limbs, their limbs hurt; if their nostrils are tickled, their nostrils tickle; and if they touch nettles with their hands, their hands itch.

No doubt one can classify sensations in more than one way. For purposes of a connective analysis locating the concept of sensation in the broader conceptual landscape, the following rough classification will prove satisfactory:

- *Localized physical (bodily) sensations* are sensations we feel *in* the body. These are such feelings as pains, aches, tickles, tingles, itches, throbbing and burning sensations, heartburn, nausea. These are traditionally taken to be paradigms of sensation.
- *Somatic sensations* are sensations *of* the body. These are such feelings as sensations of muscular strain, cramp, creaking joints, distended belly, stiff neck or pounding heart.

---

[6] See *Human Nature: the Categorial Framework*, ch. 8.

- *Sensations of overall bodily condition* are such as feeling well or ill, fit or weak, sleepy or wide awake, sensations of lassitude, giddiness. These do not generally allow the transformation pattern: I have a pain in my leg – my leg hurts; I have an ache in my back – my back aches; I have a tickle in my throat – my throat tickles. If I feel well, no part of me feels well, and if I feel sleepy, no part of me feels sleepy; when I feel giddy, my head spins, but it is not giddy, and when I feel seasick, my stomach feels queasy, but it does not feel seasick.
- *Kinaesthetic sensations* are sensations of the disposition and motion of one's limbs. Here there is room for mistake, and hence for knowledge. But such knowledge is immediate, not evidential. The boundary between sensation and perception blurs here.
- *Sensations of orientation* are sensations of one's overall bodily orientation. Here there is room for mistake, and hence for immediate, non-evidential knowledge. The boundary between sensation and perception blurs here too.
- *Appetitive sensations* (sensations of hunger, thirst, animal lust) are blends of *sensation* and *desire* characteristic of animal nature. They are localized. One could not have a feeling of thirst in one's belly any more than one could have a feeling of hunger in one's throat. Feelings of hunger or thirst must be distinguished from merely accompanying sensations such as light-headedness and dizziness. Appetitive sensations are forms of unease that dispose one to action to satisfy the appetite. The intensification of the sensations is progressively more and more unpleasant, and the corresponding desire is proportional to the intensity of the sensation. What is distinctive of *appetitive desires* is that they have a formal object (food, drink, sexual release), but no specific object. Hunger is a desire for food, but one cannot feel hungry for *coq au vin*; thirst is a desire for drink, but one cannot feel thirsty for a gin and tonic. Satisfying an appetite leads to its temporary satiation and so to the disappearance of the appetitive sensation. Appetites are not constant but recurrent. They are typically caused by bodily needs or hormonally determined drives.

The connection between sensations and emotions is different again. Many occurrent emotions, such as anger, fear and excitement, are bound up with distinctive sensations (see fig. 7.1). One feels 'butterflies' in the stomach when excited, one feels one's mouth dry and one's hands trembling when afraid, and one feels one's heart pounding and one's temples throbbing when one is enraged. Overall bodily sensations are typically involved in the syndromes of some moods, such as depression and anxiety.

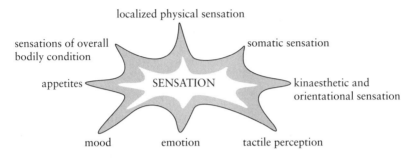

Figure 7.1 *The domain of sensation*

Sensation compared with perception Sensations, like perceptions, are not perceived, but had. Unlike perceptions, they are not only had, but felt. Indeed, there is no difference between having a pain (tickle or itch) and feeling one. Feeling a sensation thus is unlike feeling a tactile quality. Feeling hot (which may be a localized sensation, as when one's feet are burning, or a sensation of overall bodily condition, as when one feels hot after vigorous exercise) is not the same as feeling the thermal qualities of things. One may feel heat without feeling hot, and one may feel hot without being hot or feeling heat. Feeling a sensation is also unlike the tactile perception of an object. Feeling a pain is not akin to feeling a pin, for there is no such thing as seeming to feel a pain and not having one. But it can seem to one that one can feel a pin in the futon without there being a pin. One cannot have a pain in one's foot without one's feeling it, but there may well be a pin in one's futon without one's feeling it.

Having a sensation is not owning a sensation It is the sentient creature, the animal with a sensitive body, that *has* sensations. There are no sensations that are not sensations *of* some sentient being. The subject of a sensation is the being that manifests it. But to *have* a sensation, contrary to what has often been suggested, is not to *own* a sensation.[7] Ownership is a relation between an owner and the thing owned (which may be a chattel or a right), and since it is not an internal relation, ownership is generally transferable (and commonly shareable). Even if property is legally inalienable, it *makes sense* for it to be alienated. To have a pain is not to possess anything, just as to *have* a colour (to be of a certain colour) is not to *own* anything. Different people may have the same pain, itch or feeling of giddiness – not numerically the same (as when husband and wife *share* the same car), nor qualitatively the same (as when two people each *own* a car of the same make, colour, etc.), but just the same. Of course, if A and B have the same pain, for example a throbbing headache in the left temples, and A takes an aspirin, he will cease to have a headache, although B's headache will continue. This does not mean that they didn't have the same pain – it means that they did but no longer do. Similarly, if two chairs are the same colour and we paint one chair a different colour, the colour of the other chair will not change. This does not show that they did not have exactly the same colour – on the contrary, it shows that they did and no longer do.

Location of sensations   It always makes sense to ask where it tickles, what part of the body itches, where the pain is located. The criteria for the location of a sensation is where the subject of the sensation points, what part of his body he nurses, assuages or scratches, where he says it hurts. The location of sensation may be distinct from the locus of the cause of the sensation – as is evident in the case of reflected pains. Sometimes the location of a pain or itch may be hallucinatory, as in the case of a phantom pain or itch felt by an amputee 'as if in his leg', even though he has no leg. But there is no such thing as a hallucinatory or illusory pain – phantom pains really are pains. Although neuroscientists and some philosophers have been induced by such phenomena as phantom pains to suppose that pains are located in 'the body-image in the

---

[7] Frege held that 'ideas [sensations, feelings, moods, inclinations, wishes] are something we have', that 'ideas need an owner' and that 'every idea has only one owner; no two men have the same idea' ('Thoughts' [1918/19], repr. in his *Collected Papers on Mathematics, Logic and Philosophy* (Blackwell, Oxford, 1984), pp. 360f. (original pagination: pp. 67f.). Peter Strawson held that states of consciousness or private experiences are logically, non-transferably, owned by their possessor (*Individuals* (Methuen, London, 1959), p. 97).

brain', that is mistaken.[8] There are no pains in the brain – although pressure on the brain will cause a headache (which is in the head, not in the brain). There are no pains in 'body-images in the brain', but only in bodies.

Varieties of locative uses of 'in'

Of course, to have a pain in one's knee is not at all like having a silver penny in one's purse. Both phrases involve a locative use of 'in' (as opposed to non-locative uses, such as 'in the story', 'in May', 'in my dreams'), but of logically distinct kinds. To have a pain *in* one's knee is not to have a pain *inside* one's knee; the knee does not *contain* the pain, and one cannot *take it out* – only make it go away. If I have a penny between my fingers and put my fingers in my mouth, there is a penny in my mouth, but if I have a pain in my finger and I put my finger in my mouth, I do not have a pain in my mouth. If I take my purse to London, then my silver penny will be in London, but if I have a pain in my hand and go to London, my pain will not be in London – *I* shall, with a painful hand. The reason is clear. 'There is a penny in the purse' specifies a spatial relation between two objects: one is contained within the other. But 'There is a pain in my hand' does not specify a relation between two objects, a pain and a hand, since a pain is a sensation, sensations are not objects and *having* here does not signify a relation of any kind.

It is noteworthy that our ability to identify the locus of a sensation does not turn on the felt character or phenomenal features of the sensation. If one says that one has a pain in one's hand (that one's hand hurts), that is not because one has a hand-indicative sensation of pain that informs one, so to speak, where the pain is. Our ability to locate the pains we have is non-evidential or 'original'.

The criteria of sameness and difference of paradigmatic sensations fall into four classes, which are shown in list 7.1.

Elasticity of criteria of identity for sensation

These criteria of identity for sensations are elastic. The pain I now have may be the same as the pain I had previously, but it has become less severe. It may have changed from being a throbbing pain to

---

[8] See J. R. Searle, 'Putting Consciousness Back in the Brain', in M. Bennett, D. Dennett, P. Hacker and J. Searle, *Neuroscience and Philosophy* (Columbia University Press, New York, 2007), pp. 116–19, and in response, P. M. S. Hacker and M. R. Bennett, 'The Conceptual Presuppositions of Cognitive Neuroscience', ibid., pp. 142–6.

being just a dull pain – but it is still the same pain. Or I may have got used to it, and find it less unpleasant than before. We measure pains (and other sensations) with an elastic ruler.[9]

- *Bodily location*: in the case of such sensations as pains, itches and tingles it always makes sense to ask 'Where?' In the case of overall bodily sensations (e.g. feeling well or ill), and some sensations of orientation, *lack of bodily location* partly determines the identity of the sensation.

- *Intensity*: it is characteristic of locatable sensations that they occur with different degrees of intensity, and can wax or wane over time. An itch can be intolerable or only mildly irritating; a pain may be unbearable or only slight.

- *Phenomenal characteristics*: the felt features of paradigmatic sensations are often characterized in terms of typical causes, for example burning, stinging, stabbing or sensations of pressure, of torsion, of release.

- *The hedonic character*: whether the sensation is enjoyable or not, whether it is unpleasant or dreadful, whether it is hedonically neutral and so forth.

List 7.1   *Criteria of identity for sensations*

Counting sensations   We can, and very occasionally do, count pains. But this should not mislead us into thinking that counting pains is like counting pins, that the distinction between numerical and qualitative identity that applies to material objects also applies to pains. One should remember that we also count colours as well as colour patches. We may count the number of people in the room who have a pain (are in pain) – but this would be misdescribed as counting the number of pains in the room, since there is no such thing as a pain being 'in the room'. We may count how many pains we feel

---

[9] Don't think that elastic rulers are odd, irrational or reprehensible. They are often exactly what we want – as in the case of measuring the value of imports and exports (the rate of exchange – the measure – fluctuates constantly), or in measuring time by six or twelve daylight hours and six or twelve night-time hours (the fixed equi-temporal twenty-four-hour day is a relatively modern invention).

at a given moment. That is to count how many parts of our body hurt (hence rather like counting the number of colour patches on a canvas). One may count the occasions or frequency of pains – and it is noteworthy that it matters not at all whether one says 'I've had three headaches in the last week' or 'I've had a headache three times in the last week'. And we may count pains *simpliciter* (rather like counting colours). In determining whether two people have the same pain, generally location (i.e. *corresponding* location), intensity and phenomenological features are the criteria employed. But sometimes location may be disregarded – as when I have the same arthritic pain in my left wrist as you have in your right one.

The concept of sensation is linked to the concepts of (i) causation, (ii) desire and (iii) behaviour.

Link between sensation and causation
(i) What caused a sensation often plays a role in determining what sensation the subject of sensation has. Pain is linked to causes of pain such as being cut, hit or burnt – that is, to various stimuli that *cause injury or damage to the tissue of the body*. These provide *a* typical context in which such-and-such behaviour *counts* as a logical criterion of pain (for not all groans are groans of pain, just as not all baring of the teeth is smiling). This causal link is partly responsible for our phenomenological descriptions of pains as burning, stinging, sharp and so forth. Tickling and itching sensations are linked to irritations of the skin the causes of which may, but need not, be external stimuli. Sensations of giddiness are associated with spinning or being spun around fast. Heartburn and nausea are linked to having eaten excessive or inappropriate food. Somatic sensations are equally bound up with causes – muscular strain with physical effort, stiff neck with poor posture or bad position during sleep and so on.

Whether the concept of sensation is further linked to that of causation because sensations are themselves causes of behaviour is moot. Certainly we commonly explain our behaviour by reference to the sensations we feel. 'I sat down because I was feeling giddy', 'He was scratching his leg because it was itching intolerably', 'She cried out because she was in pain' are all perfectly decent explanations of behaviour. The moot question is whether these *because*s are causal *because*s. 'I sat down because I was feeling giddy' specifies my reason for sitting down. 'He scratched his leg because it was itching' explains the behaviour teleologically rather than causally – the purpose of the scratching was to alleviate the itching. Does pain not *cause* one to cry out? Does it not *make* one cry out? Certainly one can very often *not help* crying out when the pain is severe. But it is not evident that this identifies the sensation as the cause of the behaviour. The pain-behaviour is an *expression* or *manifestation* of pain (just as behaviour of rage is an *expression* of rage – not the *effect* of rage). That is why we speak of 'crying out *in pain*' or 'crying out *with pain*'. (Similarly, when one feels frightened, excited or enraged, one's hands may shake, but that is not because one's fear, excitement or rage *cause* one's hands to shake. Rather one's hands shake *with* fear, excitement or rage.) – Surely, one may *fall over* because one is giddy and has lost one's balance? Does not the feeling of giddiness *cause* one to fall over? That is not obvious. The sensation is caused by the same physiological malfunctioning as causes the loss of balance (e.g. labyrinthitis or vestibular neuronitis (both being conditions of the ear) and a variety of neural malfunctions, such as multiple sclerosis, as well as a wide variety of kinds of brain lesions.

Link between sensation and desire (ii) The connection of sensation with the hedonic ensures its link to desire. Itches, smarting eyes, aches, muscular soreness are unpleasant, and one wants them to cease. Pain is essentially undesirable, even though one may voluntarily put up with it for the sake of a good. However, 'It hurts but I don't mind it' is an utterance in need of explanation (which might be forthcoming). Sensations of warmth (when it is cold) and of cold (when it is hot), erotic sensations in appropriate circumstances, are pleasurable and we characteristically desire their prolongation. Nausea and seasickness, associated with a desire to throw up, can be mildly, or extremely, unpleasant. Giddiness is typically unpleasant (although not for children on the swings and roundabouts) and is linked to a desire to keep one's balance coupled with difficulty in doing so. Itching is conceptually bound up with wanting to scratch. Hunger is essentially associated with a desire for food, thirst with a desire for drink, and lust with a desire for sexual release.

Link between sensation and behaviour (iii) The connection of sensation with desire ensures its link to behaviour in a twofold manner: to expressive behaviour and to purposive behaviour, both of which may be either voluntary or involuntary. The expressive behaviour manifests the sensation and may be spontaneous or deliberate (one may just groan, or groan to attract attention). The purposive behaviour may be aimed at terminating the sensation or at ensuring its continuation.

No organs of
sensation

While there are organs of perception, there are no organs of sensation, although one can feel sensations in most of one's organs (but not in one's brain), including one's organs of perception. One's eyes may smart and one's ears may ache; one may have a burning sensation on one's tongue (from hot coffee or from hot curry), and a sneeze-provoking itch in one's nose (if one has taken snuff).

No faculty of
sensation

To have sensations is not to exercise a faculty. Sensations belong to the category of passivity. Having a sensation is an undergoing, which may be endured, suffered or enjoyed. Sensations are not voluntary, although they may be voluntarily self-inflicted or induced. One cannot feel an itch intentionally, or have a toothache carefully and deliberately. There is no skill in having sensations, and although people's pain-thresholds may vary, the more sensitive are not *better* at feeling pain than others. To lose all sensation in one's gums and teeth after a local anaesthetic is not to be poor at feeling the pain of the drill. There is no learning to have sharper or more accurate sensations, for sensations are not accurate or inaccurate, correct or incorrect. However, one can learn to suppress one's behavioural manifestations of pain, and one may become better at tolerating pain and preventing it from dominating one's life.

Ways in which
sensations
inform us

It would be mistaken to say that sensations 'do not inform us' about how things are, that we do not learn how things are by having sensations. What is true is that sensation is not a form of perception, and that the knowledge acquired from sensations is unlike perceptual knowledge in both range and character. We acquire knowledge of the state of our body (i.e. of our somatic features), and of what is affecting our body from (but not only from) the sensations we feel. Here we draw inferences from our sensations to their causes. (It is noteworthy that this provided the model or prototype for the causal theories of perception.)

First, we learn that we have indigestion from the heartburn we feel, that a tooth is infected or a nerve exposed from the toothache we have, that we are having an attack of angina pectoris from the pain we feel in the upper left arm and chest. In these kinds of case, what is learnt commonly requires antecedent instruction on the correlation of sensations with bodily damage and disease. The correlation of sensation with its causes is inductive. In this respect, the inferential knowledge given by such sensations is unlike characteristic perceptual knowledge.

Secondly, somatic sensations inform us directly of the state of our body – of stretched muscles, of muscle spasm, of broken leg, of pounding heart, dry mouth or streaming nose, of tears in our eyes. We feel ourselves panting with effort, we can feel our arms giving way under the weight we are trying to lift or hold. Here the boundary between sensation and perception fades away.

Thirdly, sensations are experienced in the hurly-burly of life. If one falls and grazes oneself painfully, one knows one has scraped one's skin against a rough surface. If one drinks a cup of tea and burns one's tongue, one knows that the drink is very hot. If one feels one's hand stinging as one walks through a field full of wildflowers, one knows that one must have touched a nettle. If one feels slightly dizzy at a party at which the wines flow generously, one knows that the punch has more alcohol in it than one thought. If one's eyes sting badly after a swim in the pool, one may infer that the water is over-chlorinated.

Nevertheless, 'having' and 'feeling' a sensation are not connected with that-nominalizations and Wh-clauses, as verbs of perception are. To see what colour the walls are is to see that they are such-and-such a colour. To smell what is cooking in the kitchen is to smell that such-and-such food is cooking. To feel the dampness of the towel is to feel that the towel is damp. By contrast, to feel a pain, tickle or itch is to have one, not to perceive anything.

Fourthly, kinaesthetic sensations arguably, and sensations of orientation surely, are requisite for one's ability to tell how one's limbs are disposed and how one is oriented in space. But although there is here a kinship with perception, there are important differences too. In the absence of the possibility of such sensations (due, say, to a local anaesthetic), one lacks awareness of the position of one's limbs and one's orientation. But in normal circumstances, one's knowledge that one's hands are raised and that one is standing up is not *derived from* the sensations. The sensations, one might say, are not a source of knowledge, but merely a condition of its possibility. An animal's underived awareness of its bodily orientation and disposition of its limbs is crucial for its ability to engage in voluntary and purposive movement.

This connective analysis of sensation will stand us in good stead in clarifying the concept of perception, and in identifying flaws in empirical and philosophical accounts of perception.

3. Perception and sensation

Unclarities concerning sensation and perception

It was noted above that in the seventeenth and eighteenth centuries the verb 'to sense' signified sense-perception as well as having sensations. Today the verb has shrunk in its extension. It is employed primarily for cases of intuitive apprehension, as in 'I could sense the tension in the room', 'He could sense someone behind him', or 'She could sense his unhappiness'. This should have prevented the assimilation of sensation and perception in contemporary reflections. However, the unclarities that were so prominent in the seventeenth century soldier on, especially among psychologists of perception and neuroscientists. For it is sometimes held that all perception involves sensation, that when we see something, we have visual sensations, or that visual perception, for example, consists in the 'cognitive processing' of sensations (as in the standard explanation of blindsight).[10] Clarification of the matter, and the eradication of confusions requires an analytic comparison of sensation and perception.

Comparison between sensation and perception

The noun 'sensation' has widespread currency, whereas 'a perception', as in 'a visual, auditory, etc.) perception', is poor coinage, being a term of art found largely in the writings of psychologists and philosophers. It is a source of much confusion, and the technical term of art 'percept' is a source of even more. Both 'sensation' and 'perception' fulfil a role as count-nouns, taking plurals, the quantifiers 'many' and 'several' (rather than 'much' or 'little'), and the indefinite article in the singular.[11] However, while there are tolerably clear (although, as we have seen, highly elastic) criteria for sameness and difference of sensations, there are none for perceptions. The pain I now have in my knee may be the same as the pain I (or you) had in the knee yesterday. But one cannot ask, without further explanation, whether the current visual perception I am now having of St John's College is the same as the one I (or you) had last week. One can ask

[10] The standard explanation, due to L. Weiskrantz, is in terms of normal reception of visual sensations, but the failure of the neural monitoring of such sensations that is requisite for perception. That this is incoherent was shown by J. Hyman, 'Visual Experience and Blindsight', in J. Hyman (ed.), *Investigating Psychology* (Routledge, London, 1991), pp. 166–200. See below.

[11] 'There is not much sensation in my foot' is a different use. When there is little sensation in a limb, the sensations one feels in it are numbed or blunted.

only whether St John's looks the same as it did last week; or whether
it looks the same to me, that is, strikes me as unchanged; or whether
I am viewing it from the same or different vantage point; and so forth.
But whether my perceiving is the same as my previous perceiving is
a question in search of a sense, as are the subordinate questions of
whether my seeing or hearing something again is the same or different
seeing or hearing.

Table 7.1 summarizes some of the differences between sensation
and perception that we have already surveyed.

V-ing	*Sensation*	*Perception*
Subject	animal, or its sensitive parts (in the case of *verbs* of sensation[a])	animal, not its parts
Location	*in* or *of* the body	not *in*, but *with* parts of the body
Degrees	of intensity	of clarity and distinctness
Organs	✗	✓
Skill, being better/worse at	✗	✓
Opportunity conditions	✗	✓
Voluntariness	✗	✗✓[b]
Having a reason for	✗	✓[c]
Illusion and hallucination	✗[d]	✓
Susceptibility to error	✗[e]	✓

[a] Hence 'my foot hurts', but not *'My foot has a pain'; I may have a headache, but
my head does not – it aches.
[b] The answer has to be 'yes and no'. For elaboration, see the previous discussion.
[c] Only if the perceiving is voluntary – as in looking, listening, etc.
[d] But hallucination of sensation-location is possible.
[e] But error is possible in the case of kinaesthetic sensation and sensations of
orientation

Table 7.1 *Comparison of sensation and perception*

We are now in a position to examine the thought that all perception is sensation-involving.

The idea that perception involves sensation

It was commonplace among nineteenth-century scientists to conceive of perception as 'synthesized' out of sensations. Helmholtz, for example, held that physical stimuli are transmitted to the brain, where they 'become sensations'. These sensations are the raw materials which the unconscious mind combines to form perceptions of objects – which he conceived of as hypotheses. Luciani argued that visual sensations, which occur 'in the mesencephali ganglia, and more especially in the corpora quadrigemina', are processed into visual judgements. He accordingly distinguished between sensorial blindness and psychic blindness. James explained sensorial blindness as 'absolute insensibility to light', psychic blindness being 'inability to recognize the *meaning* of the optical impressions'.[12] The distinction was revived and transformed by Weiskrantz in the late twentieth century in his research into the phenomena of blindsight.[13] He explained blindsight in terms of failure in the *neural monitoring* of visual sensations which normally results in conscious visual perceptions. Sufferers from blindsight have visual sensations, but no visual perceptions. This curious conceptual framework of sensation, perceptual judgement and conscious perception seems to have been based on a melange of Locke's conception of sensation (and perception) as the causation of ideas by stimulation of the sense-organs, and Kant's conception of perceptual experience as a synthesis of intuitions and their subsumption under concepts. The following remark made by Richard Dawkins, a well-known spokesman for the scientific worldview, nicely articulates the common scientific conception of the late twentieth century:

> The sensation of seeing is, for us, very different from the sensation of hearing, but this cannot be directly due to the physical differences between light and sound. Both light and sound are, after all, translated

---

[12] L. Luciani, 'On the Sensorial Localisations in the Cortex Cerebri', *Brain*, 7 (1884), 145–60; W. James, *The Principles of Psychology* (Holt, New York), vol. 1, pp. 40f.

[13] Luciani associated visual sensations with seeing *simpliciter* and visual perception with perceptual (visual) judgement. Weiskrantz associated visual sensations with visual experience of which one is unaware and conceived of visual perception as the 'conscious' (cognized) visual experience resulting from monitoring visual sensations.

by the respective sense organs into the same kind of nerve impulses. It is impossible to tell, from the physical attributes of a nerve impulse, whether it is conveying information about light, about sound or about smell. The reason the sensation of seeing is so different from the sensation of hearing and the sensation of smelling is that the brain finds it convenient to use different kinds of internal model of the visual worlds, the world of sound and the world of smell. It is because we *internally use* our visual information and our sound information in different ways and for different purposes that the sensations of seeing and hearing are so different.[14]

It should be evident that neither vision, nor hearing, neither smell nor taste, are sensation-involving. We shall defer consideration of touch for the moment.

Organs of perception are susceptible to sensation

To be sure, all organs of perception are susceptible to sensations in more than one sense. One can have a sensation *in* our perceptual organs – our eyes may itch, our nose may tickle and we may have an earache. These are *physical sensations*. Moreover, our nose may feel swollen, and our ears may feel cold. These are *somatic sensations*. But none of *these* sensations are proper objects of the perceptual faculty in question. Nor are they either constituents of, or accompaniments of, perceiving.

What a visual sensation might be

Is there any such thing as a visual sensation? As we have seen, the uses of 'sensation' are manifold. One unifying thread running through them all is *feeling* – sensations are felt. So if there are visual sensations, they should be felt in the eyes, and they should be associated with *visibilia* rather than with *tangibilia*. The only thing that comes close to fitting the bill is the sensation of being dazzled, which is produced by exposure to excessive light or glare. We say indifferently 'I was dazzled', 'My eyes were dazzled' and even 'I felt my eyes dazzled by the glare'. Why do we speak here of 'sensation'? Perhaps because the sensation of being dazzled, like paradigmatic sensations, is exhibited by characteristic behaviour – of blinking, looking away, rubbing one's eyes to assuage the discomfort and shielding one's eyes from the glare. Though one is not dazzled *in* the eyes, the nexus with location is maintained by its being one's eyes that are dazzled when one is dazzled, and it is the eyes that one rubs to assuage the discomfort;

[14] Richard Dawkins, *The Blind Watchmaker* (Longman, Harlow, 1986), p. 34.

the link with the hedonic is maintained – since being dazzled is unpleasant. Most importantly for present purposes, when one has been dazzled by glare, one can either see nothing or see only very ineffectively for a while.

What auditory, olfactory, etc. sensations might be

Are there analogues for hearing, smelling and tasting? In the case of hearing, the sensation of being deafened by a proximate loud noise is comparable to the sensation of being dazzled. We speak of being deafened by the din, or of our ears being deafened. One naturally rubs or covers one's ears. Being deafened is, for most people, unpleasant, and one typically blocks one's ears when exposed to a deafening noise just as one shields one's eyes when exposed to glare. For some time after being deafened by a loud noise, one cannot hear at all, or only poorly. In the case of smelling and tasting, there are no *verbal* analogues of 'to be dazzled' or 'to be deafened', but there are analogues of being dazzled and deafened. Sampling a strong curry is perhaps the gustatory analogue of a dazzling glare. It reduces or obliterates one's perception of the tastes of what one then eats, and it temporarily impairs one's sense of taste. It is, for the non-addicted, unpleasant, and has appropriate forms of behavioural manifestation. Something similar applies to smell. Overwhelming smells are unpleasant and typically reduce one's olfactory sensitivity. Substances such as ammonia are not merely painful to smell, but have a numbing effect on one's sense of smell. To be sure, these are *only analogues*. Nothing in the dimensions of our hearing, smelling and tasting corresponds precisely to light in the dimension of sight.

Non-tactile perception is not sensation-involving

Clearly, in this sense of visual (auditory, gustatory and olfactory) sensation, such sensations are not only *not* constituents or constant accompaniments of visual (and other modes of) perception – they are abnormalities and *impede* perception. Obviously, this is not what was meant by philosophers and scientists holding sensation to be a constituent of every perception. Did they have any coherent notion at all? Or were they simply enmeshed in centuries-old conceptual confusions consequent upon their acceptance of the primary/secondary quality distinction and the representational version of the causal theory of perception advanced by Descartes, Boyle, Locke and Newton? As a first step to demonstrate the incoherence of the conception of sensation as a constituent of non-tactile perception, we should place pressure on the very idea of sensations of perceptual qualities that is deployed – for example, the idea of a visual sensation of red.

Is it *felt?* — No, for one does not *feel red,* let alone *have a red feeling*
either in or with one's eyes. Does one *feel a sensation of redness* in
one's brain or mind? — No, these are nonsensical forms of words.
Does a visual sensation of redness have a characteristic behavioural
expression? Does one scratch it, or assuage it? — No. Indeed, there
is no *seeing-something-red* behaviour that might be the expression of
having a sensation of red, as crying out is an expression of having a
pain. Is this visual sensation of red akin to somatic sensations, such
as cramp or a feeling of surfeit? — No, for a visual sensation of red
is not meant to be an awareness of one's bodily condition. Similar
considerations apply *mutatis mutandis* to hearing, smelling and
tasting. To hear a Beethoven sonata is not to feel a sequence of sensations in one's ears. To smell the roses in the vase is not to have a
sensation of roses in one's nostrils. And to taste the salt in the meal
is not to have a *sensation* in one's tongue and palate, but rather the
taste of salt. The grammar of visual, auditory, gustatory and olfactory
perception is not the grammar of sensations. So seeing, hearing,
smelling and tasting, are neither sensations nor sensation-involving.

Tactile perception has to be handled separately, for unlike the
other perceptual senses, feeling, in all its variety and complexity, *is*
sensation-involving.

4. Sensation, feeling and tactile perception

'Feeling' has, over the centuries, displayed powerful imperialist tendencies.[15] It subsumes sensation in all its forms, as well as tactile
perception and exploration, inclination and desire, the passions, attitudes and part of the extension of thought (see fig. 7.2). Until the
nineteenth century the perceptual use of 'feel' was even greater. One
could speak of feeling (i.e. perceiving) smells and tastes, as in 'Com
nere son and kys me, that I may feyle the smelle of the' (1460), or
'To feel how the ale dost taste' (1575). This expansionist propensity
has now been curbed.

Etymology of The roots of the verb 'to feel' and its cognates lie in Old
'feeling' English *félan* and *gefélan,* which are linked to the
Old High German *fuolen* – meaning 'to handle' or
'to grope'. The root *fôl* is connected to the Old Aryan *pāl,* hence the

---

[15] In this section I have made extensive use of *Appearance and Reality,* pp. 78–86.

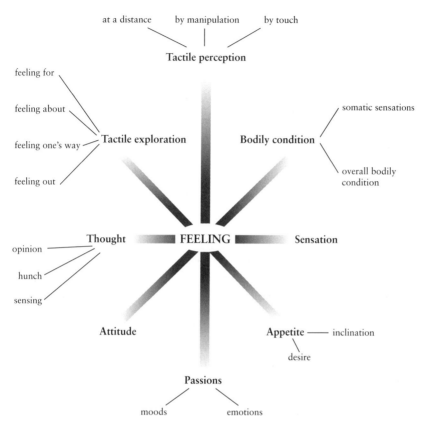

Figure 7.2 *The domain of feeling*

Old Saxon *folm*, Old High German *folma*, Latin *palma* and Greek παλαμη – signifying the hand. It is unsurprising that one focal point (or centre of variation) in the use of the verb and its cognates is that of exploratory perception by means of the hands. A variety of prepositional phrases with 'feel' signify as wide a range of quest- and task-verbs as *looking for, looking out for, looking under, looking out, looking into* do in the case of vision. For one may *feel about* one in the dark, *feel for* the keyhole with the key, and *fumble* for the key in one's pocket. One may *feel one's way* along a corridor, *groping along* in the dark. One may *feel out* the contours of an object by running one's fingers around it, *feel* the ground, test it or try it out with one's foot or walking stick. The successful upshot of these exploratory activities is finding one's way, finding the object one was groping for, finding out how things are disposed, finding what . . . , where . . . and whether . . . It is then that one feels the so-and-so, feels the F-ness of the so-and-so, feels (with one's hands) that the so-and-so is thus-and-so.

Varieties of feeling

Feeling, thus conceived, is a form of perception. It is usually denominated tactile perception or touch – although as noted above, it can also be exercised at a distance without touching anything – as when we feel the humidity of the day, the direction of the wind or the warmth of the fire. We distinguish feeling an object and its tactile qualities by touching it and manipulating it with our hands (by handling, fingering, stroking, pushing, pulling, kneading or poking it) from feeling the effect of an object on us when *it* touches us, hits us, pushes against us, crawls over us.

However, as we have noted, feeling subsumes physical and somatic sensation, appetite (as when one feels hungry or lustful), inclination (as when one feels like going out this evening) and wanting (as when one feels like a drink). Feeling is no less at home in the domain of the passions – of moods and emotions (as when one feels cheerful or depressed, anger or affection), as well as attitudes (as when one feels well disposed towards someone). Finally, as we shall see in our discussion of thought, there is a perfectly common use of 'feel' to signify opining or expressing one's hunches and guesses.

Tactile perception

Our concern here is with tactile perception and the sense of touch. The categorial range of what can be felt by touch includes objects and their properties, events (as when one feels the ground giving way or the snapping of the stick), processes (the warming up of the engine), states (as when one feels the icy state of the window-pane), and dispositional properties of things (as when one feels that *this* is elastic, or *that* the surface is slippery). We are bodies – animate, self-moving, substances consisting of matter. We move about in a world of physical objects, coming into contact with them or avoiding them. We can feel solid objects, liquids and the air through which we move. We can feel whether the air is warm and dry, cold and humid, still or moving. We can feel the relative viscosity of liquids by stirring them with finger or implement, pouring or wading through them. We can feel the spatial properties of middle-sized dry goods (as Austin put it), their height, width, length and shape. We can feel features of their boundaries or edges, whether they are pointed, sharp or dull, their location and orientation, as well as whether they are solid or hollow.

Objects of tactile perception The sense of touch is exercised by pressure and manipulation. So we can feel whether an object is compressible or not, whether it is plastic or elastic, bendable (rigid or flexible) or breakable. By pushing, pulling and tugging we can feel whether an object is movable or not, whether it fits into another object, and whether the fit is tight or loose. We can feel whether an object is moving or at rest. By fingering an object or surface, rubbing against it or walking on it, we can feel its textural qualities (smooth, rough, slippery, granular, soft or sticky), as well as its cohesive properties (solid, crumbling, cracked and fissile). By trying to lift an object, or by weighing it in our hand, we can find out whether it is light or heavy. By touching it we can find out whether it is wet or dry, warm or cold. And we can feel the number of a small group of relatively small things. One can not only feel objects and their tactile properties, but also holes (both in one's tooth and in one's sock), gaps, bumps and distances between things.

Skill, success and voluntariness of tactile perception Like our other perceptual faculties, so too with feeling there is greater and lesser skill in feeling, one's skill may improve with experience and training (think of learning to read Braille), and there is success, failure and mistake, as well as illusion. Just as we sometimes distinguish between how an object looks and how it is, so too we distinguish between how something feels and how it is. The bridge may feel safe (as when one tests it with one's foot), but not be so; the water may feel cold (if one has been sunbathing) but actually be warm, and if one moves a marble over one's crossed fingertips, it feels as if there are two marbles. As with the other senses, one may feel something attentively, carefully and deliberately, or inattentively, carelessly and accidentally.

The temptations of quality-indicative sensations It is tempting to suppose that we perceive tactile qualities of objects by *having sensations* characteristic of, or caused by, the objects perceived. It seems that we perceive by touch that something is hot or cold by having sensations of heat or cold, and that we perceive that something is rough or smooth by having sensations of roughness or smoothness in our fingertips. So we are inclined to think that tactile perception involves having tactile-quality-indicative sensations. On this conception, we are aware of, or even identify, the particular character of the sensation we have when we touch or manipulate something, and *infer* from the quality of the sensation that the thing has just those tactile qualities. Why is this so tempting?

There is no organ of sensation, and no unique organ of tactile perception. One can feel (tactually perceive) with almost any part of one's
body, and so too one can have sensations in almost any part of
one's body. We do have sensations in the organs we use to feel objects,
and often have those sensations as a result of touching the thing we
are feeling (we may burn our fingertips in feeling whether the kettle
is hot). Some kinds of tactile perception are essentially passive, as
sensations are – as when we feel the pressure of the rucksack on our
back, or the tightness of our shoes, or the heat of the day. Tactile
perceptions belong to the category of the hedonic – it makes sense to
ask what touching something felt like. Feeling the soft texture of
velvet or fur is pleasant – it gives one *a pleasant sensation* of softness,
and feeling the slimy surface of something may be unpleasant – giving
one *a revolting sensation* of slime. Indeed, the language of tactile
perception and of sensation seem interwoven. We speak of wet, slimy
sensations; it makes sense to talk of a dry sensation, as well as a hot
or cold one (as when we speak of feeling a hot flush or a cold
shudder). A limb that is numb with cold is said to be *insensible* – one
can feel nothing *with* it; it *lacks all sensation*.

Resisting the
temptation

Nevertheless, the temptation should be resisted. We
can feel the shape of an object (e.g. whether a plate is
round or square) but not by having round or square
sensations – rather by feeling the contours of the object. One must
feel that one's fingers are in contact with the edges and that they are
moving round an unbroken edge – that is, tactilely perceive that
things are so. When one feels a plate one does not have a sensation
of circularity in one's fingertips – rather, the plate feels circular. To
feel that it is thick or thin is not to have thick or thin sensations. This
is, to be sure, dependent upon kinaesthetic sensations (of the distance
between index finger and thumb) – but we feel immediately the thinness of the porcelain, and do not infer it from kinaesthetic sensations.
Similar considerations apply to the perception of qualities perceived
by manipulation, such as the compressibility, rigidity, elasticity of
things or stuffs. When one feels that a rod is rigid or flexible, that
a lump of clay is plastic, that a cord is elastic, one does not have a
sensation of rigidity, flexibility or elasticity in one's fingertips, hands
or arms. Perceiving these features involves manipulation or attempted
manipulation – pushing, pulling, squeezing or bending. So feeling that
something is rigid, plastic or elastic will indeed involve somatic sensations in one's limbs, such as muscular strain, pressure, resistance (but
only exceptionally any physical sensations, such as pains, aches,

prickles). It may well be that one would not feel these qualities of objects were one's limbs rendered insensible by anaesthetic. But it does not follow that one *must* have felt any kinaesthetic sensations, let alone that one inferred the tactile qualities of the object felt from a sensation.

How tactile perception is suffused with sensation

Neither does it follow that tactile perception is only coincidentally (if at all) accompanied by physical, somatic or kinaesthetic sensations. Is it a mere coincidence that when one's hands are insensible, one cannot feel the texture and surface qualities of the things one touches, strokes or rubs? Tactile perception characteristically (although not uniformly) involves *touch* – and hence too, sensation. Does it make sense to suppose that one might feel that a knife is sharp, even though one cannot feel that its point, pressed against one's skin, is painful? Of course, when one perceives (feels) its point prick one, one does not have a pointed sensation. One has a sensation of something pricking one, which may be painful. We recoil from the prick, for it hurts, and we perceive that the knife is sharp and pointed. But we do not perceive the sharpness of the point independently of the sensation of a prick. The sensations one has when one tactually perceives are neither a datum from which one infers the tactile quality, nor are they coincidental accompaniments of such perceptions. Rather, the concepts here intermingle. That is not to be explained by reference to the mere coordination of passive and active powers, which is coincidental and implies only an overlap in the instantiation of the distinct concepts. Rather, the criteria for having certain sensations overlap with the criteria for tactually perceiving. For example, the behavioural expression of pricking one's finger painfully is, in appropriate circumstances, also a criterion of feeling that the point of the knife is sharp. The utterance 'Ow, it's sharp' gives verbal expression both to a painful sensation and to perceptual knowledge painfully acquired.

Textures and surface qualities

Tactile perception of textures and surface qualities also exhibits a suffusion of sensation and perception. If one passes one's fingers over polished marble, sandpaper or velvet, they feel respectively smooth, rough and soft. One has a sensation of something smooth, rough or pleasantly soft. Of course, 'a sensation of softness' sounds like 'a sensation of pain'. But this is misleading. The softness is felt *with* the fingertips, not *in* the fingertips – unlike the sensation of pain caused by touching a hot kettle. If one feels a pain in one's fingertips, one's fingertips hurt or are painful. But if one feels a sensation of softness with one's finger-tips, one's fingertips are not soft. But it would be misleading here to jettison the term 'sensation' and to conceive of our perception of the softness of velvet as independent of, or merely coincidentally accompanied by, sensations of softness. To talk here, as we do, of a sensation of softness is to talk of *perceiving* the quality of the velvet – its soft feel, which is pleasant. What is enjoyed is *stroking* the velvet, which one would not take pleasure in if one's fingers were insensible. Perception and sensation are here fused, and any attempt to drive a wedge between them, to view that former as *inferred* from the latter, or the latter as a merely coincidental *accompaniment* of the former, would distort our concepts.

Stickiness   Stickiness is different again. We speak of a sticky feeling and a sticky sensation. A surface feels sticky to the hand when one's fingers stick to it (however slightly), and one feels a slight resistance to detachment. Stickiness is an adhesive power of surfaces. One feels the stickiness of a surface by touching it to discern whether it adheres to one's fingers. Here bodily feelings are essentially involved, although feeling one's skin slightly pulled is not the same as feeling the stickiness of the surface. Nor is the latter inferred from the former. One finds out whether a surface is tacky by touching it and feeling that it is (or is not) so. One does not infer that it is tacky from the slight pull of one's skin. One perceives an adhesive power by actualizing a potentiality through contact.

Wetness and dryness   Perceiving qualities in the wet–dry scale is not a matter of tactually perceiving a potentiality, even though it is true that if one feels that something is wet by touching it, one's hand or foot will become wet. When thirsty, one often has a dry sensation in one's throat or mouth – but it is not uniformly marked by lack of saliva. But when one feels whether the laundry is dry, one does not do so by having a dry sensation. One's hands or body may feel wet when one feels water on them, or dry when one does not. But we do speak of a *sensation* of being wet or dry – and here too perception and sensation merge.

Thermal qualities   Thermal qualities are distinctive. We may feel hot or cold, and our limbs may feel hot or cold – these are sensations. We may also feel that something or other (including what we are pleased to call 'the day') is hot or cold, warm or cool. We may feel something hot, without feeling hot ourselves – for we may be feeling cold as we place our freezing hands on a warm surface. Our own body or brow may feel hot to the touch (as when we have a fever), including our own touch, without our feeling hot at all. Indeed we may feel cold and shiver with cold as our fever rises. But it would be mistaken to suggest that our perception of heat and cold or of the thermal qualities of objects were *inferred* from heat-indicative sensations. But it may well be the case that we would not be able to perceive thermal qualities but for the sensations of heat and cold in our body.

To be sure, none of this shows that we *never* infer perceptual judgements from our feeling certain sensations. We often feel a tickling sensation on our skin – and sometimes this feels just as if an insect were crawling on us. We say, 'It feels as if something is crawling on my neck' – and if there is an insect there the movement of which caused the sensation, then we did indeed feel an insect crawling on our neck. But one should not take this to be the conceptual prototype of all tactile perception.

8

Perception

1. Perceptual organs, the senses and proper sensibles

Subject terms for sensation and perception verbs
Animals, including ourselves, have sensitive bodies. Verbs of sensation can be predicated of parts of the body. One's foot may hurt, one's neck may itch and one's tooth may ache. By contrast, possessive phrases with sensation-nominals, such as 'having a pain' or 'having an itch', are predicated only of the animal as a whole, not of its parts. It is the human being or dog that has a pain in its leg (its leg does not have a pain in its leg, or even *have* a pain). Verbs of perception, on the other hand, cannot intelligibly be attached to names of sense-organs. One's eyes cannot be said to see,[1] nor can one's ears be said to hear, one's nose to smell or one's tongue to taste. Nor can perceptual nominals (e.g. 'visual experience') be attached to names of sense-organs. One's eyes cannot be said to *have* 'visual experiences' any more than one's nose can be said to *have* 'olfactory experiences'. Rather, a sentient being perceives whatever it perceives *with* its sense-organs. It is the animal as a whole that perceives and has perceptual experiences.

Cartesian view that the mind perceives
Descartes, and those influenced by him, held that it is the mind that perceives. For perceiving, or properly speaking *its seeming to one just as if one were*

---

[1] Save metonymically – as in 'Mine eyes have seen the glory of the coming of the Lord'.

The Intellectual Powers: A Study of Human Nature, First Edition. P. M. S. Hacker.
© 2013 John Wiley & Sons, Ltd. Published 2013 by John Wiley & Sons, Ltd.

perceiving . . . is a form of thought. Thinking is the defining essence of the mind. One cannot think without being conscious of thinking and of what one thinks. Animals, according to Descartes, do not, *in this sense*, perceive at all, since they are not conscious and they have no thoughts. Animal perception is merely mechanical responsiveness to stimuli. It is unaccompanied by consciousness of sensory experience, that is, by the thought that it seems to one just as if one were perceiving. To ascribe perception to human beings is, in effect, to ascribe perception to the mind that is attached to (and intermingled with) the human body. We have seen ample reason for rejecting this conception, both in this volume and in *Human Nature: the Categorial Framework* (chapter 8).

Why it is not the brain that perceives
It might seem, in an age mesmerized by cognitive neuroscience, that it is the brain that sees and hears, feels, tastes and smells. So, for example, eminent scientists, such as Francis Crick, aver that 'In perception, what the brain learns is usually about the outside world. This is why what we see appears to be located outside us, although the neurons that do the seeing are inside the head.'[2] Neuroscientists, such as Antonio Damasio, hold that 'When you or I look at an object outside ourselves, we form comparable images in our respective brains . . . But this does not mean that the image we see is the copy of whatever the object outside us is like.'[3] This is confused seventeenth-century metaphysics, not twentieth- and twenty-first-century scientific discovery. Although one can perceive nothing without an appropriately functioning brain (as indeed one can do nothing without one), it is not one's brain that sees, hears, smells, tastes or feels. To predicate verbs of perception or cognition of one's brain and parts of one's brain, as neuroscientists commonly do, is mistaken. It is to commit a *mereological fallacy* of ascribing properties to parts of a substance that can only intelligibly be ascribed to the substance as a whole.[4] As G. H.

---

[2] F. Crick, *The Astonishing Hypothesis* (Touchstone, London, 1995), p. 104.

[3] A. Damasio, *The Feeling of What Happens* (Heinemann, London, 1999), p. 320. Of course, looking inside ourselves, for example, in our brain, will not disclose any images either, for there are no images on or in the brain.

[4] Such mereological constraints are not restricted to living organisms and their parts. Aeroplanes cannot fly without engines, but it is the planes that fly, not their engines. Bracket clocks cannot keep time without a fusee, but it is the clock that keeps time, not the fusee.

Lewes observed in 1877, 'It is the man and not the brain that thinks; it is the organism as a whole, and not one organ, that feels and acts.'[5] Wittgenstein was subsequently to elaborate: 'Only of a human being and what resembles (behaves like) a living human being can one say: it has sensations; it sees, is blind; hears, is deaf; is conscious or unconscious.'[6] There is nothing arbitrary about this. Nor can it be dismissed as 'folk-psychological theory', since it is not a theory, but a grammatical observation, that is, a proposition characterizing what does and what does not make sense.[7] The grounds for ascribing perceptual verbs to animals in general and to humans in particular consist in behaviour in appropriate circumstances. And *there is no such thing* as a brain's *behaving*, let alone displaying perceptual behaviour (such as looking, listening, tasting, smelling, feeling) in the circumstances of life.

Organs of perception

As noted, one can have sensations in most organs and parts of the body, but there are no organs of sensation. By contrast there *are* organs of perception – specific parts of the body that are:

(i)   sensitive to a certain range of stimuli in certain circumstances;
(ii)   employed in distinctive ways in discriminative behaviour appropriate to the stimulus;
(iii) the sole source of our knowledge of correlative *proper sensibles* (see below).

Eyes, ears and nose, as well as hands, are used in exploratory behaviour. We orient our head, follow a moving object with our eyes, put our eyes to the keyhole or telescope to look through it. We cup our ear or move our head closer to the sound source to hear better. We may be able to smell the roses in the room, but we move our nose

---

[5] G. H. Lewes, *The Physical Basis of Mind* (Trübner & Co., London, 1877), p. 441.

[6] Wittgenstein, *Philosophical Investigations* [1953], 4th edn (Wiley-Blackwell, Oxford, 2009), §281.

[7] To remind readers: grammatical propositions or observations are expressions of *rules* for the use of words in the guise of descriptions of possibilities and impossibilities. They in effect specify what combinations of words are licit and what forms of words are ruled out as senseless (e.g. 'being red all over, and simultaneously green all over', or 'checkmate in draughts', or 'trisecting an angle with a compass and rule (in Euclidean plane geometry)'.

close to the roses to smell them better. There is no unique organ of touch, although the hands dominate in perception of tactile qualities of objects, such as texture, solidity, malleability, wetness and dryness, shape and thermal qualities. Unlike sight, hearing and smell, feeling is for the most part, not *at a distance*.[8] We feel tactile qualities of objects by touching, manipulating, running our fingers over the surface of a thing and so forth. So, of course, we cannot feel the tactile qualities we have detected better by 'touching more closely', but only, if at all, by further contact and manipulation. Taste *is* uniformly by contact. We taste *with* tongue and palate. So we may lick a substance or insert a quantity of it into our mouth. If we are unsure of the taste, there is no 'more closely' or 'in better light'; rather, we taste again and perhaps take a larger sample or sip, or we cleanse our palate.

Goodness of perceptual organs and faculties

Organs of perception have both morphological and functional features. Deformation of a perceptual organ typically affects its functioning, and harmful deformation affects the exercise of the perceptual faculty the organ subserves. The eye, an organ of perception, may be good or weak. The goodness of the organ is distinct from the goodness of the faculty, although it is internally related to the normal exercise of the faculty. If one has good eyes, one's eyesight is normal (20/20 vision) – there is nothing wrong with one's eyes, and one sees (perfectly) well. If one has weak eyes, one's eyesight is poor. Good eyes are not good at seeing, but the person with good eyes (non-defective organs of vision) performs satisfactorily at spotting, discriminating, discerning or descrying. Someone who has very good eyesight is exceptionally good at these tasks. Good eyes are eyes that perform their function *normally*, without strain or pain. The optimal functioning of our eyes (or ears) is tested by reference to *standards of normalcy* among human beings in seeing (or hearing). Curiously, we rarely speak, in English, of good or weak ears, or of a good or feeble nose, or of a good or weak palate. We do say of a person that he has a good ear – but that is a remark about the niceness of the discriminations he can make by the exercise of his faculty of hearing. Rather, we say that someone's hearing is good or poor – evaluating the auditory faculty rather than the auditory organ. Similarly, 'he has a good nose for . . .' has a use, but not one that has anything to do

---

[8] But not always – we can feel the heat of the stove without touching it.

with the olfactory organ. We evaluate the olfactory faculty rather than the organ and speak of a good or poor sense of smell.

Defects of organs and faculties of perception

The normality of a perceptual organ is an innate endowment. But that does not mean that the organ can be used at birth in the optimal exercise of the faculty. Nor does it mean that a normal organ of perception may not deteriorate. Weak or poor eyes, for example, may be innate, but they may be the result of illness, injury or ageing. Defects of eye or of hearing may be permanent or temporary, partially remediable by surgery or artificial aids such as spectacles or hearing-aids. Such remedies enable a person to exercise the faculty in question better than he would otherwise be able to, given the defectiveness of the organ. While one may be endowed from birth with normal sense-organs and sense-faculties, one can be trained to perceive better for certain purposes, that is, to detect, discriminate or distinguish more by the use of one's sense-organs. One can acquire a trained eye or ear, a discriminating palate or nose.

Organs and instruments of perception

Because instruments (such as spectacles or hearing-aids) improve our perceptual abilities (in the case of defects in our sense-organs), and extend our perceptual range and acuity (in the case of microscope and tele-scope, or stethoscope and amplifier) it is tempting to conceive of sense organs as bodily instruments. This temptation should be resisted. Organs are not designed, instruments are. Organs are parts of substances, but not substances themselves; instruments, by contrast, are substances.[9] Organs are internally related to the *beneficial*, to the good of the animal whose organs they are. Their proper functioning contributes to the animal's successful engagement in activities characteristic of its kind. The function of artefacts, by contrast is related to their *usefulness* when employed for the purpose or purposes for which they were made. Good organs, including good organs of perception, are healthy organs that perform their function optimally. The goodness of organs in general, and of organs of perception in particular, is privative. Good eyes are eyes that are not deformed, diseased or defective – they function well. Good instruments, by contrast, are not normally functioning instruments. A good knife not one that is all right, and that there is nothing wrong with one's car does not imply that it is a good car. The goodness of instruments, unlike the

---

[9] For elaboration, see *Human Nature: the Categorial Framework*, pp. 42–5.

goodness of perceptual organs, is not privative. A good instrument of a given kind is one that *can* be used (by someone with the requisite skill) to serve well, or even exceptionally well, the purpose for which they were designed[10] (see table 8.1).

	Organs	*Instruments*
Designed	✗	✓
Have a purpose	✓	✓
Substances	✗	✓ [a]
Parts of substances	✓	✗
Internally related to the beneficial	✓	✗
Internally related to the useful	✗	✓
Goodness of	Normally functioning	Serve their purpose excellently

[a] That instruments are substances, whereas body parts (attached or detached) are not, was shown in *Human Nature: the Categorial Framework*, ch. 2.

Table 8.1 *Organs and instruments compared*

The 5 senses   The perceptual organs are used in the exercise of the corresponding perceptual powers – the senses. The senses are faculties for the acquisition of knowledge about what is currently perceptible to the sentient agent. We traditionally distinguish five senses, five perceptual faculties – sight, hearing, smell, taste and tactile perception (touch, feeling). For certain purposes, in experimental psychology for example, it may be desirable or even necessary to distinguish more senses, or to break *feeling* down into a multiplicity of distinct senses. Our purposes here are restricted to clarification and mapping of the conceptual scheme we have and employ, not of an alternative one employed by psychologists for specialized purposes. The traditional distinction of five senses turns primarily on:

[10] See G. H. von Wright, *The Varieties of Goodness* (Routledge & Kegan Paul, London, 1963), ch. 3, section 8.

- the association of each with a specialized sense-organ that is used by an agent in the course of perceiving (the issue is blurred in the case of feeling);
- the proper sensibles appropriate to, and discriminable by, each sense (i.e. sensible qualities of objects that can be discerned and distinguished by only one sense, and hence can be checked for validation (by oneself or by another) only by the same sense);
- the distinctive pleasures (and displeasures) – visual, auditory, olfactory, gustatory and tactile – associated with the senses. As Aristotle sapiently observed, where there is sense-perception, there is also both pain and pleasure. This does not mean that every perception is enjoyable or unpleasant, but only that it makes sense for it to be.

Non-perceptual senses   Of course, apart from the five senses, we also speak of a sense of time, a sense of direction, a sense of distance and so forth – but these do not involve sense-perception by the use of a *perceptual* organ. They are spoken of as senses largely because of their cognitive associations. They involve the *ability* to give a *reliable estimation* of the correlative quality. In a different vein, we also speak of a moral sense and an aesthetic sense. A moral sense is so conceived neither because there is a moral perceptual organ (a conscience is not an organ), nor because someone with an acute moral sense is able to *estimate* reliably, but because such a person is *sensitive* to moral concerns, *knows* what is morally fitting and *acts* accordingly.

Proper and common sensibles   Each of the senses involves a power to detect, discern and discriminate qualities unique to it – the so-called *proper sensibles* or *proper objects of the senses*: colour for sight, sound for hearing, smells for smell, tastes for taste and a wide range of properties, for example wetness, dryness, warmth, cold, smoothness, softness, roughness and solidity, for touch (feeling). Since the proper objects of a given sense modality can be detected and differentiated only by the exercise of that faculty and no other, and since no sense is infallible or incorrigible, the only way to check one's perception of such a quality is by perceiving it again or asking another person, or, in the case of the senses that operate at a distance, by coming closer to see, hear or smell better.[11] In addition to the

---

[11] It is sometimes thought that *whenever* one exercises a sense-faculty one perceives its proper sensibles. That does not seem quite right. One can see at night without seeing *the colours of things* or indeed *any* chromatic colours.

proper objects of the senses, Aristotle pointed out, there are numerous qualities that can be detected by the use of more than one sense (the so-called *common sensibles*).[12] One can detect motion or rest by sight, hearing and touch. One can detect size and shape by sight and touch.

Proper/common sensibles and primary/secondary qualities   It has been suggested that the Aristotelian distinction between proper and common sensibles was the same as the seventeenth-century distinction between *primary* and *secondary qualities*. Primary qualities were metrical, and provided the basis for physics and the natural sciences. For mathematics (especially geometry) was held to be the language in which God has written the book of Nature. The primary qualities included size, shape, number and motion. These are indeed common sensibles. Sometimes solidity (Locke) and texture, that is particulate structure, was added (Boyle); weight, for the most part, was left in limbo. Despite being, *on some accounts*, extensionally equivalent, the primary-/secondary-quality distinction is *not* the same as the proper/common sensibles distinction. Primary qualities, as understood in the seventeenth century, were held to be 'real qualities' (Locke), qualities that material objects possess independently of our perception of them. Secondary qualities were strictly speaking mind-dependent. They were held to be qualities objects *appear* to possess, but do not really. For they are actually no more than the effects of objects upon our sensibility, that is, *ideas* of secondary qualities. (As they are 'in objects', secondary qualities are no more than powers to affect our sensibility.) However, the proper/common sensible distinction had nothing to do with the distinction between objective monadic properties of things as opposed to subjective relational properties (powers to produce impressions or sensations *in us*). What was crucial for the primary-/secondary-quality distinction was that primary qualities are *mathematical* (arithmetical and, above all, geometrical) and *quantifiable*. Secondary qualities, it was held, are not. The science of nature requires primary qualities, Galileo and Descartes argued, but not secondary ones. Primary qualities are essential, constitutive, determinables of material objects, it was argued; secondary qualities are not. No such conception was involved in the distinction between proper and common sensibles. Moreover, in a world without light, or in a world of the blind, shape would no longer be a common

---

[12] Aristotle, *De Anima*, 418ª7–418ª19.

sensible. It would be a proper sensible. But it would remain a primary quality.

Objects of perception

Although each of the senses has a proper sensible or proper sensibles corresponding to it, what we perceive ranges over a wide variety of categories other than objects and their perceptual qualities. Any investigation of perception must keep this in mind and avoid too narrow a diet of *perceptual qualities* and *material objects*. Not only do we perceive *that things are so*, or *things' being so*, we also perceive events, acts, actions and activities, processes and states of affairs, dispositions (e.g. fragility, elasticity) and abilities (e.g. of one thing to fit into another). We perceive differences and similarities, distances and proximities, likenesses and aspects. We perceive 'disturbances' to things, such as waves, bumps or knots, not to mention such 'non-things' as holes, gaps, spaces and absences. Bearing this in mind may curb over-hasty generalization, for example that whatever we perceive causes us to perceive (or seem to perceive) it – which is clearly a non-starter for perceiving holes, or the matt black colour of the blackboard.

2. Perceptual powers: cognition and volition

Perceptual powers, behaviour, pleasure and pain

Possession of a sense-faculty is manifest in behaviour. The sighted are identified by their competence in finding their way around without bumping into, or falling over, things, by ducking to avoid missiles or impediments (such as branches or lintels), by their searching for and finding things by looking, by following things with their eyes and by positioning as well as orienting themselves accordingly to facilitate this. Their power of sight is dependent upon the presence of light, illumination or luminosity – and, unlike echo-location, cannot be exercised in pitch dark. The sighted are responsive to optical stimuli such as lights, glimmers and flashes, and are able to discriminate the colours of things. They take pleasure in looking at, observing and watching certain things in their visual field, and may be disgusted or revolted by certain kinds of *visibilia*. Hearing is exhibited in responsiveness to sounds and voice and to the things that make or emit sound or speech, and in the pleasure or displeasure taken in listening to *audibilia*. The behaviour that manifests possession of a sense faculty consists in degrees of efficiency in discernment, the manifestations of pleasure or displeasure at sensing what is sensed, pursuit of certain goals and exploration of the environment. Of course, there is no unique form of behaviour that manifests perceiving innumerable objects of perception. How an animal reacts to perceiving a thing or its qualities, the sound made by a thing or a smell of something depends not only on the nature of the thing, but also on the circumstances and the desires and purposes of the animal.

Primacy among the sense-faculties Does any one of the sense-faculties enjoy primacy over the others? It depends how one takes the expression 'primacy', and also whether the question concerns us humans, or animals in general. One is strongly inclined to think of vision as 'the most important' of the senses. If that means that most of the information *we* gain about our immediate environment is derived from using our eyes, then this seems correct. On the other hand, most of the information we gain *from others* in our environment, which may or may not be *about* our environment, is gained by hearing. But if the question concerns which senses are essential for the existence and maintenance of life-forms – then it seems clear that touch and taste (and their associated pleasures and pains) enjoy evolutionary priority. For, as Aristotle observed, sensation and tactile perception are requisite for motion, and taste for differentiating the edible from the inedible.

1-way and 2-way powers Are the sense-faculties one-way (natural) powers, like the powers of the inanimate, or are they two-way (voluntary) powers that can be exercised at will (like characteristic human powers to act)? One-way powers (e.g. of acids to dissolve metals, of plants to grow, of one's stomach to digest food) are such that given the conditions for their actualization, the action or process will ensue. The subject has no power *not* to act in these circumstances. There is no such thing here as having a choice, no such thing as refraining or abstaining from action. Hence one cannot speak here of *opportunity-conditions* for acting – but only of *occasions* for the relevant action that exemplifying a one-way power. Two-way powers are powers of voluntary action ('volitional powers'), since they are powers to do things the agent can do or refrain from doing at will. One can be said to forbear or omit acting only if there is an opportunity available to one. Confronted by a recognized opportunity, an agent with the appropriate ability has the choice of whether to take advantage of the opportunity or not. Forbearance and omission presuppose both ability and opportunity – one cannot omit doing something one cannot do, nor can one refrain or abstain from acting if there is no opportunity to act anyway. Opportunities are agent-relative – what is an opportunity for the skilled and proficient may not be for the novice or poorly endowed.[13]

Perceptual powers qua passive　It is evident that, in one sense, perceptual powers are one-way powers, and in another, two-way powers. In one sense, which impressed the British empiricists, sense-perception is not a matter of choice. If one's eyes are open, one cannot choose what to see (but only what to look at). One cannot intentionally see something, although one can try to see something, and intentionally look at, watch or gaze at something. One cannot voluntarily hear (as opposed to listen to) the noises in one's locality, decide not to taste what is in one's mouth (only whether to taste the food) or not to smell a strong odour in one's vicinity (only to hold one's breath). To be sure, one does not *necessarily* perceive what is immediately perceptible in one's environment, even if it is salient. But that is not because one can voluntarily refrain from perceiving. Rather, non-voluntary failure to perceive something salient depends on the direction and intensity of one's attention.[14] One needs an opportunity to see something (there has to be light, the object must not be occluded, etc.), but it does not follow that one normally has a *choice* whether to see something or not to see it. Mesmerized by such facts, the British empiricists thought of perception as a *passive power*.

Perceptual powers qua active　On the other hand, nouns signifying perceptual powers are also linked to verbs of voluntary perceptual attention. To that extent, perception is an *active power*. Sight is linked to the voluntary activities of looking (looking at, for, in, up, through, out), as well as to observing, gazing, glancing, scrutinizing, peering, peeking and watching. In this sense, given an opportunity, one can choose whether to look, observe, scrutinize or not. Similarly, hearing is linked to harkening and listening to or for,

---

[13] For a more detailed discussion of powers, see *Human Nature: the Categorial Framework*, ch. 4; see also A. Kenny, *Will, Freedom and Power* (Blackwell, Oxford, 1975).

[14] This is made wonderfully vivid by the 'gorilla in our midst' experiment. When exposed to a film of a basketball match and told to count the number of passes one side makes, most people will fail to see a man dressed in a gorilla costume who walks slowly onto the playground, waves his arms at the camera and walks off again. See D. J. Simons and C. F. Chabris, 'Gorillas in Our Midst: Sustained Inattentional Blindness for Dynamic Events', *Perception*, 28 (1999), pp. 1059–74.

smell to sniffing and sniffing for, taste to tasting and savouring, and feeling to feeling for, fingering, touching, rubbing, stroking, poking, pushing, pulling and so on. English (like German) possesses the peculiar modal forms *can/could* see, hear, feel, etc. (*kann/könnte sehen, hören*, etc.) which do service, among other things, for the absent progressive form *'I am seeing M (hearing S)'. 'I can see M', said while scanning a landscape, signifies the same as 'I have M in sight' or 'I am looking at M' – and, of course, I could cease looking at M if I pleased. To say 'I could hear S' indicates that I was listening to something continuously, as 'I could smell S' signifies a continuous perceptual awareness of a smell. If we bear this in mind, we shall not fall into the mistakes of supposing that perceptual verbs must be either *task verbs* (akin to 'travelling' or 'hunting'), such as 'look for', 'watch for', 'listen for', or *achievement verbs* (akin to 'arriving' or 'finding'), such as 'see', 'smell' or 'hear' (in certain sentential contexts), and hence of supposing that seeing, smelling and hearing are primarily culminations of tasks or quests, signifying successful outcomes of directed activities. One must bear in mind that one can not only *look for* something (a quest-verb), but also *look at it* (a scrutiny-verb), not only *watch for* or *watch out for* something (task-verbs), but also *watch it*, not only *listen for* a sound, but also *listen to* it. The exercise of the faculty of vision may result in the achievement *at a time* of seeing, spotting or descrying, but it may also be exercised in seeing (for example, an aspect), watching, observing, gazing at, scrutinizing something, *for a time*. Perceptual *achievement* (result, upshot) *verbs* or uses of perceptual verbs do not admit volitional adverbs such as 'voluntarily', 'intentionally', deliberately', but perceptual *task-, quest-* and *scrutiny-verbs* do.[15]

One cannot *voluntarily see* something in one's visual field, or *intentionally hear* what is within one's auditory field.[16] But one can voluntarily, intentionally or deliberately look at something, watch, observe or scrutinize someone at will, just as one can decide to listen to something or someone and find joy in doing so, resolve to smell the roses and taste the apples and deliberately indulge one's senses, as one may decide to feel the silk and enjoy doing so, finger the velvet and take pleasure in feeling it.

[15] See F. Sibley, 'Seeking, Scrutinizing, and Seeing', *Mind*, 64 (1955), pp. 455–78.

[16] And, as we noted above, for quite different kinds of reasons, one cannot voluntarily notice, recognise, realize or become conscious or aware of something. For these are forms of cognitive receptivity (see chapter 1).

Perceptual powers are cognitive

The senses are faculties for the acquisition of knowledge. One may, of course, perceive something without recognizing what one perceives; and one may misidentify what one perceives. One may perceive a shadow in the trees and take it to be a person, or perceive a person and take him to be a shadow. So one may perceive something without *knowing* what it is, but one cannot perceive something that is not present in one's perceptual field.[17] So '. . . *perceives such-and-such a thing* or *object*' is factive, but not cognitive. On the other hand, one may perceive *that something is so*. In this case, it *follows* both that it is so, and that one knows that it is so. So '. . . perceives that things are so' is both factive and cognitive. To perceive that something is so is to discern, apprehend, observe or recognize, by the use of one's senses, *that things are so*. The nexus of perception and cognition is marked by the fact that the generic verb 'to perceive', as well as the more specific verbs 'to see', 'to hear', etc., all take sentential, infinitive and nominalized clauses as grammatical objects: as in 'A perceived things are so', 'A perceived things to be so' and 'A perceived that things are so'. Perceptual verbs also take relative Wh-clauses as grammatical complements: as in 'A saw who was in the car', 'A heard what was said' – the use of which likewise implies acquisition of knowledge by the use of the senses.

Learning the language-game with perceptual verbs

Mastery of the use of observation-sentences describing what is in the field of perception logically antecedes mastery of the use of perceptual sentences. Only after the child has learnt to say what he can see, can he learn to say that he sees it. For perceptual verbs are predicate-forming operators on nominals specifying an object of perception (e.g. 'see *the tree*'), on sentences, specifying a state of affairs (e.g. 'see *there is a tree in the quad*'), on verbal nouns specifying an event perceived (e.g. 'see *the felling of the tree*') and on nominalized sentences (e.g. 'see *that there is a tree in the quad*'). Of course, the self-predication of a perceptual verb does not rest on observing one's own perceiving, but only on perceiving what is in one's field of perception. The child learns the proper use of the verbs of the different sense-modalities by reference to what is perceived or perceived to be so (*visibilia*, *audibilia*, etc.), and what organ of perception has been

---

[17] Except, as mentioned, in the occasional intentional uses of verbs of perception that are typically paraphrasable into statements of how things sensibly seem to one to be.

used in doing so (hence 'I spy with my little eye . . .'). Of course, in third-person ascriptions one observes others seeing, hearing, smelling, tasting or feeling, and typically also what they perceive. It is but a short step from this rudimentary skill, to a further move in the language-game, namely answering the question 'How do you know?' with respect to observation-statements. Since the senses are cognitive faculties, their exercise is properly cited as a source of knowledge. 'I can see M', 'I saw that things are so' are not themselves used on the grounds of observing one's own seeing. To say that one saw something, or saw that things were so is not to give one's *evidence* for judging something to have been present or for taking things to be so. It is to specify the sense-faculty by the use of which one came to know what one says to be so. The perceptual operator 'I V . . .' affixed to 'M' or to 'that things are so' is not employed on the basis of evidence or grounds. In particular, it is mistaken to suppose that 'It sensibly seemed to me just as if I V-ed . . .' is *the justifying ground* for 'I V . . .', or is *a criterion* for me to say that I V . . . , or is *presumptively good evidence* for my V-ing . . ., let alone for things being as they V-ly seemed to me to be.[18]

Modifying operators on perceptual sentences Because our perceptual faculties are fallible, and because observation conditions are often less than optimal, we have good reason for making use of modifying operators on perceptual verbs, such as 'It seemed to me just as if I V-ed M // that *p*' or 'It V-ly seemed to A that . . .', and 'A thought he could V . . .'. These have as one of their functions the cancelling of the factivity of 'perceive (see, hear, feel, etc.) that . . .'. One may think one perceived something, or think one perceived something's being so, just as it may seem to one perceptually as if things are so, even though one knows that they are not (as when one looks as the Müller-Lyer lines, knowing full well that they are the same length).

Trying, succeeding and failing Since the senses are cognitive faculties, and since they are not infallible or incorrigible, it is hardly surprising that they are bound up with notions of endeavour,

---

[18] Wittgenstein briefly toyed with the idea that seeming to see is a criterion of seeing (*The Blue and Brown Books* (Blackwell, Oxford, 1958), pp. 51f.), but quickly abandoned this misguided view. Strawson advanced the idea that 'its sensibly seeming to you just as if you perceived a material object array' presumptively implies that you are perceiving such an array ('Causation in Perception', repr. in *Freedom and Resentment and Other Essays* (Methuen, London, 1974), pp. 66f.).

success and failure. One can try to perceive and attempt to discern better. One may look, listen or grope *for* something or other, try to smell what is for dinner or to detect what spices are in the food. One may do so carefully or carelessly, deliberately and attentively – even though one cannot *see* something carefully (but only *watch* or *try to see* something thus), or *hear* something attentively (but only *listen to* something thus). Where there is trying, there is also success, failure and mistake. One may perceive, fail to perceive or misperceive – for one may see M, fail to spot M despite looking hard or see M and mistakenly take it to be N. The successful upshot of looking, listening for, feeling for, trying to smell, are seeing, hearing, feeling or smelling, or more generally descrying, recognizing, discerning, detecting or distinguishing. But one may detect, discern or recognize something without trying to do so.

Normal observers, normal observation conditions

Precisely because our sense-faculties *are* cognitive faculties, and because they are fallible and corrigible, it is useful to have a battery of concepts that partially explain perceptual successes and failures as well as perceptual opportunities and impediments. So we have concepts appertaining to the perceiving agent, to the perceptual conditions and to the nature of the object. We have the notions of *normal observer* (and correlatively a *poor* or *deficient observer*, who suffers, temporarily or permanently, from poor or defective organs of perception). Of course, a normal observer may suffer from momentary impairment of the functioning of his sense-organs – as when one is blinded by a powerful light or deafened by a very loud proximate noise, or when one's hands are freezing cold, and so forth. So we have concepts pertaining to *normal conditions of observation* – these being conditions under which a normal observer is able, relative to a given sense-modality, to perceive things to have the perceptual properties (colours, shapes, motion or rest, making sounds, smells, thermal qualities and so forth) they have. These conditions will involve the medium of perception at a distance – good light or illumination, clear cold air, as well as absence of various masking circumstances (noise, flashing lights and so forth). Other conditions of observation concern the object observed – the saliency of its perceptual qualities, its size, its orientation and so forth. What is important is not to fall into the common error of explaining a perceptual quality F or *being* F in terms of a thing's *appearing to be F to a normal observer under normal observation conditions.*[19] On the contrary, the concepts of the perceptual qualities (of colour, sound, smell, taste, thermal qualities, etc.) are explained (by ostensive definition) *in* normal conditions, but not *by reference to* normal conditions. So, for example, we explain colour words such as 'red' or 'magenta' by reference to colour samples visible from close proximity in good light, as we explain what 'one metre' means by reference to a ruler in one's hand (not on the other side of the street), and so on. *Then* we may go on to explain that *normal observation conditions* are those in which red things look red, sour things taste sour, hot things feel hot, and so on. And we further explain that a *normal observer* is one who can perceive things to have the perceptual properties they do in normal observation conditions.[20]

3. The classical causal theory of perception

The representative causal theory of perception

The early modern representational causal theory of perception originated with Galileo and was further developed by Descartes. It became philosophical orthodoxy through Locke and scientific orthodoxy with Newton. It was challenged only by various forms of idealism (e.g. Berkeley and Hume). The idea was that perception consists of having an experience (an impression or idea) *caused* by a material object, or by a material object's reflecting or generating light-, sound-, or heat-waves, or by corpuscles in the air or in liquid. The agitation of our nerve-endings involves the transmission of animal spirits (neural impulses) to the brain, where, according to Descartes, they give rise to *thoughts* that are characterized as 'seeming to oneself to see (hear, smell, etc.)'. According to Locke, they give rise to *ideas* – which are apprehended or perceived by the mind. This empiricist conception was memorably represented by Locke's *camera obscura* analogy:

> That external and internal Sensation, are the only passages I can find, of Knowledge, to the Understanding. These alone, as far as I can discover,

---

[19] See e.g. G. Evans 'Things without the Mind', in Z. Van Straaten (ed.), *Philosophical Subjects: Essays Presented to P. F. Strawson* (Clarendon Press, Oxford, 1980), p. 98n.; C. McGinn, *The Subjective View* (Clarendon Press, Oxford, 1983), p. 6.

[20] For further defence of this claim, see my *Appearance and Reality* (Blackwell, Oxford, 1987), pp. 125–9.

are the Windows by which light is let into this *dark Room*. For, methinks, the *Understanding* is not much unlike a Closet wholly shut from light, with only some little openings left to let in external visible Resemblances, or *Ideas* of things without; would the Pictures coming into such a dark Room but stay there, and lie so orderly as to be found upon occasion, it would very much resemble the Understanding of a Man, in reference to all Objects of sight, and the *Ideas* of them.[21]

In the seventeenth century it became obvious, from research into vision, that a complex causal process was involved in light's being reflected off an object into the eye and onto the retina. It became equally clear that consequently something (animal spirits, neural impulses) was transmitted along the optic nerves. What happened thereafter remained obscure. Descartes thought that an image or impression was produced on the surface of the pineal gland, where 'it is presented to the soul'. Willis held that an image is produced on the corpus callosum, where 'the soul beholds the image of the thing there painted'. (In the twentieth century scientists were able to take the story further – as far as the 'visual' striate cortex.) But one thing *seemed* clear: at some point or another, this process must yield something *mental*, non-mechanical (non-physiological): a *visual experience* – the perception of a visual impression or idea in the mind.

Reasons for the classical theory

In the seventeenth century there were powerful reasons for construing 'a perceptual experience' as something that falls short of a perception. Sense-impressions (ideas) were held to be *caused by* objects of perceptual experience. Impressions of secondary qualities are not perceptions of colours, smells, tastes, sounds, etc. *of* objects – since objects are not really coloured, noisy, smelly, etc. – but rather the effects of the particulate structure of objects on our sensibility. Moreover, one could enjoy the very same perceptual experience as a result of illusion, dream or nightmare. Ideas (sense-impressions) are what we *immediately* perceive – both in the case of illusion, dream and hallucination, and in the case of genuine perception of items in our perceptual field. As Locke remarked: ''Tis evident, the mind knows not things immediately, but only by the intervention of ideas it has

---

[21] Locke, *An Essay concerning Human Understanding*, 4th edn [1700], II. xi. 17, quoted in *Human Nature: the Categorial Framework*, p. 246n.

of them.'[22] What we perceive 'directly' are ideas. These ideas are caused by objects. Some of them (ideas of primary qualities) are caused by resembling qualities of objects, others (ideas of secondary qualities) are caused by the particulate structure of objects and do not resemble anything in the objects themselves. The classical causal theory of perception was the product of synthesizing a rudimentary neurophysiological explanation of perception with (a) a metaphysical distinction between how we perceive the world and how it is independently of our perceptions of it (the primary-/secondary-quality distinction), (b) a misconceived notion of what is given in perception, namely ideas, that are the immediate objects of perception, and (c) the supposition that words are names of ideas.

5 objections to the classical theory
The objections to this classical representational causal theory of perception are well known.

(i) If it were true, it could never be known to be true – since one cannot correlate impressions or ideas with the qualities of which they are impressions or ideas in order to give inductive confirmation to the postulated causal connection.

(ii) If it is a hypothesis – an inference to the best explanation – like the inferences to the existence of Uranus or Vulcan, it is not a hypothesis that could ever be confirmed or disconfirmed in experience – unlike those inferences to the best explanation.

It was these two considerations above all that gave rise to the remarkable forms of idealism advanced by Berkeley and Hume. Weird and wonderful though they are, they also seemed to be unavoidable consequences of these objections to the representationalist causal theory of perception.

(iii) It is sometimes true that someone who has a perceptual illusion cannot distinguish his having an illusion from veridically perceiving. It is also true that when we are dreaming, we do not know that we are dreaming – even lucid dreams are not instances of knowing that one is dreaming, but rather of dreaming that one is dreaming. But this does not imply that having an illusion or dreaming that things are so, on the one hand, and actually perceiving that things are so, on the other, *are similar*, or *resemble* each other. All it means is that the difference between them may not be evident to the person suffering from an illusion, and cannot be evident to the dreamer. Nor do the phenomena of illusions and dreams show that veridically perceiving, on the one hand, and having an illusion or dreaming, on the

---

[22] Locke, *Essay*, IV. iv. 3.

other, have a lowest common denominator – namely having the idea or impression that things are so.[23] We shall explore this matter in section 4 below.

(iv) As noted in chapter 1, we do not *perceive* our experiences; we do not *perceive* impressions or ideas – we have them. I do not *perceive* my seeing the red rose or my smelling its scent. I *see* the red rose and *smell* its scent. Perceiving the rose is not *mediated* by anything, and is not *indirect*. We are only imposed on to think otherwise by three mutually supporting misconceptions: (a) misconstrual of illusions, hallucinations and dreams; (b) the metaphysical distinction between wholly subjective (mind-dependent) secondary qualities and objective (mind-independent) primary qualities; (c) misconstruals of consciousness as apperception.

(v) If the seventeenth-century tale were correct, then we should have to learn the meanings of expressions signifying our subjective experiences (perceptions and sensations alike), as well as expressions signifying the objects of our perceptual experiences (in particular names of secondary qualities), by reference to the experiences themselves. Ideas, stored in memory, would have to fulfil the role of samples in private ostensive definitions. Locke observed, 'Words, in their primary signification, stand for nothing but the ideas in the mind of him that uses them . . . Nor can anyone apply them as marks, immediately, to anything else but the ideas that he himself hath.'[24] For

> *Our Senses*, conversant about particular sensible Objects, do *convey into the Mind*, several distinct *Perceptions* of things, according to those various ways, wherein those Objects do affect them: And thus do we come by those *Ideas* we have of . . . sensible qualities . . . The other Fountain, from which experience furnisheth the Understanding with *Ideas*, is the *Perception of the Operations of our own Minds* within us, as it is employ'd about the *Ideas* it has got; which Operations, when the Soul comes to reflect on, and consider, do furnish the Understanding with another set of *Ideas*, which could not be had from things without: and such are, *Perception, Thinking, Doubting, Believing,*

[23] I have deliberately avoided mention of hallucinations. On the whole, patients suffering from hallucinations do *not* confuse hallucination with perceptions. Hearing voices is not at all like hearing someone speaking to one, and visual hallucinations, riveting and frightening as they are, are by no means always confused with visual perceptions.

[24] Locke, *Essay*, III. ii. 2.

Reasoning, Knowing, Willing, and all the different actings of our own Minds; which we being conscious of, and observing in ourselves, do receive into our Understandings, as distinct *Ideas*.[25]

Ideas, preserved in memory ('that great Storehouse of Ideas'), then function as *patterns* for the use of names.[26] Patterns are *samples* employed in ostensive definitions as standards of correctness for the application of a word, such as colour samples, or samples of lengths or weights. Patterns stored in the memory are therefore mental samples for use in private ostensive definitions. But, as Wittgenstein showed definitively, there is no such thing as a 'private ostensive definition', and there is no such thing as a 'mental sample' (any more than there is any such thing as *checkmate* in draughts).[27] There is no such thing as explaining, even to ourselves, what we mean by 'see', 'hear', 'taste', 'feel', let alone 'think', 'doubt', 'believe' and 'reason', by reference to mental patterns or samples stored in memory. Perceptual verbs and their cognates are *essentially* bound up with *perceptual behaviour* in appropriate circumstances. They are self-ascribed without any grounds whatsoever, but that is possible (intelligible) only because they are, and are known to be, ascribable to others on the grounds of their behaviour. To possess concepts of perception requires mastery of both their groundless self-ascription and their ascription to others on the grounds of behavioural criteria. To possess concepts of perceptual qualities defined or explained by reference to samples or patterns requires the availability of *public* samples that *can* function as objects for comparison, and that are standards by reference to which the use of such expressions *can* be judged correct or incorrect.

The survival of the classical theory among neuroscientists

So the classical *philosophical* causal theory of perception is incoherent. It is, however, striking that it soldiers on in the thought and writings of distinguished contemporary neuroscientists, who embrace the representative theory of perception. So, for example, Kandel (a Nobel laureate) and Wurtz, in a paper tellingly entitled

---

[25] Locke, *Essay*, II. i. 2–3.

[26] Locke, *Essay*, II. ix. 9.

[27] Wittgenstein, *Philosophical Investigations*, §§243–315. For detailed explanation and defence of his arguments, see P. M. S. Hacker, *Wittgenstein: Meaning and Mind* (Blackwell, Oxford, 1990), essays 1–7.

'Constructing the Visual Image', asked: 'How is information carried by separate pathways brought together into a coherent visual image? . . . How does the brain construct a perceived world from sensory information and how does it bring it into consciousness?'. And they concluded that 'Visual images are typically built up from the inputs of parallel pathways that process different features – movement, depth, form and colour'.[28] In a like manner, Smythies and Ramachandran averred that 'we do not see what is actually out there but what the brain computes is most probably out there', and declare that 'the phenomenal object is a construct of the central nervous system'.[29] Crick (another Nobel laureate) averred:

> What you see is not what is *really* there; it is what your brain *believes* is there . . . Your brain makes the best interpretation it can according to its previous experience and the limited and ambiguous information provided by your eyes . . . what the brain has to build up is a many-levelled interpretation of the visual scene.[30]

Frith has recently written that 'our brain creates the illusion that we have direct contact with objects in the physical world'.[31] Contemporary neuroscience has doubtless added much to our empirical knowledge of the neural processes involved in perceiving. But neuroscientists are still entrapped in a demonstrably misguided seventeenth-century conceptual framework for the articulation of their discoveries about perception and the neural structures and processes that make it possible.

So much for the classical causal theory of perception that still flourishes. That it is conceptually incoherent is indisputable. But the question of whether our perceptual *concepts* are causal ones must be separately addressed.

---

[28] E. R. Kandel and R. H. Wurtz, 'Constructing the Visual Image', in E. R. Kandel, J. H. Schwartz and T. M. Jessel (eds), *Principles of Neural Science*, 4th edn (McGraw-Hill, New York, 2000), p. 502.

[29] J. R. Smythies and V. S. Ramachandran, 'An Experimental Refutation of the Direct Realist Theory of Perception', *Inquiry*, 40 (1997), pp. 437–8.

[30] Crick, *Astonishing Hypothesis*, pp. 30, 32f.

[31] C. Frith, *Making up the Mind: How the Body Creates our Mental World* (Blackwell, Oxford, 2007), p. 17.

4. The modern causal theory of perception

The modern causal theory of perception (Grice/Strawson) In the second half of the twentieth century, the causal theory of perception was revived by Paul Grice and subsequently elaborated by Peter Strawson. They detached their analyses from empirical explanations of the psychology and neuroscience of perception. They were concerned only with showing that an *a priori* constituent of our ordinary perceptual concepts is that what we perceive causes our perceptual experience of it. They eschewed the idea of impressions, ideas or sense-data as immediate objects of perception. What we *perceive* (immediately, directly) are objects, properties and relations in the world around us. What we *have* are perceptual experiences. Perceptual experiences, they argued, are described by various *non-factive* forms of words, such as 'It seems to me just as if I were seeing . . .', or 'It sensibly seems to me as if I were seeing . . .'. This is strikingly reminiscent of Cartesian perceptual 'thoughts', which were also held to be described by such forms of words. This might give us pause.[32] Unlike the Cartesian doctrine, however, the modern causal analysis of perception is not essentially linked to the classical distinction between primary and secondary qualities.

The basic pattern of analysis According to the modern causal analysis of verbs of perception, a perceptual experience amounts to a perception only if it is caused by the object which the perceptual experience seems to be an experience of. The general pattern of the analysis therefore is as follows.

A perceives that things are so if and only if:

(i)   it sensibly seems to A that things are so;
(ii) things are so;
(iii) that things are so is causally responsible for its sensibly seeming to A that they are.

---

[32] I first expressed my doubts about the modern causal theory of perception in *Appearance and Reality*, pp. 227–38, intending at the time to write a further volume on the subject. This I never did. John Hyman pursued the quarry with great subtlety in a series of papers, especially 'The Causal Theory of Perception', *Philosophical Quarterly*, 42 (1992), 277–96; '-ings and -ers', *Ratio*, 14 (2001), 298–317; and 'The Evidence of Our Senses', in H.-J. Glock (ed.), *Kant and Strawson* (Clarendon Press, Oxford, 2003), pp. 235–54 – to all of which I am indebted.

So, to describe someone as perceiving something, or to characterize something as a perception, is to describe an event (of perceiving) in terms of its cause, just as to describe something as a footprint, sunburn or raindrop is to describe something in terms of its cause. With appropriate terminological adjustments, Descartes would have little to quarrel with this.

Presumptive implication
Like the classical causal theory of perception, the modern version too offers an epistemological account of perceptual knowledge. Grice held that one normally makes perceptual claims 'on the evidence of certain sense-impressions', but denied that this is an inductive inference or an inference to the best explanation (as the neo-classical empiricists, Ayer and Mackie, had argued it to be). Rather, he insisted, this evidential nexus must be conceptual. Strawson held that sense-impressions 'presumptively imply' the corresponding perceptual belief, the corresponding perceptual statement, and the corresponding statement of how things are. This relation of *presumptive implication* (reminiscent of Wittgenstein's conception of a logical criterion) is a *conceptual* (non-contingent) one. One may enjoy a perceptual experience without believing that things are as they sensibly seem to one to be (if, for example, one has been forewarned), but normally if it sensibly seems to one just as if one perceived that things are so, one believes that one perceives them to be so, and one also believes that they are so.

Grice's argument
Grice argued that a perceptual experience does not amount to a perception if what one seems to oneself to be perceiving *merely corresponds* to what is in one's environment. For there may be, for example, a *trompe l'œil* painting between oneself and what one wrongly takes oneself to be perceiving. In that case, it will seem to one just as if one were seeing, say, a clock on the mantelpiece, even though one does not actually see one, but only the deceptive painting that stands between one and the actual clock on the mantelpiece. Nevertheless, one has exactly the same 'subjective perceptual experience' as one would have had were one actually seeing the clock on the mantelpiece. What is needed for one's perceptual experience to amount to a perception is that the experience be *caused* by what one takes it to be an experience of. This causal nexus between experience and object, Grice held, is built into our ordinary perceptual concepts.

Riposte to the Gricean argument
To this one may reply that all the argument shows is that what one perceives must be perceptible to one. In the case of vision, for example, it must not be occluded.

But it does not show that what one sees must cause a perceptual experience allegedly described by the words 'It seems to me that I see . . .', or 'It looks to me as if . . .', let alone that this is part of the meaning of 'to see'. The grammatical truth that one can perceive only what is perceptible gives no support to a causal account of the concept of perception.

Strawson's argument
Strawson argued that a perceptual experience is a 'subjective episode' that is accurately described by a form of words shorn of the factivity characteristic of such perceptual judgements as 'I see such-and-such a material object array' or 'I see that things are so'. The 'best possible way' to describe one's perceptual experience, he averred, is of the general form: 'It sensibly seems to me just as if I were seeing . . .'. The curious Cartesian phrasing is deliberate. It may visually seem to me just as if I were seeing such-and-such, even though I know perfectly well that I am not (as when I look at the familiar Müller-Lyer lines). So 'It sensibly seems to me just as if . . .', unlike 'I see . . .', does not *entail* that I know or believe that things are as they visually appear to me to be, or that things are as it seems to me that I see them to be. Nevertheless, a 'subjective' perceptual experience (a sensible seeming), thus conceived, confers a *belief-title* that one is actually perceiving things. A subjective perceptual experience, on this view, is a *constituent* of every perceiving. What makes a perceptual experience a perception of what it seems to be of is that it is *caused* by the appropriate material object or material object array.[33]

Chinks in the armour
This is elegant, and powerful. It is comprehensive. It seems to capture what the classical causal theorists were fumbling for, without falling into their errors. It seems overwhelmingly plausible. – In fact it is mistaken. It involves subtle and wonderful conceptual confusions. The heart of the matter lies in the use of the phrases 'It sensibly seems to me just as if I were perceiving . . .' ('It visually seems to me just as if I were seeing . . .', etc.) and 'perceptual experience'. The former phrases (and variants on them) are, in Strawson's tale, cast in the role of *descriptions* of a subjective ('mental') episode. This should be investigated. The moot questions are whether the actors can play the roles, whether they are on the right stage and whether they are in the right play. Furthermore, *its sensibly seeming to one just as if one perceived* is held to be a

---

[33] P. F. Strawson, 'Perception and its Objects' (1979), repr. in *Philosophical Writings* (Oxford University Press, Oxford, 2011), pp. 127f., 136–8.

perceptual experience. This should be challenged. For it is not obvious how one could have a perceptual experience without perceiving anything, any more than it is obvious how one could have the experience of childbirth without giving birth to a child or the experience of listening to Beethoven's Fifth Symphony without listening to it.

Misconceptions about illusions, hallucinations and dreams   One reason why it seems plausible to conceive of perceptual experience thus is because of a misconstrual of the concepts of illusion, hallucination and dream. Philosophers since antiquity have been plagued by the thought that illusions, hallucinations and dreams are (or can be) indistinguishable from veridical perception. It seemed that all four cases may involve exactly the same perceptual experience. This thought was *one* of the roots of scepticism – and was brought onto centre-stage in the early modern era by Descartes. But it needs to be examined. In one sense, it is patently false. Looking at the Ames Room through a pinhole aperture does not *resemble* looking at a room. Nothing could be more *dissimilar* than someone's hallucinating a dagger and someone's really seeing one – for in the latter case, there is a dagger before him, and in the former there is not. (Macbeth does not look as if he is seeing a dagger – he looks as if he is having a hallucination.) Nothing could be more *different* than the slumbering person dreaming that he is perceiving such-and-such and someone perceiving such-and-such.

One may grant this, and insist that the similarity of the experience is not objective ('third-personal'), but purely subjective. But is this true? Does seeing a dagger before one *resemble* hallucinating one? – Obviously not! For one cannot juxtapose one's perceiving a dagger and hallucinating (or dreaming of) a dagger and compare them for similarity and difference as one can juxtapose two pictures, or a picture and what it is a picture of. So in so far as the experiences are indistinguishable, it is not because of *perceived resemblance* or *perceptible similarity* – for one cannot perceive one's experiences. One may grant this too. But still, the subject cannot (or may not be able to) *distinguish* the experiences. Ordinarily, if not forewarned, he actually believes that he is perceiving. So surely, both in the case of veridical perception and in the cases of illusion, hallucination and dream, the subject has an experience describable as *its seeming to the subject just as if he were perceiving* thus-and-so. Is at least this true?

We can put dreaming aside. When someone is sleeping, he cannot distinguish anything, only dream that he distinguishes something.

Even a so-called lucid dream is misdescribed as *being aware* that one is dreaming. When one has a lucid dream, one *dreams* that one is dreaming. (This contentious matter will not be further discussed here.) So let us turn to illusion. Normally, unless one is forewarned or has had prior experience of similar illusions or the setting (at the oculist's) prepares one, one *believes*, at least initially, that one is perceiving things to be thus-and-so. Things appear to one just as they would if one were really perceiving things to be so. It *seems* to one just as if one were perceiving things to be so – one has a Cartesian 'thought'. So, the moot question is whether *the experience* one is undergoing (the experience of being subject to an illusion) is describable by the phrase 'It sensibly seems to me just as if I were perceiving things to be so', and whether this phrase *also* describes the experience one enjoys when one actually perceives things to be so.

Describing perceptual experiences It is difficult to keep tabs on an expression as unnatural and unwieldy as 'It sensibly seems to me just as if I were perceiving that things are so'. Let us start with something simpler. What might one *call* 'the description of a perceptual experience'? Even this is cumbersome. So let us simplify further. First, how would one naturally respond to the request: 'Describe your seeing . . .', or, to be more concrete, for example, 'Describe your seeing the Sistine Chapel ceiling for the first time', or 'Describe your hearing Callas in *Tosca*'. And secondly, how would one naturally respond to the request 'Describe your hallucinating a bloody dagger before you' or 'Describe your hallucinating the voice of the dead Banquo'. Undoubtedly the most natural forms of words to select would be whatever one may give as an answer to the question 'What was it like for you to see // hear // . . . ?' and 'What was it like for you to seem to see // hear // . . . ?'. Two points should be noted. First, the answers to these two questions are likely to be *very* different. Secondly, neither question could conceivably be given the answer 'It (sensibly) seemed to me just as if I were perceiving . . .'.

'Describe your seeing the Sistine Chapel ceiling for the first time' may be answered by such forms of words as 'It was quite overwhelming – I gasped with wonder'. But one form of words that is quite *definitely* excluded is 'It seemed to me just as if I were seeing the Sistine ceiling'. 'Describe hearing Callas in *Tosca*', or, more naturally, 'Tell us what it was like to hear Callas in *Tosca*', may be answered by 'It was wonderful // amazing // sheer perfection', but *not* by 'It seemed to me just as if I were hearing Callas in *Tosca*', let alone 'It *sensibly* seemed to me that I was hearing Callas in *Tosca*'. For these are *not* descriptions of perceptual experiences. Similarly, 'Describe your experience of seeming to see a ghost', or 'What was it like for you to have a hallucination of a ghost?', could be answered by 'It was terrifying // weird // bizarre', but not by 'It visually seemed to me just as if I saw a ghost', nor by 'It visually seemed to me just as if I saw NN'.

All right, it may be replied, but that was not what was meant. What was demanded was an 'internal' or 'essential' description of a perceptual experience – a description that states what the experience was or seemed to be an experience of. Whether it was enjoyable, wonderful or terrifying is a further question – for these are non-essential, external, characteristics of an experience. What is being demanded is in effect a description of the *content of a perceptual experience*. If we juxtapose such a description with a description of the content of a *perception*, it will be evident that they are the same. That is why causal theorists go on to claim that every perception 'contains' a subjective perceptual experience, and why they are inclined to explain the difference between a subjective perceptual experience and a corresponding perception in causal terms. A perception is a perceptual experience that is caused in appropriate ways by the object it seems to be a perceptual experience of.

Contents are answers But it is evident that the 'content' of a perceptual experience, on the one hand, and the 'content' of a perception, on the other, are simply *what is given in answer to the questions* 'What did you seem to perceive?' and 'What did you perceive?'. It is true that the answers to these questions may well be the same, for example 'such-and-such an object' or 'that such-and such is the case'. But the fact that the answers are the same does not imply that the answers describe a perceptual experience common to both perceiving and to seeming to perceive. The question 'What did you *not* perceive when you did not perceive Jack go up the hill?' has the same answer as the question 'What *did* you perceive when you perceived Jack go up the hill?' – namely 'Jack going up the hill'. But this answer does not describe something common to perceiving and to not perceiving something – it is a common answer to two different questions! Seeing something is not seeming to see something plus a causal condition. One cannot have a *perceptual experience* without perceiving something. And one cannot have an illusion and also be perceiving what one is having the illusion of perceiving, any more than one can be having a hallucination and simultaneously be perceiving what one is hallucinating.

Confusions about seemings   Finally, modern non-representationalist variants of the causal account of perception, unlike the classical accounts, insist that we do *directly* or *immediately* perceive material objects and material object arrays. *Normally*, Strawson argued, our perceptual experience *seems to be* a perception of a material object or material object array. Every perception is at the same time a perceptual experience – of seeming to perceive. Not every perceptual experience, however, is a perception – hallucinations and illusions are not. But this cannot be right. For if we construe 'a perceptual experience' as *seeming to perceive*, then that in turn cannot also *seem to be* a perception. Its seeming to A as if he perceived such-and-such cannot itself seem to A to be anything. Seemings are not things that seem.[34]

The roles of 'seeming to perceive'   We are now in a position to dismiss the claim that seeming to perceive is *a priori* (presumptively good) evidence for perceiving, or that seeming to perceive gives one a defeasible title to believe that one perceives whatever one seems to perceive. 'It seems to me as if', 'It looks to me as if', 'It sounds to me as if' and their numerous cousins have multiple roles.[35] But among them, one will not find the role of functioning as *a priori*, presumptively good evidence for things being as they subjectively seem to be. Among their various roles is the paradigmatic one of qualifying a claim to have perceived something, to block the factivity of perceptual statements, and hence to indicate room for doubt. (This is, of course, what Grice denied – but wrongly so.) Far from signifying the bedrock of evidence in *seemings*, they signify the questionable exercise of our perceptual faculties. The answer 'I saw it' to the question 'How do you know?' does not give *evidence* for things being as I saw them to be. On the contrary, it explains why no evidence is needed, since I *saw* the object, or *saw* that things were so. It gives the *source* of my knowledge – namely, my use of my perceptual, cognitive, faculty of sight. Though a cognitive faculty, sight is neither infallible nor incorrigible. *One* function of 'it seems

[34] See J. Hyman, 'The Evidence of Our Senses', pp. 249–52.

[35] Explored in detail in *Appearance and Reality*, ch. 6.

(looks, sounds, feels) to me as if' is to indicate a reason for questioning the exercise of my cognitive faculty, not to indicate the bedrock of indefeasible evidence.[36]

Bearing of our account on neuroscience and psychology
Finally, where does this leave the empirical theories of perception constructed by psychologists and cognitive neuroscientists? It leaves their experimental work intact, and their genuine discoveries unblemished. But it leaves much of their theorizing about their experimental work and discoveries in tatters. One way in which they *cannot* argue is as Professor Richard Dawkins did in the following passage:

> Objects are 'out there', and we think that we 'see' them out there. But I suspect that really our percept is an elaborate computer model in the brain, constructed on the basis of information coming from out there, but transformed in the head into a form in which that information can be *used*. Wavelength differences in the light out there become coded as 'colour' differences in the computer model in the head. Shape and other attributes are encoded in the same kind of way, encoded into a form that is convenient to handle. . . . It is because we *internally use* our visual information and our sound information in different ways and for different purposes that the sensations of seeing and hearing are so different.[37]

Nothing in our philosophical survey of the conceptual character of perception suggests for one moment that perception could take place without our perceptual organs being causally affected by objects, light- and sound-waves and so forth. Our detailed demonstration that the philosophical causal analysis of perceptual concepts is mistaken shows nothing at all about the empirical causal investigations of the neural processes of perception. Nothing even intimates that we could perceive anything without the appropriate functioning of our brain. Nevertheless, it is not our brain that perceives things – we do. We do not perceive things *with* our brain, but with our sense-organs. But,

[36] To be sure, sensible seemings may indeed be evidence, but not *a priori* evidence, and not evidence for things being as they seem to be either. They may be evidence for deficiencies of one's sense-faculty, or of its exercise, of defects in one's sense-organ, of sub-optimality or abnormality in observation conditions, or of things being *other* than they sensibly seem to be (e.g. 'If it looks red in these conditions, then it is almost certainly green').

[37] Richard Dawkins, *The Blind Watchmaker* (Longman, Harlow, 1986), p. 34.

of course, we could not do so without our brain (we walk with our legs, but couldn't do so without the normal functioning of our brain).

The great discoveries of psychologists and neuroscientists over the last century and more have immeasurably increased our knowledge of how perception is physiologically possible and of what goes on in our brain when we perceive things. What they have *not* discovered is presented in list 8.1.

 (i) That it is the brain that perceives, let alone that it constructs hypotheses of perception.

 (ii) That it is the mind that perceives.

 (iii) That what we perceive are percepts, images or other similar ephemera in the brain or mind.

 (iv) That the terminus of the neural processes of perceiving is a perception or percept in the brain.

 (v) That the terminus of the neural processes of perceiving is a sensation in the brain.

 (vi) That perceiving involves the neural transformation of sensations into perceptions.

 (vii) That perception involves 'bringing together' information concerning colour, shape, motion, etc. to form an internal representation of the external world.

 (viii) That perception is description formation or hypothesis formation.

List 8.1 *What the empirical sciences of perception*
have not shown

The classical causal theory of perception and the modern causal analysis of perceptual verbs are alike misconceived. They need to be abandoned – not only because they are conceptually incoherent, but also because they are an impediment to decent science. They stand in the way of a cogent empirical account of the neural processes requisite for us to perceive what we perceive.

9

Memory

1. Memory as a form of knowledge

Memory, articulate memory and humanity

Without articulate memory, we should have no concept of the past. For we learn what is past, as well as what the past is, by learning to remember – by learning to answer past-tensed questions ('Who did it?', 'When did it happen?' and 'What happened?'); to use past-tensed sentences in relating what we have been doing and what we have or haven't done ('Look at what I've done', and 'I didn't do it'), to describe what others have done ('He did it'), to respond to questions not only with 'I don't know', but also with 'I don't remember'. Without articulate memory, we should have little worthy of the name of knowledge, other than awareness of what is present, recognitional abilities, some forms of know-how and inchoate expectations resulting from past experience. We should be like other animals. There would be no great fund of common knowledge that can be passed from generation to generation, freeing us from the constraints of mere evolutionary development and emulation. Even though memory is not a necessary condition for personal identity (amnesiacs do not cease to be the persons they were), without articulate memory there would be no persons.[1] Our memories are the bedrock of our *sense* of our own identity, the seedbed of the friendship and

---

[1] See *Human Nature: the Categorial Framework*, ch. 10.

The Intellectual Powers: A Study of Human Nature, First Edition. P. M. S. Hacker.
© 2013 John Wiley & Sons, Ltd. Published 2013 by John Wiley & Sons, Ltd.

comradeship that grow out of shared experience, and the repository of our culture and cultural traditions. It is because we are blessed with memory and mastery of linguistic skills that we, unlike other animals, can have an 'autobiography'. For unlike them we can not only remember, but, as Aristotle pointed out, we can also *recollect*. It is because we have an articulate memory that we can take responsibility for our deeds, feel guilt and remorse at our sins and misdeeds, feel satisfaction at having fulfilled our obligations and take pride in our achievements.

It is not surprising that a cognitive faculty so central to our nature as human beings, rational creatures and moral agents should have attracted the attention of philosophers ever since antiquity. Memory is a faculty that commonly fails in old age. It can be lost through brain damage. So it also attracted the attention of physicians and physiologists in the ancient world and early modern era, and more recently, of psychologists and neuroscientists too. The concept of memory is problematic. It is not readily surveyable. Like its sibling, the concept of knowledge, it has been the source of extensive confusions and misunderstandings throughout the ages. Indeed, it is one of the tasks of philosophical enquiry into the nature of memory to keep scientific research on the rails of sense. So, for example, memory does not consist in 'performance changes as a result of experience'.[2] If it did, then limping after having hurt one's foot or going deaf as a result of over-exposure to noise would be forms of memory. To remember does not consist in being 'conscious of some past experience'.[3] To remember Jill is not to be conscious of her, to remember being in love with her is not to be conscious of having been in love with her, and to remember that she went up the hill is not to be conscious of her having gone up the hill. For remembering such facts does not imply that they are occupying one's mind or weighing with one in one's deliberations (see chapter 1, section 3) Unless the concepts of memory and of remembering are tolerably clear, empirical investigations are unlikely to achieve their aims.

The remembering subject

It is the human being, or animal, *as a whole* that remembers – not parts of one, such as its brain or heart. It makes no sense to speak of the brain as

[2] B. Milner, L. R. Squire and E. R. Kandel, 'Cognitive Neuroscience and Memory', *Neuron*, 20 (1998), p. 450.

[3] J. LeDoux, *The Emotional Brain* (Phoenix, London, 1998), p. 69.

remembering or forgetting something, although it is, of course, true that one cannot remember anything if one's brain is damaged in certain ways. The reason for this is obvious: we say of a creature that it remembers something, remembers something to be so or remembers doing something, on the grounds of its exhibiting in its behaviour previously acquired knowledge and current knowledge of its past experiences. But there is no such thing as a brain's *behaving*, let alone as behaving in ways that would license saying that it remembers something, is trying to remember something, has forgotten something it previously learnt or has suddenly recollected something. It is equally senseless to attempt to investigate 'how the nervous system learns and remembers',[4] since the nervous system neither learns nor remembers anything. Nor can the brain be said to be the organ of memory in the sense in which the legs are the organ of locomotion and the eyes are the organ of sight. But there is no conceptual objection to holding that parts of the brain (such as the hippocampus and medial temporal lobe) are the vehicles of memory – the structural basis of the faculty and its exercise.

Some suggested analyses   It is possible to remember only what one experienced, did or underwent; what one previously perceived, was aware of, noticed or realized; and what one learnt, found out, discovered or discerned. For *memory is a form of knowledge*. But what form? Some plausible suggestions have been advanced.

Memory is knowledge of the past. Aristotle declared that 'the object of memory is the past'.[5] Cicero wrote that 'Memory is the faculty by which the mind recalls what happened'.[6] Despite all the sophisticated mnemonic techniques of the so-called *artificial memory*,[7] employed in the ancient (and medieval) world for remembering facts (about the present and future no less than the past), reflections on the nature of memory were generally dominated by the idea that the object of memory is the past. This tunnel vision continued, from the early modern era to this day. Locke asserted that memory is the power 'to revive ideas [the Mind] has once had, with this additional

---

[4] Milner et al., 'Cognitive Neuroscience and Memory', p. 446.

[5] Aristotle, *On Memory*, 449[b]25–6.

[6] Cicero, *De Inventione*, II. liii. 160.

[7] For the detailed history and description of such techniques, see Frances Yates, *The Art of Memory* (Routledge & Kegan Paul, London, 1966).

Perception annexed to them, that it has had them before'.[8] Leibniz agreed: memory is the recurrence of a prior perception without the object perceived, coupled with knowledge that one has had the perception before.[9] Reid averred that 'The object of memory, or thing remembered, must be something that is past'.[10] James held that 'memory proper . . . *is knowledge of an event, or fact*, of which meantime we have not been thinking, *with the additional consciousness that we have thought or experienced it before*'.[11] Russell, following Bergson, distinguished 'habit memory' from 'memory proper', and held that 'When we remember, the knowing is now, while what is known is in the past'.[12] There appears to have been a widespread confusion of *when one experienced* or *came to know* what one remembers with *what it is* that one remembers. Of course, knowledge of past experience involves memory, but not all memory is knowledge of past experience. We shall explore this below.

Three alternative suggestions emphasize the nexus of memory with knowledge previously acquired, rather than with knowledge of the past. They are closely related.

To remember something is to have learnt it and not forgotten. This is apt for what one learns to be so, and indicates the possession of information acquired. It also fits the acquisition and retention of skills and mastery of techniques, as when we ask 'Can you remember how to solve quadratic equations?'. But it is obviously misplaced when one remembers engaging in some activity, or experiencing something, or when one remembers thinking, wanting or intending something. For these are or need not be a matter of learning something to be so.

To remember is to retain information previously acquired. This is clearly correct for many kinds of case. If you tell me that things are so, and tomorrow I tell another what you told me, then I retained the information you gave me and was able to pass it on to someone else. Nevertheless, this analysis is quite out of place for remembering one's experiences. One may enjoy a concert, and remember enjoying it, but

[8] Locke, *An Essay concerning Human Understanding*, II. x. 2.

[9] Leibniz, *New Essays on the Human Understanding*, II. xix. 1.

[10] Reid, *Essays on the Intellectual Powers of Man* [1785] (Edinburgh University Press, Edinburgh, 2002), Essay III, ch. 1, p. 254.

[11] W. James, *The Principles of Psychology* (Holt, New York, 1890), vol. 1, p. 649.

[12] B. Russell, *The Analysis of Mind* (Allen & Unwin, London, 1921), p. 173.

to enjoy the concert is not to acquire the information that one enjoys it, and to remember enjoying it is not to retain a piece of information that one acquired. The analysis is also incorrect for retention of skills acquired, in cases in which *knowing-how* cannot be reduced to *knowing-that*. Similarly, to remember someone's smile or the sound of their voice would be misdescribed as the retention of *information* (in the sense in which one remembers information imparted to one).

To remember is to know now something one knew previously and to know it now because one knew it previously. This too is obviously right for many kinds of case. To remember that the battle of Hastings was fought in 1066 is to have retained the knowledge previously imparted to one. One knows it now *because*, that is, in virtue of the fact that, one knew it previously (and not because it is written on the blackboard). But this analysis is equally obviously incorrect for other kinds of case. Remembering that one had a headache yesterday is not to know now something one came to know yesterday. For as we have seen, it makes no sense to speak of coming to know that one has a headache. To remember one's youth is the ability to dwell on, recollect and recount experiences enjoyed or undergone in one's youth – one's falling in love for the first time, the excitement of youthful adventures, the delight in coming to understand things. This would be distorted by being represented as knowing now something one knew previously.

So, there is much to investigate and unravel.[13]

2. The objects of memory

The objects of memory What is it that one remembers? As we have just seen, from Aristotle to the present day, there has been a proneness to conceive of memory as being exclusively *of the past*. Broadly speaking, the thought is that perception gives us knowledge of the present, expectation gives us opinion of the future, and memory gives us knowledge of the past or 'access' to past experience. Current experience is 'laid down' in the memory (the storehouse

---

[13] The best guides are Reid, *Essays on the Intellectual Powers of Man*, Wittgenstein, *Philosophical Investigations* and his various writings on the philosophy of psychology, and Norman Malcolm, *Memory and Mind* (Cornell University Press, Ithaca, NY, 1977). For detailed scrutiny of Wittgenstein's contribution, see my essay entitled 'Memory and Recognition', in *Wittgenstein: Mind and Will*, part 2: *Exegesis §428–693* (Blackwell, Oxford, 1996).

of ideas) in the form of representative images (species, appearances, ideas, impressions) which exist there *in potentia* as it were, and can be 'called to life' in recollecting or reminiscing. How this is possible was commonly answered by trace theory, which originated with Aristotle and is explored by current neuroscientists. But, as we shall see, in one sense this seems obviously true; in another it is highly problematic. We shall start by examining the idea that all memory is 'of the past'.

It is evident that while the *source* of our memories is past experience and learning, the *objects* of memory are manifold. They include, of course, past experiences that were enjoyed or undergone, and what they were experiences of, as well as past acts and activities. But it is mistaken to suppose that one cannot remember what is present. One may encounter and recognize people – remember who they are. One may remember someone's smile or laugh, their voice and manner, when one re-encounters an old acquaintance whom one has not seen for years. One can remember forthcoming events, such as one's appointments and engagements. One may remember omni-temporal things, such as the laws of nature, as well as atemporal things, such as the laws of logic and the propositions of mathematics. And one may remember skills, techniques and languages.

A brief grammatical survey of a range of possible objects of memory will help keep us on the track of our quarry. It is displayed in table 9.1.

So much for a range of accusatives of the verb 'to remember' and its cousins 'recollect' and 'call to mind' and the corresponding range of objects of memory. This should suffice to rid one of the illusion that memory is essentially *of* the past, as opposed to being essentially acquired *in* the past, and of the idea that it is essentially *retention of knowledge* previously acquired, rather than also being a matter of currently possessing knowledge of what one previously did or experienced. It should make one aware of the motley of memory and beware of hasty generalization.

3. The faculty and its actualities

The faculty and   We distinguish between:
its actualities

  (i)   the faculty of memory;
  (ii) the retention of acquired knowledge and the ability to call to mind one's past experiences;

(iii) the actualization of these abilities when remembering and recollecting.

Grammatical form	Objects of memory
'To remember N', where 'N' is a proper name, or definite description	People, animals, places, things, sounds, smells, tastes, etc.
'To remember *e*' where '*e*' is an event designation // 'to remember A's V-ing'	Events; actions and reactions of others
'To remember the F-ness of // N // A's V-ing // e'	Modes of substances and characteristics of actions and occurrences
'To remember that *p*'; 'to remember *p*'	How things were, are, will be, are omni-temporally or atemporally
'To remember the proposition // story // rumour // that *p*'	A sayable; something said
'To remember that the proposition that *p* is true/is false'	The truth or falsity of a sayable
'To remember what one learnt // learnt by heart //'	Facts, dates, verses, melodies, tables, lists, etc.
'To remember French'	A foreign language; how to speak a foreign language
'To remember V-ing // being V-ed'	What one did, experienced, underwent
'To remember Wh- . . .'	The answer to a Wh-question
'To remember how to V'	Previously acquired skills and know-how
'To remember to V'	Acts, actions and activities known to be called for

Table 9.1 *A variety of grammatical forms and objects of remembering*

The faculty of memory is a *capacity – an ability to acquire an ability.* It is a second-order cognitive power. It is the ability to retain information acquired, to call to mind one's past actions and experiences, to acquire recognitional abilities and to retain learnt skills. The faculty is *exercised* whenever one comes to know something and does not forget it, learns something and retains it, experiences something and can later recollect what one experienced. The scholastics called this the 'first actuality' of the faculty. The present tense frequentative 'NN remembers who // why // where // what // when // whether // how //' is often used to signify such *mnemonic abilities*. Like 'knows', 'remembers', thus construed, lacks duration in the following sense: just as one cannot ask 'When do you know how to play chess?', so too one cannot ask 'When do you remember how to play chess?'. One cannot ask when remembering, in this sense, occurs, since abilities are not occurrences.

Mnemonic abilities are *actualized* whenever one calls something to mind, reflects on one's past experience, engages in reasoning from what one has learnt, recognizes something previously encountered or engages in skilled activities once learnt. Scholastics deemed this the 'second actuality' of the faculty. Mnemonic abilities are *manifest* in one's statements about one's past experiences and activities, in one's expression of previously acquired knowledge, in acting on the basis of what one recollects, and in the exercise of one's previously learnt skills. The past tense non-frequentative ('I remembered . . .') is often used to signify the actualization of what was impressed upon one's mind. 'Recall', 'recollect' and the progressive form 'is remembering' (as in 'He lay in bed remembering the events of the evening') are apt for current actualization, as are 'recount', and 'reminisce' for its verbal manifestation. It is in such cases that one *can* ask when someone remembered, how long it took him to remember, and how long he spent going over some episode in his mind or in his tale.

Why remembering is not an act That one remembers something (the first actuality) consists in being able to do a wide variety of things, such as call something to mind, visualize a face or remember someone's voice, say what one remembered, answer pertinent Wh-questions, reason and act on the grounds of what is remembered, inform or correct others, exercise acquired cognitive skills, instruct others how to do what one remembers how to do and so forth. Nevertheless, contrary to what has commonly been suggested,[14] remembering something (the second actuality) is not a

---

[14] For example, by Aristotle: 'to remember, strictly speaking, is an activity which will not occur until time has elapsed' (*On Memory*, 451^{a}29) and 'the act of recollecting ought to be distinguished from these acts [of relearning and rediscovering]' (451^{b}8). See also Reid: 'We may remember anything which we have seen, or heard, or known, or done, or suffered; but the remembrance of it is a particular act of the mind which now exists and of which we are conscious' (*Essays on the Intellectual Powers of Man*, Essay III, ch. 1, p. 253).

mental act or activity. One cannot deliberately, intentionally or voluntarily recollect something or remember to do or how to do something, any more than one can deliberately, intentionally or voluntarily know something. But, of course, one can often call things to mind when one wants to, and things previously experienced or learnt often come to mind without one's wanting them to. This seems paradoxical, until one adverts to the fact that remembering is a sibling of knowing, and neither knowing something nor being aware of something one knows is an act. To call something to mind, to bear in mind something one previously came to know, is not an act that consists in doing anything – apart from calling something to mind. What actually *happens* when one remembers something may be nothing other than that one acts on information previously acquired. But whatever one does could be done in different circumstances without its constituting remembering anything. Even if remembering someone's saying something involves 'hearing' his voice in one's imagination, this too could occur without its being a case of remembering. While forgetting to do something is to omit the performance of an act, it is not to omit the performance of an act of remembering. Although remembering something often (but by no means always) occurs at a time, there is nothing one *does* that constitutively *is* the remembering.[15]

Memory and its actualization   Consequently, the relationship between remembering and 'actualizing' one's memories is not the same as that between being able to do something and doing it (e.g. being able to shut the door and shutting it, being able to solve quadratic equations and solving one). Knowing at a given moment that something is so is not an act of any kind. So too, remembering at a given moment that something is or was so is not a determinate act or activity that instantiates an ability. That I remember the date of Agincourt is shown by my replying to the question 'When was the battle of Agincourt?' by saying '1415'. But saying '1415' might also be the answer to the question 'What is the sum of 1205 and 210?' or 'What is the time?'. Remembering to turn off the lights may consist in nothing more than knowing that one has to turn the lights off, and turning them off. No further 'act of remembering' need take place. What counts as a manifestation of remembering is context-dependent, and the manifestations of remembering are polymorphous.

---

[15] See Malcolm, *Memory and Mind*, pp. 74–7, for detailed examination.

Is remembering an experience? If remembering is not an act, surely it is an experience! After all, one remembers something at a given moment. Surely Russell was right to query 'What *is* the present occurrence when one remembers?'.[16] Remembering is something mental, something 'inner'! So it is an experience. And if it is an experience, it must surely have some characteristic that marks it out from all other experiences. — These *surely*s are marks of overused tracks. One may remember something at a given moment, but equally, one may bear in mind all day the fact that one has an appointment this evening. There need be no special occurrence that is the remembering. There may be experiential accompaniments of remembering something – one may feel sad or glad, amused or confused when one remembers what happened or what is going to happen (e.g. tomorrow's party). But (i) there need not be any such accompaniments; (ii) these accompaniments are not the remembering. The verb 'to remember' is not the name of an experience and it is not used to describe an experience. Remembering *as such* 'has no volume of experience'. When one says 'I remember seeing Jack', I am reporting a past experience, not a present one. 'He left abruptly because he remembered his engagement' explains why he left abruptly, not by reference to an experience he had, but rather by reference to something he knew and suddenly realized. But knowing, realizing, that he had an engagement is not an experience, even though it may be accompanied by a sense of alarm. But surely something happens when one remembers something? — All manner of things may happen, and one may do all sorts of things. If one remembers where one left one's keys, one may sigh with relief, or one may go to the drawer and get them, or one may telephone one's wife and tell her where to find them, or one may answer 'Yes' to the question 'Did you leave them in the drawer?' (or one may lie, and answer 'No'). But none of these is an 'experience of remembering'. Do they not all 'flow from an act of remembering'? — Only in so far as they flow from an act of knowing! But there is no such thing as an act of knowing.

One might object: surely, one often visualizes something when remembering. When one remembers her face a mental image may come before one's mind. Is this not an experience? — One may concede that visualizing is an experience that occurs at a time. When one remembers how she looked, her face may come before one's mind. But note three points. (i) The mental image may occur without

---

[16] Russell, *Analysis of Mind*, p. 173.

one remembering anything (one may be imagining how one is going to paint the face of a figure). (ii) The mental image is not a picture by the use of which one remembers. If it were, then the image would be a reminder (like a photograph), and one would have to remember that the image is an image of her face and not of someone else's. (iii) The mental image is an image of what one remembers, just as a memory statement is a statement of what one remembers. Having the mental image is no more the remembering than saying what one remembers is the remembering. The image and the utterance are on the same level. Remembering does not consist in behaving, but it does not consist in having images either. So what does it consist in? As Wittgenstein queried: Why should it *consist* in anything?[17] — So are there only manifestations of memory, and no remembering? — Are there only numerals and no numbers?

Virtues and defects of memory

Qua faculty, one's memory may be good or poor. Loss of (personal) memory is amnesia. A poor memory is a proneness to forget things, to forget how to do things and to forget to do things. A poor memory is a proneness not to remember or to remember only vaguely – just as poor eyesight is not a matter of 'seeing' things that are not there, but of not seeing, or not seeing clearly, things that are there. The exercise of one's memory in recollection of one's past experience may be more or less vivid, detailed and accurate. These modes of recollection are *features of the account one can give* of the experience and its objects – not features of mental imagery that may sometimes accompany remembering. To remember vividly is to be able to give a vivid description of what happened (as Proust was able to do). To remember a past experience or previously acquired information accurately and in detail is to be able to give an accurate and detailed description of it.[18] These are the virtues of a good memory. But one may also misremember or remember something incorrectly (as one may misperceive, or perceive incorrectly). To misremember, one must, to some degree, approximate the truth. One may indeed suffer from 'mnemonic hallucinations', as George IV did, when he sincerely recounted his deeds at the battle of Waterloo. These are not instances of misremembering, any more than perceptual hallucinations are cases of misperceiving.

---

[17] Wittgenstein, *Zettel* (Blackwell, Oxford, 1967), §16; *Philosophical Grammar* (Blackwell, Oxford, 1974), pp. 79f.

[18] For elaboration of these points, see chapter 11.

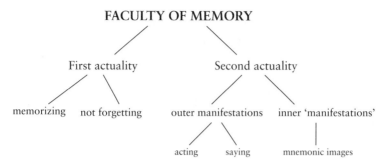

Figure 9.1 *The faculty of memory and its forms of actualization*

Trying to remember — Although remembering is no more an act than knowing, and although one cannot try to know but only to learn, one *can* try to remember. This may take two forms (see fig. 9.1). On the one hand, one can be ordered to remember something (not to forget it) and one can be told to memorize something – to learn it by heart. Here, one is required to exercise one's capacity (the faculty of memory) in order to acquire a mnemonic ability (the 'first actuality'). One can do so, or try to do so and either succeed or fail. One can likewise be ordered to remember to do something. On the other hand, there is a sense in which one cannot be ordered to remember (the 'second actuality'), that is recollect, something, any more than one can be ordered to know something (as opposed to being ordered to learn something). 'Remember what she said!' is not like 'Write down what she said!' but akin to 'Bear in mind what she said!'. One can be *asked* whether one knows or can say, and one can be asked whether one remembers or can tell, but one cannot be *ordered* to remember, only ordered to tell what one remembers. In the case of trying to recollect one's past experiences, one is often asked to *cast one's mind back*, to *look back on* something or to *hark back to it* and to recount what one recalls. If one's mnemonic efforts succeed, one remembers what one was trying to remember. If one fails, then one may have misremembered, that is remembered incorrectly, or one may have forgotten. Forgetfulness may take two forms: remediable by a reminder, or irremediable. Irremediably forgotten facts can be relearnt; irremediably forgotten experiences may be learnt from hearsay or records, but cannot be retrieved. This is then marked by 'I remember that I did . . .' (or 'I know that I did . . .')

rather than 'I remember doing . . .', and 'He remembers that he did . . .' rather than 'He remembers doing . . .'.

The factivity of 'remember'   Mnemonic verbs are factive. What one remembers, recollects or recognizes is as, or what, one remembers, recollects or recognizes it to be. If it is not, then one misremembered, thought wrongly that things were so, failed to recognize someone or something. Misremembering is a form of mnemonic failure. (One may be good at remembering, but not at misremembering.) The reason for the factivity is because memory is a cognitive faculty. One cannot remember something or remember something to be so, and not know it or know it to be so. But one may not be sure, just as one may not be sure that one knows something. Remembering correctly is compatible with doubt and uncertainty, but the statement that one remembers is not. This is parallel to knowing. If one doubts or is unsure whether things are or were as one remembers them as being or having been, one should not claim to remember. As with other cognitive verbs, the factivity of 'remember' is cancellable. When we are unsure of ourselves, we qualify a memory claim by '*As* I remember', '*As far as I can* recollect', 'I think that' and so forth. This is parallel to 'As far as I know' and 'To the best of my knowledge'.

4. Forms of memory

Personal memory   Philosophers have nicely differentiated between different forms of memory. *Personal* or *experiential memory* is distinguished by its characteristic grammatical form, namely, the verb 'to remember' followed by a gerund that specifies a previous experience, act or activity of the subject (viz. to remember V-ing). This may be perceiving, feeling or doing (including learning), as well as undergoing. Here one may remember not only what one experienced or did, but also the experiencing or doing of it. For one may often remember the distinctive experiential characteristics of doing or undergoing something (e.g. of its being exciting, frightening, wonderful, awesome, ghastly, painful, amusing, boring). The gerundive form of the expression of personal memory indicates that one experienced or did something, and has not forgotten (or not irretrievably forgotten) that one did. A criterion for whether one remembers doing or undergoing something is the open-ended multiplicity of one's recollections of the experience.

It is striking that, contrary to what many philosophers have supposed, the gerundive form is *not* indicative of mnemonic images associated with remembering doing or experiencing something. One can remember doing or experiencing things without having any mnemonic images of one's doings or experiencings. In some cases, one's experiential memory may have as its object episodes that *cannot* be pictured, as when one remembers thinking something, or intending to do something. Experiential memory has mesmerized philosophers, sometimes leading them to overlook all other forms or to relegate other forms to inferior status (e.g. of habituation (Bergson, Russell, Broad)).[19] Remembering one's experiences can be adverbially characterized as 'fondly', 'bitterly', 'happily' or 'sadly', which signify attitudes to the experience remembered. This form of memory is also a main source of the ideas that the essential object of memory is the past, that memory is a storehouse of past experience, and that to remember is to have a present representation of a past experience. We shall examine these ideas below.

The reproductive imagination

A form of memory that is connected with experiential memory is the ability to remember appearances: to recollect a person's face or facial expression, to visualize a landscape seen, to remember a person's voice, to conjure up in one's imagination sights and sounds, smells and tastes and so forth. This mnemonic power, traditionally referred to as the 'reproductive imagination' is unevenly distributed. Some have clear and distinct mental images of people and places; others are bereft of such powers. Some can accurately rehearse in their imagination a piece of music they have heard; others may be able to recognize the piece of music when they hear it anew, but be quite unable to call it before their mind. Some people can vividly relive in their imagination the experiences they have undergone.[20] It is not uncommon for people who have experienced something impressive (enchanting, horrendous) to be unable to banish the image of what they saw or heard from their mind. One may be haunted by the visual images of

---

[19] H. Bergson, *Matière et mémoire* (Alcan, Paris, 1910), pp. 75–7; Russell, *Analysis of Mind*, pp. 166f., 175; C. D. Broad, *Mind and its Place in Nature* (Kegan Paul, London, 1925), p. 270.

[20] Note that 'in their imagination' here, as in the phrase 'the reproductive imagination', does not refer to the faculty for thinking up new possibilities (see chapter 11), but rather to the image-generating faculty.

dreadful things one has seen or done, that press to one's memory 'Like damned guilty deeds to sinners' minds'.[21] But so too one may joyfully or longingly recollect in tranquillity, and call to mind, the beauty of the sights one has seen, the faces and voices of those one loves or has loved. We shall examine the concept of a mental image in more detail in chapter 11.

It would be mistaken to suppose that all forms of experiential memory are bound up with the reproductive imagination. 'I can remember breaking my leg when I was six years old, but I cannot visualize it' seems perfectly intelligible. 'I can remember Finals vividly – I can tell you exactly what it was like' may well be true even if one has no mnemonic images of the experience. However, the nexus between remembering someone's face or voice and the ability to conjure up mental images is clearly a conceptual one. 'I can no longer recollect her face' does not mean that I do not remember that she had blue eyes and long eyelashes, and so forth, but that I can no longer visualize her. So too, 'I cannot remember her voice' implies that I can no longer hear it in my imagination.

Factual memory

Experiential memory is commonly contrasted with *factual memory*, that is, remembering *that* things are thus-and-so. Here, as we have already noted, what is remembered may be past, present or future, omni-temporal or timeless. This form of memory is indeed a matter of retention of knowledge acquired, of what one has learnt and not forgotten (even though one may need a reminder). Clearly, personal, experiential, memory presupposes factual memory inasmuch as if one remembers V-ing, one also remembers that one V-ed. But one may remember that one V-ed without remembering V-ing. One may know simply because one has heard the tale from one's parents. It is noteworthy that 'I remember that I . . .' intimates recollection. Hence, other things being equal, 'I know the date of my birth', but 'I remember the date of my spouse's birth' – although if one's memory is failing, one may no longer remember the date of one's birth.

Recognitional and practical abilities

Factual and experiential memory merge with recognitional abilities. To remember Jill's voice may be the ability to hear it in one's imagination, but it may be just the ability to identify it when heard. To remember the

---

[21] Shakespeare, *Romeo and Juliet*, III. ii. 110.

taste of a certain wine may be no more than being able to recognize it on tasting it anew; to remember a place is often no more than to be able to recognize it on seeing it again. Recognitional abilities themselves merge with practical abilities and know-how. For while to remember a melody may be no more than being able to recognize it, it may also involve being able to hum or whistle it aloud, or to play it on an instrument. To remember Venice may be to recognize landmarks when one sees the city after fifty years' absence, but it may also involve knowing one's way around it.

Remembering how, and to do Retention of skills, that is, *remembering how* to do something, is yet another form that memory may take, a form that corresponds to *knowing how* to do something. Precisely to the extent that knowing-how is not reducible to knowing-that (see chapter 4, section 9), the corresponding remembering how to do something is not *reducible* to remembering that it is done in such-and-such a way. We have already noted *remembering to do* something, which is quite unlike remembering how to do something. It is not a retained practical skill, but a matter of not forgetting what must be done, and doing it.

It is evident that the contours of the various forms of memory are not sharp, and the different forms are often intermingled. It is also clear that it would be misguided to try to reduce the various forms to a single most fundamental one.

Misleading distinctions Other distinctions that have been drawn may be misleading. Scientists distinguish between short- and long-term memory, conceiving of these as different kinds of memory inasmuch as they are dependent on different parts of the brain. But these are not different *kinds* of memory. They are merely different memory *spans* (a short piece of string and a long piece of string are not two different kinds of string). Philosophers, such as Bergson, Russell and Broad, and following them, some scientists, have tried to distinguish between true memory and 'habit memory', reserving the former for remembering experiencing, doing or undergoing things (experiential memory). But remembering one's experiences, doings and undergoings is not *more properly* the exercise of one's memory than learning something and retaining what one learnt. Forgetting something one learnt is not the same as changing one's habits. Neither remembering that things are so, nor remembering something by heart, is a habit. Nor is evincing one's factual memory a habit, but rather a manifestation of one's cognitive powers. Remembering how to do something is no habit either, but rather the retention of a skill. Remembering to do something is not a habit, although it may become one.

Neuroscientists distinguish between declarative and non-declarative memory,[22] and suggest that this demarcates a 'fundamental distinction in the way all of us process and store information about the world'.[23] Declarative memory is held to be 'what is ordinarily meant by the term memory'; it is 'propositional' ('memory-that'), can be true or false, and is involved 'in modelling the external world and storing representations about facts and episodes'.[24] Non-declarative memory is held to be concerned with the retention of motor skills such as are involved in driving a car ('memory-how' or 'habit memory'). It is held to be manifest in priming, and exhibited in classical conditioning and sensitization (strengthening of a reflex response to a previously neutral stimulus, following the presentation of a noxious stimulus). This is sorely confused.[25] The research work on the gill-withdrawal reflex in *Aplysia*, the tail flick in crayfish, the eye-blink response in rabbits and so forth is not on memory. For changes in reflex-reaction speed do not manifest the retention of knowledge of any kind, nor do they manifest the retention of an acquired skill. (To test the changes in a person's blinking in response to a puff of air blown into his eye is not a test of his mnemonic abilities in *any* sense of the word.) The crude distinction between declarative and non-declarative memory fails to distinguish between non-cognitive one-way powers and non-cognitive two-way powers (see *Human Nature*, ch. 4, section 6), between non-cognitive and cognitive powers and between non-cognitive acquired abilities and cognitive skills. Most important of all, it fails to discriminate between forms of memory that presuppose mastery of a language and those that do not.

[22] N. J. Cohen and L. R. Squire, 'Preserved Learning and Retention of Pattern-Analyzing Skill in Amnesia: Dissociation of Knowing How and Knowing That', *Science*, 210 (1980), pp. 207–9.

[23] Milner et al., 'Cognitive Neuroscience and Memory', p. 450. To be sure, we do not 'process' information in the ordinary sense of the word, and we do not 'store' information in our brain (see below).

[24] Ibid.

[25] For detailed description and criticism of neuroscientific research on memory, see M. R. Bennett and P. M. S. Hacker, *History of Cognitive Neuroscience* (Wiley-Blackwell, Oxford, 2008), ch. 3.

5. Further conceptual links and contrasts

Knowledge and memory compared

Memory is a form of knowledge. It is therefore unsurprising that memory and knowledge have similar representational forms. Like knowledge, memories are acquired, possessed, retained, shared or kept to oneself. Like knowledge, one's memories may be detailed and precise, or fragmentary and incomplete. On the other hand, there are also marked differences. There is a faculty of memory, but no faculty of knowledge. There are exercises in remembering, but no exercises in knowing, only in learning. One can know, but not remember, a subject thoroughly, and one can have a profound knowledge, but not a profound memory, of a subject. If one cannot remember something, one has forgotten it. If one does not know something, one is ignorant of it (and that may not be because one has forgotten it – it may be because one never knew it). One can remember, but not know, something incorrectly. The question 'How do you know?' is a request for the sources of one's knowledge or for the evidence supporting a knowledge-claim. The question 'How do you remember?' is quite different. It is a query about mnemonic techniques and devices. The reason is obvious: knowledge has sources or grounds, but memory is, metaphorically speaking, a *store of knowledge*, not a *source of knowledge* (in the sense in which perception is). (See table 9.2.)

Just as knowledge has a kinship with ability, so too memory, being a form of knowledge, is akin to an ability. If one retains information acquired then one can use it, draw inferences from it, act on it, make use of it in one's practical and theoretical reasoning. If one learnt something, and one still remembers what one learnt, it is available to one in one's thought, feelings and actions. One can answer questions about it, and correct others' mistakes. If one learnt how to do something and has not forgotten, then unless one has lost one's powers, one will be able to exercise one's skills and the mysteries of one's craft. If one *has* lost one's powers, one may still be able to teach others how it is done. If one experienced something, either as agent or as patient, and remembers doing so, one can call the experience to mind, reflect on it, answer questions about it, recount and reminisce about it. As we have already noted, the relationship between 'remembers' and 'recollects' (like 'knows' and 'is conscious of') is not as straightforward as that between being able to do something and doing it.

	Knowledge // know	Memory // remember
Can be acquired, possessed and lost	✓	✓
Can be shared, or kept to oneself	✓	✓
Can be detailed, precise, or vague, incomplete	✓	✓
Faculty of	✗	✓
Cancellable factivity	✓	✓
Can be thorough , profound	✓	✗
Can be incorrect, mistaken	✗	✓
Can be lively, vivid	✗	✓
Not to V is to be // to have	ignorant // forgotten	forgotten
How do you V?	grounds for // source of	techniques and mnemonics
Try to V	✗	✓
Exercises in V-ing	✗	✓

Table 9.2   *Comparisons between knowledge and memory*

Memory and belief
Some forms of memory are, like knowledge, linked in subtle ways to both thought and belief. What I remember is also something I can then think about and reflect on. It is obvious that misremembering involves having a false belief. Interestingly, we normally characterize this as 'just imagining things', or as *thinking* that things were so, rather than as *believing* that they were. The moot question, however, is whether remembering that things are so implies believing that they are. Just as philosophers have, for the most part, thought that knowing implies believing, so too they have, for the most part, held that remembering implies believing. Reid observed that 'Memory is always accompanied with the belief of that which we remember . . . every man feels that he

must believe what he distinctly remembers'.[26] A century later, James averred that 'Memory is then the feeling of belief in a peculiar complex object . . . *the object of memory is only an object imagined in the past* (usually very completely imagined there) *to which the emotion of belief adheres*'.[27] And Russell held that

> Memory-images and imagination-images do not differ in their intrinsic qualities, so far as we can discover. They differ by the fact that the images that constitute memories, unlike those that constitute imagination, are accompanied by a feeling of belief which may be expressed by the words 'this happened'. The mere occurrence of images without this feeling of belief, constitutes imagination; it is the element of belief that is the distinctive thing in memory.[28]

There seem to be two main grounds for the idea that remembering something to be so implies believing it to be so. The first is bound up with the imagist, representational conception of memory and imagination, which we shall address below. For if both remembering and imagining are essentially image-involving, then it seems natural to differentiate between them by reference to the fact that when one imagines an event, one does not believe that things were as one imagined them as being. So surely, when one remembers an event, one's memory-image is accompanied by a belief that the event in question did occur. If the representational conception of memory is ill-conceived (as we shall see it to be), then this consideration evaporates. The second reason for the doctrine is that since misremembering implies false belief, remembering implies true belief. This is mistaken.

As we have seen in chapters 4 and 5, there are reasons for being sceptical about the parallel claim that knowledge implies belief. If those qualms are correct, then similar qualms are warranted in the case of remembering. 'A remembers that things are so' implies that A knows that they are. If A misremembers, it follows that he believes, wrongly, that things are so. But neither believing rightly that one did or underwent something, nor even believing truly with justification, suffices for remembering doing or undergoing it – since one may believe that one did something only because one was just told, or

---

[26] Reid, *Essays on the Intellectual Powers of Man*, Essay III, ch. 1, p. 254.

[27] James, *The Principles of Psychology*, vol. 1, p. 652; emphasis original.

[28] Russell, *Analysis of Mind*, p. 176.

shown an old photograph. Is belief a necessary condition for remembering? Only if knowledge implies belief. Of course, 'I remember
things were so, but I don't believe they were', like 'I know things
were so, but I don't believe they were', is a kind of contradiction.
But it is not obviously a formal contradiction like 'Ibp & ~Ibp'.
Rather it is akin to 'You can take my word for it, but I don't underwrite it'. We should reflect on the differences between remembering
and believing something to be so. These are displayed in table 9.3.

This wide and ramifying range of differences suggests that, at the
very least, we should hesitate before embracing the view that remembering that something is so implies believing that it is.

'I remember that things were so, and I also believe they were' is
no less aberrant than 'I know that things were so, and I also believe
that they were'. 'He believes things were so, and he also remembers
that they were' seems utterly bizarre. Grice would explain the oddity
on the grounds of the redundancy of uttering the weaker statement
when one is in a position to utter the stronger. But we have seen
reason to question this move in parallel cognitive contexts (chapter
6, section 1), and we have advanced an alternative explanation of the
aberration. To be sure, we must recognize the legitimacy of both 'I
don't believe it – I remember it' *and* 'I not only believe it – I remember
it'. But we have an explanation of these grammatical possibilities. 'I
don't believe it – I remember it' implies that this is not an *opinion* of
mine, it is solid knowledge – for example, that I don't merely think
that this is what happened – I witnessed it. On the other hand, 'I
don't only believe it – I remember it' signifies that I don't just *subscribe* to things having been so – I actually remember (know) that
they were. Memory is not a form of belief. It cannot be analysed as
justified true belief retained.

Memory and recognition
A final important connection that should be brought
upon the carpet is between memory and recognition. To
recognize is a form of cognitive receptivity. As the etymology suggests, *re-cognize* is a matter of 'knowing again'. One
recognizes what is sensibly presented to one when one *realizes* that
one has encountered it (or a representation of it) before, or that it is
of a type that one has encountered before. It is therefore a form of
memory, restricted in its object to *what is present before one*, and
temporally limited *to the time of presentation*. For one can encounter
someone and realize *only later* that one has met him before – in which
case one did not recognize him. Again, one may have *been told* whom
one is about to encounter and that one has seen him before. So one

	remember // remember that	believe // believe that
Grounds for V-ing	✗	✓
What is the reason you V-ed ?	What reminded you?	What grounds do you have for believing?
What made you V?	What reminded you?	What convinced you?
How can you V?	By what means (mnemonic techniques) do you . . . ?	Why do you overlook all the countervailing evidence?
Try to V	Try to call to mind what happened // something you previously knew	Try to disregard the apparent countervailing evidence
To cease to V	To forget	Loss of conviction // convinced by countervailing evidence
Falsity of what is V-ed	Implies that one did not V, but mis-V-ed	Does not imply that one did not really V
Sincere utterance of 'I V'	Not a criterion for remembering	Is a criterion for believing
Do you V?	Query concerning information retention or ability to recount experiences	Query concerning credulity // opinion // one's stand
Do you V who // when // where // whether // why // how?	✓	✗
Modes of V-ing	Clearly, distinctly, vividly, vaguely	Wholeheartedly, passionately, unwaveringly, obstinately, obtusely, foolishly, reasonably

Table 9.3 *Comparisons of remembering and believing*

may know the person again, but without recognizing him. For the recurrence of the knowledge to constitute recognition, one must realize, *at the time, on the basis of a perceptible feature or features* of the person or object, that one has encountered him or it before.[29] Note that one can recognize people and things from photographs, as one can recognize voices from recordings. One cannot intend to recognize any more than one can intend to notice.

Because recognition is a form of cognitive receptivity, hence a form of knowledge, one can no more falsely or incorrectly recognize something, than one can falsely or incorrectly realize (notice, be aware of, be conscious of or know) something. If one mistakenly thinks one has recognized something, one has *misidentified* it – not incorrectly recognized it. But can one not speak of misrecognizing? One can now, it seems, but it is an unfortunate linguistic innovation that obliterates nice distinctions.[30] It is merely a synonym of 'misidentify'. Why then do we speak of mistakenly or incorrectly remembering something as well as of misremembering? Perhaps because, as previously noted, when one misremembers, one gets *something* right. If one is asked 'When was Waterloo?' and one replies 'It was a battle between the British and the French in 1814', that is a case of misremembering; but if one answers 'Oh, wasn't it last week?', that is not.

The investigation thus far has dealt with the Analytic of Memory. It has furnished us with a conceptual map with which we can find our way around (see fig. 9.2). With this in hand, we can turn to the Dialectic of Memory – the logic of conceptual illusions. Our task is to plot some of the dead-ends philosophers have found themselves in, the false turnings they have taken, and the chasms and crevasses into which psychologists and neuroscientists have fallen.

6. The dialectic of memory I: the Aristotelian legacy

5 influential errors   In his short treatise *On Memory*, Aristotle made five profoundly influential and largely mistaken moves. First,

---

[29] See A. R. White, *Attention* (Blackwell, Oxford, 1964), pp. 58f.

[30] The first recorded occurrence of the verb is in 1962, in the *Bell Systems Technology Journal*, the second from the *Philosophical Review* 1970 (see *OED*). The noun 'misrecognition' is recorded in 1843; it does not mean misidentification, but rather failure to achieve public acknowledgement.

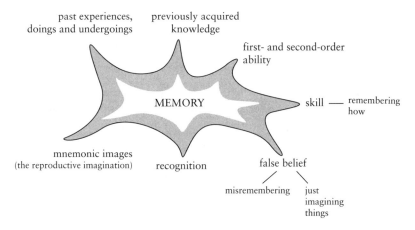

Figure 9.2 *Features of the landscape of memory*

as we have already noted, he mistakenly held that the object of remembering is the past. Secondly, he mistakenly held that remembering something is an experience – an affection of the mind. Thirdly, he advanced a mistaken representationalist analysis of memory. Fourthly, following a metaphor used by Plato, he originated trace theory as a physiological hypothesis. Finally, he is a source of the misleading metaphor of memory as a storehouse of ideas.[31] (This is not surprising, since he was fully familiar with the mnemonic techniques of the artificial memory that were taught by rhetoricians, in

---

[31] In *De Anima*, 429ª27, Aristotle remarked that 'it was a good idea to call the *psuchē* "the place of forms [seat of species]" ', sapiently adding that 'this is the forms only potentially, not actually'. For all it really means is that we have the *power* to call up these 'forms', 'species', 'ideas' or 'images'. Augustine, in the *Confessions*, writes that memory is 'a storehouse for countless images of all kinds which are conveyed to it by the senses'. Aquinas enlarged: 'From its nature the memory is the treasury or storehouse of species' (*Summa Theologica*, Q79, art. 7, sed c). Locke describes memory as being 'as it were the Storehouse of our Ideas', it being necessary 'to have a Repository, to lay up those *Ideas*, which at another time it might have use of' (*Essay*, I. x. 2). He too added that 'this laying up of our *Ideas* in the Repository of the Memory, signifies no more but this, that the Mind has a Power, in many cases, to revive Perceptions which it once had, with this additional Perception annexed to them, that it has had them before'. The caution was admirable, but the metaphor was nevertheless misleading. As we shall see, it encouraged the conflation of storage and retention, as well as the metaphor of copies.

which ideas were, as it were, *placed* in an imagined location, such as an amphitheatre, and, so to speak, *stored* there. *On Memory* is not intelligible unless one bears these ancient mnemonic methods in mind.) These five moves have distorted reflection on the nature of memory ever since.

Having committed himself to the view that 'there is no such thing as memory of the present while present' and 'that the object of memory is the past', Aristotle noted that remembering is *an occurrence* at a particular time. It is also something *psychological* – the actualization of a power of the *psuchē*. Without qualms, he took it for granted (in the very first sentence of *On Memory*) that remembering and recollecting are *experiences* or *affections of the mind*. But if they are experiences, they must, it seems, possess some feature that makes them experiences of *remembering the past* as opposed to being other kinds of experiences, such as imagining, or expecting. This nicely illustrates Wittgenstein's remark, 'The decisive movement in the conjuring trick has been made, and it was the very one that seemed to us quite innocent.'[32] For the supposition that remembering is having a current experience forces one down pathways one should not tread. Memory, Aristotle concluded, 'must be some such thing as a picture', 'image' or 'impression' generated through previous sense-perception (450^{a}26–31).

The origin of trace theory

Plato had likened memory to an impression of a seal on wax.[33] The metaphor is a natural one, invoked throughout the ages. When what we perceive impresses us, we remember it. With time, the impression made by the thing we witnessed may fade, until we can no longer recollect it. Writing on wax tablets is a way of making a record and storing acquired information for future use. As long as the wax impression remains, the record of the past can be retrieved by reading it off the tablet. So the image presented to us when we remember a past event not only resembles the past event as a picture resembles what it is a picture of – it also functions as a *reminder* of the past event. Memory, conceived as an aspect of our faculties of sense, *represents* its proper object, viz. past events experienced and the experiences of them.

---

[32] Wittgenstein, *Philosophical Investigations*, §308.

[33] Plato, *Theaetetus*, 191c–e.

What was a metaphor in Plato became a physiological hypothesis in Aristotle. Thinking mistakenly that the seat of psychological faculties is the heart, he suggested that sensible experiences are imprinted upon its moist tissues. If these are too dry and hard, as in the aged, the impression does not take; if they are too wet and soft, as in the very young, the impression does not last. Here we have the first trace theory of memory. Questions immediately flow from it. First, *what* we remember is clearly not an invisible trace on the wet tissues of the heart (or on the soft tissues of the hippocampus or amygdala). So how is the trace related (i) to the remembering and (ii) to what is remembered? Secondly, if remembering is apprehending an image, what makes the image an image of the past? Clearly, 'whenever one actually remembers having seen or heard or learned something, one perceives in addition . . . that it happened before' (450^{a}18–20). One perceives the impression *as related to a past experience* (451^{b}21–30). How can *this* be? Aristotle did not explain. He concluded bluntly that 'remembering is . . . the having of an image, related as a likeness to that of which it is an image' (451^{a}15–16). What one remembers is in the past, but remembering it involves perceiving something present that *resembles it* and that functions as *a reminder* of it (450^{b}15–451^{a}3).[34] This is made possible by the fact that perceptions leave traces in the functional seat of memory. Presumably the traces are causally responsible for the generation of the memory-impressions we have when we have memory-experiences. But what certifies pastness is unclear.

Parallels with the dialectic of intentionality

Thus far the ancient dialectic of memory – the conceptual illusions concerning the faculty and its exercise. It is remarkable that this conception repeats the dialectic of intentionality, but in reverse. As we saw in chapter 2, the central problems of intentionality arise from the thought that, for example, one can now expect something that has not yet occurred. But if it has not yet occurred, then how can one possibly expect *it*? For what one expects does not yet exist. What does not exist is nothing. But when Jack expects Jill to go up the hill, he expects something, not nothing. How can this be? Moreover, how can one *know* what one now expects in advance of the fulfilment of

---

[34] According to Aristotle, we perceive the memory-impression *directly*, but what we remember is the past occurrence (415^{b}14).

one's expectation, given that what one expects does not yet exist. Surely there must be a surrogate of this non-existent object of expectation *in* one's expectation – it must enjoy 'intentional in-existence'. Then one can come to know what one expects by reading it off its surrogate. That there is such a surrogate would also explain how one knows that one's expectation is fulfilled, for what happens *fits* what one expected (as an object fits its mould). It seems similar with memory, *once one limits the objects of memory to the past*, and thinks of remembering as *an occurrent experience*: (a) The memory experience must have, or be accompanied by, some feature that determines it as a *memory* (as opposed to imagining, perceiving, or expecting something – it must carry a *pastness certificate*. (b) It must contain a surrogate of what is remembered, otherwise one would not know *what* one was remembering. (c) In order for one's memory to be correct, the memory surrogate must correspond to the past.

Aristotle's representational analysis raises insuperable difficulties.

6 objections to Aristotle's representational analysis

(i) If remembering a past experience or its object consists in having a current mental image that resembles it, how could one know that it does, other than by memory? After all, one cannot compare one's memory image of a past event with what it is an image of, as one can compare a picture of a persistent scene with what it is a picture of.

(ii) Even if we disregard the fact that memory need not be of the past, there are things that occurred in the past that one may remember which *cannot* be re-presented by means of a memory image. These include remembering thinking, hoping for, wishing or expecting something; or remembering what one's duties and obligations were when one held such-and-such an office; or remembering what someone said without remembering their words (as when one heard a lecture in German and recounts it in English).

(iii) If remembering consists in having a mental image that resembles what one experienced in the past as a picture resembles what it is a picture of, then one does *not* remember what one experienced at all. For the memory-image, like a photograph of a long-forgotten scene, would in effect be *evidence* for what one experienced and for one's experience of it. It would be something *off which one reads the past*. It would provide one with information about the past. But that is precisely not to remember what occurred, but to learn it – as from a long-lost diary. When we remember a past occurrence, what we remember is that very occurrence, not some *ersatz* stand-in for it and not a reminder of it. We remember the past 'directly', not via an intermediary.[35]

(iv) A diary, and so too a picture or photograph, may indeed function as a reminder. But a reminder is something that *causes one to remember*. So it cannot explain what it is to remember, but rather presupposes it. Moreover, apprehending a reminder is neither necessary nor sufficient for remembering. One can remember things without being reminded; and one may apprehend a reminder (a knot in a handkerchief, or a picture of a scene) without remembering what the reminder was supposed to remind one of or what the picture was a picture of.

(v) We do not judge whether someone can recollect a past event or experience by reference to the liveliness of the mental images he avows that he can conjure up, but rather by the detail in which he can correctly recount what happened. Avowed lack of mnemonic images does not defeat a memory claim.

(vi) If remembering consists in having mnemonic impressions, there must be some way of determining that these impressions are *of the past*. Aristotle's suggestion that it is a matter of the way in which we *view* the impression, how we *take it*, is obviously incorrect. For when one remembers a dated past experience, the mnemonic impression (if there is one) carries no date or time reference on its face.

Hume: Memory ideas and vivacity

We must pursue this latter point a little further. Hume realized that while it is true that memory, unlike imagination, must preserve the order of the past events recollected, this cannot be a distinguishing mark of remembering. He made a notorious suggestion:

> We find by experience, that when any impression has been present with the mind, it again makes its appearance there as an idea; and this it may do after two different ways, either when in its new appearance it retains a considerable degree of its first vivacity, and is somewhat intermediate betwixt an impression and an idea, or when it entirely

---

[35] This too has generated confusion. If what we *directly* remember is the past occurrence, then surely that past occurrence must, in some sense, really exist (realism about the past). For are we not 'directly aware' of the past when we remember a past experience? Are we not 'in direct contact' with the past? — No! That we 'directly' remember the past means no more than that the grammatical object of 'What I remember is . . .', in such cases, designates a past occurrence. To be aware of what happened is not to be aware of its occurring, but to be aware that it occurred – the 'what' is an interrogative pronoun, not a relative one. (See B. Rundle, *Space, Time and Metaphysics* (Oxford University Press, Oxford, 2009), pp. 110–12.)

loses that vivacity, and is a perfect idea. The faculty by which we repeat our impressions in the first manner, is called the memory, and the other the imagination. (*Treatise of Human Nature*, I. i. 3)

So the mark of pastness is the relative vivacity of the idea of memory.

Reid's response was merciless. First, Hume's explanation of memory presupposes memory. For how could we find out *by experience* that past impressions reappear in the form of copies, that is, current vivacious ideas, *unless we remembered the impression*? Secondly, the suggestion that an idea of memory is, as it were, a faded impression assumes that impressions can literally be stored in the mind, where, with the passing of time, they may fade. But when one ceases to have an impression, the impression 'ceases to exist'. There can be no such thing as *storing impressions* in the mind (a point which, as we have noted above, was widely acknowledged). Hume might reply that his description was merely figurative. Strictly speaking, the mind receives impressions in the course of sense experience, and then has the power to produce weaker and weaker impressions of memory and imagination. To this Reid responds:

> When we are said to have a faculty of making a weak impression after a corresponding strong one, it would not be easy to conjecture that this faculty is memory. Suppose a man strikes his head smartly against the wall, this is an impression; now he has the faculty by which he can repeat this impression with less force, so as not to hurt him; this, by Mr Hume's account, must be memory. He has a faculty by which he can just touch the wall, so that the impression entirely loses its vivacity. This must surely be the imagination; at least it comes as near to the definition given of it by Mr Hume as anything I can conceive.[36]

A powerful criticism indeed. But the search for memory certificates went on.

The quest for pastness certificates   James noted that having a reproductive idea is not sufficient for remembering the original experience. For an idea, as such, has no reference to the past. Hence he suggested that mnemonic ideas must be accompanied by 'a feeling of pastness', 'an intimate association with oneself', a 'warmth and intimacy', as well as a belief that things were as one's mnemonic image represents them as being. To this, Russell added a 'feeling of familiarity', a 'feeling of belief which may be expressed by

---

[36] *Essays on the Intellectual Powers of Man*, Essay III, ch. 7, p. 289.

the words "this happened" . . . The pastness lies, not in the content of what is believed, but in the nature of the belief feeling'.[37] But how is one to recognize such feelings if not by remembering them? One can connect a tingling sensation with touching live wires by inductive association, but how could one possibly connect a feeling of pastness with the past independently of memory? And how does one identify such feelings of pastness?

The root of the trouble The pursuit of memory-certificates for memory-experiences is futile. For, as we have seen, remembering something *is not an experience*. There may be memory-experiences, as when we remember something sadly or joyfully. But these are *accompaniments* of remembering: feelings of sadness or of joy as we recollect past times. The question of what makes an experience a memory-experience sets us off on the wrong trail before we have even had time to take our bearings. One may, in certain cases, visualize what one is remembering, or run over a memorized tune in one's imagination. But the idea that the mental image must be certified as a memory-image is as misconceived as the idea that before one can rightfully say 'I saw such-and-such', one must certify that one is remembering something. The memory-image is an image *of what one is remembering*, not a *reminder* of it – it is mnemonics that are reminders. The memory-image may be correct or incorrect, no less than one's memory assertion, whereas mnemonics cannot be correct or incorrect, only efficacious or not efficacious. There is no such thing as confusing remembering something correctly with imagining something, for to do so would be to confuse knowing something with thinking up a possibility – and there is no such thing. Of course, one cannot distinguish, in one's own case, between remembering and misremembering that things are so. But misremembering (i.e. 'merely imagining') is not a successful exercise of the faculty of the imagination, but a faulty exercise of the faculty of memory. It *cannot* be confused with imagining, any more than failing to take action can be confused with intending.

7. The dialectic of memory II: trace theory

The revival of trace theory As noted, trace theory was mooted by Aristotle. However, once Nemesius (fourth century AD) had

---

[37] Russell, *Analysis of Mind*, p. 176.

established the ventricular doctrine, locating the functions of the mind in the ventricles of the brain, it fell out of fashion. The liquid in the posterior ventricle was hardly suited literally to receive *impressions* (although scientists continued to speak of *depositing* memories there). Trace theory was seriously revived only when Thomas Willis (1621–75) turned attention to the substance of the brain, in particular to the gyri of the cortex:

> for the various acts of imagination and memory, the animal spirits must be moved back and forth repeatedly within certain distinct limits and through the same tracts or pathways, therefore numerous folds and convolutions of the brain are required for these various arrangements of the animal spirits; that is, the appearances of perceptible things are stored in them, just as in various storerooms and warehouses, and at given times can be called forth from them.[38]

He started a tale that is with us to this day. Storing ideas in the mind is problematic, but storing 'representations' in the brain seemed a more straightforward business. At the end of the nineteenth century, James summarized the hypotheses of his day:

> The *retention* of *n*, it will be observed, is no mysterious storing up of an 'idea' in an unconscious state. It is not a fact of the mental order at all. It is a purely physical phenomenon, a morphological feature, the presence of these 'paths', namely, in the finest recesses of the brain's tissue. The recall or recollection, on the other hand, is a *psychophysical* phenomenon, with both a bodily and a mental side. The bodily side is the functional excitement of the tracts and paths in question; the mental side is the conscious vision of the past occurrence, and the belief that we experienced it before.[39]

It is noteworthy that, according to James, the memory-trace is not a *condition* for retaining acquired information (i.e. a condition of being able to do various things), but rather it *is* the retaining of acquired knowledge. It is the cortical storage of a memory.

The same conception is patent in the twentieth-century writings of Wolfgang Köhler, the great *Gestalt* psychologist:

---

[38] Thomas Willis, *The Anatomy of the Brain and the Nerves*, trans. of *Cerebri anatome, cui accessit nervorum descriptio et usus* (1664), Tercentenary Facsimile edn, ed. William Feindel, vol. 2 (McGill University Press, Montreal, 1965), p. 65.

[39] James, *The Principles of Psychology*, vol. 1, p. 655.

All sound theories of memory, of habit and so forth, must contain hypotheses about memory-traces as physiological facts. Such theories must also assume that the characteristics of traces are more or less akin to those of the processes by which they have been established. Otherwise, how could the accuracy of recall be explained . . . ?[40]

This conceptual framework continues to inform current empirical research, for example in the writings of Eric Kandel, who won a Nobel Prize for his work on memory, and in the writings of his colleagues and pupils. The hippocampus, he asserts, *stores information.*[41] The ancient picture still continues to dominate current thinking, albeit wrapped up in current scientific jargon:

Since the episodes that give rise to memories involve a variety of perceptions, it seems likely that the laying down of such memories involves nerve cells in the association areas and in secondary or higher order cortical areas concerned with the different senses. . . . It is also likely that recalling memories involves recreating something like the original pattern of activity in those same sets of cells, or at least some of them. . . . Initially then, both the hippocampus zone and the neocortical zone must act together. Eventually, when consolidation is complete, the memories are stored in such a fashion that they are available without the involvement of the hippocampal zone, implying that storage is then wholly in the neocortical zone.[42]

The trace-theoretic conception

Let us put the picture upon the carpet. What is remembered are past experiences. The experiences leave brain-traces. If these are stored in the form of long-lasting circuits, then they become memory-traces. Memory-traces are representations of what is remembered. These are available for recall. Recall occurs when a current experience activates the memory-trace. This happens by means of a perceived reminder, which produces a brain-trace that fits part of the previously imprinted memory-trace, and activates the whole memory-circuit.

---

[40] W. Köhler, *Gestalt Psychology: An Introduction to New Concepts in Psychology* (Liveright, New York, 1947), p. 252.

[41] E. R. Kandel, *The Age of Insight* (Random House, New York, 2012), p. 308. For a more detailed discussion of contemporary trace theory, see Bennett and Hacker, *History of Cognitive Neuroscience*, pp. 103–12.

[42] Ian Glynn, *An Anatomy of Thought* (Weidenfeld & Nicolson, London, 1999), p. 329.

Successful recall consists in having current mnemonic experiences, which are faint reproductions of the previous experience. Recognition consists in the coinciding of a neural trace currently caused by what one perceives with a memory-trace. This produces a recognitional experience.

This picture has mesmerized scientists for centuries. The only differences are in the sophistication of the physiology. The conceptual presuppositions of the picture, however, remain the same. They merit scrutiny.

What is remembered, the object of memory, is past experience.

That, as we have seen, is mistaken. Still, we may consider the picture to be limited to experiential memory (and recognition). But even for this restricted range, the conception is obviously flawed. To remember V-ing (doing, undergoing, experiencing), is to remember *one's* V-ing (and not merely *that* one V-ed). I remember seeing the Sistine Chapel, hearing Callas sing, breaking my arm and so forth. But the only thing that could possibly leave any brain-trace is *what* was seen, heard or felt (perhaps with a penumbra of further feelings registered by the nervous system). For *only the perceptual input could leave any brain-trace. My* experiencing whatever I experienced, as Hume already noted, could not be registered. But if all that can be stored in the form of a trace is *what* I experienced – the sight seen or sounds heard, then all that could be revived in the form of a memory is *what was experienced*, not the experiencing of it. But to remember that things were perceptibly so is not the same as remembering perceiving that they were so. It is striking that the picture is more apt for recognition, since one can recognize someone without necessarily remembering previously encountering this person.

> *Every sensible experience involves cortical changes. These cortical changes, once 'consolidated' (imprinted), are stored memories. The consequent theories of memory explicitly insist that 'the resulting memories are stored as changes in strength at many synapses within a large ensemble of interconnected neurons'.*[43]

---

[43] L. R. Squire and E. R. Kandel, *Memory: from Mind to Molecules* (Scientific American Books, New York, 1999), pp. 212f.

There can be no conceptual objection to the idea that sensible experience involves cortical changes or even to the idea that the power of memory requires the preservation of certain cortical connections.

Storage distinguished from retention
But the above conception is moot, for two reasons: (i) it conflates and confuses storage with retention; (ii) it fails to make clear what 'storing past experiences in memory-traces' means.

(i) We have noted that to remember is, roughly speaking, to retain knowledge acquired and to be able to recollect one's past experiences. But retention is not the same as storage. Storage implies retention, but retention does not imply storage. Memory is the *retention of an ability* just to the extent that knowledge is an ability; but it is not the *storage* of an ability, since there is no such thing as *storing an ability*. One cannot store the horsepower of a car beneath its bonnet.

(ii) One can store information by writing it down and storing the inscription, recording it and keeping the recording, or entering it onto a computer and preserving the hard drive. For certain kinds of information, one can take a photograph, and preserve it. The information thus stored is *contained* in the information storage: in a book, in a filing cabinet, in the recording device, on the hard drive of the computer, or in the photograph album. Being thus stored, the information is then *available* to one: one can read the inscription, listen to the record, open the computer file and read what is on the screen, and look at the photograph. Of course, all these operations presuppose memory and cannot explain it. They also presuppose the use of a language or of a recognizable pictorial representation. It should be immediately obvious that there can be no such thing as storing information in the brain, let alone of storing information in the brain in the form of strengthened synapses and neural circuits. Why so?

First, such a putative store of information is *not* available to the person remembering. One cannot read, see or hear a neural trace. But a store of information that is in principle unavailable is not a store of information at all. Secondly, a store of information *contains* information, but it does not *possess* any information. But to remember something is to possess and retain, not to contain, information. If one remembers that things were so, one knows that they were.

The picture underlying trace theory is that a memory-trace represents stored memories.

How can memories be stored? We have dealt with storage. But no less difficulty attends the idea of *representation*. The suppositions of trace theory are:

(a) that what is stored in the brain are memories;
(b) that the memory-trace is a representation;
(c) that what it represents is an antecedent perceptual experience.

We must approach this cautiously.

First of all, what is a 'memory'? We speak of having many happy (or sad) memories of past times enjoyed or endured. Here, 'a memory' signifies *what is remembered*, that is, *that such-and-such*, or *having such-and-such an experience*. It is clear that a memory is no more a *representation* of what is remembered than knowledge is a representation of what is known, or a belief a representation of what is believed. If anything, it is the verbal expression of what one remembers that is a representation. Moreover, a memory (in this sense) is not even a candidate for storage. There is no such thing as storing *that such-and-such happened*, let alone any such thing as storing *having an experience*. The most one can store is the verbal expression or pictorial representation *of* one's memory, and one cannot store that in the brain.

Secondly, it would be absurd to suppose that brain-traces are English (French, etc.) sentences or pictures. One might object that memory-traces are *encoded* sentences or pictures. For do we not encode sentences and pictures in our computers? Of course, we do. But this is not a possible model for memory-traces. For it is wholly unclear what is meant by 'encoding one's perceiving something (or perceiving that things are so)', for perceiving is not a picture, and it is not even perceiving a picture. And although what one perceives can be described by a sentence, perceiving it is not describing it.

Can a brain-trace represent anything? Thirdly, it is completely opaque what is meant by saying that a brain-trace is a representation of what is remembered. Whatever 'trace' an experience may leave, that trace is neither semantic or iconic. It is no more than a causal effect. But the causal effect of an occurrence (like a footprint) is not a store of information, even though we may derive information from it *if we can perceive it*. One might say that a brain-trace is a representation, if by 'representation' one means only a causal effect. But then the hypothesized memory-trace would not represent anything. In the customary sense of 'representation', nothing *could be* a *neural representation* of a past experience or indeed of anything else remembered. One may remember *being told* that the battle of Hastings was fought in 1066, and one surely remembers *that* the battle was fought in 1066. But nothing short of a sentence in a language or a picture could be a representation of what one remembers.

> *The memory-trace is a representation in so far as it was caused by a past experience and is the cause of a current memory experience that is of the past experience.*

This thought is pervasive. It is well expressed by Köhler:

> Much time may pass between an original experience and the moment in which there is unmistakeable evidence of its delayed effect. Some authors seem to think that we need not assume an entity which survives during the interval as a representative of that previous experience, and which becomes effective when present circumstances are favourable. They ought to realize what this view implies: a first event would influence a second, even though between the two there is an empty period, no connection and no continuity, sometimes for hours, days, and occasionally for years. I should hesitate to adopt this notion which is so strikingly at odds with all our fundamental ideas of functional interdependence or causation.[44]

Köhler's idea was that the past experience is the cause of the current remembering. But this can only be so if there is a brain-trace that can function as a cause or at least as a causal condition of remembering. Otherwise we would, it seems, be committed to a mystery of causation at a temporal distance.

What one experienced is not the cause of remembering it

This is confused. *What* one remembers is something one came to know or a past doing or undergoing. But neither what one came to know (viz. that things are, were or were going to be so) nor one's experiencing what one remembers experiencing are causes or causal conditions of recollecting. What I experienced *is* what I remember when I remember experiencing it; it is not *the cause* of my remembering, but its object. What I learnt, when I learnt that

---

[44] W. Köhler, *The Place of Value in a World of Facts* (1969), pp. 234–5, quoted in Malcolm, *Memory and Mind*, pp. 173–4.

the battle of Hastings was fought in 1066, is not *the cause* of my now remembering the date – it *is* what I remember. The relationship is logical, not causal. Why should one think that it is causal? The root of the confusion lies in the mistaken supposition that recollecting something is an *experience* (of having a memory idea, impression, appearance or species). On that assumption, it seems to be reasonable to ask for the cause of the experience, and to suppose that the memory experience might be the terminus of a causal chain that originated with the experience remembered. But remembering is not a current *experience*, but a current *knowing* – and knowing is no experience.

Are there no causes of remembering? Of course there are. Reminders, in all their variety can be said to cause one to remember something or other, to make one remember. But what one remembers is not a reminder, and it is not a cause of remembering, but its object. Brain-traces are causal conditions for the possession of mnemonic abilities, not representations of what is remembered. The brain is not a store of memories, but it is the vehicle of mnemonic abilities.

PART II

The Cogitative Powers

10

Thought and Thinking

1. Floundering without an overview

We readily tell others what we think of, or about, someone or something. We offer others a penny for their thoughts, and they usually tell us what they have been thinking of and what they thought about it. But when we are asked what thinking is, or what exactly it is that we do when we think, we have the greatest difficulty answering. Why should that be? We are, after all, as familiar with thinking as we are with walking or talking. Our difficulties cannot be a consequence of unfamiliarity. Nor can they be the result of any inadequacy in our mastery of the concepts of thought and of thinking.

Introspection does not show what thinking is

How should we find out what thinking is? It is tempting to suppose, as William James did, that all we need to do is to introspect, to observe ourselves when we are thinking.[1] We are to take note of what happens in our mind when we think, and what we observe will be what thinking is. However, what we note is disappointingly unhelpful: jumbles of disconnected words, occasional mental images flashing through our mind, fragments of an internal monologue. Moreover, sometimes there is nothing to note at all – nothing *happened*. We just thought, and said what we thought. But then, what *was* the thinking?

---

[1] W. James, *The Principles of Psychology* (Holt, New York, 1890), vol. 1, ch. 9.

The Intellectual Powers: A Study of Human Nature, First Edition. P. M. S. Hacker.
© 2013 John Wiley & Sons, Ltd. Published 2013 by John Wiley & Sons, Ltd.

fMRI scans do not show what thinking is

So introspection may well be useless. Should we then turn to science? Will a brain scan not reveal what thinking really is? Neuroscientists, when they display an fMRI scan of someone's brain while he is thinking, declare in triumphant tones, 'Here, for the first time, we can *see* thinking!'. But what they show us is merely a computer-generated image of increased oxygenation in select areas of the brain of someone engaged in some cogitative exercise. Whatever thinking of, thinking about, thinking through and thinking up may be, they are surely *not* emitting BOLD (blood-oxygen-level-dependency) signals.

Our defective conception of thinking

We possess the concept of thinking. We apply it unreflectively and correctly in our daily discourse. But we have no clear *conception* of what thinking is – and when confronted with conceptual questions about the nature of thought, we flounder and falter. For we have a mistaken *picture* of thinking – we *represent* thinking to ourselves in misconceived ways. We picture thinking as the discourse of the soul with itself (Plato) – hence as an inner process, an activity of the mind. Or we picture it as a cerebral process, an activity of the brain. When we reflect on the relation between thought and action, we imagine thinking as an activity that accompanies doing things with thought. The difference between behaviour with thought and behaviour without thought seems to be a matter of the presence or absence of this inner accompaniment – which sometimes seems to be inner speech, and sometimes seems to be accompanying mental images. We conceive of ourselves as thinking *in* our head. Indeed, we pictorially represent thinking by means of 'bubbles' coming out of the head of a person, in which what he is thinking is written, as opposed to the balloon that emerges from his mouth – which signifies what he is saying. To be sure, this cartoon is a more correct picture of thinking than the neuroscientist's fMRI (fig. 10.1).

Sources of our misconception

Just how defective our conception of thinking is will become clear in the sequel. As a preliminary step to clarifying these confusions (for that is what they are), we should take note of their sources. It is, of course, true that the surface grammar of 'thinking' resembles that of 'speaking' – and speaking is certainly an activity (but we forget that 'sleeping' shares the same surface grammar, and is equally certainly *not* an activity). We take figurative speech literally, for example, 'Use your head!' and also 'Use your brains!' – quite forgetting that, apart from scratching it, there is nothing that one can non-figuratively do with one's head,

 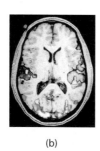 

(a) (b) (c)

Figure 10.1 *Three pictures of thinking: (a) an iconographic representation of thinking a specific thought; (b) a computer-generated image of increased oxygenation in the prefrontal cortices while thinking; (c) an image of someone sunk in thought*

let alone with one's brain, to think one's way through a problem. We say 'I wonder what is going on in his head' – but, of course, we should feel cheated if we were told that there was sudden increase of oxygenation in his prefrontal cortices. We labour under the influence of a host of idioms such as 'A thought flashed through his mind', 'The thought lurked at the back of my mind', 'She has got a first-rate brain'. Of course, they mean no more than 'Something occurred to him', 'I was suspicious', 'She is very intelligent' – but they are all bound up with misleading pictures that induce us to suppose that we think *with* or *in* our brain or mind. We shall investigate what could possibly be meant by such suppositions below.

Thinking as an inner activity   It is almost impossible to avoid the idea that thinking is an inner activity or process that accompanies speaking. We can make dolls or toys that can emit sequences of words. But these are just noises. A parrot can utter words, but it cannot *make statements*, or *tell us* anything. It cannot mean or understand the words it utters – it does not *think* what it squawks. The sounds it emits are, as it were, dead. But when we utter the same words in appropriate contexts, our words are alive. What animates them, we are inclined to suppose, is *thought*. Thinking seems to be an inner activity that informs, and breathes life into, the outer activity of speaking. But if so, does the thinking that accompanies intelligent speech consist of words? To be sure, we do say such things as 'I can now think in German'. But if thinking consists of words – what animates *those* words? Or does thinking consist of something else, such as ideas, images or (non-linguistic) concepts? For do we not often struggle to find the right words to express our thoughts? Do we not then often say in response to the remark of another 'That is exactly what I had in mind – what I was thinking?'? This makes it look as if thought needs to be *translated* into spoken language. We shall give the matter scrutiny.

The pseudo-mysteries of thought It is hardly surprising that we find thinking mysterious. Frege held thinking, which he conceived to be a process of grasping 'a thought' – an atemporal, non-spatial, object – to be 'perhaps the most mysterious [process] of all'.[2] This, as we shall see, is a paradigmatic example of interpreting our own mystification for a mystery about what bewilders us. But in philosophy, there are no mysteries. First, thinking is not to be confused with 'grasping' or understanding. Secondly, although thoughts are the *formal* object of thinking, as dreams are the formal object of dreaming – what one thinks is not an abstract object, entity or thing, because it is not an object, entity or thing at all. To tell another what one thinks is not to put him into contact with an abstract object which one has 'grasped'. But nor is it, as the linguistic idealists supposed, causing one's hearer to have the qualitatively identical array of ideas before their mind as one has before one's own mind. Different people's ideas can be the same or different, but they cannot be numerically identical or different or qualitatively identical or different, since that distinction, which applies to substances, has no application to ideas (*pace* Frege). Moreover, to impart one's thoughts to another does not mean that he now has the same thought – only that he now knows what one thinks. But it is true that thinking *can* readily seem mysterious.

It can seem mysteriously fast: sometimes one 'sees' the solution to a problem in a flash – and then it takes one an hour to explain it. How can this be? Mozart was rumoured to be able to think through a whole concerto in a flash – to hear it in his mind at a stroke. The distinguished mathematician and physicist Roger Penrose supposed

---

[2] G. Frege, 'Logic' [1897], in *Posthumous Writings* (Blackwell, Oxford, 1979), p. 145. By contrast, Thomas Reid had held that 'Thinking is a very general word, which includes all the operations of our minds, and is so well understood as to need no definition' (see *Essays on the Intellectual Powers of Man* [1785] (Edinburgh University Press, Edinburgh, 2002), p. 22).

that we would not be able to understand this until we had a correct theory of quantum gravity and of multiple time-streams.[3] But, as we shall see, that is confused.

Something that can seem equally mysterious is the intentionality of thought. One can touch someone only if he is in one's vicinity. One can shoot someone only if he is within range. But one can *think of* someone even if he is on the other side of the globe – 'For nimble thought can jump both sea and land.'[4] And, what can seem even more mysterious, thinking seems like super-archery that *always* hits its target. I can think of NN in New York and 'hit' just him and no one else, even though he looks just like his twin brother! How can one think of someone, even though he no longer exists – such as Solon or Solomon? How can one hit one's target in thought when it isn't there? Even more mysteriously, one can think of someone even if they never existed – such as Adam and Eve! We can think of what is the case. But we can also think of what is *not* the case. And that too can seem mysterious. We can think either truly or falsely. If we think falsely that such-and-such is the case, then it is not the case. But if it is not the case, how on earth can we think it? – There is, so to speak, nothing to think! – We have examined the problems of intentionality in sufficient detail in chapter 2 to realize that these are not mysteries, but only mystifications rooted in grammatical confusion. It is striking how powerful the illusions are.

We also mesmerize ourselves with reflections upon the *intangibility* of thoughts. We think thoughts, but thoughts in themselves appear to be intangible. So we think, with Frege, that 'The thought, in itself imperceptible by the senses, gets clothed in the perceptible garb of a sentence, and thereby we are enabled to grasp it'.[5] But this is to magnify the mystery. For how can we tailor the garb to clothe the imperceptible body of a thought? How can we find the right words to fit the thought that we think? Here we have the unexpressed thought – and there we have our language: but how on earth do we translate our thought into language? Are some languages isomorphic

---

[3] R. Penrose, 'Précis of *The Emperor's New Mind*', *Behavioural and Brain Sciences*, 13 (1990), p. 653.

[4] Shakespeare, Sonnet 44.

[5] Frege, 'Thoughts', repr. in *Collected Papers* (Blackwell, Oxford, 1984), p. 354.

with thoughts, and hence *better* for translating thoughts than others? Of course, this is a muddle. But it is not easy to see *why*; or how to unmuddle ourselves.

Another factor that exacerbates the mystery of the intangibility of thought is its *elusiveness*. We speak of thoughts as lurking at the back of our mind – just out of reach, of thoughts flitting across our mind – sometimes so quickly that we cannot quite catch hold of them. We say, or are told, that certain thoughts are buried deep in our unconscious mind, and that it is only after the greatest of effort (with the aid of a psychoanalyst) that we can bring them to the surface – to consciousness. So thoughts must be very strange things (see list 10.1).

- How can one 'grasp' an abstract object?
- The speed of thought.
- The intentionality of thought.
- The intangibility of thoughts.
- How can one match a sentence to a thought?
- The elusiveness of thoughts.
- The privacy of one's thought's.
- How can one know the thoughts of another?

List 10.1   *The 'mysteries' of thoughts*

Finally, thinking can be made to seem to be the prototypical *private* activity of the mind, and the thoughts we think the prototypical *private objects* that are visible to the mind's eye, but concealed from the eyes of the world. In thought, we say things to ourselves, which no one else can hear – just as in imagination we picture things to ourselves, which no one else can see. We sometimes wonder whether we can ever *really* know what another person is thinking, and we often wonder what is *really* going on in someone's head. We do not pause to wonder at these *reallys*. We do not raise the question of whether *we* can hear what we say to ourselves, or see the pictures we conjure up. We do not puzzle why, if thoughts are so well hidden, it is often so *difficult* to *conceal* our thoughts from those who know us well. We shall examine the epistemology of thought and its contribution to the formation of our conception of an 'inner life'.

So: thinking seems to be an extraordinary process or activity of the mind or the brain. Thoughts seem to be elusive, intangible, secret objects that pass through our minds. It seems obvious that *we* know what we are thinking – and that others cannot really know, but only guess. This is the *picture* we construct for ourselves – and it holds us in thrall. To show that and why it is misconceived is one of the purposes of this chapter.

2. The varieties of thinking

Our aim: an overview of the grammar

It should by now be obvious that the above pseudo-mysteries and confusions stem from lack of an overview of the concepts of thinking and of thoughts. To have mastered the use of the verb 'to think' and its cognates does not require one to have an overview of its use, let alone of its comparative use – that is, of the logico-grammatical similarities and differences between 'to think' and other cogitative verbs and their cognates. Thinking pervades our lives. It is hardly surprising that the concepts of thinking constitute a complex network connecting a multitude of diverse phenomena. It is equally unsurprising that we lack an overview of this conceptual network. The *only* way to obtain a surveyable representation of thinking is to examine the logical grammar of the expression and to elaborate its logical connections, its affinities with related concepts, its implications, compatibilities and incompatibilities, and to clarify its point and purpose.

The different grammatical forms are straightforward, and their polysemy turns largely on the prepositions to which the verb is attached, the sentential context and the context of use. Just as we can know something to be so, so too we can think something to be so (think Jack is in London) or think *that* something is the case (think that Jill is in London). Like 'to know' and 'to believe', *this* use of 'to think' does not admit of a progressive form: there is no 'I am thinking Jack is in London' or 'He is thinking that Jill is in London'. One may think (but *not* be thinking) well or badly of someone, and one may instruct another to think nothing (but *not* be thinking nothing) of some act or event. However, most phrases with 'think' followed by a preposition do have progressive forms. One may think, or be thinking, *of* someone or something. One may think, or be thinking, *about* some someone or something. Like 'to know', but unlike 'to believe', 'to think' can be affixed to Wh-pronouns. One can think (or be thinking) how to do something, whether to do something, what to do, as one can think when or where to go. One cannot order someone to know or believe something, but one can order someone to think (rack his brains), to think of something or to think about something, and one can ask someone to think how to V, what to do, when and where to go. To comply with the order or request is to think of the answer to the corresponding Wh-question. To do that may require one to be thinking how, what, where, when to V. One can think (or be thinking) *through* a problem and think (or be thinking) *up* a solution.

Because the verbs 'to know' and 'to believe' are stative verbs lacking progressive form, we are strongly inclined, quite wrongly as we have seen, to conceive of knowing and believing as mental states. Because 'to think' (in most of its constructions)[6] does have a progressive form, because one can be interrupted while one is thinking, and can later resume thinking, because one can voluntarily think of someone, and intentionally engage in thinking about something, we are inclined to conceive of thinking as an activity of the mind or brain. This too, as we shall see, is at best misleading, at worst a blunder. We *model* thinking on the pattern of an activity (as we model knowing on the model of possessing), but thinking is, in important ways, very unlike characteristic activities (see section 3).

What then are the major landmarks in the cogitative terrain? As with other epistemic concepts, here too we find multiple centres of variation. (These are displayed in fig. 10.2.)[7]

Multiple centres of variation　The cogitative powers of man consist above all in the ability to grasp, assess and solve problems, and to engage in problem-posing tasks successfully. Thinking

---

[6] Namely, thinking of, about, how, what, when, where, up, through and over. But not thinking well/ill of . . . , or thinking nothing of it.

[7] I have found the following most helpful in mapping the terrain: B. Rundle, *Mind in Action* (Clarendon Press, Oxford, 1997), *passim*; G. Ryle, *Collected Papers*, vol. 2 (Hutchinson, London, 1971), essays 30–7, and *On Thinking* (Blackwell, Oxford, 1979), essays 1–5; A. R. White, *The Philosophy of Mind* (Random House, New York, 1967), ch. 4; L. Wittgenstein, *Philosophical Investigations* [1953], 4th edn (Wiley-Blackwell, Oxford, 2009), §§316–62, and *Remarks on the Philosophy of Psychology*, vols. 1 and 2 (Blackwell, Oxford, 1980), *passim*. I have also made use of my own writings on this subject: M. R. Bennett and P. M. S. Hacker, *Philosophical Foundations of Neuroscience* (Blackwell, Oxford, 2003), and P. M. S. Hacker, *Wittgenstein: Meaning and Mind* (Blackwell, Oxford, 1990).

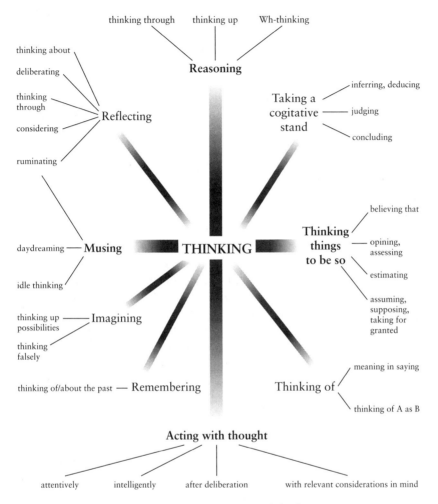

Figure 10.2 *The varieties of thinking*

may involve ratiocination – reasoning from grounds to the conclusion they support, or from data to their explanation. This may take the forms of inferring, deducing or deriving. Thinking may involve recollecting, thinking of, what one has previously learnt, including answers to questions and facts pertinent to the problem one confronts. It may involve practical reasoning – forming intentions and plans on the basis of reflection and deliberation. And it may involve attentive execution of intentions and plans, and concentrated engagement in tasks undertaken. Our cogitative powers are at work in all our skilful, non-mechanical, activities, where attention, awareness of possibilities that may arise and readiness to encounter them is needed for success-ful exercise of the skill. From this complex core, the concept ramifies in a variety of different directions.

Reasoning   So, the first centre of variation on which to focus to gain an overview of cogitative concepts is that of reasoning. We reason our way to a solution – thinking through the problem and thinking up a solution to it. We deliberate (think on the problem), and consider (think of) various alternatives before arriving at our solution. We reason from premises, derive conclusions from evi-dence, draw inferences from data, deduce consequences. We form plans (think what to do and when to do it), and reflect on means (think how to do it). Thinking here is solution-seeking and problem-solving. So it is *activity-like*, but, as we shall see, it is at best mislead-ing to conceive of it as an activity of the mind or brain. Nevertheless, it is something one does. One can be occupied with it, engaged in it and sunk in it, like *Le Penseur*. One may be disturbed while thinking (by a telephone call), and one's thinking may be interrupted (by a knock on the door), only to be later resumed. Thinking, in this sense, is purposive, goal-directed. So it is something that can be (but need not be) voluntary and intentional. One can be asked or ordered to think through a problem, to reflect on a conundrum, to come up with a solution. Depending upon its upshot, thinking can be successful or fail of its objective. It may be engaged in with concentration, tenacity and determination. It can be intuitive or discursive. If it is discursive, it may be methodical, systematic and rigorous. It may be intelligent, brilliant or pedestrian – hence one may be good or poor at it. At its most mechanical, it involves calculating or computing in accordance with familiar rules. At its most creative it involves the use of the imagination in thinking up new possibilities.

Our ratiocinative problem-solving powers are partly inherited and partly acquired. Learning expands one's powers of thought, and practice strengthens what one has learnt. Good habits of thought can be acquired through education, even though, as we shall see, there can be no exercises in thinking in the manner in which there are exercises in ballet dancing or horse riding. Methodical thinking *about a given subject matter* can, of course, be taught, and one's problem-solving abilities *in a given domain* can be cultivated by instruction and practice. One's thought may be conventional in style, going down well-trodden paths competently or incompetently, skilfully or clumsily. Or it may be original, pioneering new routes and exploring new possibilities.

Thinking, reasoning, can be done aloud or silently. One can engage in thinking through a problem alone, or with another. It may take a moment, as when one sees the solution in a flash, or be prolonged, as when one painfully thinks one's way to the solution. One may think clearly and incisively, or one's thought may be unclear, unfocused and indecisive. One may be too tired to think clearly, or too frightened to think at all. When one is still thinking, one does not yet know what to think. When one knows what to think, no further thinking is needed.

Ruminating, musing, idle thinking   Given this centre of variation, it is unsurprising that the use of the continuous tense of 'to think' should drift: from reflecting to ruminating, musing, daydreaming and idle thinking. These progressively move away from the purposive problem-oriented character of reasoning. Reflecting on something, turning it over in one's mind, considering it, may be no less goal-directed than reasoning. But it need not be. To have thought about something, a proposal or plan, may not be a matter of having arrived at a decision or to have reasoned from evidence to a conclusion. It may involve no more than a readiness to discuss the matter. 'Have you thought about it?' may amount to no more than 'Are you ready to talk it over?'. Ruminating, musing and daydreaming all involve thinking about something or other. Here too one may be lost or sunk in thought. So they too are activity-like. They may be voluntary and intentional, as well as involuntary, and in certain cases, compulsive (as when one can't help thinking about Jack or Jill). They take time, can be interrupted and later resumed. But they are not generally goal-directed. One cannot daydream methodically or systematically, and there are no standards of excellence to strive for in musing or to achieve in ruminating.

Thinking, imagining, recollecting   We noted that reasoning may be more or less mechanical and computational, or original and creative, involving the use of the imagination. We shall examine the imagination in the next chapter. For the moment, however, it should just be remembered that one use of 'to imagine' signifies *thinking of* new possibilities. To think what it would be like to V is to imagine V-ing. To think what will happen if . . . is to imagine future possibilities. To have imagined something differently is to have thought of it differently. If something is just as one imagined it as being, then it is just as one thought it would be. A different use of 'to imagine' signifies *thinking falsely* – as when we say 'You are just imagining things'.

Just as thinking is linked to imagining, so too it is linked to remembering and recollecting. To think of something may be merely for something to come to mind randomly or by association. But it may be a recollection, of which one was reminded by something that made one *think* of the past. It may be idle ruminations about last year's holidays or last week's party. But it may be the result of endeavour, the upshot of thinking – trying to recollect – who V-ed or what exactly happened, what those thingumabobs are called, where Jack is meeting Jill.

Thought and Thinking is connected not only to ratiocination (reason-
action ing) but also to *action*. One may not only think how to
do something, and think of doing something – one may *do it* with or without thought. This is a quite different centre of variation. To do something with thought, to think of what one is doing while one is doing it, is to concentrate on what one is doing, to attend to the task at hand. Mechanical tasks can be engaged in without thought. Waxing the furniture, cleaning the windows or polishing the silver are tasks that require little concentration and minimal attention. They are tasks one commonly engages in without thinking. This does not mean that one may not be thinking while one is waxing the sideboard or cleaning the silver – when engaged in such tasks one will typically be thinking of *other* things. It means that one need not 'be on one's toes', since the task is more or less mechanical. But the more complex or delicate the task, as when one is mending a watch, conducting a refined experiment or doing a surgical operation, the more it demands concentrated attention and thought. It requires one constantly to be aware of, and to take into account, possibilities that may obtain and difficulties that may arise. This does not mean that one is talking to oneself about these possibilities while one is engaged in the activity. It means that one is alert to them, takes precautions against them if necessary or is ready to take advantage of them should they arise. By contrast, to engage in such activities without thought, or thoughtlessly, is to engage in them mechanically, without due care and attention. 'Thinking' in this sense, is an *adverbial verb* (Ryle). It does not signify what one is doing but how one is doing it.

Related to, but slightly different from, such cases, is engaging in an activity not merely with care and attention, but with cunning and ingenuity, applying one's intelligence swiftly to circumstances that are changing in unanticipated ways. A thoughtful performance in such cases does not merely not fall short of adequacy. Rather one performs it intelligently and cleverly, as does the outstanding tennis player or ingenious chess-master, as well as the skilful debater in the cut and thrust of disputation. Rather differently, the brilliant actor playing Hamlet, and the pianist playing the Hammerklavier Sonata, manifest the thoughtfulness of their performances not by swift and intelligent responses to changing fortune and circumstance, but by the intelligence, originality and sensitivity of their rendering.

Thought and speech

In close proximity to these kinds of case are the manifold forms of intelligent speech. To speak *without thinking* does not mean speaking without an accompanying inner activity of thinking. It may be to speak without taking into account factors that one should have borne in mind and which, had one attended to them, would have led one to speak differently or not at all. To speak thoughtlessly may be to speak insensitively, tactlessly or inconsiderately. A thoughtless person is not a mindless person, that is, someone who does not reflect or plan when thought and planning are called for, but someone who does not attend to the sensitivities of others. In quite a different sense, a thoughtless person is one who acts imprudently, on the spur of the moment, without adverting to consequences. To speak without thinking may be to speak absent-mindedly, while thinking about something else. But it may also be to speak impulsively. In short, the various forms of speaking with thought, thoughtfully and intelligently are speaking with one's wits about one.

Thought, belief, opinion

Yet another, familiar centre of variation in the cogitative landscape is that use of the verb 'to think' in which it lacks a progressive form. Here thinking converges on believing in one of *its* uses. One may think that things are so, just as one may believe that they are. One may tentatively or hesitantly think or believe things to be so, or that things are so. Both 'think' and 'believe' function as the default position in the absence of knowledge. Both function in the first-person present tense as modifying operators on declarative sentences to signify that one is not in a position to exclude alternative possibilities. A blunt assertion is generally meant to impart information one takes oneself to possess. The two operators serve to qualify such assertions. But 'I think' is a more decisive qualifier. One may believe with complete certainty that things are so, but one cannot think with certainty that they are (for 'think', unlike 'believe', is not linked to taking a stand on something, placing one's trust in someone or something said, or staking a claim). One may passionately believe, but not passionately think, that things are so – for one may cleave to one's beliefs, but not to one's thoughts. As noted, 'I believe that . . .' is sometimes used in the sense of 'I gather that . . .', whereas 'I think that . . .' in the same context, signifies the expression of one's own opinion or judgement.

It is unsurprising that 'to think', in one of its uses, should converge on 'to opine'. One can ask someone for his opinion on a given matter, or one can ask him what he thinks about it. Thinking, in this sense, also approximates estimating, assessing and giving one's verdict on something or someone. One can think (but not believe) well, highly or fondly of someone, or one may not think much of them. Just as one may *find* something funny, so too one may *think* it funny, ludicrous, sad or shocking. To say so is to express one's amusement, ridicule, sorrow or shock.

'To think', thus construed, is patently no activity. One is not *engaged* in thinking that the battle of Zama was fought in 202 BC. One cannot be *interrupted* in the middle of thinking something to be so, since thinking something to be so takes no time. One cannot be halfway through thinking that something is so. Depending on how one arrived at what one thinks and the kinds of grounds one has for thinking what one thinks, the upshot – which is what one thinks – may be a conclusion, a belief, an opinion, a judgement, a supposition, an assessment or a verdict. 'I thought it was safe (secure, solid, robust)', said ruefully after a mishap, need not imply that one reflected and came to a conclusion – it may mean that one gave the matter no thought, that is reflection, but took it for granted, assumed or supposed – that is *thought* – it to be thus. But it may mean that one did give the matter due attention and reflection, and came to this conclusion.

Thinking and meaning Thinking that such-and-such is thus-and-so involves thinking *of* such-and-such. Thinking of someone or something may be adventitiously calling him or it to mind. But it may be the *result* – the upshot of trying to think of who, what or where, etc. Quite differently, it may be a cousin of *meaning someone or something*. For one may be asked of whom one was thinking (whom one meant) when one said . . . We not only think *of* those things about which or whom we think that . . . – we also think of things *as* such-and-such. One may think of an unpleasant experience one is about to undergo as a rite of passage, of a painting as an allegory or of a musical phrase as a response to a previous passage. One may think of someone as a saint or a sinner, as a giant among men or a pathetic figure. Thinking of something or someone *as* something is *a way of viewing*, or *a manner of conceiving* – which may be illuminating and helpful or misguided and confused.

The polymorphous nature of thinking

It is evident that thinking is polymorphous. Each of its variants may take many different forms, so that what one does when one thinks on one occasion and in one circumstance may be done on another and yet not count as thinking at all. Saying '1314' may, in one circumstance, constitute having thought of the date of the battle of Bannockburn, but in another it may be mechanically counting from 1 to 20, telling the time or giving someone one's telephone number. Equally the form thinking takes on one occasion may be quite different from the form thinking the very same may take on another. Thinking that one must tell one's friend something may take the form of telling him then and there, or of picking up the telephone, or of making a note in one's diary. Note that the forms of a polymorph are not species of a genus.

It is equally clear that thinking that something is so may be doing any number of different things. It may be concluding, assuming, conjecturing, recollecting, believing, judging or opining. Similarly, thinking of something is equally varied. It may be associating one thing with another ('That made me think of . . .'), it may be recollecting ('I have just thought of who said that'), it may be referring to something or having something in mind ('What were you thinking of when you said . . . ?'), it may be finding an answer ('I have just thought of the solution'), it may be forming an intention or plan ('I am thinking of going to St Petersburg') and it may be daydreaming ('I was thinking of last year's holiday in Florence'). Note that these may all be considered species of *thinking-that* and of *thinking-of*.

3. Is thinking an activity?

Both the Greek and the Judaeo-Christian traditions fostered the picture of thought as an activity of the spirit or soul, separable from the body and its activities, and so more pure and incorruptible, enabling us to contemplate eternal truths that transcend the ever changing, destructible world of matter. The idea resonated in early modern philosophy. Descartes held that thinking was *the* essential and defining attribute of the mind – and that the mind is *always* thinking. Locke averred that it is an *activity* of the soul – and that the soul *sometimes* thinks. Today we are more prone to conceive of thinking as an activity of the *brain*. The moot question, however, is whether thinking is an activity at all.[8]

Similarities between thinking and activities   It is easy to see why one is inclined to suppose that thinking is an activity. Like 'to talk' and 'to speak', the verb 'to think' – at least when used to signify reasoning, reflecting, deliberating, ruminating, musing, as well as V-ing with thought or thoughtfully – has a progressive aspect, an imperative mood, can form a pseudo-cleft sentence with a Do pro-form ('What I did was to think hard'), can be qualified by manner adverbs ('quickly', 'laboriously', 'reluctantly') and takes 'for . . . sake' constructions ('I thought hard for Jill's sake'). Grammarians hold these syntactical features to be marks of what they call 'activity-verbs'. Philosophers hold them, in the material mode, to be marks of activities. After all, if asked 'What are you doing?', one may intelligibly reply 'I'm thinking about tomorrow's party'. Thinking is something we engage in. It can absorb us. We may think with intense concentration. It takes time, can be interrupted and later resumed. One may think voluntarily or involuntarily, willingly or reluctantly. It can be hard work and is sometimes exhausting. How could anyone deny that thinking is an activity?

Differences between thinking and activities   To this one may reply that *thus far*, thinking (reasoning, V-ing with thought) has *affinities* with activities. Indeed, for the most part it is quite harmless to allow oneself to be over-impressed by the affinities. There is nothing awry with explaining that one suffers from insomnia because one's mind is too active when one goes to bed. But to attain a correct conception of thinking and to guard against false inferences that may be derived from the idea that thinking is an activity of the mind, we must cast our net wider and explore differences. Thinking and activities differ as it were *topologically*, both 'in the large' and 'in the small'.

(i) Activities are the activities they are in virtue of being more or less unified sequences of acts. The sequence may be repetitive (e.g. digging), an ordered sequence of different acts (e.g. dismantling a

---

[8] It was Wittgenstein who first raised and explored this question. For detailed examination of Wittgenstein's account of the matter, see my *Wittgenstein: Meaning and Mind*, part 1: *Essays*, pp. 149–55. See also S. Schroeder, 'Is Thinking a Kind of Speaking?', *Philosophical Investigations*, 18 (1995), pp. 139–50, for an illuminating elucidation.

mechanism), or an unordered sequence of acts given their unity by the purpose and circumstances. So if one is engaged in an activity continuously, then, unless there is a hiatus, there is at any given time an answer to the question 'What is going on?' or 'What is he doing now?'. One can give a running commentary on what is happening. By contrast, nothing *need* go on in one's mind when one thinks. Let me explain.

(a) In the case of 'adverbial' thinking, for example when one speaks with thought, nothing typically *goes on* in one's mind. All one's attention is upon what one is saying, and any image that may cross one's mind, or any inward speaking that may occur, typically marks a lapse of concentration. To speak with thought is not to accompany one's speaking with a simultaneous inner activity of thinking. To V thoughtfully is not to do two things.

(b) In the case of non-'adverbial' thought, for example of *Le Penseur*, thinking does not have the structure of an activity. At any given moment while *Le Penseur* is thinking his way through a problem, *nothing* need be going through his mind, no mental imagery, no talking to himself in the imagination – and yet he is thinking continuously for all that. That he is thinking is determined by the context, by what happened previously, by what he can consequently do, as well as by what he would do were such-and-such circumstances to arise.

(ii) Interior speech ('the discourse of the soul with itself') is neither necessary nor sufficient for thinking (musing, reflecting). It is not sufficient, since repeating the multiplication tables to oneself in one's imagination is not thinking, and reciting Hamlet's 'To be or not to be' soliloquy in one's imagination is not thinking whether one should commit suicide, even though someone who was contemplating suicide might indeed recite 'To be or not to be' in his imagination. Interior speech is not necessary, since someone's report of what, after reflection, he thought about a given problem would not be undermined by his denial that he talked to himself in his imagination when he thought of the solution. But even if one does say something cogent to oneself, it does not follow that what one says to oneself is what one thinks, since one may not have meant what one said (as when one says to oneself of a very boring lecturer 'Oh, if only you'd drop dead'). Much of what we say to ourselves in our imagination is said thoughtlessly! The criteria for what someone thought, as well as the criteria for someone's thinking are not the criteria for an inner activity.

(iii) Even if something *is* 'going on' in one's mind while one is thinking, one cannot read off from that what one is thinking. Even if God could see what is flitting through one's mind (e.g. saying to oneself 'That's him!', 'I must do it', 'Some hope!' or 'Oh yes, of course'), he could not see there what one is thinking.

(iv) That activities and thinking differ 'in the small' (topologically speaking) should not be surprising. While there is such a thing as half a sentence, there is no such thing as half a thought. So one can have got halfway through uttering a sentence, but not halfway through thinking a thought. If one does say to oneself what one is thinking, at what point has one completed the thought? Only when one has finished saying it to oneself? Does that mean that one does not know what one is thinking until one has finished saying it to oneself? That seems as absurd as the suggestion that one does not know what one is going to say out loud until one has said it. So has one completed the thought even *before* one says it to oneself in the imagination? If so, where has the activity of thinking now disappeared to?

One may respond to the question 'What is he doing?' by answering 'He is thinking how to . . . // who // when // . . .'. But this answer gives no information about what is concurrently going on in his mind. What the answer tells one is *what he is aiming at* – a solution, answer, plan or project. One may respond by answering 'He is daydreaming – thinking about last year's holiday in Venice' – but, unlike 'He is reciting the alphabet in his imagination' or 'He is counting sheep in order to fall asleep', that is not the specification of a mental activity engaged in. It is something that happens to one in the course of more or less random association.

An objection   A natural objection to these considerations is that when someone is engaged in reasoning, thinking through an argument, surely he goes through a definite activity of thinking first that *x* follows from *a* and *b*, then that given *x* and *c* it follows that *y*, and then that *y* *implies* *z*. This is an ordered sequence of thoughts and an ordered sequence of transitions in thought. — But that is misleading at best. If one has thought through an argument, then the *expression* of what one thought will be an ordered sequence of sentences. In so far as there is anything that can be called 'the structure of thought' or 'the structure of thinking', it is the structure of the expression of the argument which is thought through. But one must not conflate the *logical* stages of an argument with a psychological process or activity. To report what one thought when one thought through an argument is neither to describe what one said to oneself, nor to describe a series of mental images that crossed one's mind. Of course, one may be interrupted, and asked how far one has got. And one may reply that one has got through these and these steps. But this does not mean that thinking through these steps involved a structured internal monologue – only that one knew how to proceed from *a* to *g* (but had not yet worked out the last three moves in the argument).

These categorial reflections have non-trivial consequences. They shed light on some misconceptions and explain some of the puzzling features of thought and thinking.

Thinking is not a specific technique Activities that are voluntary are commonly taught. Thinking is often voluntary. But there are not, and could not be, special lessons in school in thinking, over and above the run-of-the-mill lessons in arithmetic, physics, history and literature. One learns to think, to use one's wits more effectively, in the course of learning these subjects. In this sense, all lessons are lessons in thinking, but there are no thinking lessons. For thinking is not a specific technique with teachable procedures which one can learn. If one is faced with a difficult problem in arithmetic, physics or history and asks a friend how to solve it, the reply 'Try thinking – it sometimes does the trick!' is at best a poor joke.[9] And learning the predicate calculus in order to improve one's skills as a historian would be absurd. Activities can be practised, but one cannot practise thinking as such.

The stream of thought William James fostered the illusion that what he called 'the stream of thought' – the sequence of images and words crossing one's mind when one is thinking – constitutes thinking.[10] But the stream of thought is largely a meaningless babble and kaleidoscope of images. The 'stream of consciousness' authors in the early twentieth century may have supposed that a description of a stream of thought is a description of the real activity of thinking. But all it *could be* is a description of the words and images that flitted across someone's mind *while* he was thinking, or a statement of what he said to himself – which need neither be nor express *what* he was thinking. The best description of what someone thought is an accurate *expression* of his thoughts, and the best

[9] See J. F. M. Hunter, *Understanding Wittgenstein* (Edinburgh University Press, Edinburgh, 1985), pp. 173–85.

[10] W. James, *The Principles of Psychology*, vol. 1, ch. ix.

description of his reasoning is a precise statement of his arguments. If we want to know what Kant thought, we do not need a description of his 'stream of thought', but access to his complete works and correspondence.

Asking the scientists A similar confusion is manifest in mathematicians', physicists' and other scientists' reports that they do not think in language.[11] Francis Galton reported that

> It is a serious drawback to me in writing, and still more in explaining myself, that I do not think as easily in words as otherwise. It often happens that after being hard at work, and having arrived at results that are perfectly clear and satisfactory to myself, when I try to express them in language I feel that I must begin by putting myself upon quite another intellectual plane. I have to translate my thoughts into language that does not run very evenly with them. I therefore have to waste a vast deal of time in seeking appropriate words and phrases.[12]

Einstein recorded that

> The words or the language as they are written or spoken, do not seem to play any role in my mechanism of thought. The psychical entities which seem to serve as elements of thought are certain signs and more or less clear images which can be 'voluntarily' reproduced and combined.[13]

More recently Roger Penrose said that

> Almost all my mathematical thinking is done visually and in terms of non-verbal concepts, although the thoughts are quite often accompanied by inane and almost useless verbal commentary . . . the difficulty that these thinkers have had with translating their thoughts into words is something that I frequently experience myself. Often the reason is that there simply are not the words available to express the concepts that are required. In fact, I often calculate using specially designed diagrams which constitute a shorthand for certain types of algebraical expression . . . This is not to say that I do not sometimes think in

[11] See J. Hadamard, *The Mathematician's Mind: the Psychology of Invention in the Mathematical Field* [1945] (Princeton University Press, Princeton, 1996).

[12] Quoted by Roger Penrose in *The Emperor's New Mind*, rev. edn (Oxford University Press, Oxford, 1999), p. 548.

[13] Quoted by Hadamard in *The Mathematician's Mind*, p. 142.

words, it is just that I find words almost useless for *mathematical* thinking.[14]

These great scientists noted correctly that what words cross their minds while they are thinking do not constitute the activity of thinking and do not express what they think. But they continue to suppose that thinking *is* an activity, and hence that to describe what goes on in one's mind while one is thinking *is* to describe the activity of thinking. And that is *wholly* misconceived. For it led them to the further confused ideas that one must think *in* something, that one may think *in* images or *in* non-verbal concepts and that expressing one's thoughts is a matter of *translating* them into word-language. Here it is evident that the apparently harmless idea that thinking is an activity leads to deep and non-trivial misunderstandings.

4. What do we think in?

It is tempting to suppose that one must think *in* something – if not in words, then in images, if not in images, then in concepts. Thought, we are inclined to think, must have a medium – either a linguistic medium, or a non-linguistic one.

Thinking in ideas Early modern philosophers for the most part held that we think in ideas. The empiricists were inclined to conceive of ideas as faint copies of sense-impressions. For on their view, it is sense-impressions and their mnemonic reproductions that furnish the mind with materials for thought. All thought, they supposed, is the combining or separating of ideas. Judgement is affirming or denying one idea or another. The horizon of thought is accordingly the limits of the combinatorial possibilities of the ideas with which the mind of a thinker is furnished. Language is *strictly speaking* not necessary for thinking, but only for the communication of ideas. Hobbes wrote in 1640:

> men desiring to show others the knowledge, opinions, conceptions, and passions which are within themselves, and to that end having invented language, have by that means transferred all that discursion

---

[14] Penrose, *The Emperor's New Mind*, pp. 548f. For detailed scrutiny, see M. R. Bennett and P. M. S. Hacker, *Philosophical Foundations of Neuroscience*, pp. 337–45.

of their mind . . . by the motion of their tongues, into discourse of words; and *ratio*, now, is but *oratio*.[15]

Nevertheless, it was sometimes conceded, we do generally think *in* words. Arnauld, in the *Port-Royal Logic*, averred that:

> Had we no need to communicate, we could dispense with any consideration of thought as clothed in words or other signs. But communication requires that our thoughts be expressed by external signs; and in fact this custom of expressing thoughts in words is so strong that even when we think in solitude our thoughts are always in terms of the words we would use to express those thoughts to others.[16]

But Locke, in the *Essay*, continued to hold that words are unnecessary for thought:

> Man, though he have great variety of thoughts, and such, from which others, as well as himself, might receive Profit and Delight; yet they are all within his own Breast, invisible, and hidden from others, nor can of themselves be made appear. The Comfort, and Advantage of Society, not being to be had without Communication of Thoughts, it was necessary, that Man should find out some external sensible Signs, whereby those invisible *Ideas*, which his thoughts are made up of, might be made known to others.[17]

However, the view that we can or do think *in* images or ideas (conceived as faint copies of impressions, i.e. mental images) is mistaken.

First of all, there are numerous concepts and kinds of concepts, expressed by the words of our language, that *could not* be expressed by mental images. These include concepts of logical connectives, such as 'if . . . , then . . .' 'or' and 'not', as well as quantifiers such as 'all', 'most', 'some' and 'few' – which are pivotal for reasoning (thinking) in any form. They also include a multitude of categorial concepts, such as 'object', 'property', 'number', 'time', 'colour', 'smell', abstrac-

---

[15] T. Hobbes, *Human Nature* [1640] (Oxford University Press, Oxford, 1994), ch. 5, §14.

[16] Arnauld, *The Art of Thinking: Port-Royal Logic* [1662] (Bobbs-Merrill, Indianapolis, 1964), Introduction.

[17] Locke, *An Essay concerning Human Understanding*, 4th edn [1700], III. ii. 1.

tions of innumerable kinds (e.g. truth, goodness and beauty), as well as endless other concepts of unpicturables (e.g. the rights of man, a chiliagon, the legal system). The bankruptcy of this idealist conception of the materials of thought is too familiar to need rehearsing. Secondly, a mental image or picture may illustrate a thought, just as a literal picture may illustrate a text. But it can never be a substitute for a thought, just as a picture cannot be a substitute for the text it illustrates. For without familiarity with the text, one cannot read off the picture the text it illustrates. No more can one read off a mental image the thought it accompanies. Thirdly, although images may cross one's mind while one is thinking, and although one may use drawn or mental images heuristically, neither the images nor their descriptions are *expressions* of what one thinks. The process of images crossing one's mind is no more the process of thinking than is a succession of heuristic scribbles on paper. The train of one's reasoning is laid out in the explicit statement of one's premises and conclusion – not in a sequence of images, symbols or diagrams that may have crossed one's mind while one was thinking. Saying what one thinks is not describing the ideas (mental images) before one's mind when one is thinking. Thoughtful speech is not a description of a private peep-show that only oneself can see. Telling another what one is thinking is not a running commentary on what images are before one's mind.

Thinking in words   So, if one does not think *in* images, does one not think *in words*? A number of considerations support this conception. One is the indisputable fact that we do talk to ourselves in our imagination. This phenomenon was sufficiently captivating to induce Plato to suppose that thought is the discourse of the soul with itself. Secondly, when learning a foreign language we commonly say such things as 'I can speak German, but I cannot think in German' or 'My German is now getting better: I can even think in German'. George Orwell was sufficiently mesmerized by the turn of phrase 'to think in' to write of Joseph Conrad:

> He used, I believe, to think in Polish and then translate his thoughts into French and finally into English, and one can sometimes follow the process back at least as far as French, for instance in his tendency to put the adjective after the noun.[18]

[18] G. Orwell, *The Collected Essays, Journalism and Letters* (Secker & Warburg, London, 1968), vol. 4, p. 489.

Thirdly, as we have seen, it is very tempting to suppose that the difference between a human being's speaking and a parrot's uttering the very same words, as well as the difference between speaking with thought and speaking mechanically and without thought, is that one's thought *accompanies* one's speech. It seems that one must surely think the words while one says them. That idea is further supported by the fact that one can say something other than what one thinks – what a deceiver says in his heart is one thing; what he says out loud another.

As noted, talking to oneself in the imagination is neither necessary nor sufficient for thinking. One may recite the alphabet to oneself in one's imagination in order to stop oneself from thinking. To run through one's impending after-dinner speech in one's mind is not to think through it afresh – it is to repeat it to oneself without further thought. Conversely, one may do something with thought, speak thoughtfully or think of the answer to a problem without saying anything at all to oneself. One may realize, or come to the conclusion that *h* on the basis of the evidence that *e* without saying anything in one's imagination. All that is necessary is that thenceforth one be willing, other things being equal, to assert that *h* on the grounds of the evidence. Of course, one *may* say to oneself exactly what one is thinking. But what makes what one says to oneself *thinking such-and-such* is not that one says it to oneself, but that one be willing to reason, act or react in the light of it.

We are over-impressed by turns of phrase such as 'I can // cannot // think in . . .'. For an English speaker to say 'I can speak German, but I cannot think in German' signifies that before he can say something in German, he must, by and large, decide what he wants to say (and *be able* to say it in English) and then struggle to find the right German words. It does not follow that it makes sense to say of a native English speaker that he thinks in English, unless all that means is that he talks to himself in his imagination in English. We do indeed say 'My German is improving – I am even thinking in German now'. But that, if it does not simply mean that he talks to himself in his imagination in German, just means that he does *not* first have to think of what he wants to say and then pause to try to think of the German words in which to say it.

It is true that a parrot produces English phonemes without thought. It does not think what it says. But it is mistaken to suppose that when we speak with thought, we accompany our words by an inner, covert, activity of thinking (speaking in our imagination). Speaking with thought should be compared not to singing to musical accompaniment, but rather to singing with expression.[19] For to sing with expression is not to do two things, singing and expressing, and to speak with thought is not to do two things, speaking and thinking, either. As we have seen, to speak with thought is to speak with understanding, reflectively, having reasons for what one says, taking into account the relevant factors, and so forth. One can imagine people who can think only out loud (as there are people who can read only aloud). That does not mean that when they speak with thought, they say everything twice.

Thinking in concepts or senses Do we then think in something less phenomenal than images and more abstract than words – in concepts? That idea was advanced by Kant and attracted the attention of many nineteenth-century German philosophers. Lotze, for example, argued that

> the train of ideas alone is not *Thinking*, and does not itself discharge the offices which we require of the latter. . . . the mere presence of . . . images – products of the mechanical course of ideas – is not equivalent to the possession of *Concepts*, in whose form Thinking refers the manifold content to its corresponding *Universal*. For in the latter is always implied the subsidiary thought of a determining rule.[20]

Like Arnauld, conceptualists made concessions to our all too human nature and recognized our need for language. Hamilton, writing in 1837 (and much influenced by German philosophy) wrote:

> though, in general, we must hold that language, as the product and correlative of thought, must be viewed as posterior to the act of thinking itself; on the other hand, it must be admitted that we could never have risen above the very lowest degrees in the scale of thought, without the aid of signs. A sign is necessary to give stability to our intellectual progress.[21]

Frege went down a similar road. Although he gave the term *Begriff* (concept) a non-Kantian, technical, use, he held that the constituents

---

[19] See Wittgenstein, *Philosophical Investigations*, §332.

[20] H. Lotze, *Microcosmos: An Essay concerning Man and his Relation to the World* (T&T Clark, Edinburgh, 1885), II. iv. 4.

[21] Sir William Hamilton, *Lectures on Metaphysics and Logic* (Gould & Lincoln, Boston, 1865–6), vol. II, p. 98.

of thoughts and judgements are senses – abstract entities that are modes of presentation of their designata. A thought, he supposed, is *composed* of senses (which are 'thought building-blocks'). To understand a thought is to 'grasp' such a composite sense. Like his predecessors, Frege (writing in 1924–5) held that although thinking is in principle detachable from language, nevertheless, language is necessary for us mortals. He averred

> That a thought of which we are conscious is connected in our mind with some sentence or other is for us men necessary. But that does not lie in the nature of thought but in our nature. There is no contradiction in supposing there to exist beings that can grasp the same thought as we do without needing to clothe it in a form that can be perceived by the senses. But still, for us men, there is this necessity.[22]

As we have seen (in figs 2.4 and 3.3), Ferdinand de Saussure's speech-circuit presupposed that we think in concepts which are 'facts of consciousness' in the brain, and 'are associated with representations of linguistic signs or sound patterns by means of which they may be expressed'.[23]

The supposition that we think *in concepts* has its attractions. After all, if Hans and Jean both think that things are thus-and-so, then surely they think the very same thought, even though Hans speaks no French and Jean no German. Language *represents* the concepts in terms of which they think, and the validity of their reasoning is determined by the relationships between the concepts that make up their judgements. Moreover, since languages differ in their grammatical forms and structures, it seems that one language is logically superior to another to the extent that its forms and structures approximate the forms and structures of the concepts constitutive of the judgements expressed in it. This picture is sufficiently beguiling to have led the early twentieth-century French prime minister, Aristide Briand, to assert that French is the best of all languages, since its word-order mirrors the order of thinking as it takes place in our minds. This is a psychologist misconception. Frege was not immune

[22] Frege, *Posthumous Writings*, p. 269.

[23] F. de Saussure, *Course in General Linguistics* [1915], ed. and trans. R. Harris (Duckworth, London, 1983), pp. 11f.

to a comparable Platonist misconception. He held that natural languages are not isomorphic with the thoughts (conceived as abstract objects) expressed in them, but his concept-script *is* a faithful reflection of the structure of thoughts.

The supposition that we think in concepts lives on. Some cognitive neuroscientists hold that:

> concepts are not, in the first instance, sentential. That is, concepts are not propositions in a language . . .; rather they are constructs the brain develops by mapping its responses prior to language. . . . Concepts, in our view, precede language, which develops by epigenetic means to further enhance our conceptual and emotional exchanges.[24]

Lexicons and concept-stores in the brain This idea is rooted in the writings of Wernicke and Lichtheim in the late nineteenth century.[25] It was developed by psycholinguists from the 1960s onwards, in whose work talk of mental dictionaries and concept-stores in the brain became reputable (Triesman, Morton, Levelt and Coltheart). Words were held to be names of concepts, speech to be the translation of concepts into words. Some forms of aphasia were explained in terms of retention of concepts stored in a concept-module in the brain but disconnected from the word-module. For certain aphasic patients can remember the concept of, say, a horse (since they could characterize what they were thinking of as 'the animal men ride at the races'), but they cannot remember the word 'horse'. This is explained by reference to lesions resulting in blocking the connection between the concept-module and the word-module that contains *the labels* for the concepts! Linguists, such as Chomsky and his followers, for quite different reasons, joined the flood-tide. Chomsky argued that

> the speed and precision of vocabulary acquisition leaves no real alternative to the conclusion that the child somehow has the concepts available before experience with language and is basically learning

---

[24] G. M. Edelman and G. Tononi, *Consciousness: How Matter Becomes Imagination* (Allen Lane, London, 2000), pp. 215f.

[25] For detailed critical discussion, see M. R. Bennett and P. M. S. Hacker, *History of Cognitive Neuroscience* (Wiley-Blackwell, Oxford, 2008), ch. 4.

labels for concepts that are already part of his or her conceptual apparatus.[26]

The ideas that words name concepts or are labels for concepts, that concepts can be stored in the brain and that one thinks in concepts and then translates one's thought into words are now rife among psycholinguists and neurolinguists.

Why thinking seems language-independent   What speaks for this evidently captivating conception? A variety of phenomena and various turns of phrase suggest that thinking, in itself, can be, or perhaps essentially is, both wordless and imageless. We are all familiar with the phenomenon of looking for the right word to express our thought, and with the experience of having the word 'on the tip of our tongue'. So too we have all from time to time found someone expressing exactly what we wanted to say but couldn't; or expressing the thought we were thinking so much better than we could have done ourselves. We are often amazed at the speed of thought. Sometimes someone may see the answer to a complex problem in a flash – and take half an hour to rehearse his reasoning and to spell out his conclusion. He obviously could not have said all that to himself in a flash, let alone had a high-speed sequence of images, just as Mozart could not possibly have heard a whole concerto in his mind in a moment.[27] Nevertheless, although all this may suggest that we think in some non-linguistic medium, such

---

[26] N. Chomsky, *Language and the Problems of Knowledge* (MIT Press, Cambridge, Mass., 1988), pp. 27f. It is remarkable to find the idea of innate possession of concepts revived in the twentieth century as an empirical hypothesis. It is, in effect, an inference to the best explanation. But an inference to the best explanation is coherent only to the extent that the 'best explanans' has been given a sense. However, it is totally obscure what is to count as possessing concepts innately. No criteria have been laid down for the possession of an innate concept by a neonate – other than the phenomenon of language-learning that the hypothesis is meant to explain. That human beings have innate tendencies and pronenesses to respond to linguistic stimuli, to gesture, voice and intonation contour, is indisputable. But the supposition that they have actually innate concepts is a much weightier hypothesis that is supported by no empirical evidence whatsoever.

[27] All he would then have heard in his imagination would have been a crashing chord! The letter on which this tale about Mozart is based has been discovered to be a forgery. But even if it were not, and even if Mozart did *apprehend* how to complete a concerto in a flash, this would not be because he heard it in his mind all at once. Knowing *how* to go on is not a form of lightning-like *going on*.

as concepts, which we then translate into words – this is miscon-ceived. The confusion is produced by misconstrual of a range of cogitative idioms, and misinterpretation of familiar cogitative phe-nomena. It also involves a defective conception of what a concept is and of what it is to possess a concept.

Looking for the right word describes a familiar phenomenon. So does *having a word on the tip of one's tongue*. But the phenomena are *misdescribed* when said to be a matter of thinking the thought without words and then casting around for the right word or words in terms of which to express it. 'The word is on the tip of my tongue' means nothing more than 'The right word escapes me for a moment, but it will come to me shortly, I trust'. It does not mean 'The thought is complete in my mind, but I lack one of the words for its expres-sion'. 'I know exactly what I think, but I can't find the words to express it' is either nonsense, or means no more than 'Give me another moment for the thought to crystallize'. For what would 'knowing what I think' amount to, if I couldn't find the words to *say* what I think? It is common for someone to say what *I* wanted to say, but couldn't. Or for another to express exactly what I was thinking very much better than I could. But this is not because his words match my wordless thought. It is rather that his words match the phenom-enon I was trying to describe or the argument I was struggling to articulate, and do so in a way that strikes me as appropriate.

Of course, we are struck by the eureka phenomenon. We are impressed by the speed of thought. We often see how to solve a complex problem in a flash, and then take half an hour to spell out the solution we have thought of. But we misconstrue this if we take it to be a matter of whizzing through the solution in one's mind in a non-linguistic medium, and then spelling it out slowly in words. To see the solution to a complex problem at a stroke (and to see how to complete a concerto in a flash) is the sudden realization of how to do something, not the high-speed execution of what one can then do. The sudden flash of inspiration is a pointer, not a product. Whether one is right to think that one has 'got it', that one really can prove the theorem, complete the concerto, solve the problem, remains to be seen. We do sometimes think that we have seen the solution in a flash, only to discover, when we try to go through it, that we were wrong.

It is true that to think something to be so, to be thinking of some-thing and to be thinking one's way through a problem need involve no mental images, no internal monologue and no 'dialogue with oneself'. But it does not follow that we think *in* something even more ethereal, namely concepts. Concepts are not constituents of thoughts. What we think – namely that things are thus-and-so – no more literally has constituents than what we suspect or what we intend. *It is the symbolic expression of what we think that has constituents.* Although concept-possession is requisite for all but the most rudimentary forms of thinking, there is no such thing as thinking *in* concepts. To see why, we must call to mind our discussion of concepts and word-meaning in chapter 3, section 6.

Concept-possession   The handle to grasp to elucidate our notion of a concept is the idea of concept-possession. To possess a concept is to have mastered the use of a word or phrase in some language. It is to be able to use the word or phrase correctly, that is, in accordance with the rules for its use. It is to be able to explain what it means in a given context, that is, to give, or at least to recognize, a correct explanation of what it means in a sentence one understands. It is to be able to respond intelligently to its use. In short, it is to know what the word or phrase that expresses the concept means. But although knowing what a word in *a given* language (English or German) means is sufficient for possession of the concept it expresses, it is not necessary. For one may know the meaning of a (more or less) synonymous word or phrase in a different language. As we have seen, a concept is *an abstraction from mastery of the use of a word or phrase in a given language.* For many purposes and in many contexts we are not concerned with what language was spoken when a given thought was expressed. So we abstract from any specific language and focus upon logical features common to the use of more or less synonymous words and phrases in different languages. For different people speaking different languages share a multitude of concepts. A concept stands to its linguistic expression in much the way in which the powers of a chess-piece stand to the carved figure (made of wood, ivory, plastic, metal – carved or cast in any number of ingenious and amusing shapes) that possesses those powers. To have grasped a concept is to have mastered the *technique* of the use of an expression – its combinatorial powers, compatibilities and incompatibilities; implications and presuppositions that are common to words and phrases in different languages that express the same concept. A concept is not *an* anything. Of course, one might say that the concept expressed by a word or phrase is *the technique of use* that is common to all expressions, in the same or different languages, that have the same meaning – that have the relevantly equivalent use. With some qualifications, that is correct; but it does not tell us what sort of thing a concept is.[28] That is unsurprising since concepts are not kinds of things. Nor is it very illuminating. What is much more important is to bear in mind what it makes sense to say *of* concepts. They are expressed by words or other symbols; they have an extension; they stand in logical relations of compatibility, mutual exclusion, subsumption and superordination, implication and mutual implication. They are applied to things. Things are said to fall under them or to instantiate them. They are introduced by definitions or explanations of word-meaning. One concept may be substituted for another. Concepts may be extended to cover new cases. And so on.

Concepts are not constituents of thoughts
With this in mind, it should be obvious that what one thinks does not have concepts as its constituents. For what one thinks (see chapter 2) is given by the answer to the question 'What are you thinking?'. The sentence the utterance of which answers this question has constituents – but these are words, not concepts. Nevertheless, it might be argued, the words in the sentence express concepts. Does it not follow that the thought expressed has concepts as constituents? No. Concepts, in so far as they are anything, are techniques – and thoughts do not consist of techniques of word use. The answer to the question 'What do you think?' does not specify constituents of one's thought. It specifies what one thought, and may specify what one thought of and what one thought about it.

We do not think in concepts
It should be equally obvious that it is misleading to suppose that we think *in* concepts, in the sense in which we speak in English or German. The analogy between speaking in a language and thinking is deceptive. If one says something, one says it *in* a language. A language is a *medium* of expression, communication and representation. But concepts are not a medium, and one does not think in them, even though we cannot think much without them. In order to think anything beyond the most rudimentary, we must possess concepts – that is, we must have mastered the techniques of the use of words. But there is no such thing as thinking *in* the techniques one has mastered. Without the

---

[28] Obviously, 'the concept of A' and 'the technique of use of "A"' are not always inter-substitutable. Something may fall under the concept of A, but it cannot be said to fall under the technique of use of 'A'. We apply concepts, but we employ techniques of using words.

concepts of a right-angled triangle and of a square, one could not think of, let alone think up, the Pythagorean theorem. But one does not think of it *in* concepts. Indeed, one does not think what one thinks *in* anything. One *expresses* what one thinks in behaviour, and most of what we think *can* be expressed *only* in linguistic (and other symbolic) behaviour.

Not all words express concepts. Those that do are not names or labels of the concept they express. Some words are names of various things – as 'cat' is the name of a kind of animal, and 'coal' the name of a kind of matter. But names of such things are not names of concepts. Some words can be used to label things – as 'cat' can be used as the label of an exhibit in a natural history museum, and 'coal' in a museum of geology. But words are not names, let alone labels, *of concepts*.

The word-order of a grammatical utterance in a given language is determined by the syntax of the language. If it made sense to speak of the ordering of concepts in thinking, it *would have* made sense for Briand to suppose that the order of words in French is isomorphic with the order of thinking. If concept-possession were independent of and prior to mastery of a language, then cogent speech *would be* a translation from wordless thinking. But then it would have to be possible to juxtapose the spoken sentence that is composed of words with the wordless thought that is composed of concepts to check the correctness of the translation, just as one can juxtapose an English and French sentence to check the translation. But there is no such thing. 'Red', 'green' and 'blue' are translations of 'rouge', 'vert' and 'bleu'. They are not *translations*, but *expressions*, of the concepts of red, green and blue.

Concepts are not storables

The psycholinguists' notion of concept-modules storing concepts in the brain, and word-modules storing words that name those concepts is incoherent. Concepts are not storables – any more than are the powers of chess-pieces. One can store one's chess-pieces in a box, but one cannot store the powers of the pieces in the same box, or in a different box, since they are not storables. While words (word-tokens) *are* storables, the place in which they can be 'stored' is the dictionary, not the brain. A dictionary correlates words with words or phrases. But there could be no such thing as a dictionary correlating words with 'non-verbal concepts'. There is, and could be, no 'mental dictionary' nor any *analogue* of a dictionary, in the brain. A dictionary is a book of rules, correlating words with other words and phrases that specify what they mean. This correlation is a *normative* (rule-governed) one. For a dictionary entry is an explanation of meaning, and as we have see (chapter 3), an explanation of meaning *is* a rule for the use of a word. To *use* a dictionary, one must understand the rules of correlation (e.g. ⊒ rather than ⊠) and of interpretation (i.e. which of the dozen meanings or nuances of a given word is relevant for one's purpose). But there can be no *rules* of correlation and interpretation either *in* or *for* brains. There is no such thing as an inscription (coded or otherwise) of a rule in the brain. There is no such thing as a brain *following* a rule, since to follow a rule one must *know* what counts as complying with it and what as transgressing it. But this is not an ability which it makes sense to ascribe to a brain or any part of a brain. To follow a rule for the use of a word, one must use the word in accordance with the rule – but brains do not use words. It is human beings that do so. That our ability to speak and understand our language is dependent upon the normal functioning of very specific neural networks does not, and could not, show that the brain stores words or concepts, or contains 'dictionaries' correlating words with concepts.

5. Thought, language and the language of thought

We can strengthen our grip upon the relationship between thought and language by a critical examination of the idea that there must be a language of thought – that thought *must* have constituents that correspond to the words of language.[29] In 1919, the young Wittgenstein was asked by Russell whether thoughts, as conceived in the *Tractatus*, consist of words. He replied, 'No! But of psychical constituents that have the same sort of relation to reality as words. What those constituents are, I don't know.' A thought, he wrote to Russell, 'must have such constituents which correspond to the words of Language'.[30] It would be a matter for psychology to discover what sorts of things these psychological constituents are. Why did he think this?

[29] The idea is an old one, and was prominent in the work of Ockham in the thirteenth century.

[30] Wittgenstein, *Wittgenstein in Cambridge: Letters and Documents 1911–1951*, ed. Brian McGuinness (Blackwell, Oxford, 2008), p. 98, letter to Russell dated 19 Aug. 1919. The use of 'psychical' here is a Germanism.

Because a thought seems to stand in the same kind of relation to reality as a sentence with a sense that describes how things are. It is bipolar (either true or false and capable of being true as well as capable of being false). It is made true by the obtaining of the fact that is thought, and made false by its non-obtaining. It is subject *in thought* to all the logical operations. And so on. How could this be *unless* thoughts have psychological constituents in something akin to 'a language of thought'.

Language of thought hypothesis   The idea of a Language of Thought (LOT) became popular in the 1970s, quite independently of Wittgenstein's reflections in 1919. Unfortunately, it did so in total oblivion to the arguments he had mounted against it in the early 1930s. It was argued (by Chomsky and his followers) that human beings could not possibly learn a language unless they already possessed one.[31] In addition, it was argued (by Fodor and his followers), that the systematicity, compositionality and productivity of thought can be explained only on the supposition that there is a language of thought.[32] What was generally (although not universally) presupposed by proponents of the LOT hypothesis is displayed in list 10.2.

We need not follow this increasingly byzantine cognitive theology further. We can undercut the whole debate (which is indeed a long and convoluted one) by reference to the considerations we rehearsed in chapter 2. I shall recapitulate.

4 reasons why there can be no language of thought   First, it breeds nothing but confusion to conceive of thoughts as having a 'propositional content'. One may say that thought, that is *thinking*, has a 'content', namely what one thinks. For the answer to the question 'What are you thinking?' is given by a proposition (a sentence with a sense) that spells out *what* you are thinking. However, the *thoughts* one thinks do not. Thoughts (what one thinks rather

---

[31] For refutation of this idea, see P. M. S. Hacker, 'Chomsky's Problems', in *Language and Communication*, 10 (1990), pp. 141–6.

[32] By 'systematicity of thought' is meant the intelligibility of the interchange of 'thought elements', viz. if we can think aRb, then we can also think aRc, or cRb, etc. By 'compositionality' is meant the functional relationship between the content of a thought and its constituent elements and their mode of combination. By 'productivity' is meant the ability to think an unlimited number of new thoughts. These are the cogitative shadows of the 'problem' of understanding new sentences discussed in chapter 3, section 7.

- Thoughts (what we think) have 'propositional content'.
- Thoughts are 'representations'.
- Thoughts have a syntax and semantics.
- The medium of thought (of thinking) is an innate language distinct from all natural languages. It is genetically determined and species-specific.
- Thinking takes place *in* a mental language ('Mentalese') of which no one has any explicit knowledge and which no one speaks.
- The language of thought is 'semantically expressively complete', that is, it contains all the 'semantic resources' necessary for anything human beings can grasp, think or express.
- The language of thought is physically 'realized' in the brain.

List 10.2   *The presuppositions of the language of thought hypothesis*

than one's thinking them) do not *have* a so-called propositional content – they *are* propositional contents. (This jargon is altogether unnecessary. It is best to avoid talk of 'contents', with its mischievous reification, altogether.)

Secondly, thoughts, that is, what we think when we think that things are so, are not representations. This is patent from our previous discussion (chapter 2, pp. 80–2). A picture of St John's College is a pictorial representation of the College. The opening bars of Strauss's *Thus Spake Zarathustra* is a musical representation of a sunrise. Assertoric sentences (spoken or written) are (commonly) verbal representations of the states of affairs described. It is a feature of representations that they require a medium of representation (paint, notes, speech, script). And it is an essential feature of a representation that it have non-representational properties *in virtue of which it is a representation*. These are the properties of the medium of representation. There is no such thing as a representation that has no medium. Without a medium, the representation could not be perceived – and there is no such thing as an *imperceptible* representation. Non-representational properties of paintings are the canvas, wood or paper on which it is painted, the paint (oil, gouache, watercolour), the individual brushstrokes. Non-representational properties of speech are the timbre of the voice, the loudness of utterance, the speed of speaking. The non-representational properties of script are the hand-writing, the medium (ink, pencil, biro), its colour, the character of the paper. Unless a representation has non-representational properties in virtue of which it is a representation, it cannot represent anything. It follows that thoughts are not representations at all. To repeat what was emphasized in chapter 2, *they are all message and no medium.* This should have been obvious from the mere consideration of the non-perceptibility of thoughts – of one's own as well as of others. But, misled by the metaphor of introspection, it is widely assumed that we 'introspect' our own thoughts, and know what we think by inner perception.

Thirdly, any representation, hence any symbol, can be interpreted and can be misinterpreted. But thought, as Wittgenstein noted in criticism of his *Tractatus* view, is the last interpretation.[33] One can interpret (or misinterpret) a sentence in trying to determine what is meant by it. If one *says* 'I'll meet you by the bank' it may be inde-terminate whether it is Barclays or National Westminster bank, or indeed the bank of the Isis. So what one says may stand in need of an interpretation. But when one *thinks* that one will meet him by the bank, no question of not understanding or of misunderstanding and misinterpreting one's own thought *can* arise for one. To repeat, *thought is the last interpretation.* So thoughts cannot consist of symbols in a language of thought.

When one uses a sentence, one means something by it. There can be a gap between what one *says* and what one *means*. If one says 'Jack is in Cambridge', one means by 'Jack' the fellow who . . . , and by 'Cambridge' Cambridge, Mass., not Cambridge, England. But if one thinks that Jack is in Cambridge, the question of who and where one means cannot arise for one. There can be no gap between what one thinks and what one means. So thinking that Jack is in Cambridge cannot consist of symbols in a language of thought.

Fourthly, the signs of a language are extrinsically representational. The bare sign (the sound or inscription) is in itself a mere noise or mark. What gives it meaning is its use in accordance with the conven-tions that govern it in the practice of a linguistic community (or in one's own private but communicable practice). But if there were a universal language of thought, with constituent elements possessing

---

[33] Wittgenstein, *Philosophical Grammar* (Blackwell, Oxford, 1974), p. 144.

syntactical and semantic properties, it *could not be* extrinsically representational. Otherwise the question of how the signs in the language of thought come to represent what they do could arise. And there could be no answer, since there is and could be no public practice of using them, explaining their use, correcting their misuse. Nor could there be a corresponding contingently private practice – since no one knows what these mysterious mental symbols are, no one is aware of using them, and no one knows what they mean. But there is no such thing as an intrinsically representational sign – a sign can represent what it represents only in the practice of its use in accordance with the rules for its use. So there could not be such a thing as a *language* of thought.

How thought and language are related
Our investigations thus far show that the question of how thought is related to language is too general to handle. If broken down into subsidiary questions it becomes manageable. It is worth spelling them out (see list 10.3), and then summarizing our conclusions.

(i)   Is there a medium (or are there different media) of thought?

    (a)   Does one think *in* words?

    (b)   Does one think *in* images?

    (c)   Does one think *in* concepts?

(ii)   Is there any such thing as wordless thought?

(iii) Is there any such thing as an innate language of thought (distinct from natural languages)?

(iv)   Does one have to know a language in order to think?

(v)   Are the horizons of thought limited by language?

List 10.3   *Questions concerning the relations between thought and language*

We have answered most of these questions. Thought (thinking) has no medium. It is *expressed* and *communicated* in a medium. One does not think *in* anything, although one can speak to oneself in one's imagination, conjure up images while thinking and as heuristic support for one's thinking. One can say to oneself what one thinks, and sometimes picture to oneself what one is thinking of – but what makes what one says or pictures into what one thinks is not that one says or pictures it to oneself. There is no such thing as thinking *in* concepts, although there is little to be thought without mastery of concepts. One can, and often does think without words, that is, without saying anything to oneself in one's imagination. Nevertheless, it is clear that there *can* be wordless thought only in so far as the normal behavioural repertoire of the thinking being includes behaviour that *would* express it. The idea of a language of thought, we have shown, is incoherent.

Is mastery of a language a prerequisite for thinking? If 'thinking' here means thinking (believing) that something is so, then, as we have seen, the answer is 'no'. We have granted (pp. 92f.) that non-language-using animals can be said to think that something is so. The dog may think it is going to be taken for a walk when it hears its leash being taken off the peg, think that its master is about to come in when it hears his footsteps on the garden path or think that the cat it chased up a tree is still there. In all such cases, what warrants the ascription of thinking things to be so to the animal is its behaviour. It makes sense (whether or not it is true) to say of a non-language-using animal that it thinks anything that it *can* (*not* does) display in its (non-linguistic) behaviour. This is a simple application of the general principle enunciated in chapter 2 that

> *The limits of what a being can intelligibly be said to think are the limits of its possible behavioural expression of thinking.*

This is why it makes *no* sense to say of the dog that it now thinks that it will be taken for a walk next Sunday, or now hopes for a good bone next Christmas. For nothing in a dog's behavioural repertoire could possibly determine the temporal deixis of such a thought.

The limits of thought   What lies behind this general principle? That should by now be clear. Thinking, as we have seen, is not the same as talking to oneself in one's imagination. It is not combining or separating ideas or images in the mind. Whatever may be 'going on' in one's mind, we have argued, does not *constitute* but only *accompanies* thinking, either heuristically, associatively or randomly. Of course, one may say to oneself what one thinks, but that is not the same as thinking. So what *counts* as thinking that things are so, or thinking that since such-and-such is the case, therefore . . . , or inferring, or deducing? Not any inner goings-on. But, for all that, thinking is not behaving. Nor is it having a disposition to behave. There is much that a person thinks without revealing what he thinks – not necessarily because he is secretive, but because, for example, there is no point, or no occasion to do so. We do not flaunt or display our reasonings, inferrings or deducings save in public debates and in the classroom, or in arguments, in explanations and justifications. The only way to determine what a person thinks, what he is thinking, how he thought through a problem or up a solution, is by reference to what he says and does. For if something is thought, then it *can* be exhibited in behaviour – words or deeds would count as *an expression* or *statement* of thought. If one avows that one thinks things to be so, truthfulness guarantees the truth of one's so thinking (save in cases of self-deception). Although what one thinks does not coincide with what one expresses by word and deed, what one *can* intelligibly be said to think is what one *could* in principle express in word and deed. And what one *does* think is what one *would* express were one truthfully to express one's thoughts.

6. Can animals think?

Agreeing that non-language-using animals, within the constraints of their behavioural repertoire, can intelligibly be said to think that something is so, is one thing. Agreeing that they can be said to be thinking (reflecting, ruminating) is another thing altogether. Does it make sense to suppose that a non-language-using animal is thinking its way through a problem, thinking up a solution to a problem? Certainly animals have and pursue goals, and act for the sake of an end. In the case of human beings, who *are* language-users, acting for the sake of an end is one form that acting for a reason takes.[34] A further form is responding to apprehended facts that are taken to be, and can be cited as being, justifications for action. Certainly animals are sensitive to what they apprehend in their environment, and modify their behaviour in pursuit of their goals in accordance with what they apprehend. But does it follow that the facts to which they respond are apprehended as justifications for their responses? Can they act for reasons? Can they reason, draw inferences and derive conclusions – can they *think*?

---

[34] For more elaborate discussion, see *Human Nature: the Categorial Framework*, ch. 7.

Animals cannot act for reasons To be responsive to one's perceived environment in pursuit of one's goals is a form of cognitive teleological behaviour. But it does not suffice for being able to act for a reason, or for being able to act 'in the light of reasons'.[35] Acting 'in the light of reasons' is not merely being responsive to how things are or are apprehended as being. To act 'in the light of reasons' presupposes a grasp of *therefore*s and *because*s, the sole behavioural expression of which is linguistic. A being can act *for* a reason only if it can apprehend something *as* a reason – as a *warrant* justifying or explaining that for which it is a reason. A dog may apprehend a break in the path along which it is sprinting, and accordingly leap over it. It does not follow that *its* reason for jumping was that there was a chasm in the path, although *the* reason it jumped was that it perceived the chasm. The dog can neither *justify* nor *explain* its action by reference to there being a gap in the path into which it would have fallen but for leaping. There is no such thing as its *conceiving* its action (after the event) as done for the reason that it would have fallen into the chasm had it not leapt.

The fundamental notion that needs to be invoked in elucidating the idea of a reason is that of *reasoning*. A creature can do things *for a reason* only in so far as it *can reason* – deduce consequences from assumptions, infer explanations from data, derive conclusions from evidence. To come to a conclusion on the basis of reasons presupposes the ability to *weigh different considerations* for and against something's being so, or for and against doing something. That in turn requires the ability to judge that *this* course of action is better than *that* one, *because* . . . In order to be able to act or think that something is so for a reason, one must be able to *deliberate*, to *make reasoned choices* in both thought and action and hence to give *justifications* and *explanations*. In short, one must be able to answer the question 'Why?' One learns to reason only in so far as one learns to *give* reasons. A being that can act for reasons is *responsible* for its actions. To be responsible (from *respondere*) for one's actions is to be *answerable* for what one does. And that is precisely what non-language-using animals are not. For only if one *can* answer can one be answerable.

To be sure, the higher animals are intelligent. They display their intelligence in the manner in which they pursue goals. In the course

[35] For a contrary view, see H.-J. Glock, 'Can Animals Act for a Reason?', *Inquiry*, 52 (2009), pp. 232–54.

of so doing, they solve problems. Some animals use, and in some cases even make, very rudimentary tools to aid them in achieving their goal. They may even realize that one and the same tool can serve different ends. They make choices between different means to an end they are pursuing, and may even learn that one is more apt than another. It does not, however, follow that they can reason or engage in reasoning. They may be able to find ways of doing something, but in the absence of mastery of a language, there is no such thing as reasoning logically or illogically, no such thing as deducing a conclusion from an array of suppositions, or inferring an explanation for a given datum. There is no such thing as reflecting on pros and cons, as weighing alternatives and judging one to be preferable to the other *because of* such-and-such features, as taking things previously learnt into account in one's reflections and reflective decisions.

Animal attentiveness, as when a lion stalks its prey, is not a matter of *thinking of* possibilities or *taking alternatives into account*, that is, making *reasoned* choices – even though the experienced lion may be *prepared* for alternative possibilities. An animal may behave intelligently – solve its problem *in behaving*. But could it solve a problem *without* behaving? It is unclear what this means in this context. Could a thought of how to V occur to an animal and be rejected? Could a thought how to V occur to it in the absence of an opportunity to V, and be registered for future use? What would *count* as a thought's occurring to it in such circumstances? With us there is a thought that we *could* express, even if we do not do so. And we may bear our reasoned conclusion in mind for future use. With the animal there is only sensitivity to its environment and current occurrences that is manifest in its behaviour. In the case of animals the ascription of thought is no more than a redescription of teleological behaviour that carries no explanatory weight by reference to *reasoning*, but only by reference to past experience. Animals cannot deliberate, ruminate or reflect, let alone draw inferences, derive conclusions or deduce consequences – only recognize, associate, learn and anticipate.

Can one not argue that as regards context (i.e. the problem-posing situation), demeanour (e.g. head-scratching) and result (solving the problem), chimpanzee behaviour resembles that of human beings?[36] We have granted that animals confront and solve problems. No doubt chimpanzees scratch their heads – but there is no obvious reason for supposing that their head-scratching is an expression of thought. (If

---

[36] See ibid.

a chimpanzee shrugs its shoulders, that does not mean 'tant pis'.) What differentiates human confrontation with a practical problem and the behaviour of a chimpanzee lies in what the human being *can do*. And in order to qualify for the epithet of *thinking* (reflecting, deliberating, ruminating, deducing, inferring), one must *be able* to do a very wide range of things which non-language-using creatures cannot do. They cannot do these things not because it is difficult and whenever they try they fail. They cannot even try. For their behavioural repertoire contains no forms of behaviour that would count as executing or trying to execute such cogitative tasks.

Animals cannot be self-conscious   One may be over-impressed by ethologists' experimental reports and jump to the conclusion that certain animals are self-conscious and therefore capable of advanced thought. After all, it has been shown that chimpanzees, elephants and dolphins can recognize themselves in a mirror. And if they can recognize themselves, then they are aware of, indeed conscious of, themselves. So they are self-conscious. So they have a sense of their own identity. And if so, then they can surely think! – This is too quick. To recognize oneself in a mirror is to recognize *one's reflection* – not to recognize something called 'a self' that is one's own. But does the ape's recognition of its own reflection not imply awareness of *itself* as opposed to others, and hence an ability to differentiate between itself and things that are not itself? And is that not self-consciousness? — To be sure, an ape does not mistake its own foot for the foot of another ape, or its own mouth for the mouth of another ape. If that means that it differentiates between itself and others, then that is something any animal can do irrespective of whether it can or cannot recognize itself in a mirror. But surely, the ape's ability to recognize itself in a mirror is categorially quite different from that triviality? Does it not recognize that *that* ☞ is itself? Does it not recognize *who it is*? — This is a muddle. It is true that an ape does not mistake the reflection of its own face for the reflection of the face of another ape. It recognizes *its* face, and wipes the lipstick off *its* nose, not off the nose of another. But why should that be supposed to show that it is self-conscious? Only because we assume that recognizing its reflection implies *thinking* 'That's me', and we then assume that the ability to think 'That's me' is a token of self-consciousness. But both assumptions are mistaken.

First, there is no reason to identify an animal's recognizing the reflection of its face in a mirror and seeing a red spot on its nose with its thinking 'That's me', any more than there is reason to suppose that when it looks at its hand and sees a red spot on it, it thinks 'That's my hand'. There is no reason to suppose that a creature might think *'That's* ☞ me' (pointing to its reflection) without being able to think *'This* ↺ is me' (pointing reflexively). There is no reason to suppose it intelligible that an animal (no matter whether non-human or human) should be said to think 'That's me' antecedently to mastering the use of personal pronouns.

Secondly, it is an egregious mistake to suppose that being able to think something *of* oneself is a sufficient condition for being self-conscious (see chapter 1). Mastery of the use of personal pronouns is indeed a condition for being able to think such things as 'I am tired', 'I should like a drink', 'I have a headache'. As little Thomas advances from 'Hungry' to 'Mummy, I'm hungry', or from 'Want nana' to 'Mummy, I want a banana', his mother may pride herself on his growing linguistic prowess, but not on his developing self-consciousness. In order to attain self-consciousness (in the relevant sense of this polysemic term) one must be able to *reflect* on one's dispositions and character traits, one's reasons and motives, attitudes and emotions – not merely to say or think how things are with one.[37] Mastery of the use of first-person psychological utterances is necessary for self-consciousness, but not sufficient. Self-consciousness is the route to self-knowledge and self-understanding. That is not something that could lie within the reach of non-language-using animals.

7. The agent, organ and location of thinking

We can now turn to some residual questions. What is the agent of thinking? What is the organ of thinking? And where is the location of thought? Thinking, as we have seen, is not an activity *simpliciter*. Nevertheless, it is something done, engaged in. But who or what is the *agent* of thinking? Until the mid twentieth century, the received answer was: the mind. Today it is: the brain. Similarly, if we are asked what we think *with* – the natural answer today is: with our brain. For even if it is not, strictly speaking, the brain that thinks, surely the brain is the *organ* of thought? And if the question of where thinking occurs is raised, we naturally locate thought in the head, or, more accurately, in the prefrontal cortices. The brain is surely the *locus of thought*! — But this is too quick.

---

[37] For detailed exploration of this theme, see *Human Nature*, pp. 236, 240, 260–8.

The mind is not an
agent of thinking
Descartes held thought to be the essential, defining, property of the mind, and thinking the essential activity of the mind. If the mind were to cease to think, he supposed, it would cease to exist. But the mind is not the agent of thought. It is the human being that thinks, reasons, reflects and comes to conclusions. It is I who think, not my mind – for my mind, contrary to what Descartes supposed, is not a substance of any kind. Nor is it an agent. As was argued in detail in *Human Nature: the Categorial Framework*, in so far as the mind is *an anything*, it is an array of distinctive abilities of intellect and will and their exercise. But an array of abilities is no more a thing than is an array of talents. To put matters more clearly, all our talk of the mind consists of talk of rational abilities and their exercise. We *can* speak of doing things *with our mind* – just as we speak of doing things *with our talents*. We can make it up, lose it and regain it again, and give someone a piece of it. But these are just idioms signifying respectively our making a decision, losing our sanity and regaining it, and telling another harshly what we think of him. It is human beings who think, not their minds. Is that not an arbitrary stipulation? Not at all. We ascribe thought to an agent on the grounds of what the agent does and says. The criteria for thinking are manifest thoughtful behaviour and speech – and minds do not *behave* or *speak*. It is living beings that behave and speak with thought. That they think is exhibited in the intelligence of their behaviour, in the reasoning that is displayed in what they do and say.

The brain is not an
agent of thinking
Still, if it is not our mind that thinks, is it not our brain? We frequently hear psychologists, neuroscientists and philosophers asserting that it is the brain that thinks. But this is no less misconceived than the classical error of ascribing thought to the mind. The brain does not *do* anything that could possibly count as manifesting thought. It does not engage in thoughtful performances of *Hamlet* nor does it play a subtle game of tennis. It does not speak thoughtfully or thoughtlessly. It does not argue intelligently, nor yet stupidly – since there is no such thing as a brain arguing. There is no such thing as a bigoted or opinionated brain, for brains do not hold opinions; and it is not the brain, but the human being, that can be open-minded or prejudiced. Brains do not conceive of things as this or that, since brains do not conceive of anything, and brains do not suffer from misconceptions since they do not have conceptions. Nothing in the behavioural repertoire of a brain could satisfy the criteria for thinking something, since brains

have no behavioural repertoire. Brains can neither reason well nor poorly, although the brain processes and synaptic connections in the cortex of people who can reason well no doubt have distinctive features that endow them with this gift. It would be quite absurd to say (although eminent neuroscientists do say), 'My brain is thinking it over, but I don't yet know what conclusion it has reached'. It would be risible to say (as eminent neuroscientists do) 'Wait a second; my brain has not yet decided what to do. When it has reached a decision it will tell me, and then I'll be able to tell you'.[38]

The brain is not the organ of thinking

One might grant all this and yet insist, as many do, that the brain is *the organ of thought* – that human beings, who are the agents of thought, think *with* their brains. After all, do we not say 'Use your brain!'? Do we not rack our brains when we worry away at a problem? Do we not scratch our head when we are bemused or bewildered by a problem? And do not damage to the brain and senile degeneration of the brain deprive us of the power of thought? So surely we think *with* our brain! — We must take things slowly. 'Use your brains!' just means 'Think!' It no more signifies that we think with our brain than 'I love you with all my heart' signifies that we love with our heart. It is true that we sometimes scratch our head when thinking hard, but then we place our hand over our heart when we declare our love. 'To rack one's brains' means no more than to think hard and long. Still, is it not true that we cannot think unless our brain is functioning appropriately in such-and-such respects? And does that not show that the brain is the organ of thought? We would not be able to think but for the normal functioning of our brain, just as we would not be able to walk without legs. The legs are the organs of walking, and so too the brain is the organ of thinking. — Not so! It is true that we would not be able to think but for the normal functioning of the brain. But then we would not be able to walk or talk but for the normal functioning of our brain either – and that does not show that we walk with our brain rather than with our legs, or talk with our brain rather than with our mouth. What it shows is that the normal functioning of the human brain is the prerequisite for all normal human functions.

[38] This was held by Benjamin Libet in California in his research on voluntary movement, and in his consequent reflections on free will (see his *Neurophysiology of Consciousness* (Birkhäuser, Boston, 1993). His view (shared by C. D. Frith in Britain) was that the brain decides, or forms the intention, to move a part of the body before the person is aware of any such decision. For critical discussion, see Bennett and Hacker, *Philosophical Foundations of Neuroscience*, pp. 228–31.

We must recall our examination of what counts as an *organ* for a voluntary human function (chapter 7). We speak of the sense-organs: the eyes are the organs of sight, the ears the organs of hearing and the nose of smelling. We characterize the legs as the organs of locomotion, and the hands the organs of manipulation. In each case, the organ of V-ing is the organ we *use* for V-ing – we see with our eyes, bring things closer to our eyes or bring our eyes closer to whatever we are examining to see more clearly, we put our eyes to the keyhole to see through it and close our eyes to stop seeing. So too, we use our legs to walk – we move them in order to walk. We use our hands to hold things, pick things up, push them away, manipulate them and so forth. But we cannot, in this sense, use our brain in order to think – it is not an organ under our direct control and we cannot *do* anything with it. One might, of course, object that we cannot *do* anything with our stomach either, but it is nevertheless the organ of digestion. Is not the brain the organ of thought in just the same way? — No! The organs for non-voluntary functions are not organs we *use* to perform that function. I do not use my stomach to digest my food, since I cannot *do* anything with my stomach – it digests what I eat off its own bat, and can literally be observed to do so. I do not circulate the blood in my body by *using* my heart – my heart does it of its own accord, and can be observed to do so. But the brain is not an organ of thinking in this sense either, for if it were, it would think off its own bat and of its own accord. But, as we have seen, there is nothing a brain *can do* that could possibly count as thinking. BOLD (blood-oxygen-level-dependency) signals on a scanner screen are not *manifestations* of thinking, as bold judicious action in the face of danger is. The normal activity of the stomach satisfies the criteria for digesting. The normal activity of the heart satisfies the criteria for pumping blood. But the normal activity of the brain does not, and cannot, satisfy any of the manifold criteria for thinking. Rather, the various activities of the brain that are now beginning to be discovered in association with one or another form of thinking are necessary *in order for us to be able to think* in such forms. But it is no more thinking than increased oxygenation in one's leg muscles is running.

The brain is not the locus of thinking So far, so good. One might grant all this, but nevertheless insist that thinking takes place in the brain – the brain, one may insist, is *the locus of thought*. But this too is mistaken. Thoughts no more occur in one's head than opinions occur in one's brain. The answer to the question 'Where did you think of that?' is not 'In the prefrontal cortices, of course', but rather 'In my study', 'While I was walking down Piccadilly' or 'On the train to London'. The location of the event of a person's thinking something or other is where that person was when the thought occurred to him.

Not only is thinking no more located in the brain than walking – thoughts are not located there either. Thoughts – what a person thinks – are to be found written down in books, letters and diaries, but not in the brain of the thinker. Thoughts are expressed by human beings, but there is no such thing as a brain expressing a thought. Human beings, but not human brains, communicate thoughts, share thoughts or keep them secret. A thought is just what is expressible by an utterance or other symbolic representation – but there is no such thing as a brain uttering anything or as its employing a rule-governed symbol of any kind. The fact that we may think and keep our thoughts to ourselves does not mean that we keep our thoughts in our brain.

8. Thinking and the 'inner life'

It is because we can think, that is *reflect*, that we can have an 'inner life'. Animals who lack a language do not. They are conscious, and are conscious of features of their surroundings; they have and pursue ends; they feel pain and pleasure; but that does not suffice for an inner life. They cannot reflect upon their experience, cannot think thoughts and reflect upon them. They cannot dwell, in joy or sorrow, upon their past experiences. They cannot reason, reflect upon reasoning or weigh its conclusions. They have no imagination, and cannot fantasize, wonder about possibilities or imagine how things might have been. This is one kind of reason why we should not follow Cartesians in identifying *having a mind* with mere *consciousness* or *conscious experience*. Only if one can think thoughts and reason from what one thinks, imagine things and dwell upon what one imagines, enjoy and suffer experiences *and reflect on* one's joys and sufferings, can one be said to have a mind. Only creatures with a mind can be said to have an inner life.

The misleading picture of the 'inner'　Talk of an 'inner' life is, to be sure, a metaphor. It is a deeply misleading one. It presents us with a picture – of 'inside' and 'outside'. This picture has consequences. It encourages the idea that the 'inner' is hidden, that it is inaccessible to others and accessible only to ourselves. It reinforces our inclination to think that we have privileged access to our inner life by means of introspection. So only we ourselves really know our inner life. We may report to others what we perceive there, but they have no more than our word for it. So we may conclude, with John Stuart Mill, Gottlob Frege and many others, that the 'inner' is *the world of consciousness*. – Nothing could be more misleading.

If we think of the 'inner' thus, then we are extending the very idea of an inner life to the whole domain of consciousness – to experience in general. And that is what generation after generation of philosophers, psychologists and others have done. Doing so inclines one to conceive of pain and pleasure as something 'inner' and of the manifestations of pain and pleasure as *mere behaviour*. After all, one may reason, there is pretence. So what looks like pain-behaviour may be dissimulation. If one has gone thus far down this treacherous road, one will also be prone to suppose that thought is something 'inner', and that its expression consists of mere words – signs of something hidden 'within'. That idea is reinforced by the obvious fact that one can lie about one's thoughts. So only the thinker *really* knows what he thinks; others can at best only conjecture. For thoughts are concealed from all but the thinker.

We have dwelt sufficiently on this picture to know that it is misguided. It rests on a Cartesian conception of the mind and the body, and of the supposed relation between them. It presupposes an external relation between the mental and its behavioural manifestation. It cleaves to the cognitive assumption that the subject knows how things are with him, and knows his own thoughts, by introspection. We have given ample reason for rejecting these ideas. All talk of a person's mind is talk of his intellectual and volitional powers and their exercise; all talk of a person's body is talk of his somatic features; and powers and features do not stand in any *relation* to each other.[39] The behavioural manifestation of mental attributes is not inductively related to the possession of those attributes, nor is there here an inference to the best explanation. Rather the behaviour, in appropriate circumstances, is a logical criterion, logically good evidence, for the mental. Over the range of Cartesian *cogitationes* the subject cannot be said to know *or not to know* how things are with him – and others very often know perfectly well of his sufferings and joys, his thoughts and reflections. There is a role for utterances such as 'I

[39] See *Human Nature*, ch. 9.

know what I think' and 'I don't know what I think', but as we have seen, it is a quite different one from the epistemic role of 'I know what he thinks' and 'I don't know what he thinks'.

Of course, there is such a thing as pretending, hiding one's thoughts and feelings, lying and dissimulating. But under the baneful influence of the 'inner'/'outer' picture, we are prone to misconstrue the implications of such possibilities. First of all, pretence is not *always* possible – it makes no sense to say of the baby that it is pretending – one has to *learn* to pretend. And in some circumstances, there is no such thing as pretending – as when someone is sorely injured and screaming in pain. The possibility of deceit shows that our judgements about others are fallible. It does not show that the feelings and thoughts of others are hidden behind their behaviour as the movement of a clock is hidden behind its face. One may be deceived by dissimulation, but to be so deceived is not to think that there is something inner behind the dissimulating behaviour when in fact there is not. It is to think that the emotional behaviour of another expresses his feelings, that his statements are sincere. But the deceitful expression of feelings is shown to be deceitful by *other behaviour*, and his lies are exposed by *his sincere confession*. Of course people may lie, but when they tell the truth they are not reporting on anything hidden. One cannot say that their truthful utterance is mere words, and the thought they express is still hidden in their mind. When someone screams in agony, his pain is not hidden, but manifest. When someone laughs heartily at a joke, his amusement is not concealed.

Reasons for the appeal of the picture   Why then are we so susceptible to the misguided picture of 'inner' and 'outer'. One reason is that we conflate *not expressing* with *concealing*, and so we think of what is not expressed as hidden somewhere – and what better hiding place than the mind! — But the mind is not a place, let alone a hiding place. Not to tell another what one is thinking is not, as such, to conceal anything (just reflect on how tiresome it would be if everyone thought aloud). One's unspoken thoughts are not hidden anywhere – they are merely unexpressed (when one goes for a walk one may think a great deal, but nothing is concealed).

Another reason is that we are prone to think of behaviour as 'bare bodily movement'. But this is a residue of the mistaken Cartesian duality of mind and body, and the mistaken conception of both. Behaviour that manifests one's feelings is not bare bodily movement, but smiles of delight, cries of joy, screams of pain, gestures of love and affection, shaking with anger and trembling with fear.

A third is that we confuse the ability to say how things are with us with the ability to see how things are with us – by introspection. And what we thus suppose ourselves to see is, of course, 'inner' and hidden from the view of others. For no one else can 'introspect' my mind. — But, as we have seen, introspection is not an inner sense, but reflective thought about oneself.

The inner life   What then is it to have an 'inner life'? It is to have and exercise the power to reflect on one's experiences. It is to have and exercise the ability to think without expressing one's thoughts and to reflect on the thoughts one has. It is to be able to recollect in sorrow, joy or tranquillity. It is to be able to ruminate, daydream or meditate. It is to be able not only to have the wide-ranging and complex emotions of a language-using creature, but also to reflect upon one's feelings. It is to use one's imagination in thinking what one could or should have done, on what another might have said or done, and in imagining future possibilities. Is one's 'inner life' hidden? — Not if one reveals it to another. Nor is it *hidden* if one merely does not reveal or express it. To think whatever one thinks and not to tell anyone is not to hide anything. One hides one's thoughts only if one refuses to tell another what one is thinking, or when one writes one's diary in code, or when one lies about what one thinks. One does not *hide* one's feelings when one simply does not manifest them, but rather when one suppresses them or dissimulates.

11

Imagination

1. A cogitative faculty

Thought and imagination The faculty of imagination is a cogitative faculty rather than a cognitive one. One cannot acquire knowledge by the exercise of the imagination in the manner in which one can by the senses or by reasoning. The imagination, unlike the perceptual powers, is not a faculty for detecting and discriminating objects and their properties. Our powers of imagination enable us to think up new possibilities, to deviate from customary ways of conceiving, to explore new solutions. But to imagine things being thus-and-so, and to imagine *that* they are, unlike seeing that they are, does not imply that things are as they have been imagined to be. 'To imagine' is not a factive verb. Indeed, it is a paradigmatically intentional one. One may imagine things that do not exist (such as dragons and elves) as well as things that do, imagine doing things that are never done, and what one imagines may not be the case. But although not a cognitive faculty, imagination is, among other things, a cognition-facilitating one. Einstein held that imagination is more important than knowledge. For theoretical creativity and originality require bold leaps of imagination. On the other hand, Joubert warned that he who has imagination without learning has wings but no feet. The ability to find the right balance between

The Intellectual Powers: A Study of Human Nature, First Edition. P. M. S. Hacker.
© 2013 John Wiley & Sons, Ltd. Published 2013 by John Wiley & Sons, Ltd.

experience and knowledge derived from experience, on the one hand, and imagination in the pursuit of knowledge and understanding, on the other, is one of the intellectual virtues. Reason must control the flights of fancy in the light of experience, but with delicate touch lest it clip the wings of creativity, originality and discovery.

Great artists, scientists, and philosophers create original works of art, construct novel scientific theories and achieve new philosophical insights through the exercise of their imagination. The *creative imagination* is the power we have to think of, and to think up, new, interesting and pertinent possibilities, fruitful hypotheses and conjectures, original ways of doing and making things. But one exercises one's creative imagination in much less august ways too – in wit and humour, in the decoration of one's home, in the way one arranges flowers.

One's *imagination* may be rich or poor, powerful or weak, fertile or arid. One's *imaginings* may be vivid, lively, original and creative, or vague, fanciful, fantastic and even altogether ridiculous. One may be *imaginative* if one's creations, plans and projects display meritorious originality or if one's daydreams, make-believes and stories are lively, vivid, unusual and interesting. Conversely, one is *unimaginative* if one lacks the ability to come up with anything out of the ordinary, where something novel, amusing and lively is called for. Things that we do or create are imaginative or unimaginative to the extent that they display imagination. The mark of the mediocre is that it is unimaginative. The *imaginable* is linked to the conceivable, the *conceivable* to the possible. But it is moot whether, as Hume supposed, *imaginability* is a criterion of logical possibility. What is *imaginary* is contrasted with what is actual. But not everything that we imagine is imaginary, since we may imagine what is actually the case (as when we hopefully imagine My Love winning the 3.30, and My Love does win the 3.30). On the other hand, of course, everything imaginary is imagined. We shall examine these cognates of 'imagine'.

Imagination and mental images — In the long tradition of reflection on the imagination by philosophers, writers and artists alike, the faculty of imagination has been associated with the active power to conjure up, and the passive power to be in receipt of, *phantasmata*, *mental images*, *ideas* and *Vorstellungen*. Aristotle's discussion of the faculty of *phantasia* and of its objects *phantasmata* was an attempt to introduce the concept of a faculty intermediate between perception and thought.[1] He invoked the notion of *phantas-mata* to refer to the *appearances* with which he held we are presented in perceptual illusion, when things appear other than they are; when we have after-images, in delusion and hallucination, in recollection, in dreams; when we have hypnogogic or hypnopompic images; when we desire, hope and fear, in the pleasures of memory and expectation – conceiving of these *phantasmata* as causal traces of perceptions. It is perhaps misleading to render these terms as 'imagination' and 'image' as we understand them. Rather, his reflections (especially in *De Anima*, III. 3) are more helpfully viewed as an endeavour to mould a concept to meet an apparent need in articulating the anatomy of the mind, and in elucidating the materials of thought. In this respect, he sowed the seeds of confusion that were still flowering 2,000 years later. He anticipated Hobbes and Hume in suggesting *phantasmata* are 'a kind of weak perception' (*Rhetoric*, 1370a28), and Kant in suggesting that *phantasmata* are 'perceptions without matter' (*De Anima*, 432a10). The notorious scholastic dictum – 'Nihil est in intellectu quod non prius erat in sensu' – that was the inspiration of empiricism rested on Aristotelian confusions and a misconception about thinking. In the absence of a clear conception of a concept, this was well-nigh unavoidable. Philosophy in the modern era did not even approach this until Kant's distinction between *Anschauung* and *Begriff*, and a clear conception did not emerge until the notion of a concept was linked with that of a linguistic skill and mastery of the use of an expression.

---

[1] 'Imagination is different from either perceiving or discursive thinking, though it is not found without sensation [perception], or judgement without it. That this activity is not the same kind of thinking as judgement is obvious. For imagining lies within our power whenever we wish (e.g. we can call up a picture, as in the practice of mnemonics by the use of mental images), but in forming opinions we are not free: we cannot escape the alternative of falsehood or truth. . . . That imagination is not sense[-perception] is clear from the following considerations: Sense[-perception] is either a faculty or an activity, e.g. sight or seeing: imagination takes place in the absence of both, as, e.g. in dreams. Again, sense[-perception] is always present, imagination not. If actual imagination and actual sensation [perception] were the same, imagination would be found in all brutes: this is held not to be the case; e.g. it is not to be found in ants or bees or grubs. Again, sensations [perceivings] are always true, imaginations are for the most part false' (*De Anima*, 427b14–21, 428a5–12; the bracketed addenda are to orient the reader to the drift of thought here).

The early modern conception
The concept of the imagination was introduced into early modern philosophy by Hobbes[2] and Descartes.[3] Hobbes, reproducing Aristotle almost verbatim, called sensory and quasi-sensory appearances that one enjoys when one experiences 'images' or 'phantasms', and conceived of them as 'decaying sense' or 'weakened sense'. Descartes held that to imagine is to contemplate the figure or image of a material thing, and conceived of such images as *ideas* of the imagination that are presented to the 'eyes of the mind' (by contrast with non-sensory ideas of the intellect). Locke, Berkeley (with some reservations about 'notions') and Hume held ideas to be the raw materials of thought. Hume called the images of the imagination 'ideas', and held them to be faint copies of impressions (so, again, decaying or weakened sense). They are, it was supposed, perceived by *inner sense*. Words were held to stand for ideas, and imagination was conceived to be the kaleidoscopic combination and separation of ideas independently of judgement. Hume ascribed to the faculty of imagination the task of welding together our fleeting and discontinuous perceptions into a unitary whole that produces the systematic illusion of independent objects of perception by feigning the existence of unperceived perceptions. Kant conceived of imagination as 'intuition without the presence of an object'.[4] He allocated to the faculty of imagination the task of binding together (synthesizing) the sensible intuitions (*Anschauungen*) furnished by experience to constitute, with the aid of the understanding and its fund of concepts, perceptions of an object. We shall subject the notion of a mental image and its relation to the power of the imagination to close scrutiny.[5]

---

[2] Hobbes, *Leviathan*, chs 2–3, and *Human Nature*, ch. 3.

[3] Descartes, *Rules for the Direction of the Mind*, Rule 12 (AT X, 411ff.) and Rule 14 (AT X, 433); *Meditations*, 6 (AT VII, 72–4); *Passions of the Soul*, I, 20–6 (AT XI); and in his correspondence with Mersenne (AT III, 395).

[4] Kant, *Anthropology from a Pragmatic Point of View*, §15.

[5] I am, throughout the following discussion, especially indebted to the writings on the imagination of Wittgenstein, *Philosophical Investigations* [1953], 4th edn (Wiley-Blackwell, Oxford, 2009), §§363–97, and of Alan White, *The Language of Imagination* (Blackwell, Oxford, 1990). I have drawn freely on my previous writings on this theme in *Wittgenstein: Meaning and Mind* (Blackwell, Oxford, 1990), essay 10, and, with M. R. Bennett, *Philosophical Foundations of Neuroscience* (Blackwell, Oxford, 2003), 6.3–6.31.

2. The conceptual network of the imagination

Objects of the imagination The verb 'to imagine' is a predicate-forming operator on sentences, nominalized sentences in the form of that-clauses, gerundive nominalizations, and Wh-nominalizations. One can imagine things being so, as well as imagining that things were, are or will be so. One can imagine, as one can know and think, who, when, where and why (but not whether), as well as imagining how to do something or how something was, is or will be done. One can imagine NN or X-s, no matter whether he or they exist or not. One can imagine oneself, NN or an X, as a Y; one can imagine oneself, NN or an X V-ing, as one can imagine oneself, NN or an X at a certain time or place. More abstractly, one can imagine being . . ., doing . . ., becoming . . . or undergoing . . . This diversity must be kept in mind. It provides us with poles of description.

A multi-focal concept Although the concept of imagination was born of the concepts of appearing, appearances and being appeared to (as is evident in the relation between *phantasia*, *phantasma* and the verb *phainesthai*) and although it grew to maturity in relation to the concept of an image (as is evident in the relation between *imaginare* and *imago* (a likeness or resemblance)), it has spread its wings since those early days. The verb 'to imagine' and its cognates by now express multi-focal concepts with multiple centres of variation. Describing these will show how the various uses are connected, and also how they differ.

i. *The cogitative imagination*

Imagination is manifest in thought, conception and supposition. Imagination makes cowards of us all, as we *think* of what *might have happened* or *might happen* to those we love, or to ourselves – for imagination is the fuel of fear and anxiety. The torments of a Hamlet or an Othello are multiplied by their jealous imagination; so too Romeo's adoration of Juliet waxes as he imagines her in his arms. Forms of problem-solving that are not merely mechanical or computational are facilitated by using one's imagination – by *thinking of new possibilities* and by approaching the problem in novel ways (as in so-called lateral thinking). To imagine oneself in another's shoes involves *thinking* of oneself confronted by the situation in which the other is. To imagine how someone will respond to a given situation is to think through how, given his character, pronenesses and goals, and given what he knows about his situation, *he* will think, react and act. Hence imagination is also linked to empathy and compassion. A well-imagined plan is one that has been well *conceived*, just as a building of well-imagined construction is one the design of which has been well thought out. Ill-imagined modifications to good plans, and ill-imagined additions to well-designed buildings are *ill-conceived*. To be unable to imagine NN acting thus is to be incapable of conceiving of his doing so, given his character and personality. If something is larger, smaller, further or nearer than one had *supposed* it to be, it may well also be larger, smaller, farther or nearer than one had *imagined* it to be. One often imagines things to be impossible only to find out that they exist or have been done, even though one had supposed that no such thing could exist and that no such act could be done. Faced with difficult tasks one sometimes finds them easier to do than one had supposed or imagined. In such cases, the concepts of imagining, thinking and supposing touch tangentially or run for a while along parallel tracks.

Imagining and thinking compared   Nevertheless, to imagine is not the same as to think. To think that the prime minister should resign is not to imagine that he should resign, and to imagine the prime minister is resigning is not the same as thinking he is. To speak with thought is not necessarily to speak with imagination, and a thoughtful speech is not the same as an imaginative one. To think before one speaks is not the same as to imagine something before one speaks, and to imagine one is speaking is not to think that one is. To do something thoughtlessly is not the same as doing something unimaginatively, even though the unimaginable converges on the unthinkable. To do something without thinking is to act spontaneously, or automatically, or negligently, but it is not the same as acting without imagination, which is to act in a routine manner without exploring novel possibilities.

Imagining and conceiving compared   Nor is imagining the same as conceiving, even though there is extensive overlap. One can arguably imagine time travel (H. G. Wells did), but it is inconceivable. One can imagine the furniture awakening, talking, smiling and dancing in the night, but one cannot conceive it – at least as long as the conceivable is limited to the logically possible (see section 7 below). One may imagine when, where and why NN V-ed, but that is not to conceive when, where or why he V-ed. One may have some conception of the task that Churchill faced in 1940, but that is not the same as imagining the task he faced. For to have a conception of something is to have an array of informed beliefs about it, but to imagine something is not.

Imagining and supposing compared   Finally, although one may suppose or imagine that things are so, one may suppose things that one cannot imagine (e.g. one's best friend betraying one), as well as imagine things one cannot suppose (e.g. time travel, turning into a beetle, growing sixty feet tall). While we have a faculty of imagination, we have no faculty of supposition. Whereas one may try to imagine something, and either succeed or fail, one cannot try to suppose something and either succeed or fail – for to suppose is not to exercise an ability. One can be good or poor at imagining certain things, but not good or poor at supposing things. To suppose, but not to imagine, is a cousin of assuming or hypothesizing. That one cannot suppose something to be so is because there is no justification for such a hypothesis. That one cannot imagine something to be so is not because there is no justification.

ii. *The creative imagination*

Given the involvement of the imagination in thought, it is easy to see why we should associate this faculty with creativity – both with creative thought – theoretical and practical alike – and with artistic creativity. It is linked, via the notion of *being imaginative*, with originality. The power of intellectual insight, the ability to apprehend and capitalize on novel analogies (e.g. between hydrodynamics and electricity), to see hitherto unnoticed connections between phenomena (e.g. between distance and simultaneity), to see unity amid apparent diversity as well as diversity amid apparent unity – all these involve the creative employment of the imagination in the sciences, the arts, mathematics and philosophy. This may, but need not, involve any mental imagery. Great painters and sculptors, architects and landscape gardeners are rightly credited with outstanding visual imagination. They are able to think of new artistic possibilities and new ways of capitalizing on existing possibilities. No doubt they may visualize vividly their prospective creations and the progressive unfolding of their work. But it does not follow that before Turner painted *The Fighting Temeraire*, before Verrocchio modelled the Colleoni monument, before Wren built St Paul's or before Capability Brown laid out the grounds of Blenheim Palace, they must have spent time having vivid mental images of what these would look like. If anything, they would have sketched preliminary drawings in order to explore possibilities. But such drawings are not *copies* of mental images. The powerful imagination of great artists is to be seen in their creations, in the originality, power and beauty of what they have made – not hidden in the images that crossed their mind. We rightly credit Shakespeare, Milton and Dickens with supreme powers of dramatic, poetic and literary imagination, with abilities to envisage scenes vividly, to mould language to the needs of their art with unsurpassed skill, and to create characters of abiding interest and fascination. To be sure, the creation of great drama, fiction and poetry demands uncommon imagination, but the only imagery it *requires* is verbal. Telling a good story takes imagination, but one may make it up as one goes along, rather than rehearsing it in advance in one's imagination.

The performing arts, no less than the creative arts, involve imagination. A great performance of *Richard III*, such as Laurence Olivier's, stands out no less than a great painting for its originality and imagination. The dancing of a Nijinsky or Nureyev remains in the memory of those fortunate enough to have seen them no less than the music to which they danced. The dancers are memorable not merely for their amazing prowess, but also for the expressiveness and originality of what they did. And it is obvious that the imaginative interpretations of a Solomon, Brendel, or Menuhin give their audience new insights into the music they play. Interpretive imagination lies in the blending of outstanding skill with novel forms of expressiveness.

The creative imagination is no less exhibited in the crafts, in technology and engineering, in design and in style. On a more modest scale, but one that is important for all, one displays one's imagination in one's cooking, gardening, and in one's flower arrangements. For here too one thinks up new possibilities that are attractive, appealing and subtle. Without imagination, there would be little irony, wit or humour – which colour our lives, alleviating our travails, and strengthening our friendships.

iii. *The fabricative imagination*

It is easy to see how the ability to think up new possibilities, and the ability to create original works of art, including fictions, both literary and pictorial, should be assigned to the same faculty as what I shall call 'the fabricative imagination'. For it is but a short step from thinking up and envisaging new possibilities to *make believe* and to *making things up*. Make-believe, whether in play (as when a child pretends that the cardboard box in which he sits is a motor car) or in charades, requires imagination. Making things up converges on pretending, on the one hand, and on fabricating, on the other. These links, together with the connection between the imagined and the imaginary, makes clear the nexus between imagining and falsehood, which we shall examine shortly.

Imagining and pretending compared   Nevertheless, imagining is not pretending (contrary to what Ryle sometimes suggested).[6] Although what one can pretend may sometimes be something that one can imagine, pretending something does not imply, nor is it implied by, imagining something. To pretend to be a soldier is not to imagine that one is a soldier, and to imagine that one is a soldier is not to pretend that one is. There are connections between pretence and imagination, but there are also great differences between the respective abilities, executions and consequences.

Both pretence and imagination are linked to what is unreal or not actually so. Neither to pretend to do something nor to imagine doing something is actually to do it. An imaginary country (like the Never-Never Land) is not a real one. One cannot pretend to be what one knows one actually is any more than one can imagine one is what one knows one actually is. So too, one cannot imagine that such-and-such is the case, when one knows that it is, any more than one pretend that such-and-such is the case if one knows that it is.

For all that, pretence and imagination differ. The ability to pretend is an ability to perform, to act as if . . . ; but the ability to imagine is the ability to conceive or think up possibilities. So actually pretending is a performance – the execution of a sequence of actions; but actually imagining is thinking, not doing. The difficulties in pretending are difficulties in putting on a performance; the difficulties in imagining are difficulties in conceiving of alternative possibilities. To ask someone to pretend is to ask them to perform – so it is a prelude to action. But to ask someone to imagine is to ask them to think of alternative possibilities – so it is a prelude to thought, not to action. To ask someone why they pretended something to be so is to ask them for their motives, reasons or goals, but to ask them why they imagined something to be so is to ask them what led them to imagine thus. Confidence tricksters and malingerers pretend; artists, writers,

---

[6] G. Ryle, *The Concept of Mind* (Hutchinson, London, 1949), ch. 8.

hypochondriacs and neurotics imagine. Good storytellers are good at imagining, but may be hopeless at pretending. To be good at pretending is to have mastered the arts of make-believe and to possess the skill to deceive others into thinking that things are other than they are. To be good at imagining is to possess the skill of conceiving and thinking up things. One's pretending may be courageous, deceitful, dishonest, skilful or clumsy, convincing or hollow and easy to see through. Imagining can be none of these, but it can be vivid, original and lively. 'Don't pretend that . . . !' is commonly an order not to deceive others, whereas 'Don't imagine that . . . !' is more often an order not to deceive oneself.

Imagination and falsehood　　　The connection between imagining and make believe, and between imagining and making things up, on the one hand, and between imagining and the imaginary, on the other, and the nexus between the creative imagination and the fictitious, pave the way for the manifest connection between imagining and falsehood, between imagining and misremembering as well as misperceiving, and hence too, between imagining and illusion. 'You are only imagining things', we say when someone seems to hear a sound and thinks a burglar has broken in. The same remark does service when someone misremembers things – 'It was not so at all,' we may say, 'you are just imagining it.' We may imagine ourselves halfway to our destination when we have barely covered a quarter of the distance. Suddenly, we may think we see a figure in the bushes, only to realize on closer inspection that we were merely imagining things. We may claim to remember having done this or that (as George IV claimed to remember fighting at the battle of Waterloo), or to have heard this or that, only to be told that we are merely imagining it. But it is noteworthy that someone given to misperception or to misremembering, to perceptual illusions and to mnemonic delusions, is *not* said to be exercising his powers of *imagination*, or to have a rich *imagination*. Such propensity to false beliefs is *not* conceived to be a feature of the imagination *qua* faculty. The reason for this is that the faculty of imagination, unlike perception and memory, is not concerned with (or constrained by) literal truth and falsehood, but with invention, originality and creativity. But although the faculty of imagination is not involved in falsehood, the verb 'to imagine' has perfectly ordinary uses that pertain to misperception, misremembering and falsely believing. It is evident that the connection is forged by the fact that the imaginary and the fictitious (which we may have made up by the use of our imagination) are not real or actual, and exist 'only in the imagination'. We make up stories (fictions), in which the characters do not really exist and the events are fictitious. And so too we make up lies, make believe and pretend. What we imagine to be so, we often think to be as we imagine it, and if we are wrong, we are said to be *merely imagining* things, that is, misconceiving or falsely believing.

iv. *The perceptual imagination*

While Hume and Kant were mistaken to think that the imagination is involved in every objective perception, there are connections between the two faculties. It takes imagination to see or hear certain kinds of resemblances (e.g. of faces or smiles), forms of connectedness (e.g. between styles) or patterns of relationships among *perceptibilia*. It takes imagination to hear a piece of music as a set of variations on a theme (Bach's *Goldberg Variations*) or to hear a piece of music as an auditory picture (of a sunrise, as in Strauss's *Zarathustra*, or of an execution, as in Berlioz's *Symphonie fantastique*). So too, it takes imagination to see certain kinds of 'quotations' in a painting – such as Michelangelo's *Isaiah* in Reynolds's *Mrs Siddons as the Tragic Muse*, or to see forms in a Rorschach spot. Leonardo famously advised painters how to stimulate the pictorial imagination by perception:

> I cannot forbear to mention among these precepts a new device for study which, although it may seem but trivial and almost ludicrous, is nevertheless extremely useful in arousing the mind to various inventions. And this is, when you look at a wall spotted with various stains, or with a mixture of stones, if you have to devise some scene, you may discover a resemblance to various landscapes beautified with mountains, rivers, rocks, trees, plains, wide valleys and hills in varied arrangement; or, again, you may see battles and figures in action; or strange faces and costumes, and an endless variety of objects, which you could reduce to complete and well-drawn forms. And these appear on such walls confusedly, like the sound of bells in whose jangles you may find any name or word you choose to imagine.[7]

When we engage in such exercises of fantasy, we *see* the stain marks on the wall as hills and valleys, the cracks as winding paths or rivers, the crumbling plaster as figures in a landscape. Similarly, it takes

---

[7] Leonardo da Vinci, *Trattato della Pitture*, §508.

imagination to see the aspects of a double-aspect picture (a duck–rabbit), to see hidden figures in a puzzle picture, or human figures in a painting of a pile of fruit and vegetables (as in Arcimboldo's amusing paintings).

v. *Imagination and imagery*

From Aristotle onwards imagination has been associated with 'decayed perceptions', with 'ideas' conceived as faint copies of 'impressions', and with the thought that the power of imagination is constrained by the possibilities of kaleidoscopic rearrangement of ideas antecedently acquired in experience and stored in memory. The link between the phrase 'mental image' and 'imagination' proved a pitfall. For it became irresistible to associate the faculty of imagination with the mental-image-making faculty. But there is no essential link between the two. Some artists and thinkers may find that conjuring up images in their imagination facilitates creativity, and assists them in thinking up new possibilities. Others may not. One would not fault a Shakespeare's or a Tolstoy's imagination if one were to find a note in the diary of either remarking that his powers to conjure up mental images is woefully weak. Equally, the power to conjure up vivid mental images does not imply a powerful imagination. It may betoken no more than a good visual and auditory memory for past scenes and sounds. The association of mental imagery with the faculty of imagination is an unfortunate historical accident which has lumbered us with confused and confusing terminology here. For the faculty of the imagination is not the same faculty as the faculty of mental-image-making – mental images are *logically* inessential for imagining even though they may be heuristically essential, and they are no less (loosely) linked to memory than to the imagination (see chapter 9). It takes no imagination to talk to oneself in the imagination, any more than it takes imagination to talk. It takes no more imagination to conjure up an image of something seen, than it takes to see the object one saw. To have rich eidetic powers is different from, and logically independent of, having a rich imagination. We shall examine the nature of mental images below.

The network of concepts of the imagination is represented in figure 11.1. It should be evident that the core notion that unifies many of the different centres of variation is that of thinking of possibilities, of possible actions and of possible features. Other foci are linked to the thought of possibilities in various more or less tenuous ways.

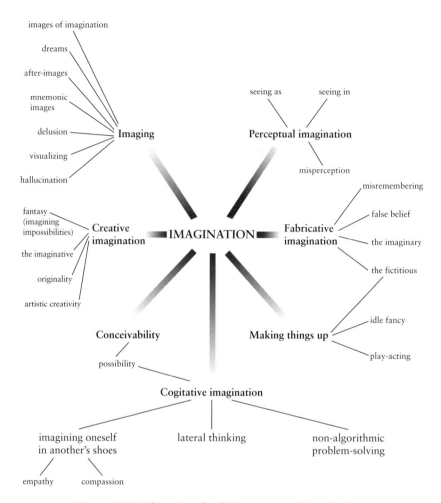

images of imagination
dreams
after-images
mnemonic
images
delusion ———
visualizing
hallucination

Imaging

seeing as   seeing in

Perceptual imagination

misperception

misremembering

false belief

fantasy
(imagining
impossibilities)
the imaginative
originality
artistic creativity

**Creative
imagination**   ◼IMAGINATION◼   **Fabricative
imagination**

the imaginary

the fictitious

idle fancy

Conceivability   **Making things up**

possibility

play-acting

Cogitative imagination

imagining oneself
in another's shoes

lateral thinking

non-algorithmic
problem-solving

empathy   compassion

Figure 11.1 *The network of the concept of imagination*

3. Perceiving and imagining

The majority of philosophers until the middle of the twentieth century supposed the faculty of imagination to be essentially bound up with mental images. Consequently, they laboured to distinguish between perceiving, which they thought to be a reception of images (ideas or impressions) caused by objects, and imagining, which they thought of as the kaleidoscopic production of images drawn from a stored reservoir. Conceiving of such images as 'decayed sense', they also puzzled over the relationship between images of the imagination and images of memory, typically taking the former to be fainter than the latter. Burdened with these misconceptions, they also drew the boundaries of the imagination erroneously, restricting the imagination to the fanciful production of mental images.

Reasons for linking imagination and imagery

There were various reasons for these misguided conceptions. First, as noted, etymology deceptively links *phainesthai* with *phantasmata*, *imaginare* with *imago*, *imagination* with *image*. Secondly, a link between the imagination and pictures or images is embedded in the forms of our discourse about imagining, what we imagine and the imaginary. We speak of picturing things to ourselves, of having, making and conjuring up images in our imagination. We refer to an accurate portrait of someone as his 'spitting image', to paintings and prints as 'images' and to sculptures as 'graven images'. We speak of the vividness and vivacity of our imagination, as we speak of the vividness and vivacity of a picture. Thirdly, there is a similar lexical association between images and perception. We speak of 'visualizing' things in our imagination, of 'seeing things in our mind's eye' and of 'hearing' a tune in our imagination. Fourthly, we misconstrue the link between names of perceptual qualities and the samples by reference to which they are ostensively defined. For we take the defining samples to be mental images (ideas) rather than objects (such as a sheet of colour samples or a metre rule). We then multiply confusion by supposing that the meanings of names of perceptual qualities are *ideas* stored in memory. We then take such ideas to be *simple* (because not lexically defined), and conceive of them as the raw material for all thought and imagination. Accordingly we are inclined to think that the limits of the imagination are determined by the range of possible combinations of simple ideas, for simple ideas themselves cannot be produced by the mind, but must be *given* in experience.

Some of these are traps laid for us by our language. But the major pitfall is one we have dug for ourselves. For it lies in the conception that we naturally cleave to when we reflect on the nature and limits of experience, thought, memory and imagination. Perception, we suppose, is the reception of sense-impressions, memory the retention of copies of impressions in the form of vivid ideas, thinking an operation of combining and separating ideas preparatory for judgement, and imagination the unconstrained combination of faint ideas. To imagine something, we are inclined to suppose, is to conjure up a fanciful image or picture, which is perceived by 'inner sense'. But this is confused. There are connections between perception and imagination, but imagining something perceptible is not at all like perceiving something. Let us first examine the connections and the differences.

Eidetic powers   Most of us are susceptible to having mental images when we remember things we have seen. We all have, to a greater or lesser extent, the power to *produce* mental images – both visual and auditory. We can picture *visibilia* to ourselves, we can talk to ourselves (or to others) in our imagination, and we all find tunes or snatches of songs 'running through our head'. So it is not surprising that the language we use in speaking of mental images, both visual and auditory, is permeated with perceptual idiom. When we imagine people, landscapes, artefacts, animals and states of affairs or events associated with them, as well as sounds and things making them, it is obvious that the perceptual vocabulary serves to describe not only what we perceive and the attributes of what we perceive, but also what we imagine when we imagine *perceptibilia*. So it only makes sense to say of a creature that it imagines the colour, sound, smell, taste and tactile qualities of an object if the creature *can* (or *could*) perceive such qualities. It is not a mere empirical matter that those blind or deaf from birth cannot imagine coloured things or sounds. It is noteworthy that if one sees a red rose, one sees something red; by contrast, if one has a mental image of a red rose, one's mental image is not red. This should be no more surprising than the evident truth that if one has 'a visual experience' of a red object, the experience one has is not red.

It is true that what can be perceived can intelligibly be said to be imagined, and can also be imagined as being perceived. It is also true that the same description can be used to describe what one perceives and to describe what one imagines. Nevertheless, the common forms of words are used very differently. The activity of describing what one perceives is *categorially*, not *specifically*, different from the activity of describing what one imagines. What it makes sense to say when describing what is perceived (e.g. 'Are you sure?', 'Did you look again?', 'Did anyone else see it?', 'Might you not have made a mistake?', 'Could you not have got closer?') makes no sense to say when describing what is imagined. We must distinguish the phenomena of perceiving from the phenomena of imagining and the concepts of perceiving from the concepts of imagining.

Phenomena of imagining and of perceiving compared The differences between the phenomena of perceiving and the phenomena of imagining are marked by the differences between the criteria that warrant saying of another that he perceives something, on the one hand, and the criteria for saying of another that he is imagining something, on the other. I shall take vision as a working example. The faculty of vision is exercised by the use of one's eyes in appropriate conditions of visibility. Someone who can see can find his way around his environment by using his eyes; he can follow moving objects with his eyes. He can also watch, observe and scrutinize. He can look for, look at, look under and look up things, as well as glance, gaze or stare at things. One can observe someone *trying* to see, or trying to see *better* – by screwing up his eyes, by moving closer to get a better view, by turning on the light or moving the object into the light. Someone who sees commonly responds to what he sees in characteristic ways – in surprise or amazement, with delight and pleasure, with fear and trepidation. He may act in response to what he sees by trying to get or to avoid, by touching or recoiling, by displaying interest or curiosity. By contrast, someone who imagines something may do so in the dark no less than in the light, and may do so by staring blankly into space or by closing his eyes. One does not observe or watch one's mental images when one visually imagines something, nor does one 'look at them' more closely, although one may imagine seeing what one imagines from closer to. The criteria for whether someone is imagining something are more akin to the criteria for thinking something than they are for perceiving something. What a person imagines and how he imagines it is visible neither to himself nor to others, unless he displays it in drawing or mime. There are no 'imaginability conditions', parallel to visibility conditions. The criteria for what someone imagines are what he sincerely says he imagines, what he draws or enacts in explaining what or how he imagines.

Concepts of imagining and of perceiving compared The concepts of perception and the concepts of the visual imagination are equally distinct. What it makes sense to say of seeing and of what is seen is altogether different from what it makes sense to say of imagining and of what one visually imagines. One can *overlook* features of what one sees, *notice* things one had not seen before, *become conscious* of things one had not noticed. By contrast, one cannot overlook, notice or fail to notice a feature of what one visually imagines. After all, one does not *see* what one visually imagines. One can imagine overlooking something, but not overlook something one imagines. What would it be for there to *be* an object (e.g. a full milk bottle) in one's mental image that one did not notice? (Could it be because one imagined it standing in front of a white door?[8]) One can find out how things are by looking, watching and observing. Imagining, however, is not a way of finding out how things are, even though things may indeed be as one imagined them to be, and imagination may help one find out how things are. One cannot ask someone to stop seeing what is before him, only to stop looking. By contrast, one can ask someone to stop imagining or daydreaming about things and get on with his work. One may be surprised or amazed at what one sees. But one cannot be surprised at what one imagines, although others may be. One may be dazzled by what one sees, or be deafened by what one hears. One can imagine dazzling or deafening objects, and one can imagine being dazzled or deafened by them. But one cannot be dazzled or deafened by what one imagines, no matter how dazzling or deafening one imagines things to be. One cannot see something differently from how it visually appears to one, but one can imagine something to be different from how it visually appears to one – for what one sees are actualities, whereas what one imagines are possibilities that may or may not be actual.

Differences between 'Look!' and 'Imagine!' All this should be obvious from reflection on the different ways in which one might teach someone to obey the order 'Look!' and to obey the order 'Imagine!'. The circumstances in which one might teach the one as opposed to the other are quite different. The first instruction belongs with such activities as finding out, observing, noting observable features, and is associated with learning to spot things, to make fine visual discriminations, to discern and detect. But the instruction 'Imagine . . . !' belongs to thinking of possibilities, of how things would be if . . . or how things would look or sound if . . . 'I can't see . . .' is altogether different from 'I can't imagine . . .', and the explanation for why one cannot see this or that despite looking as hard as one can is altogether different from the explanation of why one cannot imagine this or that (see below, p. 433).

---

[8] See A. R. Luria, *The Mind of the Mnemonist* (Penguin, Harmondsworth, 1968). His mnemonist patient explained a failure of memory in precisely this way, which Luria did not challenge. The case is discussed briefly in *Wittgenstein: Meaning and Mind*, part 1: *Essays*, p. 192 n. 6.

4. Perceptions and 'imaginations': clarity and vivacity of mental imagery

'Imaginations' is not an internal accusative of 'imagine' in the manner in which 'thoughts' and 'dreams' are the internal accusatives of 'think' and 'dream' respectively. The closest we get in English to an internal accusative is 'image': the images of the imagination. But of course, what one imagines is *not* usually an image. One *can* imagine an image, as when an artist visualizes the picture he wants to paint or the image he wants to engrave. But, in general, what one imagines is not an image. If one *has* an image when one imagines whatever one imagines, then *what* one imagines is what one's image *is an image of*. Lack of clarity here is the source of much confusion, not only in philosophy, but also in experimental psychology.

Galton's questionnaire It is very striking that Francis Galton, pioneer of the psychological questionnaire, instructed his audience as follows:

> Before addressing yourself to any of the Questions on the opposite page, think of some definite object – suppose it is your breakfast table as you sat down to it this morning – and consider carefully the picture that rises before your mind's eye.
>
> 1. *Illumination* – Is the image dim or fairly clear? Is its brightness comparable to that of the actual scene?
> 2. *Definition* – Are all the objects pretty well defined at the same time, or is the place of sharpest definition at any one moment more contracted than it is in a real scene?
> 3. *Colouring* – Are the colours of . . . whatever may have been on the table quite distinct and natural?[9]

Galton's report on the responses to his questionnaire were equally interesting:

> *Many men and a yet larger number of women, and many boys and girls, declared that they habitually saw mental imagery and that it was perfectly distinct to them and full of colour . . . They described their imagery in minute detail, and they spoke in a tone of surprise at my*

[9] F. Galton, *Inquiries into Human Faculty*, quoted by James, *The Principles of Psychology* (Holt, New York, 1890), vol. 2, ch. 18, pp. 51ff.

apparent hesitation in accepting what they said. I felt that I myself should have spoken exactly the same as they did if I had been describing a scene that lay before my eyes, in broad daylight, to a blind man who persisted in doubting the reality of vision.[10]

The moral of the tale is that, confronted by conceptually confused questions, people are likely to give confused answers. Before commencing on any such research as Galton's, one must be clear what is meant by 'mental image' or 'image in the imagination'. One must further clarify what it is for a mental image to be clear and vivid, or dim and faint, what it is for an object imagined to be well or ill defined, and what it is for the colours of an imagined scene to be distinct and natural.

Clarity in imagining   The superficial grammatical similarities between seeing and imagining derail us before we have even started moving. It is true that we may perceive something clearly and distinctly – when the air is clear, the light strong and the shadows sharp. It is also true that there is such a thing as clarity and unclarity in imagining. A theatre director, who imagines clearly the stage-set he wants, may say, when he sees the set 'That's exactly how I imagined it!' or 'That is just what I wanted'. Or he may tell his stage designer to repaint the trees in the set: 'I imagined them darker green than this', he might say. By contrast, someone who did not imagine the scene vividly or even clearly will hesitate in judging whether the effect is right. 'Is that what you meant?', his stage designer may ask, and he may reply, 'I'm not sure; let's try a bit less blue and see what it looks like.'

Vividness and vivacity   If a philosopher says that mental images are less vivid and vivacious than sense-impressions, the most he can intelligibly mean is that for most of us it is easier to discern detail in what one sees than to imagine in detail what one imagines. So too, it is, for most of us, easier to describe in detail what we see than to elaborate in detail what we imagine. To be sure, to describe how one imagines something is not to describe one's mental images of the thing. It is to describe the thing *as one imagines it*. Just as painting what one imagines is not to copy an inner picture onto a canvas, so too to describe how one imagines something is not to read off a description from an inner picture. This requires further explanation.

[10] Ibid.

Hume and Galton conceived of the 'lesser vivacity' of mental images as opposed to visual impressions as a datum (like 'Well, colour photos just do fade!'). This, of course, invites the question of what it would be like if one's mental images were very vivid indeed. Would one then mistake them for visual impressions or hallucinations? If one were to imagine very vividly a red expanse with green dots on it, would this stop one from seeing what is before one's eyes, as a strong after-image may? This is confused, since mental images are not, so to speak, 'in the same space' as sense-impressions, after-images and hallucinations. The question of whether one ever confuses the images of the imagination with sense-perceptions makes no more sense than the question of whether one ever confuses the weight of one's obligations with the weight of one's shopping bag. So if someone remarks that his mental images are much less vivid than his sense-perceptions, one cannot ask whether they are so much less vivid that one hardly notices them. For one does not notice or fail to notice one's mental images any more than one notices or fails to notice one's intentions. That the images of the imagination or of memory are less vivid than perceptions does not mean that they are less noticeable, like faint stains on one's shirt after laundering, as opposed to vivid ones before the wash.

Forms of vividness   One confusion here is over the meaning of the word 'vivid' in these contexts. *What one sees* may be vivid, as when one sees a red rose against dark green foliage, or when one sees someone vividly silhouetted against the sunset. One may indeed gain a vivid, that is, striking, memorable, *impression* of what one sees or looks at. But one does not see what one sees *vividly*; rather, one sees it *clearly and distinctly* (if it is vivid in the strong sunlight and clear air), or *dimly and indistinctly* (at dusk). What seems to be the lesser vivacity of one's mental images as opposed to the vividness of one's perceptions is not a phenomenological datum, as Hume and Galton supposed. It is a grammatical one. The vividness or faintness of the images of the imagination does not lie on the same scale as the clarity or indistinctness of a visual impression. One's mental image of A may be much more vivid than one's mental image of B, and one person may be able to visualize something much more vividly than another. But one's mental images (as opposed to one's hallucinations) can no more literally be more vivid than one's visual impressions than a negative attitude can be more negative than a negative integer.

Vividness of mental images So what does the vivacity or vividness of mental images amount to? The vividness of one's mental images, whether of the imagination or of the memory, is more akin to the vividness of a description than to the vividness of a sunrise. One could no more confuse the vividness of a mental image with the vividness of something perceived than one could confuse the vividness of what one perceives with the vividness of a description of what one perceives.

The vividness of the imagination Some things are said to be vivid if they are full of life; others, such as feelings, are said to be vivid if they are strongly felt. Utterances are vivid if they are strongly or warmly expressed; and recollections are vivid if their description is clear and detailed. Colour and light are vivid if they are bright, fresh and lively, and coloured things are said to be vivid if their colour is brilliant. A description, report or history is said to be vivid if it presents whatever it presents in a lively, clear, detailed and striking manner. Mental images cannot be said to be lively or vivacious in the sense in which what they are images of may be. Hence they cannot intelligibly be compared with visual impressions for vivacity at all. Rather whether one imagines something vividly turns primarily on one's ability to describe or represent (in acting, painting or sound) what one imagines and how one imagines it. The criterion for the vividness of one's imagination is the sharpness of the detail in which one can describe or otherwise express what one imagines. The more vividly one imagines something, the better one can describe it or paint what one imagined, or the better one can play (or identify someone as playing) a piece of music as one imagined it. The vividness of a Tolstoy's imagination is to be seen in the richness and details of his descriptions of the battle of Borodino, of the desperation of Anna or of the death of Ivan Ilyich. It is not hidden from all in the recesses of his mind – it is evident to all in his fiction. *There is no such thing* as mistaking an image of the imagination with a sense-impression. It is not that mental images are less vivid than sense-impressions, and *that is why we do not mistake imaginings for perceivings.* Rather, there is no such thing as mistaking a mental image for a sense-impression, and it is generally easier to read off a detailed description of what one sees than to think up and describe possibilities in detail. That is one reason why we are inclined to say that mental images are less vivacious or vivid than sense-impressions.

There is a very modest scrap of truth behind this venerable confusion. Sometimes we do not know whether we are perceiving something or only imagining that we are ('I am not sure whether I can see a man among the trees or whether I am just imagining it', one may say, squinting into the distance in the twilight). But here 'just imagining it' is not an exercise of the imagination at all – it is a matter of misperception. What I am unsure of is whether I can actually see a man in the distance or whether it only visually seems to me that there is a man there. But one can no more mistake imagining for seeing than one can mistake drawing for seeing or inventing for discerning.

5. Mental images and imagining

The mental image is not a picture

Mental pictures or images are not 'just like physical pictures or images', only mental. These are not two coordinate species of a single genus. They are categorially distinct. One sees pictures or images, but one cannot see – it makes no sense to speak of seeing – one's mental images. One can hold up a representational picture or image and compare it for verisimilitude to what it is a picture of. But one cannot (it makes no sense to) juxtapose one's mental image of something with the thing itself and compare it with its object for verisimilitude. For one cannot see one's mental image at all. Nor indeed can one even *have* a mental image of the object that one is concurrently perceiving (see below), which one might think to use for purposes of comparison. Of course, one can compare an object one sees with how one *imagined* it to be, but the method of comparison is quite different from the method of comparison of a picture with what it depicts. This requires elucidation.

Can one imagine what one is looking at?

One can paint what one sees, but one cannot now have a mental image of what one currently sees. Why not? The impossibility is akin to the impossibility of having a vivid mnemonic image of what one is currently looking at. To remember what the Houses of Parliament look like is to know now what they look like because one previously knew, and has not forgotten, what they look like – since one looked at them. To have a mnemonic image of what they look like is one form which remembering what they look like may take. But if one looks at Charles Barry's great building *now*, one knows how it looks *because one can see it* – not because one can remember what it looks like.

Similarly, one can say that something is exactly how one imagined it to be, but that judgement *cannot* rest on comparing one's mental image with what one sees. One cannot see one's mental images – one *has* them; one does not *see* them. One cannot visually compare something one (logically) cannot see, viz. a mental image, with something one can see. One cannot juxtapose a mental image with what it is an image of for purposes of comparison – not because it is too difficult, but because there is no such thing as such a juxtaposition. Finally, one cannot have a vivid mental image of, or visualize, what one is looking at. That would be akin to seeing how something looks and simultaneously trying to think (imagine) how it looks. There is no such thing.

Can one copy one's mental image? One can copy a painting, but one cannot copy one's mental image. A copy *reproduces* its original. But 'to reproduce one's mental image of the Houses of Parliament', if it means anything, means to imagine or visualize the Houses of Parliament again. One can paint 'from one's imagination', as opposed to *plein-air* painting (but not copying) of the visible scene. One can paint historical scenes as one imagines them to have been; one can paint imaginary mythological scenes and allegorical paintings, and genre pictures of imagined scenes. But to draw from one's imagination is not to copy or depict one's mental image. The artist depicts what he imagines (e.g. the death of Actaeon), but he does not depict his mental images. A sketch of how one imagined something is not a drawing of one's mental image, and it cannot be said to *resemble* the visual image one might have had when one drew it – for it makes no sense to say that one's mental image looks like the sketch, or that the sketch looks like one's mental image. For mental images don't look! The sketch represents what one imagined, and it may represent it well or poorly, just as one's *words* do, when one describes what one imagined. But the sketch does not represent one's mental images. Nor do one's mental images *represent* what one imagines. Just as thoughts are not representations (see pp. 80–2, 389f.), so too mental images are not representations – and for the very same reasons. Thoughts are all message and no medium, and so are mental images. They have no non-representational properties (such as brushstrokes, canvas (board or panel), paint (tempera, oil or watercolour), colour of the pencil or ink) in virtue of which they can be perceived to be representations. And, of course, they cannot be perceived any more than thoughts can be perceived.

Drawing what This has non-trivial consequences. If one draws a
one imagines picture to represent what one imagines, as a director
might do to illustrate how he imagines the stage-set,
one does not judge the adequacy of one's drawing by comparing it
with one's mental image. Rather it is judged adequate or inadequate
as one judges one's words to be an adequate or inadequate expression
of one's thoughts. One imagines whatever one imagines, and says that
this sketch is indeed how one imagined things, or that it is not quite
right and only approximates what one had in mind. How does one
know whether it is right or not, if one does not compare the sketch
with the 'inner picture' of the imagination? Well, one does not *know*
(and nor does one fail to know). One *says* so, and what one sincerely
says is decisive.

Because perceptual concepts and concepts of perceptual qualities
play such a significant role in our descriptions of what we imagine
and how we imagine things to be, we are inclined to exaggerate the
affinity between imagination and perception, and to overlook the
manner and extent to which imagination is suffused with thought.
This can be brought to light by consideration of the following examples of the perceptual imagination. When a composer conducting at
a rehearsal tells his orchestra that he had imagined *that* chord being
played louder, that is not because it sounded louder in his imagination, any more than if one thought or expected that an explosion
would be louder than it was, there was something louder in one's
thought or expectation. When a choreographer tells his dancers that
he had imagined a particular *pas de deux* much faster than they
danced it, that does not mean that they danced more quickly in his
imagination. Failure to appreciate this has led to dire confusions in
experimental psychology.[11]

Mental images Mental images may play a role in imagining things.
and imagining They may be heuristically necessary for some creative
thinkers, just as they are heuristically necessary for
some mnemonists. But they are neither logically necessary nor sufficient for imagining anything. One may have a vivid image of something one has seen – as when one vividly remembers it and can picture
it to oneself. But this is an exercise of memory rather than of
the imagination. One may have seen something horrific, and find

---

[11] See Bennett and Hacker, *Philosophical Foundations of Neuroscience*,
6.3–6.31.

that one cannot banish the image of the horror from one's mind. But this is involuntarily remembering what things looked like, not imagining anything. Conversely, one may imagine Jack going up the hill with Jill without visualizing them. So even what *can* be visualized *need not* be visualized in order to be imagined. As we have noted, one would not condemn a great artist for having a poor imagination, on the grounds that he was a poor visualizer. Furthermore, there is much that can be imagined which cannot in principle be visualized, such as a fall in the rate of inflation next year, an increase in one's duties and obligations or improvements to the legal system. One can imagine reasons for doing something, why Jack did something, what he is thinking and where he is going. One can imagine arguments, objections and difficulties. One can imagine that all, some or no As are Bs. The horizon of the imagination is far wider than the horizon of possible mental images one may have before one's mind's eye.

6. Imagination and the will

Many philosophers have been struck by the fact that our perceptual impressions (as opposed to our perceptual activities, such as looking, watching, gazing or observing) are not subject to the will. One cannot order someone to see something, but only to look at something or to try to spot something. One cannot tell someone to stop seeing what he sees, only to stop looking at it, or tell someone to stop hearing what he hears, but only to stop listening to it. By contrast, one can tell someone to imagine something, try to imagine something oneself or decide to imagine something. One can stop imagining how pleasant it will be when one goes on holiday, and banish the mental images of long sandy beaches from one's mind. This has led philosophers to claim that the imagination is subject to the will. This is true, but may be misleading. For sometimes one cannot help imagining the fulfilment of one's fondest dreams when one is full of hope, or imagining the realization of one's worst fears, when it looks as if all is lost. Mental images sometimes beset us against our will, recur obsessively and preoccupy us. One may struggle against them, try to banish them from one's mind, but then one can hardly deem them voluntary. So the relation between imagination and the will needs clarifying if we are to detect what truth lies behind the claim that imagination is subject to the will.

The voluntariness of imaging and of thinking

The voluntariness of imagining is similar to the voluntariness of thinking – and this displays the kinship of the concepts of thought and imagination. For just as one can imagine things at will, or decide to stop imagining something and get on with one's work, so too one can think of and about things at will, or decide to stop thinking of something and get on with doing. But equally, just as there are occasions on which one cannot help imagining certain things (the dreadful things that may be happening to a friend in great danger) so too there are occasions when one cannot help obsessively thinking about something. And just as some things are unthinkable, although not because of one's cogitative limitations, so too there are things that are unimaginable, although not due to the weakness of one's imagination.

The voluntariness of imagining and of acting

The voluntariness of imagining is both like and unlike the voluntariness of acting. It is like the voluntariness of acting in this sense: that what is meant by saying that they are voluntary is that it *makes sense* to say that something was done voluntarily, as it *makes sense* to say that something was imagined voluntarily. But of course we sometimes act involuntarily or non-voluntarily, just as we sometimes imagine something involuntarily. One the other hand, the voluntariness of imagining something is unlike the voluntariness of a voluntary action, such as moving one's arm. Whether one has moved one's arm may be evident to others no less than to oneself. But whether one has imagined something is determined by one's sincere word. Similarly, the voluntariness of imagining something is unlike the voluntariness of looking, observing or listening to something. For while I can look, watch or observe at will, what I see or hear *depends on what is going on*. But when I voluntarily imagine something, *what I imagine is up to me*. For imagining is not a way of finding out how things are, whereas perceiving is. Furthermore, when I voluntarily imagine someone, something or something's happening, the identity of *what* I am imagining is also up to me. What it is that I imagine is what I mean to imagine.

The kinship between imagining and depicting

Imagining, in respect of its intentionality, is more akin to depicting than to perceiving. One does not imagine whoever 'resembles' one's mental image, but rather one imagines whoever one intends to imagine, even though one may imagine him wrongly. There is here a parallel with depiction. Caravaggio painted David holding the head of Goliath. The features of the decapitated head of the Philistine resemble the features of Caravaggio himself. Nevertheless, it is not a painting of David holding the head of Caravaggio. On the other hand, there is also this difference between imagining and depicting: if one were to try to paint a portrait of A from memory, and inadvertently painted a good likeness of B, one could not say that the portrait was a poor portrait of A. Rather, one would say that one meant to paint a portrait of A, and found oneself painting a likeness of B. By contrast, if one imagines what A looks like, and inadvertently visualizes him as having the features of B, still, the person one was imagining was A. The mental image one has conjured up is an image of A, wrongly imagined to look like B. Further, a linear picture, for example ⬡ may represent various things: a closed box, a wire form, three flat quadrilaterals and so on. But one's mental image of a closed box is an image of a closed box, and of nothing else. Mental images, unlike drawings or paintings, cannot have alternative aspects. They are, as we noted above, all message and no medium.

So, the mental images one may have when one is voluntarily imagining something are images of whatever they are images of *by intention*, not *by resemblance*. That is one reason why one cannot read off what one is imagining from one's mental image. One might say that one's mental image *illustrates* the intentional object of one's imagining as a picture in a storybook illustrates the story – and although that can be misleading, there is some truth to it.

7. The imaginable, the conceivable and the possible

Philosophers have long flirted with the idea that the imagination provides the key to what is logically possible. For it has often been suggested (e.g. by Hume) that the criterion for what is logically possible is that it be *imagined*: "Tis an establish'd maxim in metaphysics, *That whatever the mind clearly and distinctly conceives includes the idea of possible existence*, or in other words, *that nothing we imagine is absolutely impossible*.'[12] And it has also been held (e.g. by Hume) that the criterion for whether something is logically possible is that it be *imaginable*: 'We can form the idea of a golden mountain, and from thence conclude that such a mountain may actually exist. We can form no idea of a mountain without a valley, and therefore may regard it as impossible.'[13] Presumably the criterion for whether

[12] Hume, *A Treatise of Human Nature*, I. ii. 2.

[13] Ibid.

something is imaginable was supposed to be that one have imagined it. The waters were muddied by lack of clarity about the relation between what can be pictured in the mind's eye and what can be imagined, and between what can be imagined and what can be conceived.

We have already seen that the fact that one cannot picture something to oneself does not mean that one cannot imagine it. For we can imagine innumerable things of which it makes no sense to suppose that they might be pictured or visualized, and there are many things which *can* be visualized, but can be imagined without being visualized. The question we shall now address is the relationship between imaginability and logical possibility.

The limits of the logically possible and of the imaginable

It seems that the domain of the imaginable far outreaches the domain of the logically possible. Novelists have imagined time-travel, and told entertaining stories about it. They have imagined disembodied beings, such as ghosts and the spirits of the dead, and thrilled their readers with their tales. Priests and prophets have imagined gods with protean powers who retain their identity throughout change of form (as Zeus became a bull, a swan or a shower of gold for procreative purposes), not to mention imagining the omniscient, omni-benevolent and omnipotent disembodied God of monotheism who exists 'outside' space and time, yet intervenes in the spatio-temporal causal order. Tellers of fairy tales have imagined the kettle calling the pot black, dolls coming to life and dancing, plants or trees talking to each other and cows jumping over the moon. *Through the Looking Glass, and What Alice Found There* is an imaginative masterpiece of philosophical wit precisely because it is not limited by what is strictly conceivable and thinkable. In this sense, the imagination – put to the purposes of religion, mythology, fairy tales and fantasy fiction – is unconstrained by logical possibility. It suffices that it capture the fancy, is awesome, wondrous and powerful, or entertaining, amusing, witty and clever. In great works of religion, mythology, fairy tales and fantasy, the predicaments, aspirations, hopes, and fears of mankind are laid bare with power and poignancy precisely by means of the transgressions of the limits of intelligibility.

Can one imagine what is logically impossible?

To this one might object. How can one imagine something logically impossible? A logical impossibility, as noted, is not a possibility that is impossible. A logically impossible object (e.g. a disembodied mind) is not an object the possibility of which is excluded by logic or 'metaphysics'. Rather, a form of words invoked in saying what one imagines seems to signify a possible object but does not. Such a description, 'a disembodied mind', is in fact a meaningless form of words (as are 'transparent white glass', 'travelling back (or forward) in time', 'metempsychosis'). Slightly differently, a picture that expresses what one imagines may seem to represent a possibility, but does not actually do so (e.g. an Escher staircase or water-cascade). Rather, it transgresses the rules of perspectival representation, and a description of what it seems to represent makes no sense. Is it not then evident that one cannot imagine something that is logically impossible, for there is nothing to imagine? — Yes and no. To imagine a logical impossibility is not to imagine a possibility. The description of what one imagines involves a form of words that makes no sense. So what seems to be a description is not one at all. But we are entertained and charmed, in fiction (Lewis Carroll, Edward Lear, Anstey, Wells), tales and mythologies, by the misleading verbal appearances, just as we are visually entertained by Escher's wonderful etchings of 'logically impossible' buildings, and by Steinberg's wonderful cartoons, for example, of a drawing of a hand drawing itself. To produce such entertaining nonsense (which, to be sure, not all of us realize to be nonsense) takes great imagination. Even more strikingly, in *great* mythology (Homer, the Norse sagas), fairy tales (the Grimms) and fiction that transgress the limits of intelligibility (Kafka's *Metamorphosis*) the suspension of the constraints of intelligibility allows the free flight of the imagination, which, in the hands of genius, illuminates the human condition. But it is evident nevertheless that the imaginable, in this sense, is not a criterion for what is logically possible. And imaginability is not a sufficient condition of possibility.

The limits of the imaginable   If the bounds of sense are not the limits of the imaginable, what are the constraints on imaginability? For we do have a use for such phrases as 'It is unimaginable that such-and-such would happen', 'I can't imagine him doing that', 'You cannot even begin to imagine . . .' and 'I can't imagine what it must be like to . . .'. Inability to imagine may (i) amount to limitations of one's ability to think of possibilities – here imaginability converges on conceivability; (ii) indicate inconceivability relative to what is known (see below); or (iii) indicate the limitations of words and thought to capture the character of certain experiences – as when we say 'You cannot imagine the glories of the Sistine Chapel ceiling – you have to see it for yourself', or 'The suffering in concentration camps was unimaginable'.

The conceivable   How then do things stand with respect to conceivability? How is the imaginable related to the conceivable, and how is the conceivable related to the possible? We are surely strongly inclined to suppose that whatever is possible is conceivable. For the limits of logic (in the customary generous sense of the word) are the limits of sense. Anything that makes sense can be conceived, and anything that can be conceived makes sense. Furthermore, what is logically impossible is inconceivable – it cannot *coherently* be thought out. We do not want to countenance the intelligibility of *conceiving* of something that is logically impossible, that is, the description of which makes no sense. At most, in such cases, we may *think* that we can conceive it – but an impossibility proof may show us that we could not really do so (e.g. squaring a circle, or trisecting an angle with a compass and rule).

We must take care here. Conceivability displays three further forms of relativity: conceptual, cognitive and personal. First, conceivability operates within available logical space (including the 'space' of mathematics). Logical space – the range of the logically possible – is determined by our conceptual scheme, which changes over time. The expansion of mathematics *is* an expansion of logical space. A new mathematical proof expands the range of the intelligible, and with it the range of the conceivable, just as an impossibility proof limits the range of the conceivable. Similarly, the invention of new kinds of number, for example signed (and hence negative) integers, expands the grammar of number and renders intelligible signs and forms of words that antecedently lacked sense. So there is nothing surprising, let alone awry, in saying that conceptual forms available to us would have been inconceivable to Greek mathematicians.

What of empirical facts? Surely, we know a multitude of facts that were not merely unknown to the Greeks, but were both unimaginable and inconceivable – such as the existence of superconductors, of black holes, of nuclear fission. We *can* conceive of them, and even imagine possibilities related to them (e.g. room-temperature superconductors). How can this be, given that we are not concerned with expanding logical or conceptual space, but with brute facts? Laws of nature that we teach to schoolchildren would have been inconceivable to the ancient world. Nevertheless, they are conceivable, and schoolchildren today can conceive of them. All that amounts to is the fact that the expression of such laws of nature requires theoretical concepts unavailable to the ancients (such as mass, gravity, electricity, conductivity, electrical resistance).

Secondly, conceivability is also constrained by what we already know. Hence the conceivable is often limited by the requirement of consistency with what is known. So it may, quite rightly, be said to be inconceivable that there be giants (they would not be able to move or even to stand) or that there be creatures like angels as we depict them (to be able to fly they would need a sternum protruding three feet). To conceive of such beings would require us to imagine the laws of nature 'abrogated' for their benefit – and that makes no sense. We can imagine angels and paint them, and imagine them flying. But we cannot conceive of such creatures consistently with the known laws of nature.

Thirdly, there is a patent use of the vocabulary of conceivability and imaginability, and their negations, that is relative to a given person. Someone may find something both inconceivable and unimaginable that others may readily conceive and imagine. Caesar found it *inconceivable* that Brutus should murder him. Hence 'Et tu, Brute!' – 'How could you!'. Caesar could not *imagine* Brutus acting thus. It was unthinkable *for him*, inconsistent with *his conception* of Brutus. It was not a possibility *he* could entertain. But others, such as the conspirators, not to mention Brutus, could and did.[14]

---

[14] For detailed examination of the dialectic of the imagination, see M. R. Bennett and P. M. S. Hacker, *Philosophical Foundations of Neuroscience*, ch. 6, where conceptual confusions in empirical psychology and cognitive neuroscience concerning mental images and the imagination are identified and diagnosed. For examination of the dialectic of the imagination in the eighteenth and nineteenth century, see my *Wittgenstein: Meaning and Mind*, essay 10. For criticism of Kant's doctrine of the threefold synthesis of the imagination (which anticipates and runs parallel to contemporary neuroscientific discussions of the so-called binding problem), see 'Kant's Transcendental Deduction: a Wittgensteinian Critique', repr. in P. M. S. Hacker, *Wittgenstein: Comparisons and Context* (Clarendon Press, Oxford, 2013).

Appendix:
Philosophical Analysis and the Way of Words

1. On method

The empirical study of human nature is the task of the human sciences. Philosophical investigation does not compete with these – any more than mathematics competes with physics. Mathematics – *inter alia*, concept formation by means of proof – provides conceptual tools for science. Philosophy – *inter alia*, concept elucidation by means of grammatical investigation – is a conceptual critic of science when it transgresses the bounds of sense.[1] Philosophical anthropology is concerned with the network of concepts in terms of which we conceive of ourselves and of the faculties that constitute our nature, and with the forms in which we render ourselves intelligible to ourselves. Its task is to describe the network and to disentangle the knots we tie in it.

There are no such things as rational beings that cannot know things, do not harbour beliefs, are not capable of thinking and forming intentions, cannot reason, and that do not think and act for

---

[1] Of course, mathematics does not supply conceptual tools *only* for science, but also for daily life and reasoning. Similarly, the domain of critical philosophy stretches much further than the realm of science and scientific reasoning. Moreover, there is more to *practical philosophy* (to use Kantian terminology) than just conceptual analysis and conceptual criticism. However, philosophical anthropology (like philosophy of psychology and epistemology which have been our concern in this book) belongs to *theoretical philosophy*.

The Intellectual Powers: A Study of Human Nature, First Edition. P. M. S. Hacker.
© 2013 John Wiley & Sons, Ltd. Published 2013 by John Wiley & Sons, Ltd.

reasons. Rationality, the power of reason and sensitivity to reasons, is a fundamental feature of human nature. We pursue knowledge, form beliefs, engage in thought and give reasons for our thoughts, feelings and actions. We understand ourselves in terms of what we know and believe, what we think and how we reason, what reasons we have for our feelings and for our decisions, intentions and actions. The quotidian employment of these *non-theoretical* concepts in mundane discourse is partly constitutive of our nature as rational beings. To investigate them is to investigate our nature.

Conceptual analysis: definitions de re and de dicto

The methods that have been used in this study are the methods of conceptual analysis and clarification. One form of analysis is definitional. It is characterized by the pursuit of analytic definitions that specify necessary and sufficient conditions for something's being so. Analytic definitions have been taken in two ways: either as *real definitions* (*definitio rei*) of things, or as *nominal definitions* (*definitio nominis*) of words. Socratic questions such as 'What is justice?' or 'What is knowledge?' were meant to elicit real definitions that would disclose the objective and language-independent essence of justice or knowledge. Real definitions were often conceived as a form of ontological decomposition of things (in thought) into component elements. Taken *de dicto*, definitional analysis is one form of conceptual analysis. Analytic definitions in terms of necessary and sufficient conditions for something's being so were taken to decompose concepts into their simpler conceptual elements.

It is doubtful whether the traditional notion of real definition is sustainable.[2] Be that as it may, it is patent that not all words can be explained by analytic definition. Some are to be explained by different forms of definition (e.g. contextual, ostensive), and yet others are not defined at all, but explained in other ways (e.g. by a series of examples that are to be taken as the expression of a rule, or by contrastive paraphrase). Even when analytic definitions can be given, they rarely resolve the conceptual problems that beset us in philosophy. For the problems of philosophy rarely arise through lack of *definitions*. A definition of 'pain' would not resolve our bewilderment over how we can ascribe pain to others. A set-theoretic definition of number does not resolve our puzzlement over the nature of arithmetical propositions. A large part of philosophy is aporetic and dialectic (in the Kantian sense). What is necessary to resolve or dissolve an aporia or

[2] It was successively and successfully criticized by Hobbes, Locke, Reid and Mill.

to lay bare the logic of illusion is very often *an overview* of the conceptual landscape in which the problematic concept is located. For, as Wittgenstein showed us, once we have an overview, we can plot the multitudinous paths leading off in all directions from the concept under investigation. Then we can see how the confusions arise.

Connective analysis The felicitous term 'connective analysis' was introduced by Peter Strawson to signify a 'more realistic and fertile' model for philosophical investigation than definitional, decompositional analysis. It is one form that conceptual analysis may take:

> Let us imagine . . . the model of an elaborate network, a system, of connected items, concepts, such that the function of each item, each concept, could, from a philosophical point of view, be properly understood only by grasping its connections with the others, its place in the system – perhaps better still, the picture of interlocking systems of such a kind.[3]

Connective analysis, thus conceived, gives us a surveyable representation of the logico-grammatical terrain and of the conceptual landscape. Connective analysis can be done in the *linguistic mode*, or in the *conceptual mode*. These are, for the most part, equivalent. Connective analysis in the linguistic mode clarifies a problematic concept by locating *the word or phrase that expresses it* as a node in the web of words, describing its pertinent grammatical features and its logico-grammatical connections with related expressions in the network, as well as its differences from those with which it is liable to be confounded. Or, *presupposing the relevant grammar*, connective analysis in the conceptual mode may locate *the concept* in the network of concepts, and describe its conceptual and logical connections with related concepts, as well as its differences.

Aristotle: the Way of Words and connective analysis There is nothing new about the Way of Words, or indeed about connective analysis. Indeed, these methods are brilliantly exemplified in Aristotle's writings. For example, he wrote:

> We use the word 'to perceive' in two ways, for we say that what has the power to hear or see, 'sees' or 'hears', even though it is at the

[3] P. F. Strawson, *Analysis and Metaphysics* (Oxford University Press, Oxford, 1992), p. 19. The text of these lectures dates from 1968.

moment asleep, and also that what is actually seeing or hearing, 'sees' or 'hears'. Hence 'sense' too must have two meanings, sense potential and sense actual. Similarly, 'to be sentient' means either to have a certain power, or to manifest a certain activity. (*De Anima*, 417*a*10)

Here Aristotle is engaged in conceptual analysis in the linguistic mode. He is pursuing the Way of Words and explicitly drawing fundamental conceptual distinctions by calling to mind and examining familiar uses of words. He is describing part of the web of words in which 'to perceive' is embedded. Consider the following remark:

Yet to say that it is the *psuchē* which is angry is as if we were to say that it is the psuchē that weaves or builds a house. It is doubtless better to avoid saying that the psuchē pities and thinks, and rather to say that it is the man who does this with his *psuchē*.[4] (*De Anima*, 408^b11–14)

This is an exemplary fragment of connective and comparative analysis in the linguistic mode. In the last remark in the *Categories*, Aristotle wrote:

Having is spoken of in a number of ways: having as a state and condition or some other quality (we are said to have knowledge and virtue); or as a quantity, like the height someone may have (he is said to have the height of five feet or six feet); or as things on the body, like a cloak or a tunic; or as on a part, like a ring on a hand; or as in a container, as with the measure of wheat or the jar of wine (for the jar is said to have wine, and the measure wheat, so these are said to have as in a container); or as a possession (for we are said to have a house and a field). One is also said to have a wife, and a wife a husband, but this seems a very strange way of 'having', since by 'having a wife' we signify nothing other than that he is married to her. Some further ways of having might perhaps come to light, but we have made a pretty complete enumeration of those commonly spoken of. (*Categories*, 15^b18–32)

This is a piece of *exploratory* connective analysis that in effect describes the possessive *form of representation* by which we misleadingly present so many logically diverse categories of things. It is preparatory to possible critical analysis (which Aristotle did not carry

---

[4] As one does things with one's talents.

through) of the apparent 'ownership' of the experiences we *have* (which no more 'belong' to us than does our spouse), or of the seeming 'ownership' of the bodies we *have* (which are not among our possessions).[5] In his objections to the Socratic/Platonic quest for the essence of things (definitional analysis), for the common features that make something virtuous, Aristotle intimated the need for connective analysis that does not consist of analytic definitions. He wrote:

> those who say generally that excellence consists in a good disposition of the soul, or in doing rightly, or the like, only deceive themselves. Far better than such definitions is their mode of speaking, who, like Gorgias, enumerate the excellences. (*Politics*, 1260ª27)

Explanation by reference to examples, which makes clear their manifold connections as well as their differences, is often the correct way to obtain an overview of a problematic concept and therewith of the nature of what it subsumes.[6]

The Way of Words among the early moderns

Although Aristotle's methods are one of the two main inspirations and guidelines for these investigations of human nature, it should be obvious that one need not go back as far as Aristotle and his great medieval followers to find philosophers engaged, more or less self-consciously, in the Way of Words. Among early modern philosophers, Hobbes, for example, wrote:

> There are two things necessarily implied in this word knowledge; the one is truth, the other evidence; for what is not true can never be known. For let a man say he knoweth a thing never so well, if the same shall afterwards appear to be false, he is driven to a confession, that

[5] That we do not *own* our body, despite the fact that we can sell it, was argued in *Human Nature*, ch. 8.

[6] It is interesting to compare Aristotle's remark with Wittgenstein's general comment on the Socratic/Platonic method in the *Blue Book*: 'The idea that in order to get clear about the meaning of a general term one had to find the common element in all its applications has shackled philosophical investigation; for it has not only led to no result, but also made the philosopher dismiss as irrelevant the concrete cases, which alone could have helped him to understand the usage of the general term' (*The Blue and Brown Books* (Blackwell, Oxford, 1958), pp. 19f.).

For a careful examination of the issue, see Oswald Hanfling, *Philosophy and Ordinary Language: the Bent and Genius of Our Tongue* (Routledge, London, 2000), chs 1–4.

it was not knowledge but opinion. Likewise, if the truth be not evident, though a man holdeth it, yet is his knowledge of it no more than theirs that hold the contrary.[7]

Of course, that he is here speaking about words does not mean that he is not *also* speaking about knowledge. Among philosophers of the Enlightenment, Thomas Reid too engages in conceptual analysis in the linguistic mode, and often in connective analysis. To give but one example, he wrote:

> I may *conceive* or *imagine* a mountain of gold, or a winged horse; but no man says that he perceives such a creature of the imagination. Thus *perception* is distinguished from *conception* or imagination. Secondly, Perception is applied only to external objects, not to those that are in the mind itself. When I am pained, I do not say that I perceive pain, but that I feel it, or that I am conscious of it. Thus perception is distinguished from *consciousness*. Thirdly, The immediate object of perception must be something present, and not what is past. We may remember what is past, but do not perceive it.[8]

He too is speaking about what we do or do not say, but, of course, *also* about perception, conception, imagination, and consciousness. Bentham, another Enlightenment figure, is at his most brilliant when he engages in conceptual analysis of actions, intentions and motives, a small fragment of which is exemplified by the following passage:

> By a voluntary act is meant sometimes, any act, in the performance of which the will has had any concern at all; in this sense it is synonymous to *intentional*: sometimes such acts only, in the production of which the will has been determined by motives not of a painful nature; in this sense it is synonymous to unconstrained, or *uncoerced*; sometimes such acts only, in the production of which the will has been determined by motives, which, whether of the pleasurable or painful kind, occurred to a man himself, without being suggested by anybody else: in this sense it is synonymous to *spontaneous*. The sense of the word involuntary does not correspond completely to that of the word voluntary.

[7] T. Hobbes, *Human Nature* [1640] (Oxford University Press, Oxford, 1994), ch. 6, para. 2.

[8] Reid, *Essays on the Intellectual Powers of Man* [1785] (Edinburgh University Press, Edinburgh, 2002), pp. 22f.

Involuntary is used in opposition to intentional; and to unconstrained: but not to spontaneous.[9]

Here the nature of voluntariness and involuntariness is investigated by nice differentiation of the use of words and their complicated connections with other words.

One could readily adduce further examples of conceptual analysis in the linguistic mode from numerous different philosophers in the early modern era, as well as examples of connective analysis in the modern era, when these forms of non-decompositional analysis were developed and cultivated.

Two reasons for doubting the Way of Words

Despite the familiarity of the Way of Words, scepticism about it persisted. Such scepticism took two primary forms. One was the widespread and perfectly correct thought that language is philosophically misleading. How then could the analysis of linguistic usage be the high road to conceptual clarity? The second was the thought that natural languages fail to mirror the nature of things. But what we are ultimately interested in *is* the nature of things! So it is *this* that we should be investigating. For the nature of things is surely independent of the forms of natural languages, the logical adequacy of which is to be judged precisely by the extent to which they mirror the nature of the things they describe.

The deceptiveness of words

Recognition of the logically and ontologically deceptive character of words and forms of words is as old as philosophy. A sharpened awareness of the misleading character of words lay at the roots of philosophy in the early modern era, in Bacon's discussion of the Idols of the Market-place:

> But the *Idols of the Market-place* are the most troublesome of all: idols which have crept into the understanding through the alliances of words and names. For men believe that their reason governs words; but it is also true that words react on the understanding; and it is this that has rendered philosophy and the sciences sophistical and inactive. Now words, being commonly framed and applied according to the capacity of the vulgar, follow those lines of division which are most obvious to the vulgar understanding. And whenever an understanding of greater acuteness or a more diligent observation would alter those lines to suit the true divisions of nature, words stand in the way and resist change.

---

[9] Bentham, *Introduction to Principles of Morals and Legislation* [1789], ch. 7 note a.

Whence it comes to pass that the high and formal discussions of learned men end oftentimes in disputes about words and names.[10]

The Way of Ideas This critical attitude towards natural languages led some philosophers to recommend that when engaged in philosophical reflection, we should dispense with words altogether in order to focus on the ideas they represent. Berkeley (like Locke before him) recommended the new Way of Ideas:

> [I]t must be owned that most parts of knowledge have been strangely perplexed and darkened by the abuse of words, and the general ways of speech wherein they are delivered. Since, therefore, words are so apt to impose on the understanding, whatever ideas I consider, I shall endeavour to take them bare and naked into my view, keeping out of my thoughts, so far as I am able, those names which long and constant use hath so strictly united them.[11]

Idealism in general, and linguistic idealism in particular, were inimical to the judicious examination of linguistic usage in order to clarify problematic concepts and thereby to shed light upon the nature of things. The Way of Ideas dominated philosophical thought until the mid nineteenth century. But when its dominance waned, the venerable Way of Words was not reinstated. Rather, avant-garde philosophers, informed by developments in mathematical logic, turned to the Way of Logical Calculi.

The Way of Logical Calculi In middle of the nineteenth century, there was a vigorous revival of the study of formal logic, informed for the first time by mathematics. Logical algebra (developed by Boole, Jevons, Venn, Schroeder and Huntington) was succeeded by function-theoretic logic (invented by Frege and Russell). Frege considered his new logic to be a *logically perfect language*. Far from having recourse to ideas in order to clarify the nature of things, Frege advocated translating sentences of natural language into his concept-script, which he held to mirror the *logical* nature of thought

---

[10] Bacon, *Novum Organum*, lix.

[11] Berkeley, *Treatise concerning the Principles of Human Knowledge*, 2nd edn, 1734, Introduction, para. xxi. It is amusing to note that in the first edition (1710), Berkeley drafted the concluding sentence of the paragraph thus: 'Since, therefore, words are so apt to impose on the understanding, I am resolved in my inquiries to make as little use of them as possible.'

and of things. He wrote: 'It is the business of the logician to conduct an unceasing struggle against psychology and those parts of language and grammar which fail to give untrammelled expression to what is logical.'[12] The logician must try to liberate us from the fetters of language. The task of the philosopher is to break the power of the word over the human mind, to free thought 'from that which only the nature of the linguistic means of expression attaches to it'.[13] So:

> It cannot be the task of logic to investigate language and determine what is contained in a linguistic expression. Someone who wants to learn logic from language is like an adult who wants to learn how to think from a child. When men created language they were at a stage of childish pictorial thinking. Languages are not made so as to match logic's ruler.[14]

A logically perfect language, such his concept-script, will, Frege claimed, avoid the pitfalls and inadequacies of natural languages.

Philosophically speaking, words and forms of words are indeed often deceptive. Words with logically similar roles sometimes look deceptively different (e.g. 'the . . .', as employed in a singular definite description, and 'there is one and only one . . . such that . . .'), and words with logically different roles sometimes look deceptively similar (e.g. 'I have a pain' and 'I have a pin'). We are commonly mesmerized by form to the exclusion of attention to use. But this means that we should pay *more*, not *less*, attention to words, to their deceptive grammatical forms, and above all to their uses. Clarification of the *logical grammar* of expressions, close attention to their *topography* in the semantic landscape, is the only way to combat their conceptually misleading features and to shed light on the concept they express and on the nature of what they signify. The Way of Words is the highway to conceptual clarity. Contrary to venerable tradition, there is (as we have seen) no such thing as thinking ideas and then translating the ideas into words. Contrary to the modern logical tradition, a concept-script is not a logically perfect language. Nor is it the depth-grammar of human languages. Translating sentences of natural lan-

---

[12] Frege, *Posthumous Writings* (Blackwell, Oxford, 1979), pp. 6f.

[13] Frege, *Begriffschrift* (L. Nebert, Halle, 1879), Preface.

[14] Frege, *Philosophical and Mathematical Writings* (Blackwell, Oxford, 1980), pp. 67f.

guage into a conceptual notation, such as the predicate calculus or the notation of modal logic, *brings us no closer to the nature of things.*[15]

The Way of Words and the nature of things

The second source of persistent resistance to the Way of Words was the perfectly correct thought that we are concerned with clarifying the nature of things, coupled with the incorrect thought that what we deem the nature of things is independent of the forms in which we describe things. Philosophical investigations into the nature of things and natural scientific investigations into the nature of things are altogether different. Philosophers do not make meticulous observations or conduct ingenious experiments with complex apparatus. They do not form hypotheses that are then confirmed or infirmed by experience. They do not discover laws of nature. They do not discover empirical truths by means of inductive, let alone probabilistic, reasoning. They aim to disclose necessary truths that hold not just in this world, but in all possible worlds. With blinkered eyes, it is all too easy to jump to the conclusion that physicists (i.e. natural scientists) investigate the contingencies of the world, and meta-physicists (i.e. philosophers) investigate the necessities of the world – the adamantine scaffolding of all possible worlds. To suppose this is to confuse the scaffolding *from which we describe the world* with the shadow the scaffolding *casts upon the world*. The world has no 'scaffolding', and what looks like scaffolding belongs to our means of representation. Conceptual analysis aims to achieve conceptual truths, not empirical ones. Conceptual truths are norms of representation. They characterize our conceptual scheme. What seem to be *de re* necessities are at best no more than misleading expressions of norms of description and rules of inference.[16]

[15] It is interesting to find the great physicist Werner Heisenberg writing: 'We know that any understanding must be based finally upon the natural language because it is only there that we can be certain to touch reality, and hence we must be sceptical about any scepticism with regard to this natural language and its essential concepts. Therefore, we may use these concepts as they have been used at all times. In this way modern physics has perhaps opened the door to a wider outlook on the relation between the human mind and reality' (*Physics and Philosophy* (Penguin, Harmondsworth, 1989), pp. 189f.).

[16] This will be briefly explained below. It was discussed at greater length in *Human Nature*, pp. 7–10. For a comprehensive discussion, see G. P. Baker and P. M. S. Hacker, *Wittgenstein: Rules, Grammar, and Necessity*, 2nd, rev. edn (Wiley-Blackwell, Oxford, 2009), in the essay entitled 'Grammar and Necessity', pp. 241–370.

Conceptual and connective analysis are conducted

The linguistic and   in the *linguistic mode* when one explicitly describes
conceptual modes   the relevant features of the use of the word or phrase
that expresses the problematic concept. It is conducted in the *conceptual mode*, when one takes for granted the logical grammar of the
term expressing the concept, and articulates connections of compatibility or incompatibility, implication or independence, between concepts. It is conducted in the *anankastic* (necessitarian) *mode* when
one characterizes objects and attributes in the form of descriptions
of *de re* necessities. In fact, as was argued in *Human Nature: the
Categorial Framework*, such anankastic descriptions are actually
expressions of norms of representation.

In practice, conceptual analysis is typically conducted in mixed
mode. This is only to be expected. In the course of this book, we
have been concerned with clarifying the *a priori* nature of knowledge
and belief, of sensation and perception, of thought and imagination.
But the *a priori* nature of things *is determined* by our norms of representation – the meaning-determining rules for the use of the words
signifying things. So alternating between the linguistic, conceptual
and anankastic mode makes no difference, as long as one is clear
about what one is doing.

The linguistic turn in the twentieth century heralded

The uses of words   a long period of methodological reflection, spear-
and the natures   headed by Wittgenstein. This brought conceptual
of things   analysis to self-conscious maturity, and brought
connective analysis into clear view. What became clear is that analysis
in the linguistic mode is the underlying template for analysis in the
conceptual mode; the analysis of concepts can in turn be cast in
the form of descriptions of natures and essences. Philosophical investigation into the nature of things is not meta-physics, let alone meta-
chemistry, but a conceptual investigation.[17] It also became clear why

[17] What Strawson, in the Preface to *Individuals*, misleadingly called 'descriptive
metaphysics' is actually no more than connective analysis of the most general categorial concepts we have. What he called 'revisionary metaphysics', as he later admitted,
'in fact always involves paradox and perplexities . . . and sometimes involves no
rudimentary vision, but merely rudimentary mistakes' ('Analysis, Science and Metaphysics', repr. in R. Rorty (ed.), *The Linguistic Turn* (University of Chicago Press,
Chicago, 1967), p. 318). However, if one is inclined to adopt the Strawsonian nomenclature, then of course the investigations conducted in this book *are* (in part) descriptive metaphysics, i.e. investigations into some of the most general concepts in terms
of which we think of ourselves.

describing the uses of the words, the contexts and purposes of their use, and the presuppositions of their use is itself to analyse the concepts expressed by those words. Apropos investigating the essential nature of imagination, Wittgenstein wrote:

> One ought to ask, not what images are or what goes on when one imagines something, but how the word 'imagination' is used. But that does not mean that I want to talk only about words. For the question of what imagination essentially is [*der Frage nach dem Wesen der Vorstellung*], is as much about the word 'imagination' as my question . . . The first question also asks for the clarification of a word; but it makes us expect a wrong kind of answer.[18]

This is of capital importance. We cannot capture imagination (or consciousness, or knowledge) in a philosophical butterfly net, transfix it with a pin, and then scrutinize it under a magnifying glass. We possess the concept of imagination (otherwise we would not be asking questions about the nature of the imagination). To possess the concept is to be able to use a word or phrase that expresses it. We know how to use the word, but we lack an overview (a surveyable representation) of its use. In the case of the general cognitive and cogitative concepts that have been our concern in this book, the difficulty in attaining an overview is exacerbated by the inappropriate pursuit of definitional analysis (nicely exemplified in the case of the concepts of knowledge and belief), and by failure to realize the structural complexity, irregularity, context sensitivity and purpose relativity of these concepts. In such cases, the only way to attain a surveyable representation is by the methods of connective analysis. So, in the case of imagination, to give an overview of the many-faceted use of the word 'imagination' *is* to give a connective analysis of the concept it expresses. To give a connective analysis of the concept of imagination *is* to clarify the *a priori* nature of what it signifies.[19]

---

[18] Wittgenstein, *Philosophical Investigations* [1953], 4th edn (Wiley-Blackwell, Oxford, 2009), §370. The phrase 'der Frage nach dem Wesen der Vorstellung' is equally properly translated as 'the question of the nature of the imagination'. The above translation is determined by the sequel in *Investigations*, §373.

[19] Of course, it *does not follow* that one's logico-grammatical remarks characterizing the nature of something are analytic, in the classical Fregean sense of being true in virtue of explicit definitions and the laws of logic. There is nothing analytic about the categorial observation that knowledge is not a mental state, or that it is akin to

The network of words The metaphor of a *network* is of great utility in grasping the character of connective analysis. The logical relationships enjoyed by such widely ramifying concepts, their connections with more or less closely related concepts, their mutual implications or mutual independence, constitute a network – a web of interwoven techniques of using words. To fall into conceptual confusion is to be caught in that web. The more one struggles, the more entangled one becomes. The 'Analytic' of connective analysis consists in describing the nodes of the web and in tracing the connecting threads between various nodes. The 'Dialectic' consists in unravelling the tangles in the web that one has tied by one's struggles. As we have seen throughout this book, many of the concepts that concern us in the cognitive and cogitative domain are not definable, or not usefully definable, by analytic definition. They are not 'focal concepts' on the Aristotelian model of *healthy*, nor yet family resemblance concepts on the Wittgensteinian model of *game*. Rather, they are *multi-focal* concepts, with a number of different, but closely connected, centres of variation. But we should note that a centre of variation need not have the structure that is exemplified by 'healthy'. It may be a focused scatter of points on a graph rather than a scatter of points with a focus.

Logical geography The metaphor of *logical geography*, introduced by both Wittgenstein and Ryle, is equally useful to illuminate the logical character of the investigation. The concepts at the centre of this study of human nature are familiar to us all. They are not technical concepts of the advanced natural sciences or of mathematics. They are not theoretical concepts. They are partly constitu-

---

an ability. Nor is there anything analytic about the grammatical observation that there is no such thing as rotating a mental image in mental space. Nevertheless, these are *a priori* conceptual truths (see *Human Nature*, pp. 17–21, for discussion of the irrelevance of the issue of analyticity to our investigations). Are they 'true in virtue of meanings' (the familiar Vienna Circle characterization of analyticity)? No, that too is confused. They are not 'true *in virtue of meanings*', but rather are *constitutive of meanings* – which should not be surprising, since as we have seen, they are *norms of representation*, expressions of rules for the use of their constituent terms. (They may be compared with 'It is true that the chess king moves one square at a time'. This is not a 'true rule of chess' (rules are not true or false), but a true statement or expression of a rule of chess. It is not 'true in virtue of the meaning of "chess king"', but constitutive of its meaning.) For comprehensive defence of this conception, see Baker and Hacker, *Wittgenstein: Rules, Grammar and Necessity*, pp. 241–370.

tive of our form of life. As mature language users, we are masters of the techniques of using these expressions. We no more need to conduct social surveys of the ways in which 'know', 'believe', 'perceive', 'think', 'imagine' are used than a chess-master needs to conduct social surveys of the moves of chess-pieces, or a mathematician needs to ask the man on the Clapham omnibus to tell him the multiplication tables. Mastery of the use of a word is exhibited in using it correctly, in giving an appropriate contextual explanation of what one means by it in an utterance and in explaining what it means in the context of the utterances of others that one understands – for these manifestations of linguistic competence are severally criteria of understanding. But to have mastered the use of a word does not mean that one can give a synoptic description of its use, any more than it means that one can give an analytic definition of the word. Nor does it mean that one can give a *comparative analysis* – describing its kinships and differences with related expressions in the same conceptual field. But it is precisely this that we need when we lose our way. We need a map of the conceptual landscape that will show us how to find our way around. We need to call to mind the familiar uses of the words that lie at the heart of our confusions and unclarities, to plot their complex logical relationships, and to note their position in their grammatical environment.

In this book I have pursued three main goals. The first was to satisfy a craving for an overview of a large and important segment of our conceptual scheme. For philosophers, there is an intrinsic interest in the way our fundamental cognitive and cogitative concepts hang together. To achieve such an overview and to map the landscape accurately is to attain a deeper understanding of ourselves and of the forms in terms of which we conceive of ourselves. The second, complementary, aim was to further the project of this trilogy – namely to present a comprehensive philosophical anthropology. To clarify our cognitive and cogitative powers *is* to characterize part of our nature as rational beings. The third aim was to help others to find their way around the conceptual landscape, so that they may avoid the quicksands and marshes into which the incautious traveller may sink.

In his *Remarks on the Philosophy of Psychology*, Wittgenstein wrote:

> In order to know your way about an environment, you don't merely need to be acquainted with the right path from one district to another;

you need also to know where you'd get if you took the wrong turning. This shows how similar our considerations are to traveling in a
landscape with a view to constructing a map. And it is not impossible
that such a map will sometime get constructed for the regions we are
moving in.[20]

My purpose has been to construct such a map for the region that is
the concern of this book. With respect to each of the concepts examined, I have endeavoured to map the terrain by plotting its salient
logico-grammatical features. In so doing, I have made use of insights
and observations of many of philosophers who traversed this forbidding landscape in the past century.

The Way of Intuitions   As the tides of conceptual analysis in philosophy ebbed
in the late twentieth century, conceptual insights were
forgotten and conceptual distinctions passed out of the
collective philosophical mind. To be sure, the Way of Ideas was not
revived. The Way of Calculi continued to enjoy some favour, but it
was gradually displaced by the new Way of Intuitions. Philosophers
began to advocate the method of consulting their 'intuitions'. Holding
that the task of philosophy is theory construction, and realizing that
their theories are not confirmable or infirmable by experiments, it
was held that if a theory squares with as many of one's intuitions as
possible, that constitutes at least partial confirmation. I shall make a
few observations on this misconception below.

Regress and loss of hard-won insights are not a novel phenomenon
in the history of philosophy: it happened to the philosophy of
Aristotle, first in antiquity and then again in the Renaissance. It happened to the logico-grammatical achievements of the medievals with
the rise of early modern philosophy. It would be unfortunate if the
achievements of analytic philosophers of the modern era, who applied
the methods of connective analysis, were to slip from sight in this
manner. The loss of conceptual insight and of indispensable instruments for philosophical understanding would be substantial. This is
already evident in current misunderstandings and misconceptions
concerning consciousness and self-consciousness that we examined in
chapter 1.

---

[20] Wittgenstein, *Remarks on the Philosophy of Psychology* (Blackwell, Oxford, 1980), vol. 1, §303.

Philosophy contributes to human understanding rather than adding to human knowledge.[21] One cannot transmit such understanding as one can knowledge. Each generation must achieve it for itself. Nevertheless, distinctions can be drawn, conceptual kinships and differences noted. These are of long-lasting value for philosophy – as long-lasting as the concepts and as the conceptual puzzles and problems they generate. In this book, I have tried to amass a large number and wide variety of such distinctions in the domain of epistemic concepts, and to show how they can be brought to bear upon a wide range of philosophical problems. I hope thereby not only to have resolved or dissolved a variety of philosophical problems, but also to have contributed to removing the need for each generation of philosophers to reinvent conceptual wheels.

Conceptual maps Conceptual cartography is as challenging as physical and marine cartography was. Moreover, there are no precision instruments to aid one. One can rely only on one's competence as a mature language-user (aided by the reminders of the *Oxford English Dictionary* and by the etymology and history of words it provides), on the reach of one's linguistic imagination, on the distinctions drawn by great philosophers of the past and on one's nose for nonsense – for transgressions of the bounds of sense. To be sure, as Wittgenstein remarked, it is easier to smell a rat than to catch one. Merely smelling nonsense is of no use – for we need to know the source of the nonsense that besets us. Otherwise, we cannot eradicate it. Hence the aporetic investigations and the examination of the dialectic of reason (the logic of illusion) in many of the chapters of this volume.

It would be more than surprising if I have made no mistakes – incorrectly located a creek, mistakenly plotted the course of a river and perhaps missed a dangerous crevasse. Nevertheless, such errors should not be thought to invalidate the maps I have drawn. They merely show that here and there the maps need correction and supplementation. However, it might be thought that I have drawn the wrong kind of maps – physical maps rather than road maps, or road

---

[21] This is, of course, an epigram, which requires qualification and explanation. I have elaborated in 'Philosophy: a Contribution Not to Human Knowledge but to Human Understanding', in Anthony O'Hear (ed.), *Conceptions of Philosophy* (Royal Institute of Philosophy Lectures Suppl. 65; Cambridge University Press, Cambridge, 2010), pp. 129–54.

maps instead of weather maps. Or it might be thought that the whole enterprise is misconceived – either because one *cannot* draw such maps, or because they are *worthless* for philosophical purposes. I confronted some such criticisms in *Human Nature: the Categorial Framework*, chapter 1. I address them afresh in the next section.

2. Methodological objections and misunderstandings

Not words but things! The most common current misunderstanding of connective analysis is represented by the indignant exclamation 'But this is just about *words*! We don't want to know about *words* – we want to know about the essential nature of *things*!'. This objection has already been answered: to describe the logical grammar of an expression *is* to characterize the concept it expresses, and to give such a conceptual analysis *is* to describe the nature of what is signified. I shall not recapitulate, but merely give an illustrative example. To note that one cannot intelligibly issue an order 'Be conscious of . . . !' (but only 'Attend to . . . !'), to remind ourselves that one can say 'For as long as I was conscious of . . .' but not 'For as long as I was being conscious of . . .', to remark that one cannot intelligibly say 'I was conscious of his anger, but I didn't know that he was angry' or 'I was conscious of his anger, but he wasn't angry' is to begin to survey the logical grammar of 'to be conscious of something'. To do so *is* to take the first steps in characterizing the concept of consciousness. For the linguistic description shows that to become conscious of something is not a voluntary act or activity that can intelligibly be ordered. It shows that the concept of transitive consciousness is both factive and cognitive, and it shows that it signifies a form of cognitive receptivity, that is, that the knowledge constituted by being conscious of something is given one, rather than achieved. But to take these steps in the connective analysis of consciousness *is* to characterize the nature of consciousness. For it is part of the nature of consciousness that one cannot be conscious of something mistakenly, and that one cannot voluntarily, intentionally and deliberately become or be conscious of something. The nature of something (that has a nature) consists of those attributes without which the thing would not be what it is. Describing the logical grammar of 'consciousness', providing a connective analysis of the concept it expresses and clarifying it's *a priori* nature are three moments in the same philosophical investigation. The first is patently prior to the other two, precisely because to possess a concept is to have mastered the technique for the use of a word or phrase that expresses it. The nature of something consists in those features without which it would not be the thing it is, and without which it would not fall under the concept that it does. Hence to clarify a concept is to clarify the nature of what falls under it.

Five objections to the Way of Words   The confused idea that conceptual analysis conducted in the linguistic mode is no more than a trivial investigation into common usage (and so just an inflated form of lexicography) is made more enticing by further mistaken objections to the *mode* of the investigation. I shall briefly address the following ones, all of which are to be found in current writings of professional philosophers.

- Although a philosopher engaged in linguistic analysis purports to describe usage, all that he actually does is record his linguistic intuitions. But why should his intuitions be authoritative?
- Although linguistic analysis purports to describe usage, all it does is present some academic sociolect, such as that of an Oxbridge Senior Common Room. To present usage responsibly, one has to conduct social surveys.
- If one is describing linguistic usage, one is confined to some particular language, such as English. Usage in other languages is usually different. Philosophy is not interested in the use of English words, but in concepts – and concepts are not words.
- If all one is doing is describing usage, then philosophy is no more than a branch of empirical linguistics, and is certainly not an *a priori* investigation into the nature of things.
- Is a philosopher engaged in linguistic analysis not just a self-appointed linguistic policeman? Who is a linguistic philosopher that he may think to tell others how they should or should not talk?

To claim, as innumerable philosophers from Aristotle to Wittgenstein and beyond have done, that we would not *say* such-and-such, or that the expression 'so-and-so' *is used* in such-and-such a way, is to make a cognitive claim. So one may ask what its warrant is. Since no sensible philosopher would engage in social surveys about common usage, it may seem that the only possible source of such claims is one's own 'linguistic intuitions'. If that is so, one may well wonder why the intuitions of a given philosopher should be authoritative; or indeed, whether they are shared by other speakers of the language (such as his readers).

Mastery of a practice and the irrelevance of intuitions

The questions are confused. A competent speaker of the language is by definition someone who knows how to use a wide range of the common, non-technical words of the language. As remarked above, he no more needs to consult others than a competent chess-player needs to ask others how to move the chess-pieces. *The warrant is the warrant of anyone who has mastered a shared practice.* In order to report that it is correct to say 'Three men were in the field' and incorrect to say 'Three men was in the field' a competent speaker not only does not need to consult others – he does not need to consult 'intuitions' either. And what goes for such morphological remarks also goes for logico-grammatical observations such as: It is correct to say 'He said something slowly', but incorrect to say 'He meant something slowly'; or 'There is no such thing as *meaning something slowly*'. One need only assemble and marshal what one already knows. Talk of consulting intuitions in philosophy is a relatively recent aberration derived from misconceived linguistic theory (Chomsky). An intuition, in one sense, is direct, unmediated, non-evidential knowledge of something. But one's knowledge of the meanings of the words one understands is not intuitive knowledge evident to the intellect – after all, one had to learn what they mean and how to use them. When one brings to mind, recollects, how a word is used, one is not having recourse to intellectual insight. In another sense, intuitions are hunches or guesses. But philosophy has no more interest in hunches and guesses than does mathematics. One's knowledge of the use of a word is no more a hunch than is one's knowledge that $2 + 2 = 4$. It is not a hunch that a vixen is a female fox, or a guess that one cannot mean something slowly. One's knowledge that a word one understands is used thus-and-so is neither an intuitive insight nor a hunch or guess. It is the knowledge possessed by any competent participant in a shared practice. Of course, that does not mean that one may not err in describing the use with which one is familiar. Nor does it mean that discussion with other competent speakers may not be fruitful in clarifying hard cases. But it does mean that one will recognize one's *error* (or oversight) as soon as it is pointed out and examples are adduced, or that one will come to appreciate significant indeterminacies in usage.

It has been objected that even if this is granted, the practice, which one has mastered, is no more than a select and unrepresentative sociolect, such as that of Oxbridge dons – and why should that command any privilege? Surely words are used differently in other sociolects! This is confused. Oxbridge dons are competent speakers of English. I am not aware of any philosophically interesting differences in the sociolects of English speakers that bear upon serious conceptual questions. But if there are, they are readily negotiable by the disputants explaining precisely what they mean. Then the conceptual problem may be reformulated in a manner that takes any such differences into account. This is unproblematic.

Differences between languages

There often are significant semantic differences between languages. If there were none, translation would not be so difficult an art. But poetry apart, the problems of translation are rarely insurmountable, although the result may be only a more or less close approximation. As discussed in *Human Nature: the Categorial Framework*, many languages have no word that corresponds exactly to the English expression 'mind'. So the problems that arise concerning our concept of mind will not be exactly the same as those that arise in ancient (or modern) Hebrew (in respect of 'ruach', 'nephesh' and 'neshama'), ancient Greek ('thumos' and 'psuchē'), or German ('Geist' and 'Seele'). But they will be analogous, precisely because the Jews and Greeks of antiquity, and German speakers of the last few centuries, raised similar questions about human nature, such as 'What is the principle of life?', 'Do we survive after death?', 'How am I related to my body?'. If we write about the nature of the mind, adjustments will have to be made in translation into German, for example, since it has only two words to do the work of the three English words 'mind', 'spirit' (which does not mean the same as 'Geist') and 'soul' (which does not mean the same as 'Seele'). The finely spun web of words in one language is very unlikely to be identical with the comparable web in other languages. But that does not mean that the conceptual distinctions, affinities and differences brought to light in English usage cannot be drawn in German, or numerous other languages *in somewhat different ways*. Lack of a progressive form does not imply that one cannot distinguish in German between states (that obtain), performances (that are done) and activities (that go on). Despite numerous non-trivial differences, Ryle's *Concept of Mind* has been translated successfully into German (and many other languages), and Wittgenstein's *Philosophische Untersuchungen* has been successfully translated into English (and many other languages).

Inter-lingual comparisons may be of great interest to the cultural historian and historian of ideas. *Some* philosophical problems and puzzles that arise in one culture may not arise in another, or may not arise in the same way. (The Greeks had no concept of a person, lacked the idea of a negative number, did not distinguish something's being voluntary from its being intentional.) In philosophy (as opposed to history of philosophy) we deal with conceptual questions and predicaments that arise for us, not with those that do not. Some of these date back to ancient Greece; others do not and could not. We resolve conceptual questions and dissolve conceptual predicaments by conceptual analysis. Our concern is with the network of our concepts, and our results will be valid for any culture that shares the same, or approximately the same, concepts. (Remember that our criteria for concept identity and difference are neither sharp nor rigid. Not *every* difference in usage is tantamount to a difference in the concept expressed.)

The atemporality of normative space A quite different objection latches onto the thought that facts about linguistic usage are historical. Usage is constituted by the rules for the use of words in a given period. It is a *contingent fact* that the word 'mind' is used as it now is. It was not so used centuries ago. The task of describing current usage, even if for purposes quite different from those of the lexicographer or linguist, is surely an empirical investigation. But philosophy is not an empirical investigation! It is not a branch of linguistics. Its elucidations are not contingent empirical truths, but *a priori* truths concerning the nature of things. But if the methods of conceptual analysis consist in describing linguistic usage, then its results are surely empirical statements about words and their time-bound uses. That is, of course, true of lexicography. A dictionary tabulates current rules for the use of the words the meanings of which it explains, and, if it is compiled on historical principles (like the *Oxford English Dictionary*), then it also records the history of the word. That there are such-and-such rules for the use of words at a given time is indeed a contingent historical fact, but the rules themselves are not facts of any kind. Lexical rules are timeless inasmuch as they *contain no time reference*. 'A bachelor is an unmarried man' states a rule for the use of the word 'bachelor'. This rule-formulation does not run 'From the late fourteenth century, a bachelor is an unmarried man'. 'To be perceptually conscious of something is to be sensibly aware of it in one's field of perception' is a rule for the use of 'to be conscious of'. But the rule-formulation does not take the form 'To be perceptually conscious of something is, from the early seventeenth century, to be sensibly aware of something in one's field of perception'. We are moving around, as it were, in *lexical normative space*, which is atemporal (not omni-temporal).[22] The statement that in the seventeenth century, the English word 'conscious' meant 'privy to' is not a statement *of* a rule, but a temporal statement *about* a rule. Of course, the rules for the use of words change. But when they change *significantly*, a different concept is expressed, and one is speaking of something else. ('She had many lovers', in Jane Austen's time, could still mean 'She was much admired and sought after by men', not 'She was promiscuous'.) Conceptual investigations in philosophy are concerned with the concepts we have, not with different concepts our forefathers had (that is relevant to the history of ideas) or with those our descendants may have. For it is the concepts *we* have that give rise to the philosophical unclarities and confusions that concern *us*. *Some* of these concepts are ancient and have not changed since antiquity. Others are novel, and would not have been understood in antiquity. The result of conceptual analysis is the clarification of the conceptual connections, of the compatibilities and incompatibilities of the concepts we have – not of some other concepts. These connections are *a priori*, not empirical. For it is not an empirical fact that, *given the rules* for the use of a certain expression, then these and these conceptual relations obtain. The expression would not mean what it does were these logico-grammatical connections not to obtain in the practice of using it.

The method of investigating concept acquisition
One might object further: linguistic philosophers since Wittgenstein have often had recourse to describing how we teach children words, and how children learn new words – but surely this is an empirical matter. So this method of linguistic philosophy is just armchair learning theory in disguise. This seems doubly objectionable. First, learning theory is a branch of experimental psychology, and not something for amateur armchair speculation. Secondly, learning theory is an empirical subject. This sits ill with the claim that conceptual analysis is an *a priori* investigation. — This objection too is mistaken. The method of drawing our attention to the ways in which children might learn the use of certain words and kinds of word does not engage in armchair learning theory. Rather, it draws attention to *logical features* that characterize the use of the expressions in question. We may explain, for example, that an expression of intention

---

[22] By 'normative' I mean no more than appertaining to rules (norms), or rule-governed.

is not a description of an inner state of intending, but heralds or presages an action. That *logical* feature of the utterance of 'I'm going to . . .' is vividly brought out by considering how a parent might teach the child how to use the phrase, namely, a mother may say to the child, 'I'm going to throw the ball', and then she goes on to throw the ball. In this embryonic language-game with expressions of intent, if one says 'I'm going to', then one must *go on to*! Similarly, one function of spontaneous utterances of 'Oh! Oh! I've a terrible pain' is as an *expression* of pain. That is highlighted by reflecting on pain-utterances as learnt extensions of primitive pain-behaviour, that is, on noting the *logical affinities* between a cry of pain and a spontaneous utterance of pain. There are here no hostages to empirical learning theory.

Not a policeman but a tribunal of sense   Does the philosopher engaged in linguistic analysis not set himself up as a linguistic policeman? — We do indeed examine the uses of words. Linguistic analysis elaborates the place of a word within the network of language. In the course of so doing, conceptual confusions are bought to light and explanations for such confusions become evident. Does this make a philosopher into a linguistic policeman? That would, of course, be ludicrous – a philosophical Canute commanding the waves of language to recede. But a philosopher who practises conceptual analysis in the linguistic mode and demarcates the bounds of sense laid down in the grammar of the language is no policeman, but a magistrate sitting on the benches of the tribunal of sense. His task is not to *prevent* people from doing anything they want to do. His task is to show when they talk nonsense. He shows that they are talking nonsense by demonstrating that *if* they are using a word in its received sense, then in saying what they say they are inadvertently misusing it, and thereby transgressing the bounds of sense. If, on the other hand, people are introducing a new use, the critical task of the philosopher is not to remonstrate against it. It is to point out when inferences are drawn from the new use that can be validly drawn only from the old use. For if one crosses the old use with the new one, incoherence results. The role of linguistic analysis is not *to stop people from doing anything they wish to do*, but *to point out what they are doing*: namely, transgressing the bounds of sense and drawing invalid inferences

4 objections to conceptual analysis   A different array of misunderstandings is evident in objections to *conceptual analysis* as such. The following are common expressions of incomprehension.

- Conceptual analysis is *about* concepts, but we are interested in the nature of things, not in concepts.
- Concepts are expressions of the ways in which we think about things, but we may be thinking wrongly. Concepts may 'get things wrong'.
- If conceptual analysis investigates current concepts by scrutinizing existing linguistic usage, then it cannot budget for conceptual revision. But conceptual revision is the go-cart of science.
- If conceptual analysis investigates current concepts, then it is time-bound to the ways we currently think, and cannot budget for new concepts.

What logico-grammatical analysis is about   The first objection has already been answered. The expression 'about' may look like a critical lever, but it is made of plasticine. A logico-grammatical investigation is no more *about* words than it is *about* concepts, and it is no more *about* concepts than it is *about* the nature of what is signified by the concepts. A conceptual investigation is indeed an investigation into the use of some expression or other. (How else might one investigate a concept?) It elucidates a given concept by describing the use of the word that expresses that concept. The concept is typically one that gives rise to philosophical puzzlement and confusion – otherwise why should one be concerned with its analysis? That concept is *likely* to be shared by many other languages, in which similar conceptual unclarities arise. Moreover, the analysis of a concept is a characterization of the nature of what it signifies, since the analysis of a concept specifies the normative grounds in virtue of which we characterize something as falling under the concept.

Concepts and ways of thinking about things   One may indeed say that conceptual investigations describe the ways in which we think about things, or the ways in which we understand things. But the very crudity of such remarks leads one immediately into confusion. For one may then object that thought, even if collective and public, is never a guarantee of truth. The fact that we collectively think about something in a certain way does not mean that things are that way. Someone may object, specifically to the project of investigating human nature, that the way we ordinarily understand ourselves is no more than how we think about ourselves. But our thought and talk about ourselves is riddled with contradictions and confusions. After all, is that not precisely one of the things that the conceptual analyst wants to show in his investigations into the dialectic of reason? Our *understanding* of the nature of things does not yield any single coherent picture. What we need is not conceptual analysis, but a *theory* that will go beyond our ordinary understanding of things.

This confuses an instrument of thought with what one does with it. When we are engaged in conceptual analysis, our interest in the words and concepts that give rise to the difficulties that beset us is in their *correct use* – not in their use in making *true* judgments, but in their use in making *true or false* judgements. Our concern is with *what makes sense*. Our conclusions, if correct, will be conceptual truths. Conceptual truths cannot be riddled with contradictions and confusions, for they are expressions of *rules*. If a conflict of rules generating a contradiction emerges in certain unforeseen circumstances, it can in practice readily be resolved. Hidden contradictions, on the other hand, are harmless – after all, a contradiction *says* nothing at all. How could a *hidden nothing* do any harm?[23] Of course, it is true that we fail to understand ourselves, both individually and collectively. We are blinkered, individually and collectively, to our own faults, and we are past masters at self-deception. But such understanding or misunderstanding is of concern to philosophy only in so far as it is investigating the nature of vice, of self-deception and of bad faith. The form of understanding that is the concern of philosophical analysis is the grasp of our forms of understanding. We are concerned with the concepts in terms of which we understand ourselves, not with the empirical facts or purported facts that we state by their means.

Conceptual analysis is not theory construction

Our investigations are not theoretical, if by 'theory' one means such things as the theory of relativity, of thermo-dynamics or of evolution. There is nothing hypothetical about our investigations, and they are not verifiable or falsifiable by experiment. They are not approximations to truth, as are many scientific theories. Indeed, they are not approximations, since an approximation to *sense* is some form or other of nonsense. They are not idealizations, as many scientific theories are, for there is no such thing as idealized sense. Our investigations are descriptive, not theoretical. Their object is not to

---

[23] A logician may insist that it is harmful, since from a contradiction one may infer anything whatsoever. So indeed one may – but, of course, not when the contradiction is hidden! And once it comes to light, one can fence it in.

construct a *theory* about linguistic usage and the conceptual network that is thereby constituted. It is, rather, to *describe* usage in order to resolve conceptual problems and to obtain an overview of a part of our conceptual scheme in order to contribute to our understanding of the *forms* of our thought, and, *in that sense*, of the nature of things.

Concepts are not right or wrong
Confusions may still persist. Surely, it will be said, concepts, prevailing and entrenched as they may be, can nevertheless get things completely wrong. The ancients thought that stars were holes in the sky. The early moderns thought that witches could cast efficacious spells. It was once believed that the sun rises and sets. Surely, such examples show that they got their concepts wrong! — It shows no such thing. In so far as the ancients thought that a star is a hole in the sky, which in turn is an inverted hemisphere, they did indeed get things wrong. However, what they got wrong were facts, not concepts.[24] For thus understood, there is no sky and there are no stars. Nevertheless, there is nothing *mistaken* about their concepts. The only thing amiss is that they are useless. On the other hand, if by 'stars' they meant no more than 'those twinkling lights one sees in the sky at night', then their concept of a star was neither empty nor useless. It was their empirical beliefs about stars that were awry, not their concepts. Similarly, if 'witch' meant someone with supernatural powers to cause harm by spells, then those who believed in witches got things wrong. But what they got wrong was not the concept of a witch, but the belief that there are any witches. Finally, it was not only once believed, but still is believed (and believed correctly), that the sun rises and sets (just as the price of butter rises and falls). This shows no conceptual error whatsoever, nor does it even manifest a false empirical belief. The sun does indeed rise in the east and set in the west (early in the morning the sun appears in the east, and in the evening it disappears over the western horizon). That is perfectly true. Error creeps in if one thinks that the sun's rising in the east is an activity of the sun (just as one would be confused if one thought that butter's rising in price was an activity of the butter). That is indeed a conceptual confusion. But *concepts* are not true or false. They are not even right or wrong – only

---

[24] One may doubt whether this description correctly characterizes their concepts of (as opposed to their empirical beliefs about) stars and firmament. For this description presents them as theoretical concepts of a false astronomical theory. Their theories were indeed wrong, but it is not obvious that 'kochav' (in ancient Hebrew) or 'stella' (in Latin) meant anything other than a twinkling light in the heavens.

useful or useless. The only way a concept can be awry is if it is incoherent. But then, strictly speaking, it is a form of words, not a concept, that is out of order. For there is no such concept as, say, the concept of white blackness, or the concept of being transparent white – these are simply useless combinations of words.

Conceptual analysis and conceptual change A further objection is that conceptual analysis of the kind advocated here is offensively conservative and time-bound. For it cannot budget for conceptual revision, on the one hand, or conceptual change, on the other. It gives one, as it were, a 'snapshot' of current usage and of current concepts. But this places us in a straitjacket. Usage changes; concepts can be improved; yet the nature of things is sempiternal. Surely we must make room for change and improvement, on the one hand, and for further and better insights into the timeless nature of things, on the other! — This is confused. The conceptual nature of things is atemporal, not omni-temporal. Conceptual analysis gives us a description of some part or parts of our conceptual scheme in order to solve or dissolve conceptual unclarity or misunderstanding, and to answer conceptual questions. This is neither more nor less time-bound than those parts of our conceptual scheme and the conceptual problems to which they give rise (which means: generally, not *very* time-bound). To be sure, as new concepts come onto the table, new conceptual problems arise. Some arise as a consequence of technical innovations: the ancients did not become confused over whether the brain is akin to a computer. Some arise over formal innovations in the *a priori* sciences: the ancients did not worry about the relationship between the predicate calculus and natural language. And some arise through advances in theoretical science: the ancients did not have to confront the conceptual problems posed by quantum mechanics. Conceptual analysis does not stand in the way of conceptual change; but conceptual change often provides fresh grist for its mills.

Conceptual revision Nevertheless, does it not stand in the way of conceptual revision? Not at all. Scientists and others are free to revise existing concepts as they please. However, conceptual analysis is concerned with mapping the concepts we have – not with revising them, but with describing them. Conceptual revision is done for a purpose (e.g. in the law, in the sciences or in mathematics). The purpose of conceptual analysis in theoretical philosophy *is* the description of concepts and conceptual networks – among other things, in order to eliminate confusions. For that purpose, no conceptual revision in the *objects* of investigation is licit – for then we should be describing something different.[25]

Introducing new concepts

Still, one might object, every science introduces new concepts for its purposes. Why should philosophy not do so too? If conceptual analysis prohibits this, so much the worse for conceptual analysis. — Conceptual analysis prohibits nothing. It may indeed introduce novel concepts for its purpose (such as the concept of *connective analysis* or of *multi-focal concepts*). What it may not licitly do is introduce novel concepts for the purposes of other disciplines (e.g. for mathematics, physics or biology) – for that is not its business. (The business of the doctor is to cure his patients, not to run their businesses.) It may show other disciplines what is awry with their concepts or with their use of their concepts. But then it is the business of the mathematician, physicist or biologist to take whatever further steps they may think fit. Nor may conceptual analysis change the concepts it is supposed to analyse (such as 'consciousness', 'knowledge', 'belief'), for one cannot clarify a concept by changing it, or disentangle a knot in a piece of string by taking a fresh piece of string. One cannot resolve Berkeley's puzzles about warmth and cold by replacing thermal concepts with the concept of temperature (as Carnap suggested we do). One cannot clean the room by brushing the dirt under the carpet.

We owe a great debt to our predecessors for introducing such analytically helpful concepts as *a priori* and *a posteriori* propositions, *tautologous* propositions, *contraries* and *contradictories*, *inductive* and *deductive* reasoning, *achievement* and *task verbs*, *illocutionary* and *perlocutionary force* and so on. There is nothing stopping connective analysts from introducing novel concepts for *such* philosophical purposes. But it is not often needed, precisely because philosophers are surveyors, not construction engineers – they are not in the business of constructing theories, but of surveying the terrain.

What we have surveyed throughout this volume are the cognitive and cogitative powers of mankind. To do this is to shed light upon human nature.

---

[25] Of course, things are not that sharp in the domain of practical philosophy. In philosophy of law, for example, philosophers have pointed out, say, that the definition of murder, or the understanding of intention, or the interpretation of *mens rea*, obliterates morally or legally important distinctions, or leads to such-and-such deleterious consequences. There is no reason why legal theorists should not recommend enlightened conceptual change for legal purposes.

Index

Pages containing significant discussions appear in bold.

The Intellectual Powers: A Study of Human Nature, First Edition. P. M. S. Hacker.
© 2013 John Wiley & Sons, Ltd. Published 2013 by John Wiley & Sons, Ltd.